Dynamo, Michael Somes

A Life in The Royal Ballet

Sarah Woodcock

Dynamo: machine converting mechanical into electric energy. Portrait late 1940s.
Photograph by Gordon Anthony.

Dynamo, Michael Somes
A Life in The Royal Ballet

Sarah Woodcock

DANCE BOOKS

First published in 2023
by Dance Books
Southwold House, Isington Road, Binsted, Hampshire GU34 4PH

ISBN 978-1-85273-187-8

Cover photograph: Michael Somes in *Horoscope*, 1937. Photograph by Gordon Anthony. Theatre and Performance Collections V&A.

Contents

Chapter One	Introduction	1
Chapter Two	Beginnings	6
Chapter Three	Golden Days	17
Chapter Four	Waiting	60
Chapter Five	War	75
Chapter Six	Return	89
Chapter Seven	New Beginnings	94
Chapter Eight	New York	121
Chapter Nine	Interlude and Across America	131
Chapter Ten	Ambition Achieved	149
Chapter Eleven	The Partnership	164
Chapter Twelve	America, America	171
Chapter Thirteen	International Stars	178
Chapter Fourteen	Assistant Director	234
Chapter Fifteen	Eminence grise	271
Chapter Sixteen	Retirement	297
Chapter Seventeen	The Method	307
Appendices	Working with Frederick Ashton by Michael Somes	322
	Music for Dancing – the Part it Plays. With special reference to 'Daphnis and Chloë' by Michael Somes	325
Index		332

Notes to the text

Abbreviations:
MS: Michael Somes
ES: Ethel Somes
FA: Frederick Ashton
NdeV: Ninette de Valois
MF: Margot Fonteyn
nd: no date
mss: manuscript
Somes copy letters notebook: Somes copied passages from some letters into notebooks, destroying the originals.

In quotations, original spellings and grammar have been retained.

Accurate conversion of contemporary currency to today's values is almost impossible and any such references should treated with caution and measured against current costs and wages. The original figures have been converted to 2021 levels using the Bank of England Inflation Calculator.

For permission to quote from material in their possession I am indebted to the Board of the Royal Opera House (minutes of Board and Ballet Sub-Committee meetings); The Royal Ballet School (the letters of Dame Ninette de Valois): to Lavinia Hookham (the letters of Dame Margot Fonteyn): Anthony Russell Roberts (the letters of Sir Frederick Ashton).

Acknowledgements

My thanks and gratitude to all those who gave me their time and memories: First and foremost to Wendy Ellis-Somes for giving me access to and permission to quote from Michael Somes' letters and papers and for her encouragement and that of her husband, Mervyn Wright.

To the dancers, musicians and designers: Christine Aitken, the late David Ashmole, the late Michael Boulton, Christopher Carr, the late Alan Carter, the late Mary Clarke, the late Pauline Claydon, Michael Coleman, Lesley Collier, Sandra Conley and Adrian Grater, the late Michael Crookes, the late Dame Ninette de Valois, Sir Anthony Dowell, Anthony Dowson, Wayle Eagling, the late Leslie Edwards, the late Julia Farron and Alfred Rodrigues, Barbara Fewster, the late Frank Freeman, Philip Gammon, David Gayle, the late Alexander Grant, Cynthia Harvey, Stephen Jefferies and Rashna Homji, the late Kathrine Sorley Walker, the late Leo Kersley, the late John Lanchbery, Lady MacMillan, Dame Monica Mason, the late Pamela May, the late Sir Claus Moser, Ashley Page, the late Prosso Pfister, the late Errol Pickford, the Rev. John Robson, the late Clover Roope, Dame Antoinette Sibley, Donald Twiner, Kathryn Wade, the late David Walker, Sir Peter Wright, Emanuel Young, and Somes' friends and neighbours: Michael Barrett, Roger and Patricia Connor, Jo Curtis and Darren McLagan.

In public collections: Julia Creed, Head of Collections at the Royal Opera House for her help and patience; the staff at the Theatre and Performance Collections of the Victoria and Albert Museum; Anna Meadmore, Curator of the White Lodge Museum of the Royal Ballet School. And to Jon Gray, editor of the much missed *Dancing Times*, for help with finding images and scanning.

My thanks and gratitude to my publisher, David Leonard, and editor, Elizabeth Morrell for their endless help and patience.

List of Illustrations

It has not been possible to trace all copyright holders. Should you believe you hold copyright over any of the images please contact the publisher/author.

Frontispiece: Dynamo: machine converting mechanical into electric energy. Portrait late 1940s. Photograph by Gordon Anthony. © Victoria and Albert Museum, London.

1 In a Hayward and Milbourne school show in the 1920s with Betty Hayward. Photograph by C. Sledmere.

2 *Blue Bird* pas de deux. Photograph by Gordon Anthony. © Victoria and Albert Museum, London.

3 The Young Man with the Sun in Leo, Moon in Gemini in *Horoscope*. Photograph by Gordon Anthony. © Victoria and Albert Museum, London.

4 Monseigneur in *Harlequin* in the Street. Photograph by Gordon Anthony. © Victoria and Albert Museum, London.

5 *Dante Sonata*: left to right: June Brae and Robert Helpmann as leaders of the Children of Darkness, Fonteyn, Somes and Pamela May as Children of Light. Photograph by Gordon Anthony. © Victoria and Albert Museum, London.

6 *Symphonic Variations*: left to right Moira Shearer, Somes, Pamela May, Margot Fonteyn, (back) Henry Danton. Photograph by Richardby at Baron Studios.

7 *Les Sirènes*: as Captain Bay Vavaseur with Beryl Grey as Countess Kitty, one of the few roles that allowed Somes to exercise his talents for stylish comedy. Photo: Richardby.

8 Prince Florimund in *The Sleeping Beauty*. Photograph by Edward Mandinian. © Victoria and Albert Museum, London.

9 The Prince in *Cinderella* with Fonteyn as Cinderella. Cover *Dance and Dancers* January 1953.

10 Arriving in America: de Valois, Fonteyn, Shearer, Ashton, Somes and conductor Robert Irving.

11 *Summer Interlude*: Pirmin Trecu as A Country Boy, Patricia Miller as A Country Girl, David Blair as a Bather. Photograph by Roger Wood. Arenapal/Royal Opera House.

12 Pamela May and Somes in a publicity shot promoting British fashions for the 1951-2 American coast-to-coast tour.

13 Daphnis in *Daphnis and Chloë*. Photo: Roger Wood, Arenapal/Royal Opera House.

14 Daphnis in *Daphnis and Chloë*: with John Field (on floor) as Dorkon. Photograph by Roger Wood. Arenapal/Royal Opera House.

15 *Giselle* with Alicia Markova. Photograph by G B L Wilson, Arenapal/Royal Academy of Dance.

16 Harjis Plucis rehearsing Fonteyn and Somes. Photograph by John Hart.

17 Somes with Fonteyn and Ashton. Shutterstock.

18 *Swan Lake* with Fonteyn. Photograph by Maurice Seymour courtesy of Ronald Seymour.

19 *The Firebird*: Tamara Karsavina rehearsing Fonteyn and Somes.

20 *The Firebird*: as Ivan Tsarevitch with Fonteyn as the Firebird. Photograph by Houston Rogers, © Victoria and Albert Museum, London.

21 *The Firebird*: as Ivan Tsarevitch with Nadia Nerina as the Firebird. Photograph by Houston Rogers, © Victoria and Albert Museum, London.

22 Publicising Ballet for Athletes with Olympic high jumper Dorothy Tyson. Keystone Press.

23 *The Miraculous Mandarin*: as the Mandarin with Elaine Fifield as the Girl. Photograph by Houston Rogers, © Victoria and Albert Museum, London.

24 Farewell to Melbourne, 1957.

25 Arriving in Japan, 1959.

26 *The Sleeping Beauty* with the Masahide Komaki Company, Japan 1959.

27 After receiving the CBE at Buckingham Palace with Deirdre. Keystone Press.

28 Somes coaching Antoinette Sibley for her first *Swan Lake* in 1959. Publicity shot as published in the *Daily Express*.

29 Somes teaching at the Royal Ballet School in the late 1950s, published in The Royal Ballet souvenir programme, New York 1960s.

30 International guesting in Monte Carlo at a performance marking thirty years after Diaghilev's death: left-right: Serge Lifar, Fonteyn and Somes in costume for *The Firebird*, Princess Grace of Monaco.

31 Rehearsal for the television production of *Cinderella*: Fonteyn and Somes with director Mark Stuart. Shutterstock.

32 Somes' protégés Antoinette Sibley and Anthony Dowell in *The Dream*. Photograph by Leslie E Spatt. Arenapal/Leslie E Spatt.

33 *Façade*, Popular Song danced by Somes and Donald Britton for Friends of Covent Garden Christmas Party, 1967.

34 Ashton farewell gala finale: Fonteyn as Chloë with Somes as Daphnis.

35 *O.W.*: Somes as Oscar Wilde, Stephen Jefferies as A Young Chap. Photograph by Anthony Crickmay. © Victoria and Albert Museum, London.

36 Demonstration for the Cecchetti Society with Wendy Ellis and Julian Hosking. Photograph by Jack Blake.

37 With Queen Elizabeth the Queen Mother. Photograph by Reg Wilson.

38 In costume as Lord Capulet in *Romeo and Juliet*, suggesting tips on child rearing to Princess Diana.

39 Dedication from Ashton in *Frederick Ashton; A choreographer and his ballets* by Zoë Dominic and John Selwyn Gilbert.

1

Introduction

Once upon a time there was an idealist without illusions, who knew that dreams come true not by wishing on a star, but by being practical and pragmatic. In a single generation, Ninette de Valois overturned centuries of prejudice and transformed six British dancers into a ballet company of global influence that challenged the long-established state institutions in Europe and Russia. No spells, no waving of magic wands, the story is rooted in hard grind, quiet growth, triumphs and disappointments, interrupted by cataclysmic events. Looking back, we see the light in the dark forest and the straight road, where the protagonists saw confusing multiple paths; the wolf was often behind the next tree and sometimes their fairy godmother seemed to have abandoned them, but the goal held true. There were happy events along the way, but no happy ending, because the story of The Royal Ballet is still going on.

As de Valois memorably snapped to an audience wanting to acknowledge her as the realiser of the dream, 'It takes more than one to make a ballet company.' Four names are commemorated in a memorial in Westminster Abbey and stand above The Royal Ballet masthead: Founder Director Ninette de Valois, Founder Choreographer Frederick Ashton, Founder Prima Ballerina Assoluta Margot Fonteyn, Founder Music Director Constant Lambert. But if it takes more than one, it takes more than four. This is the story of another of the 'more than one', who challenged prejudice, poverty and his own intractable physique, to become a star and a maker of stars, who served The Royal Ballet longer and contributed more widely to the company's development than anyone except its founder.

When Michael Somes was born in 1917, it was unimaginable that an Englishman could be a ballet dancer. Although in the Elizabethan age the English had been dubbed 'The Dancing English', suspicion of the male dancer was already deeply ingrained, expressed at its most extreme by the Puritan Philip Stubbs in 1595: 'If you would have your son soft, womanish, unclean, smooth-mouthed, affected to bawdry, scurrility, filthy rhymes and unseemly talking; briefly if you would have him as it were transnatured into a woman or worse, and inclined to all kinds of whoredom and abomination, set him to dancing school and to learn music.'[1] As such views extended to all theatre, it was hardly surprising that the Puritan legacy destroyed any hope of the Inigo Jones-Ben Jonson court masques, which rivalled any in Europe, evolving into national institutions as they did in Paris and Milan; there companies were fed from associated schools which provided the continuity and consistency to produce generations of quality dancers with career security. In 18th century London, the success of foreign dancers and singers engendered the belief that the English were physically and emotionally unsuited to ballet and opera. The Victorians saw the theatre as non-productive and therefore no career for an Englishman; performers were not acceptable in society and it was hardly surprising that the great 19th century actor William Charles Macready described acting as 'my pariah profession'. John Ruskin spoke for many Victorians when he wrote that watching dance was like 'seeing into an abyss of human life, both in suffering and in crime'.

Prejudice against the male dancer was, therefore, part of a deeper mistrust, amounting to revulsion, against all branches of theatre. So the first battle had to be for the recognition of theatre as a respectable career, then it had to be acknowledged that dance and opera were as much the province of the English as the exotic foreigner. Only then could the recognition of the male dancer in Britain be addressed.

This is not to suggest that there were no English successes. In 1725, John Weaver's ground-breaking *The Loves of Mars and Venus* featured Hester Santlow as Venus and in the 1790s, when the male dancer reigned supreme, Simon Slingsbury achieved international fame, although fashionable, snobbish London audiences preferred foreign stars, like Gaetan and August Vestris. Then, in the 1830s, public adulation shifted from the male dancer to the ballerina. Marie Taglioni led a succession of European stars, backed by English dancers in minor and corps de ballet roles, who, to maintain credibility assumed foreign-sounding stage names. In the late 1840s, fashionable audiences abandoned ballet for opera: elsewhere in Europe, dancers found year-round employment in the opera ballets, but London's opera season lasted only a few weeks in the summer.[2]

Other factors militated against dance establishing deep roots in Britain. Nineteenth century professional dance schools in London were linked to theatres, like Mrs Conquest's at the Grecian, and most disappeared when speculators acquired theatres as commercial premises for hire, with no continuity or long-term policy.

English dancers survived in popular theatre, where the male dancer shone in the Harlequinade, which, by the late nineteenth century, had

1   Philip Stubbs, *The Anatomy of Abuses*, 1595

2   Thus ballet became 'operatic dancing', a term which persisted into the 1930s. 'Classical' meant Greek dance, which enjoyed a revival in the early 20th century.

been absorbed into the Christmas pantomime; every major city and town mounted its own spectacular production, running for up to six months and providing employment for thousands of actors, singers and dancers, especially children. To supply the required hordes of child performers, the first stage schools were established in the 1890s, including Italia Conti, John Tiller and the Lila Field Academy.

Ballet maintained a toe-hold in London in lavish productions at the rival Alhambra and Empire music halls, which continued to maintain their own schools, although the ballerinas were still engaged from abroad and the predominately male audience went mainly to admire the girls' physical charms. Production values were high, but it was not a system designed to produce substantial works to test and develop dancers.

Although society looked askance at ballet, all well-bred girls learned to dance, mostly social or 'fancy' dancing, but by the 1890s, a new generation shocked their parents by demanding to learn the latest stage dance crazes, like skirt dancing or the rumbustious Tar-ra-ra-boom-de-ay with its naughty high kicks. Teachers responded by offering tap, Greek, national dance and ballet, although few had experience of most of the styles and teaching standards were generally low.

In 1895, the theatre took a huge stride towards respectability when actor-manager Henry Irving was knighted and a new generation of university educated playwrights and actors emerged. Yet, as the prejudice against the theatre declined, that against the male ballet dancer intensified and in Paris and London he all but disappeared, replaced by the *travesti*, a sturdy girl dressed as a man. In ten years as star at the Empire, Adeline Genée never had a male partner and not until 1914 did London see her dance with the fine, Moscow-trained Alexander Volinine. Men could be choreographers and ballet masters, character dancers and 'eccentric dancers' on the music halls, in Harlequinades, musical comedy and revue, but there was no public respect or structured career.

Public perception of both ballet and the male dancer began to shift in the early 20th century with the arrival of the Russian dancers. London audiences so adored Anna Pavlova's partner, the glamorous Mikhail Mordkin, that when she publicly slapped his face for getting the most applause, it was headline news. Never again would she tolerate a partner who would offer any challenge to her star status. Her success inspired thousands of mothers to send their daughters to ballet class, but few boys.[3] In 1911, the Alhambra brought in a complete Bolshoi production, *The Dance Dream*, starring Ekaterina Geltzer and Vasili Tikhomiroff, with English dancers in all other roles. Later that year, when Diaghilev brought the Ballets Russes to Covent

---

3   Frederick Ashton being a notable exception, after seeing Pavlova in Lima.

Garden, the real sensations were Nijinsky and, especially, Adolph Bolm's virile, anarchic Warrior Chief in the *Polovtsian Dances*. After the great Tamara Karsavina, Diaghilev's most praised dancers were male: after Nijinsky and Bolm came Leonide Massine, who remained a huge star into the 1950s, as did the charismatic Serge Lifar; among his brilliant technicians and character dancers were George Rosai, George Gavrilov, Leon Woizikowski, Stanislas Idzikowski and Anton Dolin.

On the negative side, their success reinforced the perception of ballet as the province of exotic foreigners; Diaghilev and Pavlova insisted that their English dancers assume Russian names, although many knew that Lydia Sokolova was born Hilda Munnings, Anton Dolin was Patrick Healey-Kay and Alicia Markova was Alicia Marks. The prejudice was so ingrained that Arnold Haskell refused to accept Markova as English, pointing out that she was Irish-Judaeo-Polish. It also established a not always justified link in the public mind between the male dancer and homosexuality.

Diaghilev, however, always believed that England would be the next country to take up the torch. Bolm recognised that 'The English are, by racial instincts, a dancing people. You have a splendid rhythmic sense, a natural grasp of beautiful plastic movement.'[4] Karsavina was equally encouraging: 'You are ... a people with such aptitude for dancing ...' but stressed that the prejudice against male dancers had to be overcome.[5] By 1914, Russian dancers teaching in London included Pavlova, Seraphina Astafieva, Nicholas Legat, Laurent Novikoff and his wife Anna Pruzina, Alexandre Goudin, Alexander Gavrilov and Serge Morosoff. Enrico Cecchetti opened a school in 1918 and in 1922 the Cecchetti Society was founded to promote and preserve his teachings; his English pupils included Margaret Craske and Errol Addison, who might have been one of England's great dancers if he had had more than a virtuoso technique at a time when just technique was not enough.[6]

The impetus that put teaching on a firm foundation in Britain came from Philip J. S. Richardson, founder and editor of *Dancing Times*. In school displays he saw the results of uncontrolled teaching without structure, understanding of underlying principles or even knowledge of the correct dance terms. In a *Dancing Times* editorial of August 1913, he laid down the principles for a 'Royal College of Dancing' as the foundation of a national school 'to see that the traditions which have been handed down to us from the great masters of the past ... should remain inviolate'.

In December 1919 an Association of Teachers of Operatic Dancing in

---

4   *Dancing Times*, September 1920, p.906

5   *Dancing Times*, December 1920, p.178

6   Asked why Addison had never worked for long with a ballet company, Markova replied 'Music hall, dear,' in the hushed tones of one imparting something shameful.

Britain (AOD now Royal Academy of Dance) was proposed to raise teaching standards. Every major dance school was represented, Danish by Adeline Genée, Italian by Lucia Cormani, Russian by Tamara Karsavina and French by Edouard Espinosa; Phyllis Bedells, the first twentieth-century ballet dancer to succeed under an English name, represented Britain. A syllabus was drawn up with agreed terminology, analysis of every step and exercise and their execution.

Examinations of teachers were first held in 1922 followed by the examination of their pupils to countercheck teaching standards; pupil examinees rose from 544 in 1924 to 3,987 in 1929, revealing a significant number of talented children, which raised the question, how to develop their gifts and what future could they expect? Prejudice aside, dance was an uncertain and short career; in 1933, Haskell estimated that only one dancer in a hundred could expect to work for one month in any year. The answer lay in two schools, established in the mid 1920s by former Diaghilev dancers Ninette de Valois and Marie Rambert. The battle for the acceptance of the British dancer had begun.

2

The Beginnings

The name Somes is place-derived, a corruption of the Cambridgeshire district of Soham. It is the less familiar spelling of Soames, and many never made the distinction, including various official bodies, critics, journalists, historians, minor Royalty, the British Council, fans and, inevitably, The Royal Ballet and the Royal Opera House Board. There was even confusion with Christopher Soames, Winston Churchill's portly son-in-law, who, according to one biography of Princess Grace of Monaco, danced at her wedding gala – a good dining out story for Somes and Soames. Soames was the usual misspelling, but other, what must charitably be called typos, included Sones, Homes and Somers, though none quite beat a Dublin paper's review of Gomee.

Everyone who met Somes was struck by his gentlemanly, almost patrician, manner. His family had already played its part in London history. In the mid 18th century, Thames lighterman Samuel Somes built up a fleet of ships, one named the Samuel and Sarah after himself and his wife Sarah Green, daughter of a coal-meter. Lightermen transferred goods from ships anchored in the Thames to the dockside. Coal meters assessed the weight or volume of quantities of coal. Son Joseph became a leading figure in English shipping, promoting the new Lloyd's Register of Shipping in 1834 and investing heavily in companies developing the colonies. During his time as deputy-governor and financer of the New Zealand Company, much of the greater Wellington region came under the company's control, including the island Matiu, renamed Somes Island after Joseph, who may also have been instrumental in naming the capital after the Duke of Wellington.[1]

By 1842, Joseph ruled one of the world's largest private shipping empires, chartering ships to the government for the transport of troops, stores and convicts. On his election as Conservative MP for Dartmouth in 1844, he had to disengage from his maritime interests or be disqualified as a government contractor; having only daughters, he transferred his fleet to his nephews, under whom the company virtually collapsed. Although Joseph left his widow, Maria, a personal fortune of £434,000 (in excess of £36.8 million today) when he died in 1845, little seems to have filtered down to his

---

1   In 1997, the official bilingual name of Matiu/Somes was assigned to the island 'in recognition of the island's colourful European and Maori histories'.

extensive descendants, except, maybe, the family pride.[2] The feeling was that fate would, or indeed should, provide.

Michael Somes' legacy from his father's family included good looks and musicality. Grandfather Joseph, a pawnbroker and silversmith by profession, was an exceptionally gifted amateur musician: a photograph shows the perfect Victorian male pin-up, with long hair, flourishing moustache and velvet jacket, a violin tucked under his arm. He married Alice Parsons, and their first son, Edwin, was born in Chelsea in 1882. Edwin was a handsome spoilt and indolent child, but musically gifted, playing both piano and organ. He briefly became a schoolmaster but simply could not keep order, and for most of his life he held various posts as church organist or piano teacher, feared for his dauntingly high standards. Those Michael also inherited, though not the inability to impose discipline.

Edwin settled in the West Country, where he met a distant relative, Ethel Pridham, daughter of a police sergeant in Weston-Super-Mare. Born in 1889, Ethel had trained as a teacher in Bristol at the Diocesan Training College at Fishponds (now part of the University of the West of England), where working class girls were trained as elementary school teachers.

Edwin and Ethel married in Taunton in 1912. Although they were not closely related, intermarriage was not uncommon among the Somes family and possibly contributed to the instability exhibited by some of the extensive family, manifested variously as eccentricity, obsessiveness, unworldliness, impracticability or volatile temper. Their first child, Lawrence, was born in 1913. Edwin was stationed in Gloucestershire as a Private in the Army Ordnance Corps when Michael George was born at 4.15am on 28 September 1917 at School House in Horsley. His surviving Progress Book records that he weighed 7 lbs and was 18 inches long with a chest measurement of 13 inches; Ethel later noted under Hereditary Peculiarities 'fond of the "cupper"' and, significantly, 'Hearing: exceptionally quick'. On 1 October, the baby suffered a near-fatal internal haemorrhage, but by his first birthday, he had become 'very jolly & sturdy, with four teeth and weighing 21 lbs'. He first stood alone on 11 October 1918.

The anxiety of the first months might be expected to account for Ethel's later assertion that Michael was, from birth, the centre of her world, but his childhood perception was that he came a poor second to his brother's angelic choirboy looks, and only became her emotional focus after Lawrence was removed from school for disruptive behaviour. Ethel's love was overpowering and not selfless; driven and neurotic, her frustrations found an outlet in her younger son. He was devoted to her, although found her constant demands

---

2   One of Joseph's descendents married into the Colyer-Fergusson family, who owned the delicious Kentish moated manorhouse, Ightham Mote, where a Somes hatchment still hangs in the chapel.

for proof draining, and fond of, if exasperated by, his ineffectual father, but he knew how much he owed them for their encouragement and support.

Home was Taunton, the county town of Somerset, which was even quieter than most county towns in the 1920s. The Lyceum Theatre did not host major tours, there was no musical tradition and new luxuries like the gramophone and wireless were not within everyone's reach, yet Michael's childhood was filled with music: his father played piano and organ, there were school concerts, bands in the parks and, above all, music in church: he was not the first, nor the last, performer whose introduction to spectacle and performance was church ritual.

The family's main income came from Ethel's small preparatory school, Eastcombe House, Edwin contributing his earnings as a church organist. In addition to her commitments to school and church, Ethel immersed herself in local theatricals, producing musical plays, as well as arranging school displays. Michael's introduction to dancing was unspectacular. Kathleen Hayward and Kathleen Milborne offered ballroom, ballet, classical (Greek), character dancing, fencing, deportment, remedial gymnastics, Swedish gymnastics, massage and Electric Treatment to their pupils, most of whom wanted to learn social skills and graces at a time when the dance hall was the likeliest place to meet the opposite sex; the local gymnasium provided a sizeable space with a good floor. Here Ethel took her pupils for lessons, with toddler Michael in tow, 'mainly', he surmised, 'to keep me out of mischief', but soon he was joining in and made his debut in the school show at the Lyceum Theatre as Little Boy Blue. He was four years old. Many years later he referred to catching 'that dreaded disease – stage fever ... the stage ... was the personification of glamour and a road, the end view of which was that splendour of lights and the smell of greasepaint – a heaven wherein dwelt ... gods and goddesses. The audience – that mass of inferior beings who sat and worshipped our every move ... when we had given them a sufficient glimpse of our glorious genius, would clamour for more and shout our names and live for the time when they could ... share another hour or two of our immortality and dwell with us in those realms of perfected technique or inspired make-believe. Now – the only problem was the slight one of getting there ...'[3] He always believed in the magic of theatre, not as escapism, but as something life-enhancing.

Children learning ballet in the 1920s had no context: Michael never saw a ballet company until the De Basil Ballets Russes in the 1930s so he had little idea what the end product of all those exercises could be except in terms of dancing school displays or pantomime. It was through *Dancing Times* that he discovered the wider 1920s dance world, laying the foundations of his life-long regard for the dancers he read about in his youth.

---

3   MS Stagecraft lecture to Royal Ballet School students 1971

1 In a Hayward and Milbourne school show in the 1920s with Betty Hayward.
Photograph by C. Sledmere.

Being one of the few boys in a dancing class never troubled Michael; he
was not the first nor the last to realise the advantages – special attention
from teachers and examiners and from the girls. He did everything –
character, national, musical comedy, Greek and ballet. Over the next decade,
he appeared in myriad school shows as Pierrots, drummer boys, toys and
nursery rhyme characters, as a newspaper boy and an Onion Boy, in dances
on May Day, Easter and Christmas themes, in the Gavotte Pavlova, ballroom
exhibition dances, as Pan, a Jester, a Spinning Top, a Lobster, Mickey Mouse
and in Russian dances – delighting audiences with his high leaps. A review
of him as the Prince in *Cinderella* was, in brevity and content, the forerunner
of many: 'Michael Somes as the Prince was excellent'.

Photographs in the programmes suggest he was a star pupil, sometimes
pictured with his first partner, Betty Hayward ('two of the most successful
of Miss Hayward's younger pupils ... presented amusingly and with marked
ability'). He stands out from his chubby and stiffly-posed contemporaries, a
good-looking boy, with a natural sense of line and an easy self-possession.

Performing was not limited to school displays. In 1928 he appeared
as Beelzebub in *Defendamus – a Pageant of Taunton*, one of the monster,
loftily-intentioned community pageants which were popular in the 1920s
and 1930s. Another activity was folk dancing. Cecil Sharp founded the

English Folk Dance Society in 1911 and by the1920s there were branches throughout Britain. The Taunton section was founded in 1925 with Ethel as secretary, and at their first demonstration Michael performed two Morris jigs – Shepherd's Hey and The Fool's Dance. He took part in folk dance festivals and huge folk dance parties, involving over a thousand local dancers and later boasted that Cecil Sharp said he would make the 'finest Morris dancer in England if he gave his time to it'.[4]

Dance became so time-consuming that Michael, although clearly exceptionally musical, never learned to play the piano or read music. He could play by ear, but described himself as a 'poor pianist' and, given his perfectionism, he would never have been satisfied unless he could be world class. Ethel was, however, right to record his 'exceptionally quick' hearing – his ear was more acute than many professional musicians.

Michael was one of the first generation to benefit from the teaching reforms when Miss Hayward became a Member of the AOD and her pupils embarked on the examination treadmill. He claimed that he was not particularly good, even at dancing school level, but got by because 'I naturally saw to it that I was made a great deal of fuss of by the dancing-teacher – by which practice I managed to secure from the visiting examiners ... high, & I'm sure quite unmerited marks!'[5] He took Grades I and II in December 1928, III a year later and IV and V at six-monthly intervals after that, scraping honours in every grade except Grade IV, and by 1933 had gained his Intermediate; all examiners praised his elevation while noting a tendency to strain his head back.

In 1930, Margot Hawkins took over the studio; she was a member of the Imperial Society of Teachers of Dancing and Espinosa's British Ballet Organisation, so Michael took BBO exams as well.[6] Now his examiners were men, including Espinosa himself, and reports more detailed: he began with Grade V in 1931: 'Good consistent work – has the making of a nice dancer – good elevation & ballon ... throws head back too far.' He had started to show off his praised jump, and Espinosa cautioned him not to 'use exaggerated (sic) elevation on all steps'. His Intermediate exam comments noted, for perhaps the first and last time in his life, 'All work needs to be *broader* and more virile ... not a girlish carriage of arms'; boys taught by women and working alongside girls easily absorbed feminine ways of moving.

There never seemed any question that Michael would be a professional dancer. To say it was an extraordinary act of faith on his parents' part is

---

4   Anon, *Michael Somes as Choreographer First Ballet is praised, Somerset County Gazette*, 8 April 1950.

5   MS British Council lecture 1961

6   Espinosa had resigned from the AOD 1930 and established the British Ballet Organisation with its own syllabus and examinations system.

putting it mildly, given existing prejudices and no clear career path: by the 1920s, ballet had disappeared from the Empire and Alhambra, the Harlequinade was dying, musical comedy and revue needed few dancers. Diaghilev's death in 1929 (aborting plans to set up an English branch of his company) and Pavlova's in 1931 closed those doors.

Then, in 1933 the De Basil Ballets Russes, led by Leonide Massine, hit London and ballet exploded. The company inherited much of Diaghilev's repertory while creating works that aroused both admiration and passionate controversy. The public idolised the 'Baby Ballerinas', Irina Baronova, Tamara Toumanova and Tatiana Riabouchinska, pupils of the great Russian émigré ballerinas in Paris, Mathilde Kschessinska, Olga Preobrajenska and Lubov Egorova; barely in their 'teens, they were a sensation, not just technically brilliant, but with an emotional and theatrical maturity beyond their years. The Russian Ballet was back.

Its success was a double-edged sword, reinforcing the perception of Russian supremacy in dance, while keeping the spotlight off two embryo British companies, allowing them to grow quietly and slowly. Small performing groups had evolved from the schools established by Ninette de Valois and Marie Rambert in the 1920s. Rambert's Ballet Club was based at the Mercury Theatre in Notting Hill Gate with a mostly subscription audience. De Valois had seen the advantages of working within a repertory theatre and her company and school were part of Lilian Baylis' organisation, dedicated to producing Shakespeare, opera and ballet for the local communities around the Old Vic at Waterloo, south of the Thames, and Sadler's Wells in Islington, north of the Thames – hence the Vic-Wells Ballet. Neither company performed every night, so the few English dancers appeared for Rambert and de Valois as well as the Camargo Society,[7] taking jobs in the commercial theatre to tide them over lean patches between seasons.

Michael's focus, however, was still local. As dancing became a popular childhood activity and the number of accredited schools increased, the dance competition flourished. Michael regularly entered the Bristol Eisteddfod in Operatic, Classical, National, Character and Musical Comedy; the judges were not always flattering, noting weak back and line, a lack of strength, not much expression and that tendency to hold the head back, though all were complimentary about his elevation and, in Duet, his most highly scored category, Felix Demery noted his good ballon. He was not often a winner – 'Glynis used to win everything before I arrived, but they used to let me win a few prizes to encourage me' – Glynis being an extraordinarily talented child called Glynis Johns. Most memorable was his first encounter with Karsavina: he recalled with awe how she made him stand behind her,

---

7   The Camargo Society, established in 1930, produced occasional evenings of ballet, commissioning English composers and designers to work alongside young choreographers.

'(my) hands reaching up to her waist ... (as) she demonstrated and explained the intricacies of the glissade. My thoughts flew to those magical ballets performed during Diaghilev's first invasion of Paris, and just what it really must have felt like to be her partner.'[8] He particularly remembered her elegant, red high-heeled shoes. Though not overwhelmed, she noted '... he is shapely and has very good elevation, which are the most important qualities for a male dancer ...'[9] Her encouragement was a great boost to his ambition and he became her slave for life.

How to fit school around all these activities was a question that exercised Arnold Goodliffe, headmaster at Huish's Grammar School for Boys, where Michael went after receiving his early education at his mother's school. Goodliffe, a strong disciplinarian, with a variety of canes to hand, was no philistine, being a former choral scholar at King's College, Cambridge and a member of the local Madrigal Society, but when considering his pupils' careers, he thought traditionally – a steady job in a bank, insurance or, this being Somerset, agriculture. He was bewildered, scandalised even, that three pupils refused to conform – Gerald Hooper, later Abbot of Buckfast Abbey, Arthur C. Clarke, doyen of science fiction writers, and Michael Somes.

Inevitably, Michael's dancing invited taunting from his schoolfellows, but he could usually out-run his tormentors. His PT teacher, an ex-army sergeant, with a splendid waxed moustache, encouraged boys to settle disputes with the boxing gloves, although there is no evidence that Michael ever resorted to this expedient. He described himself as a 'quite an ordinary, rather brainless, school-boy'[10] whose father often did his homework, while his French teacher, Reginald Trevett, recalled him as a 'dapper, gentle, quiet, and highly intelligent little boy ... His sensibility, courage and pertinacity were ... obvious.'[11] Eventually Goodliffe demanded that either Michael concentrate on his lessons or leave school and get on with his dancing.

Michael was too young for a BBO scholarship and AOD scholarships were only available for lessons twice a week in a few major cities, and neither were geared to the potential professional. Ethel wrote for advice to Espinosa, who reiterated that, with hard work, Michael should have a successful professional career but that he must go to London. Demery advised him to continue studying a wide range of styles, '... (with) Operatic as a primary subject ... one has to be very versatile and the elocution would be useful' (in fact, he was already taking Guildhall elocution exams) and suggested writing to Ninette de Valois.[12]

---

8   Foreword to *Theatre Street*. ts in MS papers
9   Tamara Karsavina to ES, 1 March 1933
10 MS British Council lecture 1961
11 Reginald Trevett, notes for dinner honouring Somes, Huish's Grammar School nd
12 Felix Demery to MS 2 April 1932

It was Kathleen Gordon, Assistant Secretary of the AOD, who suggested he become a student assistant with an established dance teacher, specifically Katharine Blott, a successful teacher in Weston-super-Mare since 1912. Dancer and choreographer Clover Roope, daughter of Blott's partner, Rita Watts, remembered her as 'incredibly strict and quite frightening' but her school shows 'were always beautiful and the costumes were exquisite'.[13] In September 1933, Michael left school to work full-time with Blott.

Surviving notebooks record his activities: between two and four classes a day, six days a week, itemising various dances, Hornpipes, Harlequin, Tap Dance, Hiawatha's Lullaby, Duet, Classical, Tap, ballroom and timetables for Elementary and Advanced exams: references to 'students' and 'babies' suggest that he was also teaching. In the Bristol Eisteddfod, he won the under-17 Classical (Greek) section, which earned him his first solo news story headlined 'The Only Boy – And 50 Girls' over a photograph which is notable for enthusiasm rather than line. *The Weston-super-Mare Gazette* reported that 'Michael Somes showed that he is a dancer of great promise, and this was especially noticeable ... when he did some clever tap dancing in the course of a traditional jig number.' He began practising his autograph.

Miss Blott was highly impressed with Michael's character, enthusiasm and capacity for hard work. She was a good teacher, but, like most, had little experience of teaching the exceptionally talented, so, early in 1934, Ethel wrote to de Valois. De Valois was interested: the Vic-Wells Ballet was desperate for male dancers, though not as desperate as Michael liked to make out when he said they would take anyone. The fees were £14 14s (£700) for a 12 week term, covering Operatic dancing, theory, character, plastic movements and mime; an extra inducement was the chance of stage experience.

An interview was arranged for 1 February 1934 with de Valois' assistant, Ursula Moreton. He made such a good impression that they offered to halve the fees, but even so, the family could not afford the other half. Disappointed, Michael returned to the daily trek to Weston.

Ethel now sought the advice of Arnold Haskell, who had just published the first (and last) ballet best-seller, *Balletomania*. She stressed the financial problems, but pleaded 'He has the highest ideals & is longing for a chance to really work.'[14] Haskell reiterated that Michael should be in London with, he suggested, Rambert, Nicholas Legat or Lydia Sokolova, former leading dancer with the Diaghilev Ballets Russes, who had just opened the Cecchetti-Diaghileff Rehearsal School. He estimated that training would cost £60 (£3,000) a year plus living expenses and enclosed a letter of introduction to Sokolova, adding the warning 'Guard at all costs against effeminacy. There is

---

13 Interview with author
14 ES to Arnold Haskell, 1934

no future for the effeminate male dancer.'[15]

He might as well have suggested flying to the moon. Ethel was losing pupils to a rival school and money was tighter than ever. Lawrence had been diagnosed as schizophrenic and was not working, but loans raised for his education still had to be paid back, and Ethel's mother, who lived with them, required frequent medical attention. With an income of only about £100 (£5,000) a year to support five adults, the family was practically destitute, yet they never considered Michael taking a job to help out. He saw the strain his mother was under and the sacrifices being made for him, and his fellow students remember him vowing that he would pay his parents back some day.

Suddenly, events started to move very fast.

Their plight came to the attention of J. L. Lloyd, Vice Principal of Ethel's old college, Fishponds. Impressed by Michael's intelligence and determination she resolved to help. Knowing all about financial struggle, she was full of practical sympathy; she had extensive experience of trusts and charities, but most had specific aims which were unlikely to include ballet training for a boy.

Then an advertisement appeared in the *Daily Telegraph* for 'an exceptionally talented boy dancer to train'. It had been placed by Jill Argyll, who had worked on the first AOD Children's Examinations syllabus, and whose school had branches in London and Europe. It was too good an opportunity to miss and an audition was fixed for 2 December. Using Haskell's introduction, Michael arranged to see Sokolova the next morning and de Valois in the afternoon. He sold his bicycle to fund the train fare.

Jill Argyll and Michael were so taken with each other that he nearly cancelled the other appointments. However, the next day he presented himself at Sokolova's. The school exuded expense, was well equipped and promised the best teachers from all over the world. Quaking, Michael joined Sokolova's Cecchetti class, which was very advanced for him, but, he wrote to grandmother Somes, she praised his 'wonderful jumps and very good turns etc etc (don't think I'm boasting, I'm only telling you what she said, personally I think myself awful at present, but have faith in myself & physique & capacity for hard work for the future).'[16] However, the class started late and he was worried that he would miss his 1 o'clock appointment at Sadler's Wells.

The Finsbury Town Hall clock was already showing 1pm as Michael dashed up Rosebery Avenue and he hesitated, fearing he had missed his chance, but at Sadler's Wells he found the clock was always fast and de Valois

---

15 Arnold Haskell to Edwin Somes, 8 November 1934

16 MS to Alice Somes, 14 December 1934

was, anyway, running late.[17] She seemed impressed with his elevation, and then asked for a pirouette; despite the unfamiliar stage rake, he executed one of the best pirouettes of his life. She asked about his finances, assuming, in spite of his protests, that Miss Lloyd was 'Mr' Lloyd and his headmaster, an error she blithely perpetrated in her autobiography *Come Dance With Me*, to the annoyance of Somes and Miss Lloyd. Overall, he felt he had made a good impression.

A few days later, Jill Argyll wrote to Miss Blott promising him solo dancing in Europe with a salary from £10 (£500) a week. Then Miss Lloyd wired that she had heard from Lilian Baylis.

Brisk and business like, Baylis promised nothing. De Valois thought Sones (sic) very talented and that, with 'severe' training, he should go far: 'He has natural talent and grace, seems intelligent and hard working, and has a very good appearance.'[18] She now offered a scholarship covering full year's tuition valued at £44 (£2,200); he would be bound to the company for two years with an option on a further year, earning 10/6d (£25) for ballet performances, 5/- (£12) for opera ballet, although a permanent place in the company could not be guaranteed.

Michael, his heart set on the Russian ballet, thought the conditions 'very one-sided, for they will work hard with me to attain *their* only reward, no fees, but my ability'.[19] Baylis admitted that the 'binding' clause seemed selfish 'but it is a big thing for us to give a scholarship, and we are only justified in doing so if we stand to gain something for the work'.[20] Michael was the first boy whose talent justified them making such an offer.

It took both Miss Blott and Miss Lloyd to convince him that the long-term offer was best, although he still had to find living expenses. Baylis's handwritten postscript threw the lifeline: 'About two years ago a Mr Leo Glyn ... wrote to us offering to help a clever boy dancer if we had one ...'[21]

In fact, Glyn didn't really care for ballet (he was practically blind) and didn't even think Michael would make much of a dancer, but he believed that 'people who have ideals ought to be encouraged'.[22] He proposed a generous allowance, rather than a loan, allowing for extras, like massage and even clothes. Of the £180 (£9,000) needed for living expenses, Glyn promised £100 (£5,000) and friends raised the remainder. He was longing to get away from the anxieties at home and concentrate on his dancing and artistic

---

17 The experience left him with a lifetime intolerance of inaccurate clocks

18 Lilian Baylis to J. L. Lloyd, nd

19 MS to Alice Somes, 15 December 1934

20 Lilian Baylis to J. L. Lloyd, 12 December 1934

21 Lilian Baylis to J. L. Lloyd, 12 December 1934

22 Quoted in letter from J. L. Lloyd to ES, 29 December 1959

education; he started planning museum and gallery visits and learning languages. In a state of euphoria, he wrote thanking Lilian Baylis and she replied that she was glad they could offer him the chance: 'I know that you'll work hard, and be happy in your work.'[23]

'I only hope' Michael wrote to his grandmother, 'I shall be able to reward all these people, I shall try & do more than my best ...'[24] He never lost touch with Miss Blott, Miss Lloyd or Glyn.

There was hardly time to draw breath for de Valois wanted him in London on 27 December for coaching before the school term started.

There were no regrets for the lost dream of the Russian Ballet. Characteristically, Michael immediately gave his whole-hearted loyalty to the Vic-Wells; because he had chosen them, they must be the best, although there was little evidence to support his prescience when he wrote to his grandmother in December 1934: 'It will be nice to think I was a member of them in their early days when they become world famous, as they will in time ...' In two weeks his life had turned around. Predictably, but understandably, he called it 'the most wonderful fairytale.'[25]

23 Lilian Baylis to MS, 19 December 1934
24 MS to Alice Somes, 15 December 1934
25 MS to Alice Somes, 15 December 1934

3

Golden Days

In 1971, Somes spoke to the Royal Ballet School: 'To justify all that anxiety and headaches – not only of yourself but of your parents and those who have maybe made a lot of sacrifices ... not a second should you lose in acquainting yourself with all aspects of the theatre and what it takes to become not just dancers, but artistes'; being an artist imposed a huge responsibility 'of immeasurable depth' to themselves and the company to 'equip yourself with knowledge (and) experience ... in every aspect of ... our art'.[1] In 1934, when the Vic-Wells Ballet was only three years old, Somes was about to assume something of that responsibility as one of the first generation of dancers who, in Frederick Ashton's words, 'just didn't want to dance, they had to dance to guarantee the right of existence of ballet'.[2]

'We were rich in the stature of our leaders & teachers,'[3] Somes acknowledged. Foremost among them was the indomitable Lilian Baylis. All who worked with her were steeped in her ideals, and her driving mission and commitment intensified Somes' own. Neither particularly well-educated nor musically highbrow, she believed God had sent her to enrich the lives of the deprived communities living around the Old Vic and, after 1931, Sadler's Wells, through Shakespeare, opera and ballet, although, when she became manager of the Old Vic in 1912, Shakespeare was unpopular and the prejudice against English singers and dancers was strong. Her policy was simple – to give her people the best and have God as Chairman of the Board. 'The best' carried no overtones of superior patronage or elitism – she wanted to give something over and above mundane existence at a time when not everyone had a radio and travel was so restricted that many living around the Vic had never even crossed the Thames and there were Islingtonians who had never been further west than King's Cross, just over a mile away. As for God, faith, in the sense of a fixed purpose and strength of mind, often triumphed over the lack of resources and certainly someone seemed on the side of the Vic-Wells.

---

1 MS Stagecraft lecture to Royal Ballet School students 1971

2 *An Interview with Sir Frederick Ashton*, Hans-Theodor Wohlfahrt, Ballett-Journal/Das Tanzarchiv, 1 December 1988

3 MS British Council lecture 1961

In her unfashionable theatres Baylis offered what, elsewhere in Europe, was the province of state theatres. The Old Vic and Sadler's Wells were a registered charity, administered by a Board of Governors for the Charity Commission, with Baylis employed as General Manager. Although ballet and opera are ruinously expensive, they were committed to low seat prices, there was no subsidy and Baylis was answerable to the Board for every penny. It was no wonder that she was obsessed with money and could not pay big salaries so her famous prayer, 'Dear God, please send me some good actors cheap' was practical not parsimonious. By the 1930s, if the stalls were often sparsely filled, the cheap seats were packed with a supportive, yet not uncritical audience, mostly white collar workers, products of the new Education Acts, hungry for culture, but uncomfortable with the expensive West End or Covent Garden.

Baylis' triumph is that it was not through the pamphleteering and committees of brilliant theatrical geniuses, like George Bernard Shaw and Harley Granville-Barker, that the national theatre was achieved, but was born out of those 'amateur' beginnings. Today, when stress is put upon having the right building and funding, it is salutary to remember that then the 'national' theatre, opera and ballet were not buildings but people. Baylis and her colleagues were doers.

Baylis shrewdly appointed people to perform her miracles. In 1926, she chose Ninette de Valois to arrange opera ballets and work on movement with the actors and singers at the Old Vic. De Valois' first hand-experience of the problems of the later Diaghilev Ballet had convinced her that every company needed a school to ensure a continuity of dancers trained in the same style; in 1926 she founded her Academy of Choreographic (sic) Art as a first step to a company. Stars pass; companies move an art forward. Baylis agreed to absorb de Valois' school and fulfilled her promise to establish a ballet company once Sadler's Wells was rebuilt in 1931. Baylis was much in evidence around her theatres, a 'remarkable, – & for us boys, – rather fearsome character, who seemed able to appear in several places at once ... We were her family, – & no one was too humble to receive a kind word from her, – or too eminent to be reprimanded.'[4]

Somes arrived at a significant time. The embryonic years, when the ballet company didn't even have a name (programmes merely announced 'ballet' or 'opera') were over. Drama was settled at the Old Vic, ballet and opera at Sadler's Wells. The ballet had grown from six girls in 1931, with male dancers contracted as necessary, to twenty-five in 1935, including many who were to be the backbone of the company over the next decades, and would later become teachers of future generations. Original ballets were

---

4 MS British Council lecture 1961

being produced, rather than recycling existing ideas and scores and taking over Camargo Society productions. Engaging 24-year-old Alicia Markova allowed de Valois to mount *Casse-Noisette*, *Swan Lake* and *Giselle*[5] and usually guaranteed a full house.

By 1935, two performances a week (Tuesday and either Friday evening or Saturday matinée) plus dancing or walking on in the operas, kept the dancers busy for at least four nights a week during the eight-month season. Once annual provincial tours were organised from autumn 1935 (by Van Damm Productions and, from 1936, by Daniel Mayer), the dancers were employed on annual contracts and no longer had to take jobs to tide them over the summer. Following the usual theatre practice, rehearsals were partly unpaid, partly on half pay; holidays were unpaid. Security was de Valois' aim. She knew that, to be accepted as a career, ballet had to pay a living wage and, 'more important, how could we expect to have *male* dancers unless we could prove ourselves to be an accepted part of the English theatre'.[6]

Space was tight. The raked stage at the Wells was small – sixteen swans were a crowd. The opera company gave most performances, so had the most stage time; the ballet company had two hours a week. The one large rehearsal room was used by the school in the mornings and the company in the afternoons, opera requirements permitting. The Wells Room over the foyer doubled as rehearsal room during the day and coffee room in the evenings. One dancer could be rehearsed in de Valois' tiny office, if it was not needed for meetings. Somehow, classes for office workers (a welcome source of extra revenue) were also shoehorned in. This would be Somes' home for the next seven years.[7]

He proudly filled in details in his 1935 diary: 'Occupation in Ballet at Sadlers Wells Theatre, London; Health & Happiness Wonderful & lovely'. He had just enough to live on, 'but not too well, & with always that sharp reminder at the back of my head that I had to "make it" before the money ran out';[8] he always believed that things should not come too easily, a touch of fear being a spur to achievement. He lived on just 'a little too little' choosing daily between travelling to the Wells by public transport, or saving the fare for milk and a bun.

Somes had his first lesson from Ailne Phillips on Boxing Day 1934.

---

5 *Casse-Noisette* and *Le Lac des cygnes* were given their French titles in London, although *Swan Lake* was often used on tour. Not until 1963 was the latter regularly programmed as *Swan Lake*.

6 Ninette de Valois, *Step by Step*, W. H. Allen, London, 1977, p28

7 Sadler's Wells was revolutionary in being the first theatre to have a bar front of house *and* backstage. Despite Baylis' roots in temperance, she reasoned that if the orchestra was going to drink (and orchestras will), their money should go back into the theatre's coffers and not into the nearby pubs.

8 MS British Council lecture 1961

Once term started, there were two sessions each morning, elementary and advanced. The twenty girls in the school outnumbered the boys by five to one. Discipline was strict and students were so intimidated that they would never sit on the teacher's chair, even if the teacher was not there.

De Valois described the school as working on 'Russian Italian' lines. Her own classes were a distillation of her experiences of working with teachers from many different schools; fast, difficult and intense, they stressed lyricism, precise footwork and elegant port de bras. At the end 'you felt you had been tied in knots', recalled Pamela May feelingly.[9]

Representing the Russian school, was St Petersburg-trained Anna Pruzina, who had danced with Pavlova. '... absolutely crazy classes!' commented Somes. 'Her method is very strange & strenuous indeed & we shall profit a lot from it I think.'[10] Her classes were full of jumps, so Somes was immediately on her right side. She spoke little English and wasn't easy to understand: 'She used to say "Some more you come, so better it is"', recalled Alan Carter, 'Or "So high you jump so easier it is", but she didn't tell you how to do it. (But) she did give the company 'a bit of oomph'.[11] Markova later studied with her while creating Massine's *Seventh Symphony*, for the Ballet Russe de Monte Carlo, which was 'freer and more plastic ... Pruzina was wonderful in that area'.[12]

Principal male teacher was Polish-born former Diaghilev star Stanislas Idzikowski, Cecchetti's favourite pupil, an unforgettable Snob in *La Boutique fantasque*, Dandy in *Le Tricorne*, and a legendary Blue Bird; for the Vic-Wells Ballet he created the lead in Ashton's *Les Rendezvous* and danced Blue Bird, a mischievous Harlequin in *Carnaval* and a brilliant *Le Spectre de la rose*. His formidable technique, style and even lack of height 'enrich(ed roles) with a very personal quality that will be for ever, all his own ...,' recalled Somes. '(He had the) *greatest* integrity' and never vulgarised a role for personal acclaim ... (his) classes were performances, and none the worse for that'. He expected each dancer to '*reach* to exceed their *grasp*' and '... taught us to discipline *ourselves*, and it is impossible to calculate how much is owed to (him) ... in *this* country – for his *personal* example, and as a professor of dancing.' Somes was 'frightened to death of him'.[13]

Idzikowski initiated the students into the mysteries of pas de deux. In his class on 8 March 1935, Somes found himself teamed by default with a dark, exotic teenager ('beautiful' he noted in his diary); this was no premonition

---

9 Interview with author

10 Copy letters notebook dated 13 October 1935

11 Interview with author

12 Maurice Leonard, *Markova The Legend*, Hamish Hamilton, London, 1995, p180

13 MS tribute to Idzikowski at Service of Thanksgiving 1977

of things to come: Idzikowski removed Margot Fonteyn from Somes' inexperienced hands unflatteringly fast.

Mime was taught by Ursula Moreton, who had studied with the great Francesca Zanfretta, and the company's strength in this often neglected field came from her link to the Italian tradition.

How good was the seventeen-year-old Somes? For de Valois, it wasn't his technical ability but 'his extreme intelligence and musicality that told'.[14] '[de Valois] adored him of course from the word go', declared Somes' contemporary Leslie Edwards. 'She knew he was highly talented and she knew he was going to be a power in the company.' Edwards, whose own training was erratic, thought Somes well taught and 'absolutely perfect for dancing'.[15] His greatest assets were his exceptional musicality, facility in double tours and a lovely, seemingly effortless jump: 'if you hadn't got a jump you weren't a dancer', commented Leo Kersley, who saw the company throughout the 1930s before joining as a dancer in 1941. '[I]t was the thing from Nijinsky ... Somes had this incredible one that went on and on and on.'[16] Somes also set the standard for double tours: they would feature in every role Ashton created on him, becoming *de rigueur* for all male dancers. On the down side, his back and arms were stiff and his feet were weak. He did, however, have the looks: Julia Farron, Clara to his Nut-cracker,[17] '... nearly died, he was so beautiful. He really looked absolutely gorgeous before he did anything.'[18] Designer David Walker concurred: 'He was the most beautiful stage figure. And if you look at the hands and the way the legs are posed and everything it is magnificent – it is a wonderful piece of sculpture – he has an innate grace.'[19] Kersley remembered the strong masculine presence that came across the footlights, something Somes shared with Serge Lifar and Harold Turner, 'You could smell them as they came on, lovely! They were male animals.'[20] There was, however, a barrier to male technique in the 1930s, maintained Carter – the heavy wool tights, which never fit, bagged at the knees and shrank, so that the crotch ended up half way down the thighs, making it impossible to raise the leg beyond 45 degrees.

Students could join company class at midday, after which they learned their roles as walk-ons before graduating to the back of the corps de ballet and opera ballets. Somes began that priceless education that comes not just

14 Interview with author

15 Interview with author

16 Interview with author

17 Escort to Clara: the programmed role was Nut-cracker and separate from the Nut-cracker Prince, who partnered the Sugar Plum Fairy in Act II.

18 Interview with author

19 Interview with author

20 Interview with author

from doing, but by watching and listening: 'What a wonderful experience it *was*, to see Markova & Helpmann being rehearsed in a new choreographic work by F(rederick) Ashton, or a revival of some great classic under N(inette) de V(alois). To stand at the back of the Circle listening to a full orchestra under Constant Lambert, or even to watch the scenery being set was magic for us.'[21]

Markova, only in her early twenties, was undisputed ballerina and an example to dancers only a few years younger than herself, including Margot Fonteyn and her friends, the cool, beautiful Pamela May, Elizabeth Miller and June Brae, remembered as the 'sexy' one. Somes was enchanted by Markova, and idolised the brilliant, wayward Anton Dolin. For the first time, he saw a great partner at work and Dolin's immaculate, self-effacing presentation of the ballerina became Somes' ideal. Dolin honed Somes' double tours en l'air, though teaching him to land almost without a demi-plié might have contributed to later knee problems. Dolin always encouraged young dancers and was never too aloof to be polite. When Somes diffidently told his god 'that I wished we cld. all dance like he did, he said "You will some day".'[22]

Watching the remounting of Ashton's *Rio Grande*, Somes noted the sophisticated young choreographer and the beautiful teenager from the pas de deux class playing her first leading role. Ashton was part of the scintillating, stimulating core of the company along with the brilliant, witty, unruly Constant Lambert, white hope of British composers, and a superb ballet conductor, sensitive to the needs of individual dancers (he once began Odette's solo in Fonteyn's tempo, realised May was dancing, and seamlessly brought the orchestra into her tempo); he was also an unrivalled snuffler-out and arranger of music for ballets, a controversial music critic and, for Ashton, 'potentially the greatest man I have ever known'.[23] His dedication to the company's musical side, possibly to the detriment of his composing career, ensured its credibility in the musical world, but his importance was far-reaching, and he would pull dancers up over costume, presentation or behaviour. His role was so vital that, during the war, de Valois' principal prayer was 'Please God, don't let anything happen to Constant.' To Carter 'he was sort of genius, a bit of a god, and I couldn't think of anything to say to him'[24] but Somes never had that problem. Lambert's influence on his musical development was profound. Also, Lambert and his friend, artist Michael Ayrton, were champions of Berlioz and Somes absorbed their passion for a composer who would become his favourite.

---

21 MS British Council lecture 1961
22 MS diary entry 30 April 1935
23 Ashton unidentified radio broadcast
24 Interview with author

Dancers and musicians alike were in awe of Somes's musicality. Lambert declared he had the best rhythm and musicality since Diaghilev star Leon Woizikowski, whose rhythmic sense was legendary. Conductor John Lanchbery particularly admired his understanding of '... (not) only the relationship of the music to the steps ... not the structure, but the *colour* of the music, the colour and shape ... he was concerned that they wouldn't be lost in this different art form'.[25] His ear was 'second to none,' declared conductor Emanuel Young. 'I have never met in all my life any musician or conductor, and I've met some of the greatest, who had that kind of an ear. This is a thing that you don't develop, it's given by nature and God.'[26] Somes didn't read music but, when working on a ballet, he always listened to the music until it became second nature, never relying on the piano reduction in rehearsals. He had perfect pitch and phenomenal recall (he once sang the whole of Malcolm Arnold's ballet *Rinaldo and Armida* to Young from memory). Because of his exceptional memory, Young told Somes that, with a few lessons, he could be a great ballet conductor (Donald Twiner maintained that the suggestion originated with the pianist-conductors so that 'then he can't complain about us'); after consideration, he admitted 'I wouldn't have the guts'.

Many Ashton ballets were enriched by the elegantly pared down designs of his friend Sophie Fedorovitch, whose taste and judgement he trusted implicitly: she 'would ponder on things and weigh up which moment was right or which moment needed some amplification or which could be simplified,' remembered Fonteyn.[27] If anyone had a question of right or wrong, in theatre or life, they turned to Fedorovitch.

Dancer William Chappell brought friends from his art school days, including painter Edward Burra. Having worked in commercial theatre, Chappell and Ashton's horizons extended beyond ballet and equally Lambert's friends in Fitzrovia were links into the artistic world of the 1930s. Inevitably, something rubbed off onto the young dancers, making them less parochial.

There was a distinct hierarchy, with Lambert, Ashton and principal dancer Robert Helpmann at the top. Not all were aloof: 'Bobby (Helpmann) is very nice to me.' Somes confided to his diary. 'Harold Turner says I have very good possibilities. Invites me to class.'[28] Turner was the company's male virtuoso, a pupil of Alfred Haines in Manchester, who had toured variety theatres with Haines's English Ballet and appeared in commercial theatre before

---

25 Interview with author

26 Interview with author

27 Zoë Dominic and John Selwyn Gilbert, *Frederick Ashton, a choreographer and his ballets*, Harrap, London, 1971, p123.

28 MS diary entry 23 January 1935

studying with Rambert. The Blue Boy in *Les Patineurs* perfectly encapsulated his technique, buoyant character and sheer physical pleasure in dancing. Somes' contemporaries included Richard Ellis and Leslie Edwards, who became a life-long friend.

In April 1935, Somes met Leo Glyn for the first time. Glyn agreed to continue financing his training and ordered him a dress suit. References in letters to 'massages' and 'Turkish Bath' sounded warning bells to his mother, and Somes hastened to reassure her: 'I think he's alright & you needn't worry abt. him, he's only thinking abt. me & what will be good for me.'[29] They often met for a meal followed by theatre; throughout the 1930s Somes indulged in an eclectic diet of films (from *Mutiny on the Bounty* to Jessie Matthews musicals), theatre (pantomime to Shaw, Shakespeare to West End hits and musicals to a 'low revue at the Granville') and dance, including De Basil Ballets Russes, the Ballet Club,[30] Ballets Jooss and American ethnological dancer La Meri.

Music, however, was his overriding passion. After church on Sundays he visited his paternal grandmother in Putney, read musical biographies or one of the few books on ballet, and listened to music on his precious new wireless and gramophone. He had friends and relations of his own age in London, and set out to make the most of his independence. At the spectacular pantomime *Cinderella* at Drury Lane, they had a box, indulged in champagne and Somes had his first cigarette, smoking then being an accepted sign of sophistication.

But work took precedence. His diary records the breathless learning curve: on 25 February 1935 he learned the part of a party guest in Act I of *Casse-Noisette*, was shown how to make-up and made his first stage appearance the next day. On 3 April he made his opera ballet debut in Charles Villiers Stanford's *The Travelling Companion*. By the end of the season in May, he had appeared as the Innkeeper in *Coppélia*, a Huntsman in *Giselle* and the Usher who announces the arrival of Odile and Rothbart in *Swan Lake*. He learned in quick succession roles in *Rio Grande* (one of six 'Stevedores, Stokers, Loiterers and Natives'), *Les Rendezvous*, *The Jar, Job* and *Fête Polonaise*.

The dancers were always ambivalent about opera ballets: Fonteyn found them something of a joke but Somes loved them as a wonderful free musical education. The dancers could relax a little – 'We often had a giggle' reminisced Edwards, and even Somes joined in.[31] Most were choreographed by de Valois or Ashton, and over the next four years, Somes danced in *The Snow Maiden, Aïda, Die Fledermaus, Der Meistersinger, Rigoletto, The Bartered Bride, Boris*

---

29 MS to ES nd

30 Chappell remembered the Ballet Club as 'a very elegant thing .. We used to have the most fantastic, glittering audiences ...' Somes was uncompromising – 'I hate the Ballet Club really – such snobs!!' MS to ES p 3 November ny

31 Interview with author

Godunov, Carmen, Faust, Don Giovanni, Tannhauser and *The Marriage of Figaro.*

He had his first experience of creating a ballet shadowing Frank Staff as a Musician and understudying several roles in de Valois' *The Rake's Progress,* premiered on 20 May. On 25 May he recorded another milestone: 'Receive 1st pay cheque of 10/-!! v bucked!!!' However, he could not help feeling envious as the company went off to dance in Blackpool and Bournemouth, to be followed after the summer holidays by their first major provincial tour. Envy turned to euphoria when he was told that he would go as a student extra on the autumn tour (£4 a week (£200) plus fares) and Baylis confirmed that they would take up their option for next season at £3 a week (£150).

That summer Somes embarked on an orgy of De Basil Ballets Russes performances at Covent Garden. He admired Massine's controversial symphonic ballets, *Les Présages, Choreartium* and later *Symphonie fantastique,* and, like everyone, was mesmerised by his Miller in *Le Tricorne.* Whatever was happening at Sadler's Wells, this was on another planet – 'you didn't really compare it with what you did,' explained Farron.[32] Somes saw the company whenever possible and years later claimed he could still remember many ballets in detail.

Back in Taunton for the holidays, he choreographed Paper Hat Brigade for his mother's school concert, and dropped into Miss Blott's studio, where his photograph was prominently displayed ('all children v. delighted to see me ...'[33]).

*****

Somes' first tour to Glasgow, Edinburgh, Manchester, Birmingham and Leeds in autumn 1935 was a bewildering experience. There was no advice about essentials, like finding digs, so, too shy, or too proud, to ask, he shadowed Edwards and Richard Ellis as they trudged the streets of Sunday Glasgow, before Edwards recognised him as the new boy. Together they found a small commercial hotel where they lodged in the basement for two guineas a week including meals. It was the beginning of a lifelong friendship, forged in shared dressing rooms, digs, performances and holidays. Everything had the glamour of novelty – the theatres, the reserved train compartments labelled Vic-Wells, even the digs were bathed in a rosy haze, despite being often squalid and cold, with queues for the bathroom, if there was one, otherwise it was cold water in the bedroom ewer and basin and an outside lavatory.

Outside London there was little awareness of ballet, but by the late 1930s major cities could count on seeing the Vic-Wells, Ballet Rambert and Markova-

---

32 Interview with author

33 MS diary 9 July 1935. Among the awe-struck children was Deborah Trimmer. She, too, went on to the Vic-Wells School, but forsook dancing for acting and Hollywood stardom as Deborah Kerr.

Dolin fairly regularly. Many theatres were considerably bigger than Sadler's Wells but audiences were usually good and enthusiastic if not particularly knowledgeable. Reviewers preferred *Job* to *Giselle*, admiring the company's 'Englishness', richness of characterisation and youthful vitality, although the men and overall technique were often criticised: an 'English ballet ... of which we can modestly be proud', enthused R.C.R. in Birmingham, although he complained that the corps was sadly lacking in the '*diable au corps*'.[34] If finesse and polish were lacking, the company made up for it with a winning combination of sincerity, zest and a sense of enjoyment.

Tours were excellent training grounds; more performances improved teamwork and gave young dancers the chance to try out roles: by the end of the tour Somes had graduated to a Son and a Messenger in *Job*, the pas de six in *Les Rendevous*, Fencing Master and Violinist in *The Rake's Progress*, Danse Arabe in *Casse-Noisette* and a Footman in *The Haunted Ballroom*, as well as walking on in *Giselle* and *Swan Lake*.

Although shy, Somes got on with people and was quickly accepted, joining Claude Newman, John Byron and Turner on a trip to Warwick and Stratford; Dolin even introduced him to some of his 'swank' friends, offered to show him how to make-up and took him out for tea. Somes was in an ecstasy of hero-worship. However, after the last performance in Leeds, Markova and Dolin left to form the Markova Dolin company.

Markova left at the right time. She had been an inspiration in the embryonic years and without her the company could never have mounted the classics nor gained acceptance so quickly. Many dancers feared the company could not survive without her, but, as Haskell later wrote, 'The opportunity arose, and the company was ready; young, a trifle raw, but a genuine personality, where before it had been a group of schoolgirls and boys.'[35] In 1935 he was less sanguine and suggested to de Valois that she bring in an established ballerina, like Olga Spessiva: de Valois was adamant: 'If I do that, I will rob all my young dancers of their self-confidence and we shall never have a national ballet.'[36] Instead, she contracted the ravishing Pearl Argyle and the scintillating technician Mary Honer while grooming three interesting young company dancers, Elizabeth Miller, Margot Fonteyn and Pamela May.

The pressure on de Valois as choreographer was relieved as Frederick Ashton joined on full contract.

The first new star to emerge, however, was a slender young Australian, marked out by his deliberately over-brilliantined hair. This was Robert Helpmann, 'the rock upon which the Vic-Wells church is built' in Richard

---

34 R.C.R., unidentified publication, Somes press cuttings

35 Arnold Haskell, *Balletomane at Large*, Heinemann, London, 1972, p90

36 Arnold Haskell, *Balletomane at Large*, Heinemann, London, 1972, p90

Buckle's sonorous phrase.[37] 'With his small mouth, wide forehead, and huge, slightly protuberant eyes, he had a little the look of a moth on a tapestry binge', recalled P. W. Manchester, 'but it was a face that took makeup marvellously'[38] (and often a great deal of it). He was an excellent partner with a sound technique, which he knew how to make look better than it was. Above all, he was a matchless dance-actor. Assertions that he would never get into the corps de ballet today are beside the point for, as Manchester observed, 'as a performer he would still wipe the floor with almost anyone'.[39]

In an age when personality and theatricality were as valued as technique, Helpmann dominated the company – audiences adored him and throughout the 1930s and 1940s they, and their fellow dancers, thought Helpmann-Fonteyn, never Fonteyn-Helpmann. De Valois loved his unashamed theatricality and encouraged him to ever greater comic extremes. Performing was his life and his natural curiosity made him test himself, and succeed, in every aspect of entertainment – dancer, actor, film and revue star, broadcaster, director of plays, operas, musicals. '[O]nly those of us who were privileged to work & learn from him can know how much we all owe to his influence & example,' Somes recalled. 'His presence on the stage was so magnetic, that for the rest of us on there, it often felt a waste of time, & ... to follow him in a role, as I so often had to do, was a pretty hopeless task. (He was) not only a great artist, but a kind & generous human being who could share his talent for the benefit of others.'[40] When asked how they learned stagecraft, Julia Farron and Alexander Grant replied 'Watching Bobby', and doubtless Somes would have concurred.

Other changes helped the company to mature. The parochial flavour that haunted the early years began to disappear after the appointment of the formidable Tyrone Guthrie to overall charge of the Old Vic organisation. He became de Valois's boss, although he had never been bowled over by ballet, which he believed should be content to remain handmaid to the opera. There was a general rising of artistic standards throughout the whole organisation after he persuaded Baylis to bite the bullet and pay realistic wages for an efficient technical staff. Pleas to the faithful audience for old clothes to make the costumes ceased – although it wasn't easy to transform the jumble of the wealthy into dance costumes and most ballet productions had always been made from scratch.[41]

The return to London entailed a search for somewhere new to live in one

---

37 Richard Buckle, *Ballet*, Sept-Oct 1939 p9

38 P. W. Manchester, *The Royal Ballet at Fifty*, Dance Chronicle, 1982 pp111, 113.

39 P. W. Manchester, *The Royal Ballet at Fifty*, Dance Chronicle, 1982 pp111, 113

40 MS tribute in *UpROHr* nd

41 Leslie Edwards remembered being at one of Lilian Baylis's garden parties and wondering where the deckchairs had gone. Next day he saw his costume as a dancer in *Aida*.

of London's thousands of small lodging houses and hotels, which provided rented accommodation for the city's workers, and Somes simply left one when he went home for the holidays and found another when he returned. It could be expensive – leaving only £1 (£50) from a salary of £3 (£150) a week to cover living expenses. 'All our co. live from day to day financially,' he noted. 'Haven't any socks without holes.'[42] From 1935, he lived near the Wells, moving around cheerless rooms in Mecklenburgh Street, Brunswick Square, Calthorpe Street, Grange Road, Guildford Street, anywhere to sleep when real life was lived in the theatre.

Somes now had a new teacher for character dance, Nicholas Sergeyev, former dancer and répétiteur at the Maryinsky, who had mounted the classics for the Vic-Wells. He brought with him 'a selection of schoolmaster's canes with which we young boys were to become more than well acquainted as we struggled vainly to hold our legs up for 32 counts whilst dear old Matchaloff [Sergeyev's pianist] dreamed of Holy Russia & droned away his sad Russian tunes ... I often wonder what [Sergeyev] thought, used to the vast resources of the great Maryinski Theatre, struggling with us, the Opera Chorus, &, in Casse-Noisette, the Lord Mayor's Boy Players as mice & rats, reproducing those great Tschaikovski Classics.'[43] Somes was awestruck by Sergeyev's recollections of Tchaikovsky playing *The Sleeping Beauty*, meekly making alterations as demanded by Petipa. Somes' later habit of buttonholing terrified company and students and firing 'Who was ...' at them came from his appreciation and awe of these direct links into ballet's history and the belief that those who did so much to establish ballet in Britain should never be forgotten.

Thanks to his excellent memory, Somes was a quick learner and was soon appearing in ever-more substantial roles in nearly every ballet: Valse Nobles in *Carnaval*, the Fencing Master, Hornblower & Musician, Gambler and Violinist in *The Rake's Progress*, the Nut-cracker, Danse Arabe and Valse des fleurs in *Casse-Noisette*, yet more roles in *Job* (War, Pestilence, Famine), Mazurka and Czardas in *Coppélia*; he was promoted to Huntsman and Czardas (then a pas de quatre) in *Swan Lake*, joined peasants in *The Jar*, the Noblemen in *The Gods go a-Begging*, Gendarmes in *Douanes* and soldiers in *Barabau*. Audiences began to take note. In the opera ballets he walked on as a bishop in the first English production of the original version of *Boris Godunov* and, when the opera was broadcast, all the dancers joined in the chorus and did plenty of 'crashing about' so that their families listening in could hear them.

A diary entry for September 1935 reads 'Ask Fred time meet him.' Ashton, now contracted full-time as dancer and choreographer, had already noted the

---

42 Somes copy letters notebook 1935

43 Michael Somes, Twelfth Night revels anniversary gala programme, Sadler's Wells, 1981

good-looking 18-year-old. He was working on Stravinsky's *Le Baiser de la fée* for Fonteyn and Turner and invited Edwards and Somes to watch him work on the pas de deux, so long as they made themselves inconspicuous. Somes was one of eight male villagers (men were still so rare that dancing next to him was the company's property master, Harry Chatting).[44] '... (Ashton) is awfully nice to me' Somes wrote to Ethel, '& I must keep in with him, not only 'cus he'll help me but 'cus he's so nice & sympathises 'cus he was in the same boat as I was years ago before he was established.'[45]

Le Baiser de la fée, premiered on 26 November 1935, was an important work. The lyrical duet for the Young Man and his Fiancée is considered the first recognisably 'Ashton' pas de deux, although the chemistry was missing between the protagonists: Turner was an efficient partner, but, compared with Fonteyn, unmusical, although it didn't affect the success of the ballet. 'It was a riot' Somes wrote home. 'Never heard such applause from a packed house ... The critics went absolutely wild with delight!! ... I thought it would be a winner, & we all did it excellently! Freddy said he was in tears of joy!'[46] The ballet deserved a longer life, but the cost of the enlarged orchestra precluded frequent performance.

Ashton was in Manchester over Christmas, working on the new Cochran revue, *Follow the Sun* and Somes' first surviving letter to him is a thank-you for his Christmas present: '... For that, and for all your great help, good advice and kindness to me, which I have missed *very* much since you have been away, I cannot thank you enough, – I only hope you realise how much I appreciate it ... Love, Michael.'[47]

Somes' feelings were understandably complex. He was dazzled by Ashton's talent and sophistication and knew there was an element of self-seeking on his own side, but he genuinely liked Ashton and came to understand him as few others did. Ashton was drawn by Somes' masculinity and heterosexuality, the cause of attraction being the reason he was unlikely to succeed – 'Very Fred' remarked Carter.[48] 'I'm sure (Michael) was a wicked coquette when young'[49] observed David Walker, who knew him in the 1970s, and certainly Somes, flexing his sexual muscles, was not averse to flirtation and skirmishing while perhaps realising that unattainability would be his hold over Ashton. The company gossips were sure it was a full-blown affair, although nobody had proof.

---

44 Chatting later became Somes' dresser.
45 MS to ES p 14 November 1935
46 Copy letters notebook 1935
47 MS to FA 31 December 1935
48 Interview with author
49 Interview with author

Whatever their relationship at the time, it developed into a deep personal friendship with far-reaching repercussions. Despite Somes' youth, he had natural taste and the highest standards and Ashton had found another collaborator with whom he could discuss problems, rely on for honest, if sometimes brutal opinion, and who would push him to his limits. There would be times when Somes was the only person Ashton would listen to. If he sometimes bullied Ashton and treated him with less than reverence, 'almost roughly' as he himself admitted, it came from an understanding of Ashton's character, giving him the chance to play 'Mrs Tiggywinkle' and moan to sycophants how horrible Michael was to him. Sometimes it may have gone too far. Friends, hangers on and fans criticised Somes, but few had such understanding of Ashton's strengths and frailties, unquestioning, though not unqualified, devotion to his talent and a disinclination to see him give in to laziness and settle for second best.

Ashton was only one problem for the teenage Somes. His mother drained his emotions and energy. He loved seeing Ethel and was always grateful for his parents' support, but, having let him go to London, she now bound him to her with an emotional web of nervous illness and helplessness. His frustration poured out in scolding letters. 'I'm fed up with trying to be reasonable with you ... you *cannot* go on without food & that even if you *don't* want it you must eat it, & *give up things which do you harm* ... you whine because you feel lifeless & when one tells you what to do, you do it for one day ... we can't do anymore but just take no notice & let you go on your own sweet way & perhaps when you're not being taken notice of you'll realise your childishness & stupidity.'[50] After he suggested that his parents might come and live with him in London one day, it became a theme in her letters, as though reiteration would make it happen. He longed for independence, success and the good life, yet, only eighteen and embarking on an uncertain career, he accepted that he would have to assume some financial and social responsibility for his parents.

Somes passed seamlessly from school to company. His future at least looked secure as he signed contracts for the autumn tour and 1936-37 season: £4 (£200) a week to cover all performances on tour and, as customary, those earning under £10 (£500) a week gave one week of rehearsal free, the others on half salary. Although money was still tight and he often had to borrow a few shillings or £1 from his mother, it was not bad at a time when the average weekly wage was around £2 10s a week (£125). He was also promised a contract for the following year at £3 (£150) a week, 10s (£25) more than originally promised. 'I have another season to go after that haven't I? But I don't mind as its ... far the best thing I can be in every way & possibilities

50 MS to ES p 16 November 1936

of going touring abroad.'[51] The company was already receiving invitations to tour, including America, Berlin, Paris and South Africa. A group of East European foreign ministers had visited the Wells '& were simply enthralled & astounded & impressed! ... Had opened their eyes considerably.'[52] In fact, the outside world was becoming increasingly unstable. The death of King George V cast a blight over January 1936 and national mourning was succeeded by concerns over Abyssinia. The boat rocked, but life went on.

In February the company opened the new Arts Theatre in Cambridge: 'I don't think I've ever laughed & had such a good time' Somes wrote to Ethel. 'Ninette running after 1 of the buses which left without its share of people, she in evening dress running & bawling up a Cambridge street at 2 o'clock in the morning & all of us laughing our wits out ...' There was not enough champagne to go round 'as the orchestra pinched it & set up a bar in the coach going home!!!'[53]

Back in London, the big surprise he learned from the company noticeboard – that he was not only in Ashton's new ballet *Apparitions* but would understudy Helpmann in the leading role of The Poet. What the rest of the company felt about the newest member of the corps de ballet covering a leading role is unrecorded and expecting the inexperienced Somes to follow Helpmann looks like passion overcoming Ashton's judgement – the first scene was almost all mime and exploited Helpmann's particular sense of romantic fervour – but de Valois must have agreed: after all it would be good experience and the likelihood of Helpmann ever being off was nil.[54]

Apparitions took its theme from Berlioz's *Symphonie fantastique*, a poet's opium-fuelled pursuit of his ideal, but was danced to Liszt, arranged by Constant Lambert (at the first orchestra call the Galop was so infectious that the dancers got up and danced round the auditorium). But with a week to go the ballet was nowhere near finished. Nor were the costumes. To ensure that his designs were executed with the requisite chic, Cecil Beaton handed over his fee to Barbara Karinska, one of the most respected costumiers in Britain, but famous for never having costumes ready on time.[55] They were not ready for the dress rehearsal. Nor had they arrived on the day of the performance. They arrived in taxis during the interval before the premiere on 11 February.

Apparitions was a critical and audience hit. Somes was one of eight Dandies in the Ballroom and walked on as an anonymous monk in the funeral cortège,

---

51 MS to ES nd

52 MS copy letters notebook 1936.

53 MS to ES p 7 February 1936

54 Correct. Apart from a couple of performances by Chappell, Helpmann did every performance until he left the company in 1950. Somes at last got on in 1952.

55 Which is why Fonteyn had to wear an unadorned rehearsal dress for early publicity photographs.

when anyone who could move donned robe and cowl: to the company's glee, Ashton, de Valois and even rehearsal pianist Hilda Gaunt would occasionally have to 'put on cloaks & walk around trying to look solemn! – it's the funniest thing ... & none of us can keep from laughing ...'[56]

There was more laughter when the company appeared in Paul Czinner's film of *As You Like It*, starring his wife, the legendary Elisabeth Bergner, and the young Laurence Olivier. In practice this meant 'we spent most of the day in the canteen having a jolly old time laughing & slacking abt. ... The time & money they waste is unbelievable. ... We were all dismissed ... abt. 8-30 ... collected our 2gns for nothing & went home ..."[57] Somes earmarked £1 (£50) for some new clothes.

'Laughing and slacking about' seem uncharacteristic; most contemporaries, fashionably flippant about their work, were impressed by Somes' seriousness. Fonteyn remembered him as supercilious, working very hard, not relaxing and giggling with everyone else, but shyness probably accounted for the characteristic held-back head which gave the impression that he was looking down his nose at everyone. Somes, however, remembered golden days filled with laughter, the fun of sharing digs and giggling in the operas. 'He liked laughing, we all laughed in those days,' declared Edwards. 'Miss de Valois, however she might tick us off, would always be in peals of laughter the next minute.'[58] Letters home conveyed the relaxed fun, laughter and sheer joy in being young.

*****

During the summer break, Somes helped his parents move into a new house in Taunton, before a postcard peremptorily summoned him back: 'It is compulsory that every one [sic] attends.' To publicise the recently announced five-year plan for the Vic-Wells Ballet, the first class after the break was given by one of the plan's vice-presidents, the legendary ballerina and ex-mistress of Tsar Nicholas II, Mathilde Kschessinska.[59] An invited audience, including society and critics, ensured gratifying media coverage. Somes was in his usual ecstatic state faced with a legendary dancer. '[Y]ou were entranced by her all the time!! ... We cldn't understand what she meant as she spoke hardly any English, but you cld. understand by her wonderful gestures, – her whole body spoke all the time!! ... she is the most wonderful dancer, teacher

---

56 Copy letters notebook August 1936

57 MS to ES p 21 February 1936

58 Interview with author

59 The plan proposed establishing long-term contracts with rising salary scales, insurance and hopefully pension schemes, setting up the Vic-Wells School of ballet along the lines of stated-aided Continental schools, providing dance and general education, and filming important ballets.

& personality I've ever seen – her & Karsavina. I drank in every one of her lovely movements she only looked 40 & is 63 & danced like 25!! She said something v. complimentary ... something abt. us being the coming dancers & very good etc.'[60]

On the 1936 autumn tour, Fonteyn and Helpmann took top billing. 'We are now all "hardened old pro's"' Somes wrote proudly to his mother.[61] Touring brought the company into contact with the wider theatrical fellowship. Every week, hundreds of theatres through Britain offered every kind of entertainment, from Shakespeare to melodrama, musical comedy to variety and every week myriad companies and hundreds of performers were on the move, mingling on station platforms, on trains, in digs and pubs. Everyone travelled by train in specially-reserved compartments; portable gramophones alleviated the tedium of long journeys and Somes learnt to play whist. He adopted the languid, theatrical manner, easily misinterpreted by those outside, 'that sort of comic language that enclosed societies always have', explained Carter.[62]

Conditions in digs and rehearsal rooms – or rather the rooms in which they rehearsed – varied greatly, but the company was young and it was all part of the thrill of being in 'the profession'. Floors ranged from highly polished to full of splinters; in Birmingham, there was only a tiny bulb and they rehearsed in almost complete darkness. In Newcastle the dressing rooms were terrible, up long staircases on the second floor with only a few scraps of mirrors and one chair among the men. The dancers took it all in their stride – no complaining about conditions because that was how it was if they wanted to dance. Not all digs were at the lower end: in Brighton Somes and Claude Newman stayed in John Gordon's [of Gordon's gin] flat, 'wonderful furniture & every luxury!!', waited on by 'a sweet German woman ... sherry then served dinner on the most exquisite china ... I shall prob. never have such luxury again.'[63] In Bristol Somes was struck by 'mirror in the bed', though whether set into the headboard or above he does not say, nor whether he drew any conclusions. Theatres too varied – some still allowed smoking in the auditorium. The dancers fitted in sightseeing – visiting the new luxury liner the *Queen Mary* and seeing the old *Mauretania* being broken up interspersed with trips to Sherwood Forest, Loch Lomond and Whitley Bay.

There was never enough rehearsal time: 'In 'Lac' I dance the Mazurka which is very strenuous! Me & my partner knew hardly anything about it & were saying under our breath to the next couple "what comes next?" Ninette

---

60 MS to ES p 21 July 1936
61 Copy letters notebook 1936
62 Interview with author
63 MS to ES p20 April 1936

& Ursula were pleased though & said I'd picked it up very well!'[64] Several reviewers noticed him as one of the three Gendarmes in de Valois' *Douanes* and his Violinist in the Bedlam scene of *The Rake's Progress* remained in Farron's memory half a century later.

1936-37 was Somes' breakthrough season. *Casse-Noisette*, redesigned by Mstislav Doboujinski, opened the season at Sadler's Wells on 22 September, with Somes and Ellis in the showy Chinese Dance. 'Everything went excellently' Somes wrote to Ethel. '... the enthusiasm after our number!! ... Ninette said (it) was a pleasure to watch & she said she found fresh funniness in it & that we must keep it up! It was the atmosphere of the whole house though – all Russian Ballet like so diff. from drab provincial audiences ...'[65] Marlene Dietrich, Alexandra Danilova and Irina Baronova were in the audience and Danilova wrote on her programme 'On the whole the Sadler's Wells Ballet is a wonderful achievement. I have had a genuinely good and exciting evening ... It seems to me that the company has all the future before it.'[66]

The opening was not without criticism. The press had harsh words for the loyal Wells audience, which was developing a lunatic fringe. De Valois too was concerned at a lack of discrimination – good and bad were received with the same shrill enthusiasm and new ballets were inevitably acclaimed. This was another reason why tours were good, exposing the company to less partisan audiences. Then there were those who went because they thought ballet highbrow and so reflected well on themselves to appreciate it: '... the average man and woman would go and see it more if he and she wasn't put off by the halo of remoteness and aloofness that is erected like a barrier between audience and stage. And it's the audience who has erected that barrier, not the dancers.' Unspoken was the detestation of the effete young intellectuals, the corduroy and sandal brigade.[67]

Somes remembered the '... great family feeling in our audiences & amongst them some wonderful & loyal characters such as the Lady Tenterden sitting in the Stalls & steadfastly refusing to remove her large hat. She sang her way loudly through those ballets & Operas she liked, only pausing to issue a loud 'ssh' – if anyone murmured a protest. Then there was Gen(eral). Waters, one-time aide-de-camp to the last Empress of China, whose great delight was to sit directly behind Constant Lambert & out conduct him in the Mazurka from *Coppélia* much to our merriment on stage.'[68] Best remembered was

---

64 Copy letters notebook 1936

65 MS to ES [23] September 1936

66 Quoted Clive Barnes, *Dance and Dancers* July 1951 p6

67 Anon, ?*Evening World, Bristol* March 1940

68 MS Gala programme Sadler's Wells nd

the legendary Miss Pilgrim, who never missed a performance except on the night Baylis died, when she 'just sat at home and thought of that wonderful woman and of all the beauty she had brought me.'

Somes celebrated his 19th birthday on 28 September ('I hate being 19'). He had hopes that Ashton would give him his old gramophone – with his wireless it would be his lifeline to music outside the theatre. Ashton's gifts to Somes were usually luxurious and practical – he occasionally bought him clothes and had given him his first watch. Somes reciprocated with presents that were practical and professionally applicable, often records. For Christmas 1938 he gave him two volumes of Dr Oska Fisehri and Max von Boehn's standard work *Modes and Manners of the Nineteenth Century*, an invaluable illustrated source for movement and costume.

The first new ballet of the season was de Valois' *Prometheus*, set to Beethoven's only ballet score arranged by Lambert and designed by the surrealist painter John Banting. Having stolen fire, Prometheus finds his neighbours unwilling to embrace progress and when the sceptics are routed by the Spirits of Fire, he settles for domesticity with wife, six children and the 'Other Woman'. It was not one of de Valois' enduring works.

Somes was one of Prometheus's Fellow Citizens alongside new recruit Alan Carter, who remembered it as 'an immensely complicated 'counting' ballet. I counted myself silly, everyone was counting something different – I'm sure it wasn't intentionally ...'[69] Even Somes, with his marvellous memory, found it very difficult to remember.

Carter found Somes 'very nice, he was helpful'. Dressing room 5, which they shared with Ellis and Edwards, could become something of a rough house and the occasional beer was not unknown. Somes had developed a huge admiration for the Georgian-born dancer Vakhtang Chabukiani, whose soft, high jump set off a style described as 'forte-fortissimo', masculine, full of bravado and *joie de vivre* but never graceless or inharmonious. When Somes' colleagues could no longer bear his pontificating about a dancer he had never seen, they locked him out of the dressing room, which opened directly onto the gallery, treating the audience to an extra show as the half-dressed Somes tried to get back in.

He was determined to improve quickly ('Must have "outside" lessons from Legat Massine & Woizikowski & Lifar.'[70]) 'Maybe he didn't hide his ambitions', mused Carter, remembering his dedication. '(Yet) he had a great modesty, and sometimes we got angry with him because we thought it was a bit false, but I think he was genuinely modest.'[71]

---

69 Interview with author

70 Copy letters notebook dated 6 May 1936

71 Interview with author

Somes contemplated being photographed in his minimal *Prometheus* costume. He had worn his Hussar costume from *Apparitions* for his first professional photographs, taken by de Valois' brother, Gordon Anthony, but he felt these showed off the costume rather than himself. Anthony's beautifully composed, atmospheric studio photographs, with innovative shadows evoking a ballet's sets, were published in the glossy society periodical *The Bystander*, introducing British ballet and its dancers to a wider public.

His desire to show off the body beautiful may have been fired by another rite of passage. Around this time, he and Fonteyn had a brief sexual relationship – his first, although not hers – but the chemistry was missing and Fonteyn's defining relationship of the 1930s was an emotional rollercoaster with Lambert. The brief liaison did not affect their friendship, forged in the shared experiences of those pioneering years. They had private names for each other, which they used for the rest of their lives – Sam and Sarah, so private that many close friends didn't know, although a note in Lambert's *Horoscope* score, casting one scene as 'Sarah & Sam, & the followers of Virgo', indicates that at least he and Ashton knew.[72]

Somes' preference was for English blondes and he turned his attention to Fonteyn's friend, Pamela May, although she denied that they were lovers: 'A kiss and a cuddle and that was it.'[73] '[W]ith Michael we were all just ships that passed in the night.'[74] A sexual aura pervades any closely-knit working group, but in ballet the hothouse atmosphere is exaggerated – beautiful, scantily clad young bodies, close encounters in pas de deux – but any recrimination and regret had to be subsumed into day-to-day working.

Although Somes projected a maturity, sexual attractiveness and sensuality that was later variously likened to Gary Cooper, Rock Hudson and Paul Newman, it was offset by an innocence, 'a sort of purity' as David Walker described it. 'He was not a corrupt person at all.'[75] Everything was a mix. Like all successful performers, he was attractive to men and women; he was shy, but loved the attention of being on stage; he was arrogant yet humble, with a clear sense of self, his looks and talents; gentle yet with an underlying sense of violence. His ambition was tempered by idealism.

Ashton's *Nocturne* was premiered on 10 November. To Delius' *Paris: The Song of a Great City*, a 'Spectator' observes the drama of a poor flower seller enamoured of but rejected by a rich young man. Somes was one of the revellers, careless of the tragedy in their midst. A subtly moving work, deftly walking the narrow line between sincerity and sentimentality, *Nocturne*

---

72 Somes did not know until much later that the Samuel and Sarah was one of Samuel Somes' ships.

73 Interview with author

74 Meredith Daneman, *Margot Fonteyn*, p109

75 Interview with author

revealed Ashton's growing mastery of classical vocabulary to express character and mood.

Somes was not only in at the birth of British ballet, but at the birth of television. In summer 1936, the world's first high-definition programmes were broadcast from Alexandra Palace in north London, and on 11 November ('all looking like death after the late night before') Somes was Famine when the Vic-Wells performed extracts from *Job*. He described the huge cameras, 'tons of machinery, switchboards & terrific lights like a film studio. The space allotted to the dancers is tiny – that's what they're up against now – size ... They were very pleased with it as it was one of the biggest things they'd done ...'[76] There were two live performances, at 3.25pm and 9.35pm. Somes greatly enjoyed the experience, and the £3 fee (£150). There were many teething problems in those early years: feet were often cut off, close-ups were insensitively used and in *Swan Lake* the cygnets, having finished in perfect unison, had to crawl off, still on camera. The company looked forward to their occasional appearances over the next few years, but for the extra income rather than the excitement of the new medium.

Ashton's wide social and theatrical acquaintance had advantages. In January 1937, fortified by dinner and champagne, he and Somes went to the Albert Hall to see the Folk Dance and Song festival, sitting in C. B. Cochran's private box ('everyone was giving us terrific regardés!!') Somes brought his knowledgeable eye to bear: '... the Roumanians were best as they were the most primitive & had lovely rustic & earthy & unselfconscious lilting rhythm ... the other was beautifully done but too pretentious ...' Somes thought Ashton should get photographs to use as reference – 'with all his talents as choreographer something great cld. be achieved ...'[77] – but Ashton wasn't buying ('creating '"another peasant dance" often brings forth a sigh' Somes recalled[78]) until *La Fille mal gardée* in 1960.

Ashton began to introduce Somes to his society friends. '... I went to a grand ... supper party ... Alice Hoffmanstahl [sic] – Freddies friend asked me ... We went in 2 Rolls & there was Constant, Margot, Claude [Newman], Billy [Chappell], Sophie Fedorovitch, the Count [von Hofmannsthal] & many of her friends ... It seems amazing that I have sprung up into the Bobby & Freddy etc grand set & right out of the corps de ballet ... I'm getting quite accepted now.'[79]

Mixing in society needed the appropriate clothes. He was very aware of how he looked and liked clothes and longed to dress well, but his income was simply too small. Miss Lloyd helped out and Glyn especially was generous

---

76 MS to ES p 16 November 1936

77 MS to ES p 11 January 1937

78 MS *Working with Frederick Ashton*, *The Ballet Annual 15*, A&C Black, London, 1960, p54

79 MS to ES nd early Oct/mid Nov 1937

in his support: on one shopping spree they spent £16 (£780) on a new suit (dark grey, quite plain), and overcoat from Wilde's 'a very fashionable place & it's the very last word in every way, everyone at the Wells adores it & you know what conossieurs they are!!'[80] 15s 6d (£37) on three 'arty' shirts and £4 12s 6d (£233) on underwear and accessories as well as black, brown and evening shoes. Grateful as he was to Miss Lloyd and Glyn, he longed for financial independence.

In the revival of de Valois' *Nursery Suite* on 19 December, Somes was second cast to Ellis as the Prince; other new roles, included Florestan in *Carnaval*, the Yokel in Country dance in *Façade*, Mercury in *The Gods go a-Begging* and the Peasant pas de deux in *Giselle*.

He was also working on Ashton's next ballet, premiered on 16 February 1937. *Les Patineurs* put on stage a smart skating party devised by Ashton to spotlight the company's growing virtuosity, especially Turner's. The choreography had wit and style, charm without coyness and cunningly showed off the dancers' individuality. Ashton was already demanding a great deal of upper body movement and bending. As the skating instructor, he created a fiendish role for Turner, which he performed with a tongue in cheek insouciance which few others have ever come near. Honer's fouetées rivalled anything achieved by the Russians, and she and Miller remain unequalled as the girls in blue.

With so much to praise, Ashton's cunning show-off moment for Somes as one of the four men in the pas de huit went unrecorded in reviews but not unnoticed: as one dazzling sequence followed another, and the finale built to a tremendous climax, the men leapt from one side to the other, then, one by one, off stage. Somes was the last, jumping high and sensationally into the wings and into the memories of a generation of balletomanes.

Encouraged, Ashton went so far as to talk to Somes about dancing *Les Sylphides* and Vertumnus in his ballet *Pomona* on the forthcoming visit to Paris. 'I said – nonsense!! You're talking drivel!' Somes wrote to his mother, '... for a long time he's been saying how he wants me to do all these rôles ... & how he wants to teach them & do everything except dance them. You see, he's a creative artist & ... he prefers to build on someone else ... altho' he can't dance (*Les Sylphides*) very well himself,' Somes observed candidly, 'he knows how it shld. be done. Karsavina taught him exactly how Fokine originally arranged it for her Pavlova & Nijinsky, & he knows all the tricks. ... I quite thought I might do perhaps fairly small parts next season ... But to do Sylphides ... at the end of this season ... I quite believe they'll find me unable to cope with it yet ... it's wonderful really, but really so insignifigant [sic] as what I want to do is be created on.'[81]

80 MS to ES p3 November 1936

81 MS to ES p 26 March 1937

If Ashton wanted the pleasure of teaching the ballet to Somes, de Valois had her own agenda: she wanted May to dance *Les Sylphides* and Somes was a good height for her. However, Somes was right and he did not dance the ballet that season.

Ashton found other ways to further Somes' career, arranging, and possibly helping pay for, lessons with Nicholas Legat, an excellent teacher for men. 'His classes were magnificent, human and enjoyable (if impossible!),' Somes wrote later, 'and one so well remembers having finished the last pirouette ages ago, while (André) Eglevsky and Alan Carter were still spinning on and on – André ever so slowly – and both until there was no impetus left ... I also remember him showing me the step he said was the original for Albrecht in the second act of *Giselle* consisting of three renversés. Needless to say, I never attempted it in public.'[82]

In the 1930s, new ballets were planned according to the needs of the repertory, not to a choreographer's whim, and now the repertory needed something light and relaxing, so, only two months after *Les Patineurs*, Ashton produced the sophisticated *A Wedding Bouquet*, a ballet for his friends in the smart set, which didn't stop the witty, bitter-sweet joke being enjoyed by a wider audience. Lord Berners was responsible for the music and costumes (aided by Chappell) and Gertrude Stein provided the text. First nights were now important occasions and the audience on 27 April included a strong artistic contingent, including Sir Thomas Beecham, C. B. Cochran and Anthony Asquith, plus miscellaneous Princesses, Duchesses and many aristocratic ladies, who arrived late and chattered all through the first ballet.

A Wedding Bouquet presented an acutely observed French provincial wedding and the attendant embarrassments, including the Bridegroom's rejected and *distrait* mistress and her Chihuahua; one guest gets merrily drunk and 'bitterness is entertained by all'. As Ashton said, it becomes funny because 'everybody is so serious in it ... I hate people to play for laughs'.[83] The choreography amusingly translated each character into movement; Stein's witty, apposite and always rhythmical text punctuated the jokes, although the opera chorus, speaking in unison, were inclined to 'bellow industriously but unintelligibly'.[84] The critics evoked Diaghilev in praising its unity and sophistication, although those who considered ballet highbrow (and, by association themselves), were shocked at the levity and the words 'music hall' were whispered.

The choreography fitted each individual dancer like a glove, allowing

82 MS Forward *Heritage of a Ballet Master Nicholas Legat* by André Eglevsky and John Gregory, Dance Books, London, 1978, p28

83 Penelope B. R. Doob, *A Conversation with Sir Frederick Ashton*, *York Dance Review*, Spring 1978, no 7, p24

84 P. W. Manchester, *Sadler's Wells Ballet Comes West*, *Theatre World*, ? 1941, p68.

everybody to shine; Somes was Guy 'unknown' according to the text, his character expressed in light and fluent movements, soaring about the stage in breathtaking, effortless jumps, like 'an agitated stag at mating time'.[85] For P. W. Manchester, in 'style and effortless execution, he gave ... what I should be inclined to say was the best bit of English male dancing I have ever seen.'[86]

The audience acknowledged Somes' progress on the last night of the season on 21 May. 'Simply colossal enthusiasm as I've never seen before' he wrote to Ethel. 'I got a terrific burst of cheers at the end of 'Patineurs' and shouts of 'Michael' etc. I was thrilled & the Gallery people said afterwards that they were shouting for me & all that applause – just before I went off was in recognition of my thrilling dancing that season ... I must say I gave them a thrill. ... I got right to one end of the stage & jumped right across & off & even the Co were amazed & I crashed right over everyones heads in the wings eventually landing up in the scene-dock!! ... The crush outside the stage door & the autographs I signed & people yelling on all sides, "there's Michael Somes isn't he marvellous" & "give us some more elevation" ...'[87] Although he later annotated it 'Conceited letter!!' he thoroughly enjoyed his first real taste of fan adulation.

The Vic-Wells Ballet now faced its biggest challenge as official British representative in Paris during the 1937 Exposition Internationale from 15 to 20 June. Performing alongside the Royal Danish Ballet, Markova Dolin Ballet and Catherine Littlefield's Philadelphia Ballet would be a salutary guide to progress and everyone was nervous. Glyn generously suggested that Somes stay on for lessons; de Valois thought likewise and arranged for Somes, Edwards, Carter and Paul Reymond to work with Alexander Volinine.

Few had travelled abroad before, and there was the excitement of getting passports and phrase books, the novelty of the Channel crossing and the thrill of seeing Paris for the first time. The Théâtre des Champs-Elysées was huge and remembering that the Diaghilev Ballet had appeared there did nothing to allay nerves, nor did an enervating heat wave. Tension turned to drama when Helpmann developed a boil on his leg and Somes was summoned for an 8.30am rehearsal to learn Vertumnus in *Pomona*. 'I was there *all day* with only cups of coffee – absolutely "Russian Ballet" rehearsals with Fred & Margot until I nearly fainted with exhaustion & the heat!' He then went into the dress rehearsal of de Valois' new ballet *Checkmate* which lasted until 3am, and was back in rehearsal at 9am, excited yet dreading that he might have to go on in his first leading role, with Fonteyn, before a sold-out house

85 Gordon Anthony, *A Camera at the Ballet, Pioneer Dancers of the Royal Ballet*, David & Charles, Newton Abbot, 1975, p90

86 P. W. Manchester, *The Vic-Wells: A Ballet Progress*, Victor Gollancz Ltd, London, reprinted 1947, p98

87 MS to ES 23 May 1937

on such an important night. 'Ninette is worried out of her life, & I may have to do Apparitions ... I'm so het up over all this. Margot is wonderful but its so difficult & I had no chance to watch it before 'cus of Checkmate.'[88]

Deep down he knew he had nothing to fear: '... my prophesing [sic] that Bobbie wld go on even on crutches was right ... But all my work was not in vain 'cus Ninette said she thought I was very good in it indeed, & that she was going to let me double it next season!!'[89] She and Ashton were impressed by how quickly Somes picked up the roles.

Checkmate had a prestigious first night in the presence of the Diplomatic Corps with the Garde Republican in uniform lining the staircases, although backstage a strike of scene shifters meant the hastily assembled stage-hands knew neither the theatre nor the scenery. Somes and Carter were the Black Knights, their subtle make-up of curving lines down the cheeks and black lips combining with the stylised headdresses to perfectly suggest the chess figures.

That evening apart, the visit was appallingly publicised, but if the theatre was rarely more than half full, audiences were impressed and several critics declared that it was the most interesting company to appear in Paris for years: 'It opened the doors on a conception of ballet which, far exceeding all expectation, surprised with its subtlety, delighted with its youthfulness ... allying tact with daring, tradition with originality, and stylisation with measure, it glorified choreography beyond them all.'[90] The ensemble was particularly admired and Somes singled out. The genuine, if unflattering, surprise that an English company had reached such a standard and built such a varied and individual repertory in so short a time would become a depressingly familiar reaction abroad.

Nothing could dampen the joy of that first visit, certainly not the disturbingly large groups of soldiers on the streets. Somes went sight-seeing with Ashton or Edwards, lit a candle and made a wish at Sacré Coeur, window shopped in the Rue de la Paix, watched class at the Paris Opéra, poured over relics at the Archives International de la Danse and was wowed by the 70-year-old Mistinguett. He loved the pavement cafés and the food (gateaux featured prominently in letters home, although his budget prohibited such indulgences). Lady Mendel threw a reception at Versailles, but the highpoint was Mathilde Kschessinska's last night party, where Somes proudly talked French to her and her husband, the Grand Duke André: '... when you think who she was & the people she's known ... so sweet & informal & yet so regal ...'[91]

88 MS to ES nd

89 MS to ES nd

90 L. Franc Scheuer, *The Vic-Wells Ballet in Paris*, *Dancing Times*, August 1937, p557

91 MS to ES 18? June 1937

After the company returned home, Somes, Edwards, Reymond and Carter moved to a cheap hotel in Montparnasse (20 francs (about £15) a night). With a budget of 12 francs (£8) a day Somes pictured them living as 'starving artists ... in our garret eating bread & cheese!!',[92] augmented by free food samples at the Exhibition, and walking to Volinine's studio near the Bois de Boulogne. Volinine had been a principal with the Imperial Russian Ballet in Moscow, partnered Pavlova and was Adeline Genée's first male partner in London. His exercises were devised to strengthen the arms, neck and back and make the body as malleable as putty;[93] he worked everyone exceptionally hard and concentration was not helped by his mistress flitting in and out, but he was pleased with Somes and told him he had 'done in 2 weeks what he usually expected to take 2 years, & that if I did the exercises he gave me etc, I shld. get all my faults right, in time. – well I hope he's right! ...'[94]

Their education continued at the Casino, watching Maurice Chevalier, and at the Folies Bergère, where a scantily-clad Josephine Baker was thrown about in a spectacular adagio number. Somes got a seat for the premiere of Lifar's *Alexandre le Grand*. He loved the Opéra and sitting among the French aristocracy (Ashton, in Kschessinska's box, ignored him) but was less enchanted with the performance: 'I thought Lifar still had something wonderful about him,' he wrote to Ashton, 'but the women and the ballets!! – I believe even *I* could do a better ballet!'[95] On their last night, Somes and Edwards went to a 'very grand Ball' at the Grand Palais, where Lifar performed *Icare*, but Somes was more impressed by his first sight of what became his ideal ensemble – the precision-perfect, high-kicking Rockettes.

Over the summer, he kept in touch with Ashton, who was holidaying in Austria with Alice von Hofmannsthal. 'I'm afraid (your) judgement is a little out ... for (Michael Somes) could never do Pomona anything like the choreographer would wish, and I'm sure he would hate to let his ballet down so badly. Nevertheless, it is thrilling to hear you say these things, even if I know I can never do them.' Taunton was dull; he longed to get back to work and see Ashton again 'no one else ... Love (such as it is!) From Michael'.[96]

*****

The 1937 autumn tour was the prelude to Somes' most significant season yet. As his career began to take off, his letters and diaries showed a mix of self-confidence, fear, trepidation, conceit, modesty and, most of all, exhilaration. He was billed sixth out of the forty dancers who set out for the regions a

---

92 MS to ES, nd

93 *Volinine at Work, Dancing Times,* January 1928 p548-551

94 MS to FA, p 7 July 1937

95 MS to FA, p 7 July 1937

96 MS to FA 19 September 1937

2 *Blue Bird* pas de deux. Photograph by Gordon Anthony.

month later than usual – touring in early autumn ensured better houses than July, when most northern towns were on holiday. Also, from now on, the company toured its own orchestra, which was much appreciated by many regional audiences, who were used to high musical standards.

In Newcastle on 2 September Somes made his debut in the Blue Bird pas de deux, a roller-coaster learning curve of things no school can teach: 'I rehearsed ... in the costume for the 1ˢᵗ time for over a week ... Mary (Honer) has been ill & I had to do it with Elizabeth (Miller) who was awfully sweet & helpfull. At the last minute – my shoes split ... my costume which had only just come was all wrong my headgear too big & a *hole* in the new tights & I'd never done it with Eliz & it was very strange in a ballet tutu ... it was terrible & I almost wept. But Fred took me home & gave me fresh courage & all the Co. were sweet ... & according to all accounts (I) gave a marvellous performance ... we got lots of calls & shouting which they rarely do in the provinces – it was marvellous to hear them clapping me – just me! At the end I did the leap off right into Joe's arms [assistant stage manager] & my knees gave way, it was a glorious feeling ... & then had to do quick change & do Gods & then Checkmate having done Rendezvous! Fred was delighted & said it exceeded all expectations & Ninette was thrilled & the whole Co ... I've rarely heard them so profuse over anyone. I hope you don't think I'm blowing my own trumpet but I know you understand & want to hear ... Now for Pomona ... Aren't I lucky.'[97]

The next night he danced his first dramatic role, the god Vertumnus in *Pomona*, who tries various wiles, including disguising himself as a lady of uncertain age, to win the nymph Pomona, danced by Fonteyn. He was nervous of dancing with her for the first time and almost more afraid of Mrs Hookham, her indomitable mother, who was travelling with her. Ashton described the role as 'the typical young man of Greek times, the athlete, prototype of the hearty of to-day, complicated only in an athletic way ... a god to whom everything comes easily, who will have his will, and who satisfies his desires'.[98] The highlight was a tender pas de deux, full of effective lifts, in which Pomona's archaic movements softened as she fell in love. Somes managed the romantic encounters but Lionel Bradley, who meticulously recorded performances in his diaries, noted that '... the comic interlude ... showed him almost completely lacking in a sense of humour & the power of characterising mime'.[99] Nevertheless, he signed lots of autographs and de Valois 'said I looked fine & had such finish & sustained it wonderfully ...

---

97 MS to ES p September 1937

98 Mary Schroeder, *Talking with the Body, The Ballet Dancer's Language, Leeds Mercury*, 17 September 1937

99 Lionel Bradley, ballet diaries, 9 October 1937, unpublished mss, Theatre and Performance Collections, Victoria and Albert Museum

Margot & her mother were thrilled & I didn't let her down once ...'[100] Ashton gave him a book inscribed with the hope that 'my dancing of Vertumnus wld. become as ledgendary as the myths of the Gods!!' *Pomona* didn't last long enough for Ashton's hope to be fulfilled.

As the new season opened, on 15 October Somes and May made a television appearance in Joy Newton's divertissement *Strauss-Tanze* reflecting four different 'moods' expressed in basically classical classroom enchainements to Strauss's *Perpetuum Mobile, Figaro Polka, Gondellied* (adagio) and *O Schöne Mai'* (waltz). In November he repeated his success in the Blue Bird pas de deux. Bradley recorded that 'Somes already has great elevation and does his turns more neatly and perfectly than most dancers of to-day ... It may not be long before he is a quite outstanding dancer ... Like Nijinsky he is exceptionally well developed at the base of his body & that perhaps accounts for the ease with which he rises from the ground. I thought myself that it was in that he shows a marked superiority to most dancers, rather than in actually rising to an unusual height, but it is the lack of apparent effort that is the most remarkable.'[101]

By now, Somes knew he would have the lead in Ashton's next ballet, but whether it was originally conceived for him is not clear. In November 1936, Lambert wrote to Ashton: '... I shall be free to look at *Horoscope* which has naturally been at a standstill',[102] but in March 1937 Somes wrote to his mother: 'I hope Fred may give me a part or two in his new ballets next season but *that* must come later, as to be created upon you must be thoroughly developed.'[103] However, by the time the score was finished that autumn, it had become 'my new ballet'.

Carter remembered *Horoscope*'s creation as 'a terribly exciting point'. Helpmann was away, acting Oberon at the Old Vic, '... and that was very good for the Company, you could sort of move a bit ... (he was) terribly uproarious, exaggerated ... very funny, but not entirely good for the younger people ... I think Michael felt that too.'[104]

To prepare for his biggest role yet, Somes sneaked off for extra lessons from Margaret Craske (10/6d about £25 each). By December Ashton was working on the solos: '.... Being Leo subject I have to be very full of nervous energy & attack & I do terrific leaps & crash around onto my knees & am going to be

---

100 MS to ES nd

101   Lionel Bradley, ballet diaries, 28 April 1938, unpublished mss, Theatre and Performance Collections, Victoria and Albert Museum

102 Lambert-Ashton correspondence ROH – quoted Daneman. Internal references date the letter to November 1936.

103 MS to ES c26 March 1937

104 Interview with author

thrown onto the stage by my subjects.'[105] Somes was dancing twenty minutes out of thirty-five and Ashton was tapping all his youthful turmoil, energy, frustration and aggression, using the raw technique and his rough edge, but the quiet, calm ending was equally characteristic.

Unusually, Fonteyn was giving cause for concern: 'F(red). was worried because he said Margot was doing it in the same way as she did all her other ballets & it had no attack from her & if she didn't look out I wld walk away with the ballet ...'[106] Coping with a new partner was difficult enough for her, but the Lovers were also less individuals than moods and emotions, which suited Somes, whereas she liked to create a definite character. The score was dedicated to her, and, with Lambert and Ashton determined to give of their best to their relative beloveds, tension was high and in the white heat of creation emotions boiled over. With less than a fortnight to go before Somes faced the most nerve-wracking night of his life, Ashton put the emotional boot in and threatened to join the Ballet Russe de Monte Carlo if a relationship with Somes was hopeless.

On 15 January, Somes wrote to Ashton:

> Dearest Fred, ... Forgive me for all that has happened, & I mean that, straight from that *wicked, hateful* ♥, I honestly marvel at your tolerance – I *know* I'm *such* a *beast*, I hope you haven't written that letter – I would *hate* you to go away. I shall *always* think of you even if you do, & whatever happens. I need you as I always did & gross success means *nothing*, & any I get thro' Horoscope is *yours*, alone. There is absolutely *nothing* in this note & it's just the thoughts, & I'd like you to keep it with you always. I do wish I was as nice & as wonderful in every sense (looks including)! as you. Love always Micky Rooney

Given Somes' genuine liking of and overwhelming admiration for Ashton, his confusion over the sexual pressures plus the tensions surrounding the creation of any work, let alone his first big starring role, it is not surprising if the letter is a mixture of high emotion and self-interest. He liked the attention, knew what Ashton could do for him, but above all, he venerated his talent and valued his friendship. Whether the self-recrimination was justified is another matter – it sounds as though Ashton was being pretty beastly too. Somehow matters were resolved. Though never relinquishing his critical faculties, Somes put himself in Ashton's hands, which may have been Ashton's intention all along, part of his breaking down process: he once told Rudolf Nureyev 'If I work with a dancer, he has to put himself in the palm of my hand' and allow himself to be moulded to Ashton's vision. He had already relentlessly worn down the obstinate young Fonteyn until she

105 MS to ES, p 20 December 1937
106 MS to ES, p 17 January 1938

burst into tears and he knew that 'I had won the battle; that I would be able to work with her.'[107]

It all blew over.

The run through '... nearly killed me!! Fred says it's the most exhausting role he knows ... Everyone says it's F. greatest ballet & many who hadn't seen it in rehearsal (were) moved almost to tears ... they say I'm excellent ... (and) were wondering how I could go on scene after scene panting away but ... I knew it was a test to see if I could manage it ... Constant was delighted & paid me a fine tribute by telling Fred I had the best rhythm & musicality he'd seen since Woizikowski ...'[108]

'I do believe so strongly in Michael's talent' Ashton wrote to Ethel, 'that I am glad to do what I can to show it & shall share with you in your pride if he fulfills all that I expect of him ... he is beautiful in it, if he doesn't "pull it off" this time do not be & do not let him be discouraged because he will eventually & this will be of help to him always. He has worked unsparingly like a true artist & should reap his reward deservedly & his inherited musical talent will be evident to all in his rhythm which is amazing for a dancer ... I am merely giving him his due & his success will be my reward.'[109]

On 27 January 1938, he sent Somes a first night message: 'Dance like a God.'

The lovers of *Horoscope* are born under the moon in Gemini but she with the sun in Virgo, he with the sun in Leo; Virgo, timid and sensitive, and Leo, vigorous and full-blooded, struggle to keep them apart but they are brought together by the Gemini and united by the Moon. As the orchestra played an eerie palindromic prelude, the curtain rose on Fedorovitch's slate blue gauze, decorated with signs of the zodiac; the lights came up to reveal the moon in a sky of angry black and red clouds and, centre stage, the Followers of Leo, the women's flame coloured hair falling down their white bodices and flame coloured skirts draped with black; the men wore tawny tights and close fitting tunics with headdresses like broken crowns. Downstage, dominating by stillness, stood Somes, wearing a long-sleeved tunic of wide-squared mesh, grey tights and red sash, arms down, fists clenched in a defiantly masculine, heroic stance, the characteristic held-back head adding a touch of arrogance. The Followers of Leo clawed at the Young Man lest he should escape their influence, then, to a march-like theme, Somes danced his first solo, full of fierce, raw power, moderated by a recurring reclining pose suggesting unfulfilled youthful ardour. The Followers of Virgo, in flowing robes of light grey blue, established their sensitivity in an elegant, melancholic Saraband,

107 Penelope B. R. Doob, *A Conversation with Sir Frederick Ashton, York Dance Review,* Spring 1978, Number 7, pp16-25

108 MS to ES p 17 January 1938

109 FA to ES p 22 January 1938

3   The Young Man with the Sun in Leo, Moon in Gemini in *Horoscope*.
Photograph by Gordon Anthony.

with Fonteyn in a flowing dress of grey blue, her complex arm movements expressing a wavering timidity. The lovers' solos restated their characters – his aggressively masculine grace embodying frustration and anger against her shrinking delicacy. In a forceful Bacchanale, the opposing sides parted the lovers, leaving the dejected Young Man alone.

The mood changed to the serene valse of the Gemini, danced by Ellis and Carter in smooth unison.[110] Under their influence, the Lovers united in Ashton's first pas de deux for Fonteyn and Somes. They 'dance themselves into rather riotous love-making' with violent undertones, including several upside down holds and 'one surprising novelty ... as she falls full-length her partner cups a hand and neatly catches her by the nape of the neck' sliding her diagonally across the stage in a movement reminiscent of adagio dancing.[111] The fiery backcloth changed to chaste, silver-grey moonlit clouds, and the tranquil purity of May, mysterious and icily beautiful as the Moon, all curves and crescent shapes, while her Attendants stretched back in wavering lines, suggesting moonlight on water. The ballet ended with the united lovers held aloft in a pyramidal grouping.

There were more than twenty calls. Ethel was bowled over: '... all that fierce part was fine, just like a raging animal & then the way it all tamed down to that wonderful ending. And your bits with Margot ... so tender & gentle & lovely & yet not sensuous ... you *did* make love to Margot nicely, it must have been nice for (her).'[112]

Horoscope was hailed not only as Ashton's greatest ballet but the Vic-Wells' most perfect work and a real challenge to the Ballets Russes. Choreography, music and the refined simplicity of the designs fused to embody the central drama, '... the emotions which are common to us all – love, hope, despair – were sublimated into beautiful movement. It dealt with human problems in an inhuman way.'[113]

Above all, it was Somes' night: '(he) has become a star in an evening ... dominated the stage by the agility and perfect timing of his performance. His appearance is decorative, his technical skill exceptional. In time one hopes that confidence will give his movements a little more fluidity and make his expression less anguished.'[114] Girl Friday, however, pleaded for ballet to be 'danced by beautiful young men like Michael Somes, whose haunting expression of face reveals the inescapable power of that destiny that drives

---

110 Carter remembered it as 'this funny little dance ... the two of us sort of 'hopsing' around – I thought it was really rather comic to be honest ...'

111 PB, *Happy Lunacy in Brilliant New Ballet*, unidentified publication, nd 1938

112 ES to MS p 28 January 1938

113 P. W. Manchester, *The Vic-Wells: A Ballet Progress*, Victor Gollancz, London, 1947, p40

114 Our Own Correspondent *New Ballet Star Nottingham Journal*, 28 January 1938

his supple limbs in their passionate expressiveness.'[115] Dyneley Hussey recognised '... a definite stage-personality, a much rarer thing in these days than an efficient technique. And this is by far the most valuable part of an artist's equipment ... the imaginative understanding of emotion and the will-power to transform that understanding into expressive movement.'[116]

Somes' line, ballon, vigour and virile attack were widely praised, but the Sitter Out was not alone in admitting that, 'great as is the promise for the future shown by Michael Somes, at present he is scarcely finished enough in his technique to do full credit to the leading role'.[117] A. V. Coton, however, had few doubts: 'The quality of Michael Somes' playing ... ranging from frustration to high ecstasy, was an astonishing interpretation from one so young. ... In creating the major role of this important work Michael Somes had the reward that his exquisite line and "ballon" have long deserved ... marking the debut of one who cannot fail to become, with adequate guidance during the next year or so, the greatest English male dancer of this half-century.'[118]

Horoscope remained a key image for Somes' peers: Kersley remembered him 'like Vesuvius just before it erupted.' May recalled 'Positions were square and strong – which suited him very well, and sharp and strong sideways head,' and Farron remarked how he combined strength with lyricism. Carter thought Ashton used him 'brilliantly. I wouldn't call him a lyrical dancer, he gave a more tough appearance than lyrical and there were a lot of those kind of rather tough masculine and leonine [gestures] ...'[119] Ashton always saw a dancer's unique abilities: 'However tiny your talent', Somes observed, 'he found something you could do that would look good.'[120] Even 'faults' became virtues and Somes' thrown-back head, noted by his childhood examiners, became a defining characteristic of the Young Man.

Although attention focussed on Somes, *Horoscope* was no mere vehicle: Ashton equally showcased May's pure serenity as the Moon, revealed an unexpected ferocity in Miller, leading the Followers of Leo, and created some of his best ensemble work, moving the corps de ballet in lines like tossing waves before they melted into groups. Only Fonteyn seemed uncomfortable, but gradually her quieter anguish became the perfect foil to Somes' aggressive frustration and they became the embodiment of youthful love. No one else ever danced the roles.

---

115 Girl Friday, *Girl Friday Says:* unidentified publication nd

116 Dyneley Hussey, *"Horoscope" at the Wells, The Spectator,* nd

117 Sitter Out, *Dancing Times,* March 1938 p767

118 A. V. Coton, *A Prejudice for Ballet,* Methuen & Co, London, 1938, p207

119 Interviews with author

120 Zoë Dominic and John Selwyn Gilbert, *Frederick Ashton, a choreographer and his ballets,* Harrap, London, 1971, p107

As a partnership, Fonteyn and Somes would come to have a great influence on the development of Ashton's style, blending the classical with an English lyricism. His mastery of the pas de deux would develop on and through them, the pas de deux which were, in John Percival's words, 'a remarkably extensive anatomy of the nature of love, which they interpret with a touching delicacy and compassion'.[121] Somes later described their collaborations as 'creative grinding together' – she 'the important one, I was probably more difficult – though Sir Fred could be difficult too'.[122] However, as successful as they were in this first pairing, the defining partnership of the 1930s and 1940s was Fonteyn and Helpmann, or, as their contemporaries insisted, Helpmann and Fonteyn.

Whatever Ashton's personal feelings, his concern was the company and others had to be brought on. In the 1930s Fonteyn was not perceived as his 'muse' and central to his creative inspiration: after *Apparitions* and *Nocturne* (which were arguably equally, if not more, Helpmann's ballets) she concentrated on the classics while Ashton exploited other young dancers – Somes as the fulcrum in *Horoscope*, Carter in *Harlequin in the Street*, Farron in *Cupid and Psyche*, and established talent like Turner in *Les Patineurs* and Argyle in *The Judgement of Paris*.

Somes went from star to supporting role in de Valois' *Le roi nu*, based on Hans Andersen's *The Emperor's New Clothes*, premiered on 7 April 1938. In grey full-bottomed wigs and horn-rimmed glasses, Somes, Carter and John Hall were Ministers to Helpmann's Emperor, strutting around with vacant expressions, sagely wagging heads over the non-existent cloth and kept on their toes by Helpmann, who enjoyed varying his by-play at each performance. The general consensus was bright and amusing but didn't work. Somes later had the thankless task of following Helpmann. Bradley was pleasantly surprised: 'He cannot assume quite all Helpmann's air of vanity & self satisfaction but the natural woodenness of his face helps & he showed occasional traces of an ability (hitherto conspicuously lacking) to express character by facial play.'[123]

On 28 April, Somes at last danced *Les Sylphides*, partnering May. Despite an unflattering reddish-blonde wig, he succeeded in marrying languorous romanticism and virility. 'It ... has a manner all its own', wrote Elizabeth Partriége, 'rather as if you were in a trance and would never awaken.'[124] Although his deficiencies as a partner did not go unnoticed, especially in lifts, Bradley felt that he 'won't have to go far to equal or surpass the best

---

121 John Percival, *Margot Fonteyn's Partner, Dance and Dancers*, March 1959, pp16-17

122 Jann Parry, *Homage to Fonteyn, Observer*, 13 May 1990

123 Lionel Bradley, ballet diaries, 3 January 1939, unpublished mss, Theatre and Performance Collections, Victoria and Albert Museum

124 Elizabeth Partriége, Director Manchester Ballet Club, to MS, nd 1939

living exponents of the part ... The range of his leaps in the final valse was astonishing. But what really surprised me throughout was the lovely graceful sweep of his arm movements and the perfect disposition of his fingers. It was not merely a promising performance it is already a distinguished performance and may become who knows what.'[125]

May was less impressed: 'My very first *Sylphides* was with Fred and he was wonderful, so musical and light ... wonderful (partner) ... and then he taught it to Michael and they were so different. I kept saying to Michael 'Don't *try* so hard ... You're holding me too tight – I don't want to *feel* you' – cos I never could feel Fred ... I've got to look as if I'm on my own, even if you are helping me.'[126] The young Somes did not inspire confidence in his partners and, though he had no problem in ballets created for him, in classical pas de deux he was 'more of a liability than an asset to his ballerina'.[127] Whatever May's misgivings, audiences liked the partnership and Mary Clarke was not alone in speculating 'whether Pamela and Michael would be the two really important dancers. Certainly one thought of them on a level with Margot and Bobby ...'[128]

Somes spent the summer with his parents in Cornwall. Between swimming and learning to surf, he wrote to Ashton, allaying, as best he could, his insecurities and fears, but mostly just keeping in touch with occasional teasing – 'I have done nothing interesting yet – just a few farm-hands & milking maids!, but Uncles are more in my line!'[129]

****

Encouraged by his new contract for 1938-39 paying £5 a week (£135), Somes found his long-dreamed-of flat at 27 Lloyd Square, a small Georgian house with a tiny garden near Sadler's Wells. 1930s Islington was an impoverished area, its streets dominated by trams (Somes always retained a great affection for trams) but its neglected, shabby, low-key charm struck a chord and, apart from one short period, he lived there for the rest of his life.

As he rose through the company, Somes added fewer new roles to his repertoire – in 1938 and 1939 these were Edward Gray in *Lord of Burleigh*, Death in *Checkmate*, the Czardas in *Swan Lake*, Bouffon and Trepak in *Casse-Noisette* and one performance of Paris in *The Judgement of Paris*, looking,

125 Lionel Bradley, ballet diaries, 28 April 1938   unpublished mss, Theatre and Performance Collections, Victoria and Albert Museum

126 Interview with author

127 P.W. Manchester, *The Vic-Wells: A Ballet Progress*, Victor Gollancz Ltd, London, reprinted 1947, p96

128 Interview with author

129 MS to FA 24 July 1938

Bradley recorded, 'rather solemn and worried'. Although not challenging Helpmann or Turner's popularity, he had his own fans, although uncritical gush was not his style; '... such rot as you have never read', he wrote to Ethel after one fulsome letter. 'I believe these people get obsessed, & go quite mad.'[130]

Amid national disquiet, the company embarked on the 1938 autumn tour; Germany had threatened to invade Czechoslovakia unless Britain supported her take-over of the German-speaking areas along their borders and, as Somes wrote from Manchester at the end of August, 'everyone thinks (war) will come soon ... Terrific demonstrations in the streets.'[131] On a positive note, *Horoscope* repeated its London success. Somes recorded 'tumultuous' and 'triumphant' receptions, with stamping and shouting and critics hailing him as '... the personification of everything that is strong and daring'.[132]

Back in London in September, the international situation worsened in the lead-up to the Munich meeting between Britain, Germany, Italy and France. '... shops and businesses are at a stand-still ... police cars with loudspeakers are in the streets urging people to get fitted (for gas masks). People are digging trenches (in the Royal Parks) & making air-raid shelters & the railways are all prepared to take people out of London ... There was terrible gloom at the Wells today & nobody can settle to do anything ... Everyone who can is flying out of London ... All our people are wondering how they're going to get out & of course all theatres will be closed ...'[133] The Munich Agreement came as an enormous relief.

Lilian Baylis had died in November 1937 and her memorial was the Vic-Wells Completion Fund, which cleared debts on both theatres and paid for alterations to Sadler's Wells, deepening the stage and building a new scene dock, wardrobe, a dedicated ballet rehearsal studio and new dressing rooms, putting an end to the girls having to use the Dress Circle Ladies Cloakroom. Her long-term memorial was extraordinary: without her, the tradition of Shakespearean acting might have died out and English singers and dancers might never have disproved the old prejudices nor performed under their own names: Britain owes her the National Theatre, English National Opera, The Royal Ballet, Birmingham Royal Ballet, The Royal Ballet School, Opera North and the survival of the Old Vic and Sadler's Wells.

Ashton took advantage of the larger stage to improve the flow of the ensembles in *Horoscope* but his main energies were directed towards revising *Harlequin in the Street*, which he had created as a curtain-raiser for the

---

130 MS to ES p 16 May 1938

131 MS to ES 30 August 1938

132 Vic-Wells unidentified publication, September 1938, Somes press cuttings

133 Copy letters notebook 1938. The government had already decided that, in the event of war, all places where crowds might gather, including theatres, would close.

4   Monseigneur in *Harlequin in the Street*. Photograph by Gordon Anthony.

Cambridge Arts Theatre in 1937, with music by Couperin and ravishing designs by André Derain. He expanded the characters from ten to twenty-five to showcase the younger dancers, led by Carter as Harlequin, and, 'restored (Harlequin's) poltergeist's powers, resharpened the edge of his mockery' and 'let him loose upon a Queen Anne street to stick pins into pretentiousness'.[134]

Against Harlequin's quicksilver brilliance Ashton set the formal dances of Somes and Brae as Monseigneur and La Superbe, the fooled clandestine lovers. They looked stunning, even if he lacked the aplomb to carry off an 18th century full-bottomed wig convincingly. Carter remembers him having 'the most difficult solo. ... I sat in the corner balletically chiyiking him and he was doing this very elaborate dance, in a very heavy costume, beating his legs and jumping ... and I never understood why he didn't object ... but he was very good-tempered ...'[135]

'A very dull part which he performed in a very dull manner', was Manchester's verdict. 'To give a dancer of his *ballon* the *à terre* dancing which was all that was required was a sheer waste of time.'[136] For Hussey, however, Somes and Brae brought 'an elegance and a restrained passion that set one thinking of Mirabell and Millament, and lift the ballet on to the plane of true comedy'.[137] Partriége's unconsciously revealing comment was: 'You can display here the dignified, aloof and slightly miserable air that seems to become you.'[138]

The ballet was well received on 10 November and was regularly performed, but no one had the technique to replace Carter and when wartime shortages led to the scenery being painted over a delightful work was lost.

Meanwhile, the company was being enlarged to allow de Valois to mount the most ambitious production so far – The *Sleeping Beauty*, which she, following Diaghilev called *The Sleeping Princess*. Embarking on the greatest of the Petipa-Tchaikovsky ballets after less than a decade of existence, using dancers mostly trained in her own school, argues either exceptional progress or extreme arrogance. De Valois and Ursula Moreton had danced in Diaghilev's 1921 production, which had not been popular with audiences unused to a complete 19th century ballet, but she had trained her audience to watch 'pure' dance and they wanted more full-evening works. Once again, Sergeyev produced his trusty volumes recording Petipa's choreography in Stepanov notation, from which he had already mounted *Coppélia*, *Giselle*, *Swan Lake* and *Casse-Noisette*. The notation provided details of dancing,

---

134 Dyneley Hussey, *Harlequin at Sadler's Wells The Spectator*, nd 1938
135 Interview with author
136 P. W. Manchester, *The Vic-Wells: A Ballet Progress*, Victor Gollancz, London, 1947, p97
137 Dyneley Hussey, *The Sadler's Wells Company*, *The Spectator*, 14 January 1941
138 Elizabeth Partriége, Director Manchester Ballet Club to MS undated letter 1939.

grouping, processions and mime, but the actual production – entrances, exits, crowds and getting counts and timing right – was left to de Valois. 'I show steps,' Sergeyev would say. 'You make interesting!'[139] Devoid of any real stage sense, he loved the trappings of 19th century theatre, for ever fiddling with *Swan Lake*'s mechanical swans and demanding red beards for villains. More seriously, according to de Valois, he was unmusical 'to a degree bordering on eccentricity' and she held secret rehearsals to tidy up his confused fitting of steps to the music, but he was a shrewd judge of a dancer and cast well.

De Valois felt that, besides bankrupting Diaghilev, Bakst's designs had overwhelmed the dancing, and she had no intention of that happening now. She chose Nadia Benois, Alexandre Benois' niece, who had never designed on such a scale before: her unenviable task was to produce over two hundred costumes and four sets on a budget that would hardly have paid for half a dozen costumes in 1921. Her designs certainly did not swamp the dancing, but neither did they enhance; legend has it that Fonteyn wept when she saw her plain, far-from-fairy-tale princess tutus. Despite all the economies, the production all but bankrupted the Vic-Wells Ballet, as it had Diaghilev.

The jewel of the production was Fonteyn's Princess Aurora, the role that confirmed that greatness was within her grasp. Looking back, it seems impossible that the whole world had not noticed her talent, but even Ashton did not initially see her potential at a time when the ballet world was dominated by the brilliance and precocious maturity of de Basil's acclaimed Baby Ballerinas – Irina Baronova, Tamara Toumanov and Tatiana Riabouchinska. In the Vic-Wells she was not thought more outstanding than May or Brae and artistically she was in Helpmann's shadow. This slow and relatively pressure-free development may account for her astonishing staying power – the foundations were solid and she did not burn herself out like de Basil's bewitching trio.

The men, however, were far from happy. They spent most of their time miserably walking around in unflattering costumes: 'It is still a matter of surprise' wrote Mary Clarke, 'that the combined wig and headdress for the Blue Bird did not lead to mass resignations among the male dancers forced to wear it.'[140]

Somes was Cavalier to the Lilac Fairy in the Prologue, a Village Youth in the Garland Dance in Act I, a Duke in Act II and a Courtier in Act III. 'Some of ... our leading soloists to-day look back with slightly ashamed amusement at their appearance in (the Garland Dance),'[141] commented Joy Newton. Carter concurred: 'The decor and costumes were appalling and hilarious

139 John Hall, '*The Sleeping Beauty*' at the Royal Opera House, *Ballet*, March 1952, pp48-53

140 Mary Clarke, *The Sadler's Wells Ballet*, Adam & Charles Black, London, 1955, p143.

141 Joy Newton, *A Backstage View, The Sleeping Beauty*, Sadler's Wells Ballet Books No 1 Bodley Head, London 1949 p24

too ... Michael and I and Dick (Ellis) had white bloomers with very pale blue stripes ... long club cut wigs and garlands ... and we'd meet in the middle and absolutely collapse with laughter ... We used to get drunk – what the corps de ballet had to do was so appalling. By the end we just stood on stage [swaying gently] very happy. Michael then went on to do the Blue Bird – he was a very good Blue Bird – but we got so bored – endless, endless, terrible, terrible ...'[142]

The real achievement was that it happened at all and if at first performances were often far from ideal, a great classical ballet was there to learn from and grow into. The silver lining was that Acts I and III were given at a Royal Gala in honour of President Lebrun of France at the Royal Opera House. At the end of March, an edited version was televised, the biggest dance transmission yet undertaken.

Somes had high hopes of Ashton's next ballet, *Cupid and Psyche*, with a score by Lord Berners and elaborate costumes by Francis Rose, a protégé of Gertrude Stein from the fringes of high Bohemia. Psyche was the young Julia Farron, to whom Somes had transferred his affections; Cupid was Frank Staff with Somes as Pan, Ashton's intention being that they should alternate in the roles. Staff usually performed for Ballet Rambert, although he had appeared with the Vic-Wells in the early 1930s, and rejoined to swell numbers for *The Sleeping Princess*.

Psyche's lover only visits her at night, and she is ordered not to try to see him. When she disobeys and discovers her lover is Cupid, she loses him. Pan advises her to regain his love through service and, after she completes a series of menial tasks set by Venus, the lovers are reunited. It was a big production with fifty-five roles, so there was frenetic doubling amongst the townspeople and the many attendants on various goddesses. Ashton opted for a sophisticated treatment, but the result was an uneasy mix of lyrical and send-up. Starting out as straightforward narrative, the ballet degenerated from wit into a tasteless wedding scene, with drunken goose-stepping and Fascist-saluting Olympian gods. The reception on 27 April was mixed: the *Dancing Times* declared it a popular success and others reported the gales of laughter, but the boos had it.

As Pan, Somes was lumbered with a tawny-green, long-tailed costume, more lion than goat. The sideways angles of his only solo were supposedly inspired by Nijinsky's in *L'Après-midi d'un faun*, but it wasn't obvious as the stage was so dark that he was almost invisible. Bradley dismissed the episode as '(Pan) cavorting behind wall – leaps over and joined by two nymphs. Their dances bear no relation to theme.'[143] There were only four performances. Somes never danced Cupid.

---

142 Interview with author

143 Lionel Bradley, ballet diaries, 2 May 1939, unpublished mss, Theatre and Performance Collections, Victoria and Albert Museum

The ballet 'didn't seem to have any reality to it', complained Carter; everyone was in a very strange mood, unsettled by the influx of new dancers, and, even worse, Staff didn't know his steps on the first night: '... we were upset ... he came in and had big role written on him and he just couldn't be bothered.'[144] Somes was angry when he had to go on for an injured Staff in *Les Patineurs*, an injury which didn't prevent him from appearing for Rambert. Somes' wrath was always kindled by unprofessionalism.

Cupid and Psyche was a disappointment for Somes. He needed a success to allay concerns over his lack of progress. The early promise was not consolidating; while he could impress in roles created for him, in classical work there was little improvement in his technique and while he could convey emotion, his miming and characterisation were unconvincing. The fans, always ready for a generalisation, if it was bitchy enough, reduced Fonteyn to 'cotton feet' and Somes 'like a goldfish – can only do double tours'. Manchester summed up the frustration: 'I should have thought that the utmost care would have been devoted to his development after 'Horoscope' had made it clear that England at long last had found a potentially great *danseur* ... His work ... varies from the infuriatingly inadequate to the utterly satisfying. Yet always he gives one the feeling that he is a real dancer, that he couldn't possibly be anything else. This makes him almost unique amongst English male dancers, most of whom look as if they could easily have been something quite different.'[145]

In May, the company decamped to Cambridge for the annual fun-filled week. For most Cambridge was a relaxation (Fonteyn, May and Brae all met their husbands there), but Somes disliked the Arts Theatre because it was unsuitable for the repertoire: 'The S. Princess, for instance looks absolutely absurd on this tiny stage & had to be cut down of course, for the tour, & the back-cloth is too big & doesn't fit & it all looks terrible. They have also taken away the footlights because people in the front rows cannot see our feet & of course that makes the lighting absolutely futile ...'[146] For Somes, compromise was a distortion and the experience fuelled his belief that classics should not be performed in inadequate theatres.

Characteristically, Somes preferred Oxford where 'everyone seems so much more *serious*, & less *foolish*', he wrote to Ashton who was in Paris, working on *Devil's Holiday* for the Ballet Russe de Monte Carlo: '... *so* hot, – I went almost straight onto the river paddling my *own canoe alone*... I've spent my time mainly with Leslie, on the river in the afternoons. Yesterday we took

---

144 Interview with author

145 P. W. Manchester, *The Vic-Wells: A Ballet Progress*, Victor Gollancz, 1947, p 96

146 MS to ES p 2 June 1939. The stage was so small that, in the 1960s when The Royal Ballet Touring Company presented *Swan Lake* there, ballet master Henry Legerton had to rearrange it for a corps de ballet of four swans.

Doris [Pamela May] & Margot in a punt, & I taught them to punt. (I did *not* get off or try to! – I can read your mind, – Leslie will tell you!) ... I miss you, but I'm not really very pleasant to be with as I'm so mopy!'[147]

He was still bolstering Ashton's confidence: '... you're as good as any of them remember, and don't get flustered by them, as no doubt that is what they will try to do ... you see our little sessions in the Board Room crammed between 'Checkmate' rehearsals were good training for you in a way ... I'm sure what you've done is splendid, & you'll soon get it sketched out, & then you'll have plenty of time to alter & polish up ... don't worry or get inferiority complex – there's no reason at all for that ...'[148] The reference to 'our little sessions' indicate that Ashton was already using Somes as a sounding board and is a tribute to the judgement of a 21-year-old.

Somes himself was low spirited on the family holiday in Falmouth: Cornwall was cold and miserable and the ominous clause 'This contract can be cancelled in the event of war or national emergency' in the 1939-40 contracts exacerbated his depression. Everyone was resigned.

---

147 MS to FA p 8 June 1939
148 MS to FA p 12 June 1939

4

Waiting

Manchester was eerily unreal when the company arrived in the last week of August 1939: 'All the street lights have been painted out ...' Somes wrote to Ethel. 'Soldiers everywhere & all in a state of panic, but we just go on. There's also a rail strike & we may go to Liverpool by ... coal-barge with the scenery piled up front! with a horse towing us!!'[1] To general approval, he danced the Red Knight in *Checkmate*.

'It seems inevitable now,' he wrote from Liverpool on 1 September. 'They have been evacuating children all day & one sees nothing but soldiers and lorries & housewives going around with brown paper to put over windows. The roads out of Liverpool are filled with heavy guns & we have got our gas masks. We are going on with the show, but I doubt if there'll be anyone in front. Ninette is very grim & we go on rehearsing "Coppelia" ...'[2] They arrived in Leeds late on the morning of 3 September to find war had been declared. Believing that major cities would immediately be bombed, the Home Office had already announced that all entertainment venues would be closed on the outbreak of war. The cancellation clause in the contracts came into effect and the company disbanded on Leeds station.

Now facing conscription, a despairing Somes went back to Taunton accompanied by Farron and her mother. Conscription had been reintroduced in May 1939 and included all fit men between 18 and 41, the call-up starting with those aged 21 and Somes was a month away from his 22nd birthday.

On 7 September, Tyrone Guthrie, Director of Old Vic and Sadler's Wells, wrote confirming the closure of the Wells, adding that they would re-open as soon as feasible, but, with closure due to war, the management was not liable to pay salaries and the dancers were freed to work elsewhere.

De Valois, too, had no idea what the future held. 'There seems nothing to say or do,' she wrote to Somes on 9 September, 'but wait & hope that all this madness will cease before long – & enable us all to work together again. I shall always feel, and particularly during the last year, that your work & promise was turning into a perfect example of what the Vic-Wells was *meant* to produce, – as a reason for its existence.'[3]

---

1   Copy letters notebook 1939
2   MS to ES 1 September 1939
3   NdeV to MS 9 September 1939

Somes wrote to Ashton, shifting the parameters of their relationship: 'I was *so* glad to get your letter this morning, – I was in the heights, or rather depths – of depression & thinking of someone else's troubles helped me to forget mine ... I feel there's nothing to live for ... & now I'm separated from all my friends & there's no-one to moan to, I live in one of my continual stupors & my nerves kill me, & sleep never comes. However it must be *much* worse for *you*, poor Fred, with all your nerves & stomachs etc, & all your work gone to the winds.[4] ... As for *my* personal happiness, – you're *very sweet* to say what you did, & you know how I appreciate you, but I'm afraid, dear F, it's *no* good, – I have a pretty certain & shrewd idea I shall never be happy that way now. But don't you worry, I'm glad to have made *you* happy for a little while, & as long as I know *you* appreciated it, it will console me.'[5]

Hating inactivity, Somes went back to London to make arrangements about his flat: 'I also went to the Wells to collect the things in my basket ... I nearly wept undoing it all & packing it up again.' He wandered out onto the stage, did a last double tour and left.

Then Ethel phoned. A letter, dated 11 September, had arrived from the Vic-Wells with the news that, as there had been no bombing, the government would allow theatres outside London to reopen. Daniel Mayer, under whose auspices the company had toured since 1936, offered a two week engagement starting on 18 September in Cardiff 'and hopes that this will be a prelude to other dates in the less vulnerable areas'. However, '... we could only accept this provided the company were prepared to work on a co-operative basis'– a basic salary of £3 (£137) for all performances plus proportionate percentage of 75% of profits after expenses, up to a dancer's normal full tour salary, with the remaining 25% retained by the Vic-Wells. As 'The Musicians Union will not consider their members working on a co-operative basis', two pianos would replace the orchestra.[6] The tour would start in Cardiff on 18 September,

---

4   Ballet Russe de Monte Carlo had cancelled their London season, which included *Devil's Holiday*.

5   MS to FA, undated

6   There were several different versions of how the company reformed, but few seem to have had access to the official letters sent to the company, which Somes kept. According to Kenneth Clark in his autobiography *The Other Half A Self-Portrait*: 'At the beginning of the war the Governors of Sadler's Wells decided that it would be a patriotic gesture to close the Ballet down. The sum involved was small enough for Willie Walton and me to provide it, so the ballet remained in being and toured the country, performing new works by Freddie to music chosen and played on piano by Constant Lambert.' (p46-7) In *Secret Muses* Julie Kavanagh (p255) records that Ashton and Lambert planned to reassemble the company and tour with backing provided by Alice von Hofmannsthal. Neither patriotism nor finance was the issue: the Government ordered the closure of all theatres and, once the decree was reversed, it was Mayer's offer to organise the tours for the Vic-Wells that ensured the company's survival. De Valois's statement to Kavanagh: 'It was like a little concert party. I let them do it on their own, there was no point in me going', sounds as though she confused dates as the 1939 tour repertory included only full ballets; Somes

with later dates to be confirmed; later letters are full of handwritten changes as dates shifted almost hourly.

'I was *so* excited I nearly *died*' a euphoric Somes wrote to Ashton. '... I would go if it were only a week & I had to sleep in the *street*. ... I got on to Leslie & I told him what I'd do to those who wouldn't accept, & he gave up the chance of a job ... We shall have to pool all our resources *this* tour, & live in a hovel, but *I* don't care. – I would have done anything.'[7]

De Valois remained in London to run the school with Sergeyev and help her doctor husband. Ashton harshly felt that she abandoned the company, only returning when it was clear that the tour was successful; in fact, she returned after Ashton was called up, by which time Moreton was available to run the school. Ashton never understood her preoccupation with the school, nor with her husband, and his attitude affected those around him.

Eight ballets were toured – *Harlequin in the Street, Checkmate, The Gods Go a-Begging, Façade, Les Patineurs, The Rake's Progress, Horoscope* and *Les Sylphides*. With nine performances a week, everyone had to be ready to go on in any role and muck in, including wardrobe and scenery. The two pianos were played by Constant Lambert (also swanee whistle in *The Rake's Progress*) and Hilda Gaunt, the company's rehearsal pianist, with support from Harold Rutland or Angus Morrison. The basic minimum salary was considerably less than peacetime, but everyone knew that they were lucky to be working at all; some weeks they achieved peacetime wages, other times they had a few shillings extra, sometimes nothing.

In three months the company gave more performances than in a whole Wells season. Somes kept going while others dropped around him. Everyone was on edge: there was friction between Ashton and ballet mistress Joy Newton and the dancers grumbled that de Valois was merely 'teaching evacuees to keep fit!' while running the company through Newton 'which is imposs. these times especially – you must be on the spot to sense the audience & for a hundred & one reasons. No-one knew who was in charge ... & from an artistic point of view the Co was going to pieces, doing the wrong ballets badly & Joy Newton was ... doing things she neither had the right or the experience, to do with Fred & Constant there, all engineered by de Valois who was terrified *her* position might be usurped by Fred ...I think de Valois wanted to finish, but she cldn't bear to think the Co going on without her ... she apparently was all against this tour ...'[8] Lambert and Ashton appealed to Guthrie and were made directors for the tour.

---

refers to a 'concert party' performing while de Valois reformed the repertory after the return from Holland in May 1940. The Clark-Walton involvement may have been at that time or in September 1940, when Somes referred in a letter to 'Clarke & the Ensa business'.

7   MS to FA p 13 September 1939
8   MS to ES w/c 25 September 1939

Underlying everything was the unease and uncertainty; no one knew how long engagements would last and there were rumours that they would go into pantomime at Christmas. Somes now wrote less about audience reaction than the box office and the horrors of travelling. Trains readily submitted to wartime mentality, with late running and long waits, leaving the dancers to find digs in unfamiliar, blacked out towns. The 200-mile journey between Glasgow and Bradford took nine hours 'with a 2 hour wait at some unearthly place where they had to send for an engine somewhere down the line because they'd forgotten abt. us ... & we were ... left in a siding freezing with cold! We all huddled together like a lot of Russian refugees.'[9] Under these conditions the company matured, learning to be entertainers, to hold unknowledgeable and even hostile audiences without playing down.

By the end of the year, as air raids had not materialised, London theatres gradually reopened and the company returned to Sadler's Wells in December 1939. The Royal Opera House, however, succumbed to wartime needs and became a dance hall. Somes and Fonteyn paid a farewell visit, taking a turn on the dance floor while remembering the glamorous De Basil Ballets Russes seasons and their own appearance in *The Sleeping Princess* gala.

The prevailing tensions found expression in Ashton's *Dante Sonata*, premiered on 23 January 1940: private and public emotions – his mother's recent death, the break with Somes, wartime's knife-edge existence, Poland's suffering – underpinned his 'heart-cry for humanity'.[10] Direct inspiration came from Isadora Duncan's 'kind of living music',[11] Gustave Doré's engravings and John Flaxman, whose monumental simplicity also infused Fedorovitch's spare designs.

Fonteyn and Somes led the Children of Light, their tortured anguish set against the ruthless aggression of the nightmarish, snake-entwined Children of Darkness, led by Brae and Helpmann. There was no resolution; at the end Somes and Helpmann were held in crucifixion as the lonely figure of Fonteyn walked between them. The style was severe, drawing on Isadora Duncan and Central European dance tempered by the company's classical roots, within which groups flowed, dissolved, tangled and melded.

For Lambert, the ballet conveyed an 'unchained tragic force'.[12] Brae whirled maenad-like; Helpmann, every muscle writhing, embodied satanic power; May had a brief, heart-wrenching entrance of broken steps, poignantly emphasised by her loose hair as she flung her head in ecstatic torment. Fonteyn and Somes shared several memorable moments, as when

---

9   MS to ES p 27 November 1939

10 Margot Fonteyn, *Autobiograpy*, Hamish Hamilton Paperback, London 1989, p79

11 Penelope B. R. Doob, *A Conversation with Sir Frederick Ashton*, York Dance Review, Spring 1978 Number 7, p23

12 Constant Lambert,*Slightly Brutal?* unidentified press cutting, nd (?May 1949)].

5 *Dante Sonata*: left to right: June Brae and Robert Helpmann as leaders of the Children of Darkness, Fonteyn, Somes and Pamela May as Children of Light.
Photograph by Gordon Anthony.

they entered from opposite sides, he 'with head bowed as with the weight of some inexpiable sin'[13] and they gently and sorrowfully comforted each other. There was 'one brief, heart-stopping moment of ecstasy when they ran towards a shaft of golden light, their bodies seeming to cry aloud, "The sun, the sun!"'[14] For Manchester, 'Throughout the whole ballet runs a bitter sense of shame, all the more terrible because it is unexplained. This is so particularly poignant in those moments when the leaders of the white group despairingly seek each other, that one can hardly bear to watch them.'[15]

Ashton had caught the national mood. The ballet was a powerful outlet for dancers and audience: 'Most of us feel ... particularly in these days that the world is too much with us, and we would give anything to be able to roll on the floor and tear our hair and scream. "Dante Sonata" does it for us.'[16]

Dante Sonata released new depths in Somes, a tortured desperation lit by poignant flashes of child-like terror. In the controversial mimetic crucifixion, John Percival recalled him performing 'with such a conviction of sheer goodness and such burning sincerity that the scene ... could give no offence.'[17]

---

13 Lionel Bradley, ballet diaries, 25 January 1940, unpublished mss, Theatre and Performance Collections, Victoria and Albert Museum

14 Mary Clarke, *The Sadler's Wells Ballet*, A&C Black London, 1955, p151

15 P W Manchester *The Vic-Wells: A Ballet Progress*, Victor Gollancz Ltd, London, reprinted 1947, p45

16 P. W. Manchester, unidentified source

17 John Percival, *Danseur Noble*, *Dance and Dancers*, April 1959, p19

As the military call-up took its toll, every performance was overshadowed by the knowledge that it might be a dancer's last. Fearful for Somes, Ashton consulted Maynard Keynes, who consulted R. A. Butler, then Under-Secretary for Foreign Affairs. Butler put the case to the Minister of Labour, arguing that during the First World War, ballet dancers in Germany and Russia had been exempt, as were Paris Opéra dancers now; de Valois, Lambert and Ashton appealed to the Secretary of State for Home Affairs on the grounds that the company would have to disband permanently if the call-up of male dancers continued. The authorities reasonably felt that exemption would create 'bewilderment and even resentment among the general public'. The only loophole was that individual dancers could appeal on grounds of hardship, arguing that, unlike painters, actors and musicians, a break would ruin their career. Somes, due for call-up in January 1940, was to be the test case.

Support came from an unexpected quarter. On 6 February the *Daily Telegraph* published a letter from George Bernard Shaw. 'What I want to know' he thundered, 'is whether these irreplaceable rare and highly-skilled artists providing a most delectable entertainment of the highest class for our 50,000 soldiers on leave every night, are to be sent into the trenches to fill 30 places which could be better filled by 30 unskilled labourers ... Besides, if the Sadler's Wells leading dancers go, bang goes the whole concern ... There will be an end of our supremacy in one of the finest of the theatrical and musical arts.'

Shaw's letter aroused great interest and was picked up by several other papers. However, as the appeal had to be on the grounds of hardship to an individual, the committee could not take into account the effect of that loss on an organisation. Arguing that ballet in Britain would suffer was a non-starter.

The outcome was compromise. 'NO CALL-UP FOR BALLET DANCER / VIC-WELLS PRINCIPAL EXEMPTED 6 MONTHS' proclaimed the *Daily Telegraph* the next day. 'The grounds for postponement were that Mr. Somes had trained for 10 years and that prolonged absence from practice would make it impossible for him to get back to his present state of proficiency.'[18]

In fact, the tribunal had decided against postponement until Guthrie's arguments swung them round. A delighted Shaw restated his belief in British ballet declaring 'Our British male dancers are as good as any in the world.'[19] Although Somes's six months stretched into eighteen, it was only postponement and how many cases could they fight? One by one the men disappeared into the forces. As a soldier's daughter, de Valois accepted the ruling but, optimistically and pragmatically, appealed to dance teachers to

18 *Daily Telegraph* 7 February 1940
19 G B Shaw, nd unidentified pc Somes collection, possibly *Sunday Chronicle*

safeguard the future by continuing to train boys so that they would be ready at the end of the war.

A relieved Somes rejoined the tour in Liverpool. On 21 February, as Helpmann had fallen victim to German measles, he made his debut as Prince Siegfried in *Swan Lake* Act II, partnering Fonteyn; 'their acting, as well as their dancing, made these ... productions almost speak' declared the *Liverpool Evening Express*.[20]

At the end of the tour, Turner left to join the Arts Theatre Ballet amid rumours that he had been lured away by a higher salary; Somes and Carter took over his roles, Somes essaying the lead in *Les Rendezvous*, in which he could not match Turner's sparkling virtuosity. Back in London in April, *Swan Lake* was a triumph, with Somes putting life into the thankless role of Benno: 'If he has no great range of expression at least he is supreme in a sort of inarticulate yearning, which becomes this character very well,' observed Bradley.[21]

Houses were not full. The classics were most popular, and on 15 April the company mounted a new production of *Coppélia*, including Act III for the first time; Somes and Ellis led the Mazurka with Joy Newton and Palma Nye. However, in *Horoscope*: '[he] is developing both in fluidity and (I suspect) in characterisation,' wrote Bradley. 'Where before one's breath was taken by his technical accomplishment one can now take that for granted and admire the beautiful results which it produces.'[22] It seems he had made his artistic breakthrough.

Ashton was working on *The Wise Virgins*. Searching early baroque art for groups and poses to evoke the feel of religious ritual, he brought reproductions of Botticelli paintings to rehearsals. Aurally and visually *The Wise Virgins* was stunning: Lambert's selection of themes from Bach's choral preludes were orchestrated by William Walton and Rex Whistler created the ravishing set – a wall of pink, fluted bricks broken by vast, nail-studded gold doors flanked by huge winged angels, with two cherub-decorated pillars downstage.

Originally, Ashton intended to dance the Bridegroom, but in the end it was Somes with Fonteyn as the Bride. The Bridegroom first appeared in the Bride's dream, then stood beside her as cherubs dressed her in a white and gold satin robe and handed her a lily and him a sceptre. After a solemn dance punctuated with elaborate groupings, the Angels paired with the Wise Virgins and passed through the golden doors; the Bridegroom crowned his Bride as the Foolish Virgins were turned away.

---

20 Anon, *Vic-Wells Ballet Delights Liverpool Evening Express*, nd

21 Lionel Bradley, ballet diaries, 4 July 1940, unpublished mss, Theatre and Performance Collections, Victoria and Albert Museum

22 Lionel Bradley, ballet diaries, 17 April 1940, unpublished mss, Theatre and Performance Collections, Victoria and Albert Museum

On the first night on 24 April, Mary Honer's First Foolish Virgin nearly stole the show from Fonteyn's sustained ecstasy as the Bride. Somes performed with noble serenity a rather colourless role, one of many in which Ashton relied on his looks and stage presence to create an effect. His costume was sumptuously Baroque, a purple tunic and trunks overlaid with white satin and gold, gold wig, bare legs and purple boots, which contrasted with Fonteyn's deceptively simple white gauzy dress, its mass of pleats falling from under the bust and huge balloon sleeves falling over deep cuffs. Whistler sent Somes an annotated sketch of his wig and make-up, which became a treasured possession.

With hindsight, it is almost inconceivable that anyone could think of sending the company to Holland, Belgium and France in 1940, but either the phony war had lulled everyone into a sense of false security or cancelling might suggest to the Germans that the government knew invasion was imminent. It was left to the individual to decide whether to sign the contract, with the assurance that if they decided not to go it would not affect their future with the company. The contract was for a tour with the Sadler's Wells Ballet Company, (previous contracts had used general terms – 'we offer you' a contract with 'the ballet') and despite many legends about the name change, it was a management decision. Ironically, they left the Wells only a few months later.

The Hague was a revelation with no blackout or food shortages and Somes sat out in one of the pavement cafés imagining he was back in Paris. The reception for *Checkmate, Les Patineurs, Dante Sonata* and *Façade* at the gala opening on 7 May exceeded everyone's expectations (despite a dreadful orchestra), culminating in a rain of rose petals and tulips, followed by a champagne supper at the British Legation. Press and public were frankly surprised: 'To be truthful, one does not look to England for big art movements in the theatre, but the Sadler's Wells Ballet is a creation that one and all of us must accept ...'[23]

At Hengelo the dancers could see the German factories across the border; audiences were enthusiastic, though Eindhoven was more reserved. Everywhere there was barbed wire, concrete tank-traps at bridges and canals, fully armed troops and the frantic construction of air-raid shelters, all of which, de Valois recorded laconically, 'did not give us a feeling that all was too well'.[24]

On Thursday 10 May the company was bussed out from The Hague to perform in Arnhem. The reception was ecstatic and the post-show party went on until 1am. The return journey was hampered by battalions of armoured

23 Quoted Ninette de Valois, *The Sadler's Wells Ballet in Holland, Dancing Times,* June 1940 p534

24 Ninette de Valois, *The Sadler's Wells Ballet in Holland, Dancing Times,* June 1940 p534

vehicles making for the frontier. They arrived back in the Hague at 3am, as the German army crossed the border, giving rise to Helpmann's claim that the Sadler's Wells Ballet led the German invasion into Holland. By 3.30am German planes were dropping leaflets assuring the Dutch that The Hague was surrounded, the Germans were there to protect them from the English and resistance meant death. From the hotel roof, with machine-gun fire all around, Somes and Edwards watched the parachutists floating down, mostly very young men with sub-machine guns, their mission to destroy morale by firing indiscriminately on military and civilians. Somes witnessed a lot of street fighting and four bombs dropped nearby, one hitting a prison only 200 yards away. To the constant wail of air-raid sirens, the company passed the time making the hotel cellar comfortable and playing cards, while Helpmann entertained them with gems from the musical comedy *Miss Hook of Holland*, a legacy from his touring days in Australia.

Calm and efficient amid gunfire and parachutes, Dutch officials arranged the company's escape. A suggestion that the women leave first was quickly squashed; de Valois was adamant that her men were in most danger and those carrying call-up papers had to destroy them because, if caught, they would be considered prisoners of war. In a complication worthy of EU Brussels, passports were awaiting visa confirmation at the Belgian Legation, which insisted on making out and charging for the now unrequired documents.

On Saturday, the company piled into two coaches and set out for Ijmuiden, twenty miles away. All scenery, costumes and music were abandoned and they took only what they could wear and carry (de Valois saved Ashton's prized dinner jacket by wearing it over her clothes). German troops blocked all main roads and there were endless detours. Then the coaches got separated, which was disastrous as all the papers were on one; fortunately the military authorities in Haarlem were persuaded to issue duplicates. Gunfire was incessant. Above, the sky reddened as Rotterdam burned. After five hours they pulled into a large chateau-style hotel, set in idyllic leafy parkland with lake, peacocks and deer, the serenity shattered by occasional gunfire.

To pass the time, an impromptu football match evolved between the ballet and Dutch soldiers, the ballet having the advantage in cunning, the Dutch in superior weight and hefty boots. Somes scored at least one of the goals and the dancers were ahead until a former football international joined in on the Dutch side.

The next day, it took nearly three hours to cover the final four miles beneath a sky dark with German planes and parachutes. Pushing towards the coast was a flood of humanity, desperate to escape. Over 600 crammed onto an old tramp steamer without sanitation or food; most of the dancers had not eaten since Saturday afternoon. The North Sea crossing was a nightmare, their destroyer escort being under constant attack from German bombers.

After fifteen hours they arrived outside Harwich at lunchtime, only to be told they would have to wait until next morning for a pilot boat, when 'Mr So-&-So would be back' and 'they' didn't get 600 refugees arriving every day'; Lambert retorted that the Dutch didn't get invaded every day, but they had been efficient. They eventually disembarked at 8.30pm, but it was another five hours before they left for London, where anxious friends and families were waiting. Their experiences featured in local papers across the country, Somes' under the headline *Tauntonian in Holland. Member of Vic-Wells Company escapes the Nazi Hordes.*

De Valois was pragmatic. The dancers were safe even if 'We may be minus the costumes, scenery, and music of eight ballets, and we may have lost most of our personal luggage. But we were able to fulfil four engagements out of six to an audience that never failed to fill the theatre for us.'[25] The tour had shown the powers-that-be something that Germany and Russia had long known – the value of cultural propaganda. Budapest and Rome were already asking for visits.

Most of the abandoned ballets could be reconstructed but *Horoscope*'s score only existed in manuscript and it was never performed again. A concert suite survived and photographs of Somes and Fonteyn, glorious in their youthful promise. 'It is possible, however,' wrote Mary Clarke, 'that the gods loved *Horoscope*: it never suffered from indifferent casting or too frequent performance, and it lives in the memory in the full beauty of its youth.'[26] Many years later, Ashton told John Lanchbery 'I'm never going to revive *Horoscope*. I did that ballet for Michael, at a very special time.'[27]

While de Valois set about restoring the ballets and devising an alternative repertory for the booked British tour, Somes volunteered to join a small group under the auspices of ENSA, performing divertissements in garrison theatres in the Aldershot area.

Playing to service audiences was its own baptism of fire. '... I don't know how we even got on the stage, leave alone *do* anything!' he wrote to Ashton, who was keeping well out of it. 'However we went down very well indeed, – in fact, we seemed to be the "hit" of the evening, & they seemed to welcome the change ... Mind you, they weren't the toughest lot we *shall* have, by any means, we are going to have Canadians tonight! They liked things like the tumblers dance, & the czardas, & I put in double turns & grand pirouetted myself silly, & they cheered & carried on & really enjoyed it. We're jammed in between the Concert Party, who were sweet to us, & gave up their dressing rooms & generally made themselves very helpful. We have to join in the

25 Ninette de Valois, *The Sadler's Wells Ballet in Holland, Dancing Times*, June 1940 p534
26 Mary Clarke, *The Sadler's Wells Ballet*, A&C Black, London, 1955, p137-8
27 Interview with author

chorus at the end, & I can tell you we have to work like mad & just bang around to make any effect ... I hope you are resting, but at the same time you must get up in the mornings, & go out & get some fresh air, – it's terribly bad to stay in bed, like you do!'[28] Actually, the Canadians weren't as formidable as feared. '... they said, although they'd never seen ballet before in their lives, that our's [sic] was the best show they'd ever had here. They said we would go down marvelously in Canada.'[29] Other service audiences could be less enthusiastic.

Somehow the company opened as scheduled at the Wells on 5 June 1940, and on 4 July came the premiere of de Valois's *The Prospect Before Us*. It was one of her most brilliant works, a comic look at the rivalry between 18th century theatre managers O'Reilly and Taylor, with Roger Furse's elegant, witty designs based on the eponymous Rowlandson print. It was infused with 18th century raciness, rich in comic invention and delightful vignettes. The evening belonged to Helpmann, whose drunk dance as the defeated Mr O'Reilly reduced audiences to hysterical jelly, but May, as the spoilt ballerina Mlle Théodore, was never more ravishing; Somes, Ellis and Edwards had minor, but showy, roles as bespectacled lawyers, deep in ageing greasepaint and grotesquely bewigged, solemnly dancing out legal niceties with precise stiff movements and forming convoluted pyramids that neatly physicalised the complicated legal problems.

As dancers were called up, Somes took on more and more roles: in *Façade* he danced Popular Song, the Yokel in Country Dance and a Mountaineer in Yodelling Song; he danced Hymen with Palma Nye in *Coppélia*, the lead in *Les Rendezvous* and the Hussar in *Apparitions*. He particularly enjoyed understudying Helpmann as Siegfried and Albrecht, roles he longed to dance, although it all seemed rather pointless with his call-up hanging over him.

On the afternoon of 24 August an air raid warning heralded the beginning of the Blitz: '... we're having a pretty hot time of it up here now' Somes wrote, 'We had one (raid) from 9 till 4.30 in the morning yesterday & then we had another at 8.30, 10, 12, 3, 6, 9, 10 & 12 till 4 again! ... They were very near on Frid & the whole house shook. Still its no good worrying abt. it, but everyone is feeling the lack of sleep ... during the perf. ... they stop immediately & announce it, but very few leave & we resume.'[30] By the end of the season on 6 September everyone was exhausted. The next day the Blitz started in earnest and a week later the Wells became a centre for bombed-out families for the remainder of the war. Then a direct hit on the Old Vic took out the Vic-Wells organisation's homebase.

---

28 MS to FA p 22? May 1940

29 MS to FA p 28 May 1940

30 MS to ES nd [September] 1940

A seemingly insignificant memory captured the feeling of the time. De Valois remembered an evening when she, Ashton, Fedorovitch and Somes were having supper after the show. Somes was cooking corn on the cob when the raid started. Their whole world became concentrated on not the external danger, but the green shoots of corn sticking up out of the steam; Fedorovitch spoke the simple words 'It's nothing.' It captured all the reality/unreality of the time.

To fill in before the next tour, Somes and some of his colleagues volunteered for ENSA, appearing in garrison towns and military camps well off the regular touring map, billed as '26 world famous artistes'. Conditions were appalling and pay minimal – from £2.10 (£97) to £5 (£195) for twelve performances plus performing in Military Hospitals. Despite cramped stages and no scenery, many troops were far from hostile and many went more than once.

'We went down very well here,' he wrote from Devizes, '... but it has been very unpleasant in these 'digs' ... Of course, Bobby & Fred are desperate with it & its very funny to see them here mucking about ... They both say something must be decided & (the management) ought to try & get the S. American thing thro' ... They think there's quite a hope for it *now*, especially while we're doing these troop shows, & that there's obviously no reason to call up any more men ...'[31] Almost surreal episodes punctuated the gloom: a charity performance 'got us a lot of thanks in the shape of 1 glass of sherry each from Lord Howard de Walden! ... We lunched with the Ex-King & Prince of Siam who were very charming ...'[32]

In Birmingham the bombing was the worst yet: 'we're right in the thick of it ...The 'digs' we were supposed to go to have been razed to the ground! ... the camp ... was an aerodrome & we performed in a hangar! – the most primitive show we've given yet – altho' ... tonight ... all we get is a tent! ... There are fires literally all round us! Still, what's the good of worrying – we're here on business & that's that ... The hoses are playing on this place now because of sparks from the church across the road. Don't worry, as we'll be alright I know!!'[33]

In Stratford-upon-Avon there were no digs to be found, so everyone camped out in the theatre. 'It is most peculiar & a unique experience, & the place reeks with Shakespearean tradition & ghosts are supposed to walk here ...'[34] The girls slept cozily in the bar, their camp beds over the boiler rooms, while the nine men were relegated to the upper bar, sleeping on the long cushions from the gallery benches under dressing gowns and coats. But it

31 MS to ES p 20 October 1940

32 MS to ES nd c27 October 1940

33 MS to ES p 29 October 1940

34 MS to ES 24 November 1940

was peaceful. In the morning the porters woke them and ran their baths after which they had breakfast on the river terrace. However, nowhere was free from attack and there was an air raid during *Les Patineurs* and Somes, dancing the White pas de deux, had to make the announcement – somewhat awestruck at the thought of speaking from the stage of the Shakespeare Memorial Theatre.

Back on the regular touring circuit in November, things could only get worse, and did. 'Goodness knows when we shall get [to Manchester],' Somes wrote from the train on 17 November, 'we're already 4 hrs late & haven't got out of London yet! ... the main lines are smashed & we've had to make terrific detours ... have to go by canal they told us ...'[35] Rehearsals were non-stop as people fell by the wayside or left and ballets had to be revised. Even when they reached a theatre there was no guarantee that the scenery would arrive. The dancers clung hopefully to rumours of a South American tour.

December brought the relief of a month at Dartington Hall in Devon, where Leonard and Dorothy Elmhirst had established a co-operative arts and crafts centre; it was headquarters of the Ballets Jooss, Uday Shankar had worked there and Michael Chekhov ran the acting studio. It was a happy interlude and everyone benefitted from the relaxed atmosphere and better food. Somes was busy substituting for the unwell Helpmann, a typical evening being *Les Sylphides*, the White pas de deux from *Les Patineurs*, Aurora pas de deux and a role in *Façade*. Days were spent working on Ashton's new ballet, *The Wanderer* to Schubert's Wanderer Fantasie. May remembered him creating the pas de deux for her and Somes on Christmas morning, the floor strewn with Ashton's drawings of exquisite poses. It was the only time she remembered Ashton working from such a source, but he told her 'On holiday, I have a sketch book and if there's anything I see, (like) positions of bodies, I'll draw it.'

While the company had been on the road, complaining about de Valois and Guthrie and dreaming of a South American tour, the Vic-Wells organisation had been busy relocating from blitz-torn London to the Victoria Theatre in Burnley, from where Guthrie managed the drama and opera companies, while Bronson Albery took over management of the ballet. Albery offered the New (now Noël Coward) Theatre as a London base for the ballet, and the first season opened on 13 January 1941. Here a new audience grew up, almost half men in uniform, many familiar with ballet in their own countries.

News was grim, but, even as France fell, it was impossible to get into *Swan Lake. A Wedding Bouquet* was a surprise success; Lambert replaced the incomprehensible chorus, delivering the text musically and wittily while capturing the delicate bitter-sweet sting. *Façade* was always a big hit,

---

35 MS to ES p 20 November 1940

especially Somes and John Hart plumbing boredom's depths in Popular Song and the new Foxtrot, performed with incredible joie-de-vivre by Brae, May, Helpmann (also dancing the Squire in Country Dance) and Ashton (also dancing Noche Espagnole and the Dago).

The Wanderer was premiered on 27 April. Ashton described the central figure as a 'wanderer in the mind,' tormented by memories, distracted by physical joys, beset by pain, terror and compassion, before finding peace in resignation. He eschewed pure classicism for freer movements: 'Around (The Wanderer) the dance flows with an exciting surge of acrobatics adapted to classical technique ... and ... plastic groupings which have an intense and at times macabre quality of emotion';[36] other reviews saw 'writhing' and used 'acrobatic' damningly.

Fonteyn threw herself with abandon into the acrobatics and Wanderer-Helpmann held the ballet together with customary skill, but audiences were bewildered and remained bewildered even after a programme synopsis was supplied. It was generally agreed that the characters represented ideas or types, and all the pointing upwards or to the sunset on the backcloth were significant, but exactly of what was unclear. Graham Sutherland's designs were generally disliked, Dyneley Hussey describing Somes' and May's costumes as 'a crude and ill-matched pink, like that of a blancmange'.[37]

Blancmange-like or not, in their brief entries as the mature lovers 'in whom passion attains an incandescent and spiritulaised absorption',[38] Somes and May were the undisputed hit of *The Wanderer*, 'not only a ravishing pas de deux,' declared Clarke, '... it was also a beautiful partnership'.[39] Locked in face-to-face embrace, his hands moving over her body, Somes conveyed passion and tenderness, qualities that became characteristic of his pas de deux work.

The partnership continued into the London spring season when they led the revival of de Valois's *Fête Polonaise* and danced *Swan Lake* Act II. May had found a new warmth and Somes was developing into a convincing Siegfried, investing the conventional gestures with intense dramatic feeling. The season saw the last of Sergeyev's beloved jerking cardboard swans, which henceforward had to be conjured up in Siegfried's imagination.

De Valois' *Orpheus and Eurydice* was the season's other new work. Somes was one of eight masked Furies who 'tested (Orpheus's) love in menacing barefoot ensembles before softening to the sound of his music and directing

---

36 Audrey Williamson, *Ashton's "The Wanderer" Revival, Theatre World*, October 1945, p17, 32

37 Dyneley Hussey, '*Wanderer' Fantasy, ?*The Spectator, nd Somes cutting'

38 Audrey Williamson, *Ashton's "The Wanderer' Revival, Theatre World*, October 1945, p17, 32

39 Interview with author

him to the Elysian fields'.[40] As often with balletic furies, the choreography didn't reflect the music or the audience's imaginings, although Somes, Carter and Edwards were so convincing that the choreography's weakness only became clear after they left.

Maybe because time was short, maybe because he was freed from the anxieties about his relationship with Ashton, but since the outbreak of war Somes had made his greatest strides as an artist. He was dancing with passionate dedication, finding a new self-confidence and assurance; he was more relaxed and lost some of his woodenness and devastating earnestness. There was a new fluency and assurance, even signs of humour. But to what purpose with his call-up now inevitable?

By May 1941, Chappell, Edwards, Ellis, Leo Young, Paul Reymond and Stanley Hall were in uniform and John Hart in the Home Guard. Even finding four men for the pas de huit in *Les Patineurs* became a problem. Some ballets had to be dropped and Ashton had to go on in *Dante Sonata*, but Ellis and Chappell set the trend for men on leave swapping boots for ballet shoes when they danced Popular Song that season.

The knowledge that Ashton, Somes and Carter were leaving gave an unbearable emotional charge to the packed last night on 21 June. Somes was in every ballet – *Les Sylphides*, *The Prospect Before Us* and *Dante Sonata*. After her end-of-season speech, de Valois brought forward Ashton, who was too moved to speak. Helpmann was crying unashamedly. Somes was given a black cat for luck and, as the curtain fell, ran for the wings, trying to restrain his tears. 'We may never know now the full extent of his powers' wrote Manchester, 'but he has left behind the memory of three performances which no other dancers in the same roles will ever be able to erase.'[41]

Somes always remembered the 1930s, 'working with a small, hopeful band of friends,' with 'Constant Lambert "thumping it out on the piano,"' as the happiest time of his career.[42]

40 Kathrine Sorley Walker, *Ninette de Valois, Idealist without Illusions*, Hamish Hamilton Ltd, London, 1987, p228

41 P. W. Manchester *The Vic-Wells: A Ballet Progress*, Victor Gollancz Ltd, London, 1947 p98

42 James Kennedy, *Somes's hindsight*, Arts Guardian, 1 February 1974

5

War

On 27 June 1941, Michael Somes became No.1833162, in 225 LAA Regiment Royal Artillery, A section A Battery, at Newquay in Cornwall, a training regiment for Light Anti-Aircraft Gunners. 'It isn't bad & the boots don't hurt too much,' he wrote to Ethel. '... they treat us rather like convicts or inmates in an asylum & I'm not surprised when I look at the others – they're absolute morons!'[1]

'Moronic companions' is a common complaint in wartime reminiscences, along with stories of foul-mouthed intolerance, but conscripts were not all uneducated, antagonistic or philistine and some were intrigued rather than hostile, never having thought of dancing as a career for a man. Somes' unit included actors and musicians and the sergeant, a former schoolteacher, mentioned him to Lieutenant Robert Holmes, a former actor who offered him access to a local hotel room where he could practise. Apparently, he escaped the indignity meted out to Ashton and Carter when all the senior NCOs turned out to 'see the ballet dancers. They were just unbelievably beastly', Carter recalled, 'and after that I absolutely used to deny my profession',[2] which Somes never did, the worst he admitted being his sergeant's 'Taught 'em to dance yet?' He got on with people, even surviving his comrades' envy of his electric razor (a present from Ashton), which meant he could shave in bed. Above all, he was worth knowing because he would filch weekend passes and forge the appropriate signatures for his friends.

'The discomfort etc, doesn't worry me in the slightest,' he wrote, '... I hate most of all ... sitting down in rows & becoming a no. But they'll never take my individuality away.'[3] His letters and diaries are full of complaints and he went through some very dark periods, but his attitude was 'one day it will be over and I can get back to my life'. While totally uninterested in all things military, he realised that keeping occupied helped time pass more quickly and soon developed the army trick of looking busier than he was. His main worry was the effect of army boots and square-bashing on his feet.

He settled into the routine of morning exercises and afternoon assault

---

1   MS to ES p 28 June 1941
2   Interview with author
3   MS to ES p 28 June 1941

courses: 'child's play to me ... It could be pretty tough, but I liked it.'[4] Anyone thinking 'poufy ballet dancers' changed their mind during endurance training: loaded with more than full gear, Somes deliberately ran twice as far as anyone else, a show of bravado which may have contributed to his later knee problems. He was used to picking up instructions quickly and his sergeant suggested he give the orders for drill as a step towards promotion or even applying for a commission; another possibility was training in remedial work with the wounded. Brigadier Farren was so impressed that he sent a highly commendatory letter to the War Office: Somes was encouraged: '... I felt so embarrassed reading it' but 'it doesn't actually mean they'll do *anything*'.[5] He was right; it only confirmed that there was no possibility of anyone of his age and category being even temporarily released.

Christmas 1941 found Somes starring in Sgt. G. Vaughan-Jones' *Dick Whittington*, produced by Gunner Leslie Sachs, with actress-now-bus-driver Eileen Merrie as Dick and Lt. Robert Holmes as Susan the Cook. Somes was Tommy the Cat, devising a solo to Ravel's *Bolero* and dancing the Trepak from *Casse-Noisette*. Recruit Phil Fillery never forgot Somes' 'most convincing' cat, who, during his solo 'leapt so high into the air that I thought he would disappear into the flies!'[6]

Early in 1942, Somes transferred to Yeovil and then to Figsbury Barracks in the middle of Salisbury Plain to train as a PT instructor. Sessions lasted from 6am to sometimes 7pm and from the start he was leading and demonstrating ('I can do all their stuff on my head'). He learned to control groups, exert authority, often over people senior to himself, and, on the side, to play badminton.

Boredom gave him time to brood. He heard Helpmann on the radio '– they seem only out for themselves & saying how *wonderful* they all are – well, – they can keep it!!'[7] Pretending he didn't care made life bearable. In fact, weekend leaves in London were his lifeline. He saw Helpmann's first ballet, *Hamlet* ('terrific ... more miming than dancing – but *very* good theatre'[8]). Another time, he met up with Ellis, Edwards, an extremely depressed Carter and a supremely miserable Ashton ('I think he even beats *me*'[9]). The male dancer shortage was so acute that de Valois sent Somes on in *The Sleeping Princess* as Blue Bird *and* Carabosse, a role which he had never even covered before. Everyone was frantically doubling, including Helpmann, who appeared as a

4   Donald Gomery, *Why a man becomes a ballet dancer,* unidentified press cutting c1961

5   MS to ES p 12 April 1942

6   Phil Fillery to Wendy Somes, 23 November 1995

7   MS to ES p 1 July 1942

8   MS to ES p 7 July 1942

9   MS to ES p 7 July 1942

Rose Adagio prince before transforming into Prince Charming and the guest list for the wedding was severely curtailed.

Somes stayed with Fonteyn, and they sat up gossiping with Lambert until the early hours. Sleeping in a proper bed, having a lie in, playing records and chatting, interspersed with her mother's wonderful meals, was 'just heaven ... how little the Army mattered ... it was only a question of putting up with a bit more'.[10]

De Valois' optimism was being severely tested ('one does rather feel that it is all work about nothing ...'[11]). The company operated on a knife-edge, for, besides losing the men to the forces, many girls had also left and, given the risks of living in London, there were fewer pupils from the school to replace them. She brought in David Paltenghi (Swiss), Gordon Hamilton (Australian) and Alexis Rassine (Lithuanian/South African), but without Helpmann, exempt from military service as an Australian and key male dancer, the company would collapse. Long before they were ready, boys were taken from the school at 15 to get a few years' performing before their call-up, but they had to be paired with equally young girls if the ballets were not to look absurd; wartime audiences saw few mature male dancers, and detractors often confused immaturity with effeminacy.

Somes was introduced to the new audience when P. W. Manchester's *The Vic-Wells: A Ballet Progress* was published in 1942. His reaction was 'the usual type of rather "gallery-fan" nonsense, but is better than most being quite sensible in parts'.[12] Later she was embarrassed by her comment about him being more of a liability than an asset to his ballerina, though admitted it was justified at the time.

Unfortunately, plans for remedial training were put on hold when his regiment was merged with the 225th and posted to Aldershot ('Hideous'). Ashton was moving around various RAF camps, hating each more than the last. Somes shared his bitterness and sense of abandonment, and could be equally hypercritical of the company and de Valois, slewing between understanding and unreasonable railing, reflecting the unhappiness felt by all who were away. However, despite his own misery, Somes could feel sorry for those who were coping less well. Ashton never came to terms with Helpmann's exemption and his success as a choreographer exacerbated his dejection. Unfortunately, it was impossible to escape Bobby – keystone of the company who, during the war years, also managed to choreograph musicals, guest on popular radio shows, give poetry readings, perform a showy cameo in Olivier's prestigious *Henry V* film and topped it all by acting *Hamlet*.

10 MS to ES p 7 July 1942

11 NdeV to MS 2 July 1941

12 MS to ES p 30 November 1942

Ashton believed that de Valois could have kept him out of the services if she had really wanted to, but realistically she couldn't afford the luxury of a non-dancing choreographer and had not time, energy nor resources to fight the impossible. Exemptions had to be applied for through CEMA, which Sadler's Wells Ballet did not join until later in the War, and even they found it difficult to negotiate the labyrinthine red tape.[13] She also knew, from the attitude towards non-combatants in the First World War, that exemption would fuel the prejudice against male dancers. As a soldier's daughter (her father died on the Somme in 1916), she recognised there was more at stake than individual careers and had affirmed in *Dancing Times* in September 1940 that military requirements must be paramount.

Ashton didn't understand and didn't want to, and his misery and insecurity boiled over into paranoia which, Somes realised, could seriously damage him and the company. He had no compunction in pulling strings, appealing to high-up friends, including Kenneth Clark, Director of Art for CEMA, who should have known better than to take sides. A recurring theme in his wartime letters was setting up his own company with Somes as principal dancer and possibly ballet master and let him try his hand at choreography, but Somes knew the plan had no firm foundation: '... exactly what the idea is, – when it's to be brought into action ... the motives & who's at the head, & where the Co. is to be formed & from whom & what?'[14] He did not confide his reservations to Ashton, nor his own view of the future: that the Sadler's Wells Ballet would split, with Ashton in charge of one part with Fonteyn, Lambert and most of the established dancers while de Valois built up a second company.

Fonteyn tried to reassure Ashton: '... I think you are being quite ridiculously stupid about de Valois ... there is absolutely no doubt that she realises what a great loss you are to the Co & wants you back. As for your assertion that she is jealous of you as a choreographer, she makes a great effort to be as fair-minded as possible & succeeds far better than *you* do, with regard to Bobby who doesn't even pretend to rival you himself! I do think you are unjust to her & have caused a great deal of trouble by giving people such as the Clarks a completely false idea of her. Naturally she cannot say to Beven (sic)[15] or the Air Ministry that the Co will close down in 9 weeks if you are not released. It ... would only infuriate the authorities who could reasonably reply that we

---

13 The Council for the Encouragement of Music and the Arts (CEMA), forerunner of the Arts Council, was set up in 1940, dispensing government funds to promote British arts and culture. For much of the War the Sadler's Wells Ballet was commercially viable, so had no need to apply for funding.

14 MS to ES undated [1944]

15 Ernest Bevin, Minister of Labour and National Service in the war-time coalition government.

have carried on very successfully without you for 10 months. ... I am devoted to you & very worried that you should feel like that. Please, please believe.'[16]

In 1943, Ashton was released for three months to produce a new ballet. After 'the rumpus', he was apprehensive: 'Bobbie is now definitely hostile & anyway I really dread going back there now to their alien atmosphere', he wrote to Somes. 'They only resent me & only want me back from fear I think ... Have you been to the ballet these week-ends, does my name stink I bet it does & I hope so too.'[17] On a practical note, he suggested possible subjects – a pure dance work to an unnamed French score, Spenser's *The Faery Queen*, *The Carnival of Animals* or 'my funny one'. He felt that wartime called for something uplifting and patriotic which would prove his and ballet's importance and might help get others released. Privately, Somes thought this optimistic, but agreed that 'St George' in Spenser's *The Faery Queen* would be an appropriate theme and they discussed possible composers: as Britten was 'booked for Bobbie's next Ballet though I always wanted him',[18] Ashton reverted to his first choice of William Walton. Doris Langley Moore produced a scenario and designs were commissioned from John Piper.

De Valois exuded enthusiasm and dealt disarmingly with complaints and threats: 'I do not see any point in going to the Ingolsby's[19] for more great appreciation, lavish pay, and costly mounting,' she wrote to Ashton. 'Here we all wait to fight with you, underpay you & mount you for less than the Ingolesby legend spends on press night drinks.' Why should he think his production would be skimped? Standards were not ideal and audiences indiscriminate, but 'everything is a success in war time theatre – it was the same last time ... your ballets – (and for that matter mine) – suffer in presentation. They are pre-war in conception & cast ... You are unhappy, we can all deeply feel for you. But at the pace you are going now you do not give us a chance. You will tire your best friends & no doubt give much pleasure to those who would like to see us quarrel. But I have no intention of quarrelling with you. I know all your values, both as a friend & an artist. It is no good writing me the sort of letters that you would to your lady admirers when you want to get a rise out of them. The whole basis of our friendship is on a deeper better and saner standing – and you know this in your lucid moments. And here endeth the 1st lesson.'[20]

Ashton could not give up his wallowing. He sent Fonteyn and de Valois's

16 MF to FA copy letter nd

17 FA to MS nd

18 FA to MS nd

19 Ashton was always threatening to join Mona Inglesby's International Ballet. The Ingoldsby Legends was a series of stories based on Kentish folklore by Rev. Richard Harris Barham.

20 NdeV to FA, copy letter nd

letters to Somes with his own comments. De Valois' humour and tact he saw as insincere politicking and refuted her comments with miserable glee: '... my friends ... had better keep away if they are tired so easily. ... I don't want any unwilling appreciation or force my will on anything or anybody. I'm fighting for freedom so that they can all go & shoot themselves ... I'm getting so exhausted with all the coming & going and delays that I shall be too tired to do anything when the time comes. Will you see [Helpmann's new ballet] the Birds ... & tell me of the horrors of Wanderer & Dante. If only you could be St George.'[21] If anything was wearing him out, it was his own attitude.

Somes tactfully agreed with him, 'as I *do* in many respects, – but he's only being destructive to *himself*, by taking that line ... I think he values my judgement ... & will listen to *me* above anyone, – perhaps *only* to me! & I can say things to him no-one else wld. dare! – But I *didn't* oppose him.'[22] There was no point in alienating Ashton further. Even his sister, Edith Russell-Roberts, thought he was being utterly unreasonable, but Somes sensed he would see things differently once he got back to work.

Meeting in London, Ashton discussed casting with Somes. Watching *Coppélia* without the bitterness of distance and with fresh eyes and purpose, Somes admitted that the girls were 'much better nowadays... & better looking too,' while in *The Rake's Progress*, 'the cast I think even better because they *are* more character dancers now ...' De Valois took Ashton and Somes out for tea. 'They are quite reconciled now ... & I think very fond of each other *really*, & *respect* each other's qualities.'[23]

Most wartime Christmases Somes spent at Datchet with the Russell-Roberts. Christmas 1942 was far from Army life with almost pre-war abundance of food and drink and cocktails with neighbour Sam Eckman, MGM's 'big noise' in England ('with an income of £40,000 (over £1.4m) a year tax free!') Ashton then abandoned them in favour of dinner with Lady Cunard, but Somes stayed on for supper, cycling back to Aldershot in the early hours. Edith became his confidante, the only person to whom he could unburden himself about both Ashton and his parents.

Work on *The Quest* began early in 1943. With only a few weeks' rehearsal and a company he hardly knew, Ashton compounded his problems by lumbering himself with a complex narrative (possibly to show that anything Helpmann could do he could do better) and a commissioned score, which arrived in short bursts, precluding his usual practice of immersing himself in the music beforehand. Somes applied bullying tactics, which certainly got

---

21 FA to MS nd. Helpmann himself admitted to Somes that *The Birds* was '*very, very* slight'.
22 MS to ES nd
23 MS to ES nd

results: 'As he says – *I* put him right "on his toes", with that 1ˢᵗ rehearsal when I slated him so & made him weep, & when I forewarned him what he *must* & *mustn't* do ... I told him ... to do real choreography when naturally the Co. tended to pull him in the way Bobbie had them with *his* ballets, – *blitzed* him into listening to the music & the importance of musicality & rhythm throughout, & greatly influenced him with the décor etc. Even as late as last Sun. when he rang up to say the lighting rehearsal was bad – I insisted *he* shld. do it altho' he doesn't know much abt. it, & he *did*, – & the result was magnificent.'[24] Ashton dedicated the ballet to Somes.

Fedorovitch acknowledged Somes' positive influence while Piper told Ashton that he found Somes 'one of the most intelligent people he'd ever met, & that everything I said, was of *extreme* value of a fine mind, & I brought out my points with remarkable sureness & effect! That my opinion & 'heckling' must be of the greatest value to Fred, & I said things so intensely true & explanatory, seizing on the vital focal point with amazing speed & extraordinary clarity & new line of thought!!'[25]

The Quest's theme was the triumph of good over evil, good in the form of 'St George (Red Cross Knight personifying Holiness)', danced by Helpmann. It was something of a curate's egg, but Somes had no reservations: '... thrilling & *most* moving ... full of invention, & all difficulties overcome with *such* mastery ... the rather complicated plot as clear as day ... *simplicity* – so striking, as to be *far* more impressive than *all* the tricks ... I'm the *most* difficult person to please ... but it reached all my standards of a masterpiece & I cld. really find *no* flaw.'[26] Gratifyingly, Ashton's sister and Fonteyn's mother told Somes that, good as Helpmann was, he should have been St George 'which was nice, but you must on *no account* tell anyone *else* that'.[27] While Helpmann could make something of any role, walking through as an idealised saint wasn't what he did best.

The atmosphere at *The Quest*'s Aid to China gala premiere on 6 April 1943 was almost pre-war, with telegrams, flowers and a smart audience, including balletomane Minister of Aircraft Production (and a later Chancellor of the Exchequer) Stafford Cripps, the Chinese Ambassador and the cream of society, plus ballet aristocracy Lydia Lopokova, Adeline Genée, Marie Rambert, and Phyllis Bedells. The audience responded with a spontaneous ovation. In the intervals, Somes and Edith talked loudly behind the Air Marshals about the stupidity of keeping Ashton in the services. After the company party, they joined Ashton, Helpmann, Fonteyn, May, Fedorovitch and the audience

---

24 MS to ES nd
25 MS to ES nd
26 MS to ES nd
27 MS to ES nd

elite at the Savoy, where Ashton cultivated his society friends, leaving Somes to tackle the high-ups about him. By midnight only 'Bobby Sophie Margot Constant Willie Piper & one or two others' remained, and then Somes and Alice von Hoffmansthal went back to Ashton's cottage before a euphoric Somes caught the 7.24am back to Aldershot.

The Quest was a high amid many lows. Ethel continued to demand her son's attention. Suffering from palpitations and breathlessness, constantly nervous and tearful, she needed full-time nursing: at times, Somes thought she would die. He exhorted her to help herself, but 'you either expect *me* to be there, & doing it *and* in the Army, at the same time, or *else* that it will all just happen of it's *own* accord.' Then she was diagnosed with breast cancer. Thankfully, the growth was benign, but it was another strain on his taut nerves and her letters exacerbated Somes' own depressions.

Not bullying, nor cajoling, nor reasoning helped. Amid urgings to be positive and suggestions about her school, he held out the hope that one day they would be together in London against her insidious refrain that he didn't want her to come: '... you tell me the *same* (worries) *each* time ... & I *want* you to tell me them, but I *really* get so awfully tired of these "supposings" & "ifs", & predictions & "expecting the worst", which *never* happens'.[28] His parents could not even find accommodation without his help and he was also helping to support them, leaving him only 12/- (£20) from his army pay; Ashton became so concerned that he consulted de Valois about whether the Ballet Fund could help.

Then there was brother Lawrence. Invalided out of the forces and without financial resources, he nevertheless proposed studying organ at the Royal College of Music. His solution was for the whole family to live together '& all my things could be put there at *his* convenience, & the whole thing paid for by *me* – very nice!!'[29]

Somes was at a very low ebb. At Easter, a time 'I *always* find rather gloomy ... my mind wandered & worked into a frenzy, until I was driven onto my bike, & cycled & cycled, roaring away at myself with my head bursting, until I was worn out,' he wrote to Ashton. 'I'll manage *somehow*, I suppose. ... there's *so* little *consolation*, or even *hope* for *me*, – I have lost everything, because I have lost *myself* ... happiness but a very fleeting memory, already dimmed by bitterness.'[30] His lifeline was weekends with Ashton, who was now stationed in London, when they discussed possible future ballets: Somes suggested 'the Franck Variations ... I'm *sure* something *very* beautiful *cld* be arranged to

28 MS to ES p 13 June 1943

29 MS to FA c28 September 1943

30 MS to FA nd

such mystical music ...';[31] other possibilities were Richard Strauss's *Don Juan* with designs by Edward Burra, and Ravel's *Daphnis and Chloë*. Typically, it was Somes who bought the records, so that Ashton could immerse himself in the music.[32]

In September 1943, Somes went up to London to see *Swan Lake*, newly designed by Leslie Hurry. The male dancer situation was so dire that the company was close to cancelling performances, so again Somes went on, learning an unfamiliar place in the Mazurka so that the boy doing his old place wouldn't have to change. It was cheering to know that 'sitting there making up, everything seemed to come instinctively ... as tho I hadn't been away for more than a day!!'[33] It was a rare highlight in the pervading gloom.

Diaries are often confessions of loneliness, and 1944 opened with Somes resolving to keep a diary. 'Have decided at last to rouse my lazy mind in this 4th year of Hell, & hope I'll keep this up, altho' seems inevitable to be grim record of dreariness, depression, doom and doubt ...'[34] He saw no solutions to his problems and, torn between his own life and his parents, he saw his greatest failing as selfishness.

He recorded one day of D.G (dreary grind) after another, the petty regulations and mind-numbing Army life: '... no taste to anything, – the dirt & squalor. Scrubbing endless floors ... no sleep while mind & everything slowly degenerates & is starved of beauty, friends, no life, – but just backs to the wall grind & no hope – & yet there *must* be, – hope & faith'.[35] Days were restricted to road-training, 'cold & filthy' trench digging, sten gun lectures and guard duty, which at least meant longer leaves. London had the strange atmosphere of a phantasmagoria, 'empty of her true inhabitants, – only full of crazy girls & Americans & mad crowds pushing & jostling thro' the streets all out for one thing only!! Aren't we all?! – no luck my way, & feel *very* lonely and dispirited.'[36] Apparently, wartime depression was exacerbated by unrequited love, but his letters give no clue as to the beloved object.

Watching Karsavina rehearsing Fonteyn and Rassine in *Le Spectre de la rose* was a bitter sweet experience: 'Why can't it be me! – but she's divine – *what* an artist & how privilidged to see her.'[37] He saw Helpmann act Hamlet 'a real masterpiece of 'acting movement,' but his voice hasn't volume, altho'

---

31 MS to FA nd

32 *Symphonic Variations* in the Walter Giesking recording.

33 MS to ES 13 September 1943

34 MS diary 1944

35 MS diary entry 12 March 1944

36 MS diary entry 12 March 1944

37 MS diary entry 28 January 1944

you cld. hear everything ...'[38] *Horoscope* on the radio brought back memories of Arnhem '& rose petals at the Hague. How I loved doing 'Horoscope' – wonder if I cld. remember it now.'[39] Garrison concerts, occasional operas and films brought temporary relief (Fred Astaire and Rita Hayworth in *You were Never Lovelier* was a highlight). He always enjoyed introducing friends to music and one A. G. Langley acknowledged his influence in '... turning the steps of at least one very lowbrow in the direction of better things'.[40]

He saw the company at Eastbourne and the Aldershot Garrison Theatre and was immediately co-opted to dance the Mazurka and Czardas in *Coppélia*, and Popular Song with Edwards, who had been invalided out of the army in 1943. He took great pleasure in his friend's good performance as the Rake and admired the young Beryl Grey ('feels each movement well') and Moira Shearer. But the following week was almost unbearable.

He was promoted to Lance Corporal, but his spirits sank even further as D-Day approached and his battalion was ordered to Llandrindod Wells: '*What* a dump! – miles from anywhere. Usual chaos.' It was an end to the London leaves.

On 16 May he fell from the back of a truck. It was only a two foot drop, but he landed with his elbow digging into his side. As a precaution, he stayed in hospital overnight. In the early hours a small puncture in his spleen split and only the fast reaction of seven surgeons saved his life by draining two pints of blood from the abdomen and removing the spleen. At first, he feared that he might never walk again but 'I had to dance. There was nothing else by which I could earn my living.'[41] He spent his 'darkest hours ... when my life wasn't worth the stitches I was making!!' sewing a rabbit, christened Sammy Spleen, for Edith's new baby, Anthony; his determination to finish it saw him 'thro' my worst moments & somehow was a consolation & helped me to control my will-power'.[42]

Within days, de Valois undertook the slow journey from London to see him and made a lot happen in a short time. She assured herself of the extent of his injuries, reviewed his finances and offered to consult the relevant Funds, found Mr Smith, former writer on dance for *Reynolds News*, who could keep an eye on him, wrote a long letter to Ethel and offered to visit Lawrence; she left Somes £5, paper, books, magazines, the assurance that everyone was worried about him and promised to find out if the injury might mean his discharge, before making the slow journey back to London, having forgotten

---

38 MS diary entry 11 March 1944

39 MS diary entry 7 March 1944

40 A. G. Langley to MS 14 January 1949

41 Richard Hawkins, *Profile of a West-Countryman*, unidentified undated publication 1956

42 MS to ES p4 July 1944

to deliver a letter from Fonteyn ('I knew Ninette would lose that letter!').[43]

Letters and enquiries flooded in, from the Colonel down, and Somes was particularly touched by a visit from his gun-site comrades bearing a gift of a volume of Shakespeare's plays. 'I wld. never have made it without all your prayers which gave me strength & will,' he wrote to Ashton. 'God has blessed me & given me back life.'[44] De Valois was typically pragmatic: '... you are well out of worse things – which is some sort of blessing these days':[45] she was concerned about Walter Gore and Richard Ellis, who were both in the D-Day landings, and John Nicholson, who was flying Sutherlands hunting U boats. On 18 July, Rex Whistler was killed on his first day into battle.

Somes was already making 'a most *marvellous* recovery'.[46] By July he was fit enough to be moved to the Red Cross Hospital at Gregynog Hall in Monmouthshire, the home of Gwendoline and Margaret Davies, whose grandfather had made a fortune in coal, railways and docks in South Wales. Somes made a big hit with them, 'so I may be worth a million or two if I can bring it off!'[47] They were extremely cultivated having founded the Gregynog Press and the Gregynog music festival, at which Elgar, Vaughan Williams and Holst appeared, but their passion was art. An ex-pupil of Walter Sickert looked after their paintings: 'He picked up a little picture from the floor – just stacked there, – unwrapped, – he said that was worth £5,000 itself!! ... Gainsboro's, Turners, Modiglianis – strewn around the place like postage-stamps!! ... even a *da Vinci*. There is a wonderful Millet – rarely seen, – yet it's a real masterpiece & is my favourite.'[48] Amid works by Botticelli, El Greco, Blake and the finest collection of Impressionist and Post-Impressionist paintings in Britain, he was delighted to find two Burras. The sisters were pleased by his appreciation and lent him books and records, but he sensed they were unhappy: 'I'd rather be a cockney char anyday!'[49] The collection is now in the National Museum of Wales.

A leisurely convalescence in beautiful countryside helped restore health and nerves, but he was anxious about friends in London as the V-1 attacks began. Even now, he was bolstering up Ashton: '... you mustn't dissipate your mind by *worry* ... *try* & be calm & have faith, & work for the future. Our lives have been shattered, – but not irreparably ... to talk of being too old or tired is only sabotaging one from the start.'[50] There was an influx of injured from

---

43 MF to MS p 9 June 1944

44 MS to FA nd

45 NdeV to MS nd

46 MS to ES p 25 May 1944

47 MS to ES nd

48 MS to ES nd

49 MS to ES 8 ?July 1944

50 MS to FA nd

Normandy and seeing men younger than himself mentally and physically scarred, made him realise how lucky he was as he helped out making beds and washing up.

His new-found calm was, however, severely tested by his mother's worsening state: '... as usual was really *my* fault';[51] the shock of his accident affected her heart; the ensuing bed rest caused the familiar spiral of weakness, helplessness and nervous exhaustion. She was worried about her school, which would never meet the 1944 Education Act requirements for better qualified teachers, modern equipment, compulsory games and languages. Edwin was only happy playing the organ and although his charm and otherworldliness endeared him to vicars and congregations, they didn't have to deal with his inability to cope with reality. Ethel's nurses tried to rouse him into taking some responsibility 'but you know Dad, he only argued all the time'. Somes accepted that he would have to look after his parents 'because no-one else, even well-paid, – could stand it'.[52] It was hard summoning up support for others when he was going through so much himself.

Friends kept him up in company gossip. The big news from Fonteyn was that Sol Hurok had asked her and Helpmann to dance in New York with Ballet Theatre: though there was no chance of going '... it is nice to be asked ...'[53] *Carnaval* was revived: '... never one of my favourites' she admitted, 'but it seems to have been very well (received) – I can't think why ... old Sarah (is) Columbine – full of hideous false gaiety ... How I wish we could do Horoscope again together ... my God, it was difficult! No wonder we used to be a bit puffed.'[54] When *Nocturne* was revived, Somes dug into his phenomenal memory and, humming the music to himself, produced in three hours a 'choreographic score' for a ballet in which he had never danced a major role, '... not bad after 4 years!'[55]

Then came the unexpected announcement that music publishers Boosey and Hawkes had acquired the lease of the Royal Opera House from 1 January 1945 with the intention of establishing a year-round international opera house, with resident British opera and ballet companies.

Somes shared Ashton's grim joy: 'that'll shake S. Wells, – & Ninette has got quite worried, & realises at last her Co. is not the 'crack' lot she imagined ... (Ashton) said they seemed more anxious to get him out *now*! before he signs up with anyone else! ... he's not keen'.[56] Somes' wider view was that Boosey &

---

51 MS to FA 28 September 1944
52 MS to FA 28 September 1944
53 MF to MS p 9 June 1944
54 MF to MS 15 October 1944
55 MS to ES nd
56 MS to ES nd

Hawkes 'have an eye for the sincere production of good stuff, – as well as for box-office receipts'.[57] He too couldn't resist a dig at the Wells whose 'values & standards are so *low* now, – *they* don't realise that their present success is *cheaply* won. I always warned you that they would find the difference when the Soviets etc, come over, & people *really* see what dancing *is*. I agree that they must develop a *strong* corps – & pay far more attention to *technique* & above *all*, – *lead* with their choreography.'[58] However, he still had confidence '... that S. Wells has the *spirit* & the tradition (if they can *recapture* it), when the War is over, & we old things return, & with the competition from foreign Co's to buck them up, – to make a fight, – they should be an interesting & exciting Co. to work with ... (if) British ballets, dancers – *& choreographers!!* are to survive the post-war slump – they must *unite*, because they're not strong enough in *any* shape or form to be divided.'[59] The war had seen the establishment of a number of small companies, but of variable standard and all were exhausted.

In fact, Boosey and Hawkes recognised the unfeasibility of building companies from scratch and planned to take over existing organisations, which essentially meant Sadler's Wells Ballet and Sadler's Wells Opera. However, the opera was not considered of international standard, so the Vic-Wells Governors were approached about releasing the ballet.

'(Ashton) feels it would be wanton to lose such a grand opportunity, & they'd only get some foreigner instead ... Yet he says Ninette won't see sense, & yet if she had any vision she'd see it was the best thing to do ...'[60] Somes had long thought that Covent Garden and Sadler's Wells should '... combine & be toured & have seasons ... alternately with the Russians etc, & keep S. Wells as an experimental theatre & ballet-school & perhaps a small Co there for experimental purposes & small ballets'.[61] If the Governors refused to release the ballet Ashton thought he might be asked to form a company, in which case 'I would rather go with (Ashton), – &, of course, I'd be in a better position. But lets hope they *will* reach a compromise...'[62]

Though torn between loyalty to the company, to Ashton and to his own career, Somes had a firm grip on reality and urged Ashton to stay with the Wells to prevent 'a future of uncoordinated & divided strength'.[63] De Valois was 'cantankerous & insulting' to Ashton when they met, calling him disloyal. Although it is unlikely that this one meeting changed her mind,

---

57 MS to FA nd
58 MS to FA nd
59 MS to FA nd
60 MS to ES p 8 October 1944
61 MS to ES p 8 October 1944
62 MS to ES p 8 October 1944
63 MS to ES nd

'after seeing that he might go & start something new (she) got panic & is now all for it'.[64]

With hindsight, de Valois' hesitation does seem lack of vision, but it was little wonder if she felt the disadvantages outweighed the advantages. Despite Somes' contention about low values and 'cheaply won popularity,' her correspondence with Ashton makes clear that she was not smug about the company's wartime success and had no illusions about standards at a time when she had to put survival before development. Having slagged off the company (and her) for years, Ashton now wanted her to accept an offer that would expose every weakness, whereas she felt that the problems needed to be tackled slowly, out of the limelight. In some ways, her war had been more stressful than Ashton's or Somes', running a company while contending with sleepless nights, insufficient food, constant touring, entailing hours of mind-numbing travel, and the sheer logistics of living in blackout and blitz while keeping an eye on the school *and* helping her doctor husband. The men would return raring to go, but she and her company had few reserves left.

Maybe, too, she foresaw the dangers of becoming a national company – 'rigidity, bureaucracy, ossification – these are the attendant evil spirits which hover perpetually over a state theatre'[65] – but in the end she accepted the need to expand and challenge the memories of the foreign companies that had dominated ballet in England. Generously, the Governors agreed the transfer on condition that de Valois set up another company at Sadler's Wells, fulfilling Somes' vision.

Somes was jubilant: '... *my* hopes realised, – to dance the lead at *C.Garden*!!' Now we'll have a huge theatre, – stage, – orchestra, – international status, & the backing & possibilities to mount bigger productions after the War ... *if* it *works* & there's *no* reason why it *shouldn't*, it will really put British Ballet on a firm foundation.'[66]

In retrospect, Somes came to see his war as a positive experience: '... who are we to judge whether it *is* really misfortune or no, – it's what we allow it to be'.[67] He resolved never to be depressed again: he was lucky to be alive and time outside the narrow ballet world had been no bad thing. He kept in touch with some of his army comrades and many followed his career and let him know of their pleasure in his success; the Misses Davies sent food hampers.

On 11 January 1945 he was discharged from the Army, 'Cause Ceasing to fulfil Army Physical requirements'. On 13 March, Michael Somes, Rank W/ Bar, having served three years 261 days, Campaigns Nil, Military Conduct Exemplary, returned to civilian life.

---

64 MS to ES nd

65 Alexander Bland, *Twenty-five Years*, interview with NdeV, *Observer* 6 May 1956

66 MS to ES nd

67 MS to ES nd

6

Return

The Sadler's Wells Ballet was on tour in Europe when Somes was discharged, so he began carefully working back with Vera Volkova at the school and teaching pas de deux classes. 'Volkova says ... I won't know myself in a month, and how "wonderful it is to see such talent again (!) and beautiful elevation she's never seen before" (!) and she's from the Moscow State School ... Of course ... I don't suppose what I do is very *good*, – but there's no reason that *I* can see why I shldn't be fully as good as ever inside 3 or 4 weeks!'[1] He was over-optimistic: he had been warned that he must go very carefully for a long time.

Time he didn't have. He was no longer a promising young dancer: he was 27 and had to reestablish himself both with the company and a new audience. His name on posters for the spring season at the New Theatre and newspaper reports of his return were reassuring; any lingering fears that he had been forgotten were dispelled when he made his debut as Pierrot in *Carnaval* on the opening night on 17 April. A full house gave him an ovation and every review singled him out, praising his pathos and restraint and noting that he had developed a sense of humour.

Not all the company were as welcoming, especially those who saw Somes as a threat to their positions established in the years he had been away. '... I'm afraid "I've had it"' he wrote to Ashton. 'I seem to be most undesired – isn't it sad?!' but added 'Am *determined* to be happy, & *not* miserable even if certain people *don't* want me!'[2] 'Somes was not a loner by temperament but made one,' surmised Kersley. '... all those boys hating him and Fred being so very bloody cussed'.[3] Carter thought him out on a limb, and that he needed 'cossetting', but such one-to-one attention was simply not available.

Opinion is divided about Somes post-War. If some thought his technique still sound and the elevation and ballon unaffected, Kersley thought the body was less elastic and that musicality and elevation had suffered: 'I didn't think after the war ... he got much sexy pleasure out of dancing. He may have enjoyed dancing but it wasn't that physical thing.'[4] Alexander Grant, too,

---

1   Copy letters notebook 1945
2   MS to FA undated (November 1945)
3   Interview with author
4   Interview with the author

wondered if his accident had affected his jump: 'when a dancer knows they could jump and they can't any more, they strain to try and achieve it and that's not good.' Teacher Prosso Pfister, too, saw a difference: '... his leg ... looked a little drooped in many of the arabesques and his elevation wasn't what it was. He still had a certain natural ballon (but) the solos, which were adapted a bit I think in some cases, were not quite as exciting.'[5]

Audiences were glad to see him back with May in *The Wanderer*, but hopes of dancing with Fonteyn seemed doomed, for she and Helpmann were more popular than ever, *Horoscope* was lost and she rarely danced *Dante Sonata*. De Valois had hopes of a partnership with Beryl Grey, but they found it difficult to establish a rapport. Given his debilitated state and a troublesome knee, Somes was wary: '... you had to be very strong to partner her ... Beryl had a tremendous vitality and never held back. When she gripped you it was like a man taking hold of you and she had a kick like a horse. She kicked me once and I kept well clear after that.'[6] Although they eventually developed an understanding and regularly danced together, the chemistry was missing.

He partnered her in *Les Sylphides*. 'It has come as a shock to many of the Wells audience,' wrote Mary Clarke, 'to discover how much there is in the male solo in this ballet – particularly in the way of battements which Somes performs with ease and other Wells dancers actually omit.'[7] Grey was also Odette-Odile when he danced his first full *Swan Lake* on 30 April. Clearly not strong enough for the complete ballet, he concentrated on the mechanics and pacing himself rather than interpretation, but there was a marked improvement in his partnering, possibly a result of teaching pas de deux. However, the strain was obviously great and by the end of May he was off with water on the knee.

He could not let up without losing ground already gained. When the company returned to Sadler's Wells that autumn, he stretched his range, taking on the lead in *Promenade* and M. Didelot in *The Prospect Before Us*; as the Young Man in *Nocturne*, he was insufficiently heartless, but his Stranger Player in *The Haunted Ballroom* had a chillingly sinister edge, giving Bradley 'an impression (however diluted) of what Nijinsky must have been like as Faun & Harlequin'.[8] Partnering Shearer and Fonteyn in *Le Spectre de la rose*, he was less Nijinsky's androgynous spirit than Fokine's memory of the lover and Clarke felt that 'When his strength is sufficient for him to let out the stops and really dance, we should have a most memorable Spectre,'[9] but it was not

---

5   Interview with the author

6   David Gillard, *Beryl Grey*, W H Allen, London, 1977, p35

7   Mary Clarke, *Dance Magazine*, November 1945

8   Lionel Bradley, ballet diaries, 3 August 1945, unpublished mss, Theatre and Performance Collections, Victoria and Albert Museum

9   Mary Clarke, *Dance Magazine*, November 1945

revived again. Before *The Quest* disappeared, Ashton had the chance to see his ideal St George, but the role defeated Somes, as it had Helpmann.

After five years of leading the company, Helpmann was exhausted. When he had to pull out of the 1945 autumn tour, Somes had the daunting task of replacing him in his controversial, though popular, *Miracle in the Gorbals*, in which a Christ-like 'stranger' was killed by a razor-slashing gang in the Glasgow slums. 'I think he *hates* me having to do it, but was quite nice & pleased it is *me*, & not someone else,' he wrote to Ethel.[10] His Stranger had a serene beauty, calm integrity, mystical authority and sense of goodness which some, including Farron and Kersley, found more moving than Helpmann: 'Michael just looked strange – and of course he was The Stranger – Bobby was so slick, he was acting it – Michael was being it.'[11] Whenever Helpmann was absent, Somes danced the role, but it was Paltenghi who partnered Fonteyn in the classics.

During the tour, David Webster, newly-appointed General Administrator of the Royal Opera House, entertained the company to an impressive tea. A successful Liverpool businessman, whose patrician air hid a socialist heart, he had been at the centre of the city's pre-war musical life and Chairman of the Liverpool Philharmonic. Somes liked him, admiring his stylish, gentlemanly efficiency in running Covent Garden – unless it clashed with the dancers' interests.

In November the company, in uniform and with temporary officer status, embarked on a six-week ENSA tour of Germany. With meals sometimes fifteen hours apart, a combination of hunger and intense cold made sleep impossible on the slow, fog-bound train to Hamburg. They travelled on with mounting horror: 'I've seen nothing *approaching* it in England ... Miles & miles of complete flatness, & none of it cleared away ... How anyone was left *alive* I *can't* imagine ... thousand upon thousand just wandering & tramping around hopelessly, women & children with little trucks & great bundles on their backs, – nowhere to go ... We threw some stale sandwiches out of the window to some German kids & they fought to get them ...'[12]

Hamburg was in ruins; the few buildings still standing were in the hands of the occupying forces while the Germans survived in basements and cellars. The company was told to go nowhere alone: the antagonism of the Germans, who had to salute the officer-dancers and get off the pavements as they passed, was almost palpable: '... (yet) their own miseries are beyond description it's so hard not to feel sorry for them, even when one remembers all *they* did.'[13]

---

10 MS to ES nd

11 Leo Kersley, interview with author

12 MS to ES nd

13 MS to ES nd

Venues varied from garrison theatres with no scenery to a banqueting hall in Hanover and relatively unscathed opera houses in Dusseldorf and Berlin. Audiences were mostly military personnel and the reception was rapturous. At outlying aerodromes '... they were *so* thrilled ... as they hardly *ever* have anything decent come to them ... They couldn't do enough for us, & after the show gave us the most *wonderful* party, – champagne ... the most glorious trifles & cake ... grapes & pears specially flown from Brussels ... & outside in the street were people picking in the dustbins for potato peelings ... Tonight at his Schlöss Air Chief Marshal Sholto-Douglas is giving us an even more super party ...'[14] Somes became increasingly uneasy about the lavish hospitality and their own relatively comfortable accommodation when the Germans survived in such indescribable conditions.

Astonishingly, musical life survived amid the devastation. Somes raved over Karl Dammer conducting the Hamburg Philharmonic: he saw *Fidelio* rehearsals in Hanover and *The Bartered Bride* in Berlin. In Hamburg there was an eerily sad encounter when he 'heard some music from below, & discovered a ballet-class in progress in the cellar!! I was ushered in & had to watch for a while. They were *awful* poor things!'[15]

With many dancers ill or injured, Somes was filling in in both leading and corps de ballet roles. Helpmann had an attack of sciatica but kept going with injections until he contracted a virus from his own ventures into the ruins, and had to return to London. Somes took over in *Miracle in the Gorbals*. Life became increasingly unnerving as they moved into the Russian zone where their coaches were regularly searched. Unbelievably, the devastation got worse and worse: '... they'll never *begin* to clear it up in a 100 years, leave alone rebuild it. Black crosses painted on nearly all these buildings mean that there are bodies buried underneath they haven't bothered to get out, – it's too impossible, – & they just gassed them in case they were alive.'[16]

Berlin '... surpasses even what we have seen already. It's *so vast* – & the buildings *were* so big ... *all flat* ... even the few walls which *are* left are spattered & torn with gunfire ... It really is ghastly, – the stench is awful & the people *so* thin & wretched & more hostile here ... the Russians ... are a very tough lot, & add a very sinister quality to the already fearful atmosphere ... (they) shoot first & *ask* afterwards!'[17] Undeterred, Somes hitched a lift on a lorry through the dead city, littered with burnt out vehicles and guns, into the Soviet quarter, where explosions rent the air as the army searched the ruins for Hitler's body. During a visit to see what was left of the Chancellery, Somes

---

14 MS to ES nd
15 MS to ES 3 December 1945
16 MS to ES p 1 December 1945
17 MS to ES 3 December 1945

palmed a piece of glass from the huge chandelier in the conference room, one of several significant souvenirs he purloined during his career.

Heavy snow fell as the depressed, sobered company huddled together for warmth on the journey through gloomy forests across the north German plain to Dusseldorf. The whole tour seemed 'like a crazy dream, always dominated by endless ruins ...'[18] Equally unreal, was knowing that in six weeks they would be moving into a new home and new beginnings. They had received their contracts with the Covent Garden Opera Trust, Somes for £22 a week (£650); he signed readily, resignedly noting that they had spelt his name wrong again.

18 MS to ES 10 December 1945

7

New Beginnings

Victory euphoria gave way to exhaustion as Britain entered the Age of Austerity. Edmund Wilson was reminded of the Soviet Union in the 1930s: '... constant queues of shabbily dressed people ... the quietness of everybody, the submissiveness, the patience, the acceptance. ... Everything was rationed, everything was drab.'[1] Amid the drabness, the Sadler's Wells Ballet's move to the Royal Opera House was a symbol of renewal and regeneration. After a chequered history the theatre now became the national home of opera and ballet, the surrounding fruit and vegetable market countering any leanings towards elitism. Despite six years as a dance hall, it needed only an army of cleaners, some paint, touches of gilt and the removal of chewing gum to restore its glory.

During the war, the arts had proved their importance, not just keeping up morale and the idea that civilisation was not completely dead, but also as a showcase for Britain abroad; the policy of national sponsorship for the arts in Britain would continue in peacetime. The Opera House subsidy meant security – that the company was not totally reliant on the box office, allowing them room for experiment and to survive inevitable low patches. However, to justify this, they would have to prove to Government the continuing relevance of the arts in a peacetime of continuing restrictions and privations.

The company, however, was not strong; Britons generally had never been so healthy, but intense physical activity needed more than basic rations and rationing continued well into the 1950s. In the short term de Valois needed to enlarge the company in time for the reopening in February 1946, but the pool of talent was small; with few girls and even fewer boys in training, there were few native resources on which to draw.

Mary Clarke assessed the state of male dancers as 'pathetic'.[2] The first generation had lost ground; in wartime, few boys had serious training before joining the school at 15, where there were few male teachers or examples of good male dancing. Long before they were ready, they were on stage, then before they had time to polish technique or mature as individuals they were whisked into the forces. De Valois' choices were either to bring in foreign artists, or plan long-term, developing mainly native talent in the school,

---

1   Edmund Wilson, *Notes on London at the End of a War*, *The New Yorker*, 6 February 1946
2   Mary Clarke, *The Sadler's Wells Ballet*, A&C Black, London, 1956, p209

which would now be reorganised to take pupils from the age of 11. She resisted the pressure to bring in outside stars: 'If I take any of these foreign boys,' she told Fonteyn, 'it will discourage our own dancers and we will never develop a tradition for male dancers in England.'[3] At the risk of seeming parochial, she took the slow track, mortgaging the present for the future, not only keeping faith with the men who had fought in the war, but the upcoming generations whose careers would be broken into by National Service until 1960. For years the men would be adversely compared with those in visiting companies, but she kept faith.

Reinforcements came from an unexpected source; almost as soon as the war ended, there was an influx of dancers from the Dominions – including Alexander Grant and Rowena Jackson from New Zealand, John Cranko, Nadia Nerina, Patricia Miller and David Poole from South Africa, Elaine Fifield from Australia. The international examinations policy of the RAD and Cecchetti Society had born fruit and they fitted in with their English contemporaries without the joins being too obvious. Above all, they provided much-needed energy and verve, being untraumatised by war and deprived of neither food nor sleep. For nearly 25 years the Commonwealth provided a steady stream of dancers who enriched the native stock and developed into many of the stars and soloists of the company's golden years.

De Valois' energy now reignited: she was planning new ballets while keeping twenty-two others in rehearsal and staging new productions of *The Sleeping Beauty* and *Giselle*. With Covent Garden still being renovated and technical departments and workrooms moving in, the dancers were banished to cramped rehearsal rooms all over central London and didn't get onto the stage until a week before the opening. In the workrooms, designer Oliver Messel was magicking up over two hundred costumes, accessories and myriad props on a meagre coupon budget, severely testing his legendary creative use of materials. Many of the eighty dancers and walk-ons were appearing in more than one role, causing chaos for Joy Newton as she tried to coordinate fittings. Clothing coupons imposed restrictions on cast changes – at its most extreme, it meant that a role originally danced by a boot size seven had to be covered by a boot size seven, there being no reserves to allow a boot size nine to take over.

Everything down to the smallest prop had to be ready for the photocalls, which lasted two days. Somes, Moira Shearer and Gerd Larsen were photographed in Ashton's newly choreographed Florestan and his Sisters, Somes wearing a hat which P. W. Manchester described as 'lethal' and which, like so many hats in ballet, disappeared after a few performances.

Off-stage photographs show Somes looking drawn and tired, no longer

---

3   Margot Fonteyn, *Autobiography*, Hamish Hamilton paperback, London, 1989, p79

the eager youthful dancer of the 1930s, but a grimly determined older man, clawing his way back against younger competition. While he might resume roles created on him, he could not expect to oust Paltenghi and Rassine and had to contend with younger dancers like John Field and John Hart. Despite a troublesome knee, he dared not let up, especially as Ashton was choreographing César Franck's *Symphonic Variations*, one of the scores they had discussed during the war; rehearsals were gruelling and the exhausted cast were often in tears, but Somes remembered the creation as '"magical" ... They all felt it was going to be something special ...'[4]

On 20 February, the Royal Opera House reopened with *The Sleeping Beauty*. Crowds stood for hours applauding Prime Minister Clement Atlee, government ministers, ambassadors, military leaders and representatives of the arts, academe and society, before a storm of cheering welcomed the Royal Family, King George VI, Queens Mary and Elizabeth, Princesses Elizabeth and Margaret. If the audience was undeniably dowdy, the atmosphere was electric.

Inspired by Lambert's superbly authoritative handling of the score and Messel's spell-binding 'Englishisation' of the Russian classic, the company rose beyond the occasion, although they clearly needed time to adjust to the larger stage and auditorium: on the second night, Bolshoi-trained Violetta Prokhorova (Elvin) as Princess Florine showed in stage-devouring attack and personality how it should be done and over the season, there was a great improvement. To give the men more opportunities, de Valois choreographed the Act III pas de deux coda as the Three Ivans and the Jewel Fairies were replaced by Ashton's Florestan and his Sisters.

Only grim determination got Somes through. Three days after the opening, he bowed to the inevitable. 'Last night of first C. Garden season for me!' he wrote in his diary. 'Cartilage has to be removed.' This meant postponing *Symphonic Variations* and Ashton lost the honour of creating the first new ballet at Covent Garden to Helpmann's *Adam Zero*, a large company work tracing Everyman's journey through life using all the theatre's technical resources.

In great pain after the operation, Somes found inspiration in his hero, Chabukiani, who suffered a similar career-threatening injury but recovered to dance better than ever. After only three weeks he was back rehearsing *Symphonic Variations*, although his progress was slow and his role had to be constantly modified.

Ashton had used the extra time to distil and refine until only the essence remained, potent and powerful, '... through (the music), one gets the purity of the dance expressing nothing but itself, and thereby expressing a thousand

---

4 Wendy Ellis interview with Frank Freeman

degrees and facets of emotion, and the mystery of poetry of movement.'[5] He never put anything into words, even to himself, lest it become 'literary, and that the fluid nature of my inspiration might crystalise into something I did not really intend.'[6] It was his reaction to the literary, 'opulent' turn ballet had taken during the War: 'Dance seemed to be pushed aside and lose significance ... I was principally concerned to try to give pure dance again its proper validity.'[7] Six simply dressed dancers in a minimalist set was hardly a message of expansion and a horrified Webster actually suggested that Fedorovitch's designs were unworthy of an Opera House.

On 24 April, the curtain rose on a scene that reminded Christian Bérard of lily of the valley – a yellow green backcloth on which fine black lines swooped and curved and six dancers in white – Fonteyn, May and Shearer in short-skirted tunics, Brian Shaw and Henry Danton in black-edged tunics with one shoulder bare, Somes with both shoulders covered. They stood in wrapt stillness until the music impelled them into life. For eighteen minutes Ashton's discreet eloquence held the stage, like the music of the spheres made visible or, as Philip Hope-Wallace put it no less reverently '... a kind of heavenly tennis ...'[8] Teacher Winifred Edwards, likened it to 'a string of pearls, simple, lovely and everlastingly satisfying.' [9]

Ashton cunningly exploited each dancer's qualities – the 'serene excitement' of Fonteyn, the 'exulting triumph' of Somes jumping with bold assurance, the cool precision and beauty of May and Shearer, the youthful vigour of Shaw and the lyricism of Danton; together Fonteyn and Somes projected a 'passionate elegance.'[10] The dancers were exposed, emotionally and physically, unable to relax for a second, and the intense concentration required conveyed a sense of dedication and absorption in something over and above the individual – the effect gleaned by Ashton from his wartime reading of mystical texts, including St Teresa of Avila and St John of the Cross. Stillness was as important as movement in a ballet so understated that the slightest turn of the head, the placing of an arm, the shift of a body had almost epic significance; with Somes not back to full strength, lifts were sparingly used, heightening their impact. Ashton now perfected his fiendish

---

5   Frederick Ashton, quoted Clive Barnes, *Symphonic Variations, Ballet Perspectives 30, Dance and Dancers*, March 1963, p27

6   Richard Buckle and Frederick Ashton, *Abstract Ballet, Ballet*, November 1947, p2

7   Hans-Theodor Wohlfahrt, *An Interview with Sir Fredrick Ashton, Ballet-Journal/Das Tanzarchiv*, 1 December 1988.

8   Philip Hope-Wallace, *Time and Tide*, 4 May 1946

9   Winifred Edwards, Theatre Diary. Book II. 22nd July 47 – 21 Ap. 1949. mss in Theatre and Performance Collections, V&A

10 Clive Barnes, *Symphonic Variations, Ballet Perspectives 30, Dance and Dancers*, March 1963, p29

signature 'walking on air', where the supported ballerina floats just above the ground, requiring the man to carry her at hip height. Fonteyn claimed it was one of her favourite movements but only Somes' partnering skill made it possible. Fonteyn's perfection in the development of Ashton's sublime pas de deux is often acknowledged, but it is a pas de *deux* and much of their character and quality came equally from Somes.

Somes was the anchor around which *Symphonic Variations* revolved, his interplay with the girls suggesting shifting emotional relationships against the certainty of the music. 'His masculine strength, his protectiveness and authority, his tenderness, his gravity and joyousness and nobility all add richness to the ballet's texture,' declared John Percival.[11]

Symphonic Variations remains the ultimate test of stamina, style and artistic virtuosity: 'We often hear of dancers of that generation not having the technical expertise of dancers of this generation,' declared Cynthia Harvey, who danced the ballet in the 1980s, 'and I beg to differ, because ... the steps, the phrasing, the difficulty factor was all there. You have to have very good technique to do these.' RSM George Howe of the Irish Guards spotted another challenge: '... I've taken P.T. parades, King's Guards and Olympia displays. But this is a far, far harder bit of drill ... They didn't quite keep their distance – or interval. If they had, it would have been perfect.'[12] How often Ashton exhorted his dancers to 'watch their spacing' and Somes stress distance and interval as central to the ballet.

Ashton sent Somes a first night message: 'Dearest Mishky, This ballet for what it is worth is due to you. You suggested it & you bullied it out of me & if it has any merits it is due to you.' It was his tribute, not to the passionate, raw youth of *Horoscope*, but to the mature artist, acknowledging Somes' superb musicality, sculptural line, partnering skills and quietly dignified command of the stage. It has been suggested that friendship lies at the heart of the ballet, although, as Ashton admitted, 'one doesn't know afterwards what the real motivation was.'[13]

As Somes recovered, Ashton amplified the central role. The costume too was changed to match the other men, with one bare shoulder: 'I think suddenly a lot of people realised that Michael really was very dishy,' mused Clarke. 'That change of costume made an extraordinary difference to the physical attraction and one was more aware of it. From then on it was thought of him as being a very important person in the Company, carrying a lot of responsibility.'[14]

11 John Percival, *Danseur Noble, Dance and Dancers*, April 1959, p19

12 Roy Johnson, *Ballet turns to drill*, unidentified periodical, 1946, Somes press cuttings

13 Hans-Theodor Wohlfahrt, *An Interview with Sir Frederick Ashton, Ballet-Journal/Das Tanzarchiv*, 1 December 1988

14 Interview with author

6 *Symphonic Variations*: left to right Moira Shearer, Somes, Pamela May, Margot Fonteyn, (back) Henry Danton. Photograph by Richardby at Baron Studios.

Somes was on almost every night, sometimes as Florestan or a Rose Adagio Prince, mostly in *Symphonic Variations*; he danced Laertes for the first time and, with Helpmann unwell, made his London debut in *Miracle in the Gorbals* and took over in *Nocturne*. He was also working on *Giselle* with Fonteyn, noting in his diary 'Must 'chase' Margot in 2nd Act – & not arrive too soon before jetes. Must be even less stiff all thro' & project personality more & not 'flag' at end (fouettes),' and the ominous note 'watch out for flying wilis.' However, when the new production was unveiled on 12 June, Rassine was Fonteyn's Albrecht. 'Rassine was a lovely dancer,' recalled Kersley, 'maybe he danced better than Somes ever did, but it didn't matter ... when Somes came on he was somebody.'[15]

Criticism of the male dancers increased as dance companies poured into London. The men of the Original Ballets Russes were still remarkable, although relentless touring and economic hardship had badly affected overall standards. Roland Petit's youthful, artistically sophisticated Ballets des Champs-Elysées brought the sensational Jean Babilée, whose exciting technique and charismatic personality Somes rated 'excellent' – a rare accolade. Lifar returned with the Nouveau Ballet de Monte Carlo. Most significantly, Ballet Theatre brought André Eglevsky, John Kriza, Michael Kidd, Jerome Robbins and Hugh Laing in ballets like *Fancy Free* and *Rodeo*, portraying energetic men, not mythical characters or empty sophisticates. The English virtues of subtle and lyrical had never seemed so bloodless. It was a necessary wake-up call.

*****

Hardly had Somes resettled into his professional life, than there were upheavals in his private life. He had already returned to Islington and his Lloyd Square flat, but then accepted an offer to swap with a flat in a small block in the same square where, fulfilling his promise to Ethel, he and his parents could live together, they contributing income from the sale of her school and letting their Taunton house.

Another distraction was pretty and brunette. Canadian Jean Gilbert was Sadler's Wells Ballet's rehearsal and solo pianist. A war-widow, she was hardly ready to respond to Somes' desperate overtures, so he asked Ashton to intercede. Their relationship could be extremely volatile; in the early years, Somes was frequently in pain, his nerves on edge, anxious about his future, and Jean was often in tears, but the relationship endured into the 1950s.

In autumn 1946, the Sadler's Wells Ballet embarked for Vienna, staying in the Sacher Hotel, where Nijinsky had been living when the city was liberated. In Helpmann's absence, Somes was again dancing *Miracle in the Gorbals*, which was one of the great successes of the visit, along with *Symphonic Variations*. While some of the British army despised ballet, all were proud of the company's success; Russian occupation forces were more enthusiastic

---

15 Interview with author

7 *Les Sirènes*: as Captain Bay Vavaseur with Beryl Grey as Countess Kitty, one of the few roles that allowed Somes to exercise his talents for stylish comedy.
Photograph by Richardby.

and *Pravda* acclaimed the 'great English dancers' and hoped they would visit Moscow. There was sightseeing to innumerable palaces, drives in the Vienna Woods, tea with the GOC General Steele, a wine festival and the endless round of British Council parties. Here Somes began to hone his cocktail party skills, his natural good manners and charm masking his dislike of socialising. The luxurious food was in stark contrast to British rations and the poverty of the Viennese: Somes gave some of his away – 'they are *really* hungry & so nice & sweet – one *couldn't* barter with it.' [16]

Back in London, Ashton's *Les Sirènes* was premiered on 12 November. In Cecil Beaton's elegant Edwardian seaside setting, to Lord Berners's 'aqueous and romantic' music, everyone shrimped, splashed and indulged in aquatic games in the canvas wavelets as mermaids combed their hair and carried off men, watched by two seagulls 'with the interested unconcern of a Greek chorus'.[17] Sporting a fetching naval beard and heartily twirling his moustache, Somes was a dazzling Captain Bay Vavasour, partnering Grey as a frilled and fluffy Countess Kitty, but they were upstaged by Fonteyn as La

16 MS to ES nd

17 Anon, *"Les Sirènes", The Times*, nd, Somes press cuttings

Bolero, an exotic Spanish dancer, Ashton as King Hihat of Agpar (arriving by vintage car) and Helpmann as tenor Adeline Canberra (descending by balloon), who actually burst into song.

The dancers threw themselves into the ballet with all the 'wholehearted sense of fun'[18] (overplaying) that comes from sensing a work needs all the help it can get. Somes and Grey got some of the best notices, but *Les Sirènes* soon disappeared. What would have been lightly dismissed pre-war now took on greater significance: Bradley was horrified that it shared the same bill as *Les Sylphides* and *Symphonic Variations* while Haskell castigated anyone who enjoyed it. Such frivolous trifles were NOT for The National Company in The Royal Opera House. Only *The Times* felt it was a necessary corrective to everyone taking themselves too seriously.

Barely a month later, on 12 December, Lambert achieved one of his most cherished ambitions when the new opera company was launched with a spectacular production of *The Fairy Queen*, Purcell and Dryden's monster reworking of *A Midsummer Night's Dream*. He enthusiastically reduced the seven-hour score to 2½ hours, banished Dryden, restored Shakespeare and concentrated on the best of Purcell in the four masques – Night, Love, Seasons and Chinese Garden; Ashton was director and choreographer and Michael Ayrton created the breathtakingly lovely designs. While Richard Buckle called it 'a bran-tub in which everyone is sure to find something to enjoy,'[19] Caryl Brahms felt 'The playgoers will miss Shakespeare ... the music lover be maddened by the lachrymose grouping and obstinate gambolling of the dancers. While the ballet-goer will want them to cut the cackle and come down to the cavorting.'[20]

Fonteyn and Somes as Spirits of the Air were one of the highlights, their pas de deux showcasing Somes' particular partnering skills while apparently focussing on Fonteyn. 'By dint of a series of dreamlike lifts which keep the female dancer off the ground nearly all the time, Ashton has suggested flight,' wrote Buckle. 'Like some immaculate denizen of the ether, Fonteyn skims in on her partner's shoulders and executes with him the movements of a cold geometry; then, as if the earth had relinquished its right of gravity upon her, she is borne floatingly away into the upper air.'[21] The production was short-lived, but the pas de deux was too good to lose and Ashton incorporated some of the movements into *Symphonic Variations* and, later, into *Homage to the Queen*.

With the opera company installed, the battle for stage time began, a battle

18 Anon, *"Les Sirènes"*, *The Times*, nd, Somes press cuttings
19 Richard Buckle, *Commentary*, *Ballet*, January 1947, Vol 5 No 1 pp5-8
20 Caryl Brahms, *The very respectable Fairy Queen*, *News Chronicle*(?), 13 December 1946
21 Richard Buckle, *Commentary*, *Ballet*, January 1947, Vol 5 No 1 pp5-8

which Somes was still waging forty years later. Space was so tight that the ballet company had to vacate dressing rooms after a performance if the next night was opera, and vice versa (at the Paris Opéra stars had a three-roomed suite for life). There was no rehearsal studio, so the company spent their days in a succession of gloomy rooms, including the basement of the Kingsway Hall, the Stoll theatre, the Inns of Court, a pub behind Bow Street police station and a 'hall in Bloomsbury' the location of which no one seems to remember; as none had a canteen, more time was wasted changing several times a day.

During November and December Somes forsook stage for film studio, partnering Fonteyn in *Les Sylphides* in the educational film *The Little Ballerina*. Not long after, however, he asked to be taken out of *Les Sylphides*, feeling that he could no longer meet his own high standards, an extraordinary request, especially when the establishment of the opera company meant fewer performances and even more competition for roles.

In the revised *Swan Lake* on 19 December, Somes was in de Valois's rearrangement of the Spanish dance (which in wartime had shrunk to two girls), with Hart, Farron and Palma Nye. Somes always had the rhythm and weight for character dances and was so successful that, at this time, some felt this was his true forte.

His ambition, however, was to dance the great classical roles and he turned his energies towards his first Albrecht on 11 January 1947, with Grey as his Giselle. His technique had improved, he was lighter, his dancing had clarity and moments of brilliance and if his mime was not particularly expressive nor his acting subtle, he had the right Romantic style. His success came as a surprise to many, especially his spectacular dance to the death. '... it seems as if a successor to Helpmann has at last been found.' wrote Clarke. 'He looks the complete ballet aristocrat, dances very well (it seems worth recording that he performs an excellent *entrechat huit*) and, particularly in Act II, gives a moving interpretation ... it does not seem an exaggeration to say that, quietly but decisively, Somes is now taking his place among the tiny band of English male dancers who really matter.'[22] He looked well in the James Bailey-designed peacock blue tunic in Act I and the black tunic, trimmed with yellow rather than the obvious white in Act II (the yellow 'reading' as soft white under the blue lights). At least he didn't have to cope with flying wilis, which had been abandoned after one had crashed into another Albrecht as he prayed at Giselle's tomb.

Having settled the company into Covent Garden and launched the replacement Sadler's Wells Theatre Ballet at the Wells, de Valois reassessed the repertory. Ballets from the 1930s that made little impact in the larger

---

22 Mary Clarke, *Massine at Covent Garden*, *Ballet Today*, April-May 1947 Vol 1 No 5, p7

Opera House went back to the Wells or disappeared; she now had to acquire works to suit the enlarged Covent Garden company and wanted to acquire significant works from the Diaghilev period to give her dancers experience of working with other great choreographers. To this end, early in 1947, she invited Leonide Massine to mount and dance in his masterpieces *The Three-Cornered Hat* and *La Boutique fantasque.*

Somes was overjoyed to be chosen to understudy Massine as the Miller. However, there didn't seem much likelihood of him even learning the role, as he told Wendy Ellis: '... whenever it came to the Miller's dance Massine used to say "Cut" and nobody saw him do this damn dance ... the final rehearsal in the studio, he came to it and (I) said "If he doesn't do it this time how can I ever ..." and (Massine) said "I do" and I didn't learn a step because I was just mesmerised.'[23] Somes learnt it by watching every performance from the wings.

Massine had the desired effect: 'Never did London appreciate more the colour, verve and *joie de vivre* which came tumbling over the footlights as if from another planet,'[24] although the dancers couldn't colour the steps and rhythms as the Ballets Russes had done, and everyone looked rather clean compared with memories of their predecessors' scruffy ruffians. The champagne effervescence of *La Boutique fantasque,* however, just eluded them. The only consensus was that Somes, in the small part of the Cossack Chief, was 'gloriously "right"',[25] a nice showy role, which always merited a mention in reviews.

He added the third classical Prince to his repertory on 29 April, dancing Florimund to Fonteyn's Aurora. For Clarke, Somes 'really brings the nebulous Florimund to life – giving him his Louis Quatorze air and suggesting first the *ennui* and then the magic of the forest scene. Seeing is not necessarily believing with a ballet audience,' she added dryly, 'but Somes' Prince Florimund may help to convince people that he is now no mean partner.'[26] Manchester's 'more of a liability than an asset' had become something of a mantra, but, as he regained strength his potential as an outstanding classical partner became blindingly obvious and in his dancing and characterisation he set a high bar for his successors in the role.

After having closed down for the duration of the War, television was now on air again, though few people had access to it. In the 1930s, all transmissions had been from the studio, but new developments now allowed more outside broadcasts. On May 23, Somes took part in another significant date in television history when *Symphonic Variations* and *The Three-Cornered*

---

23 Interview with author

24 L. J., *"The Three Cornered Hat"*, Theatre World, March 1947, p7

25 Mary Clarke, *Massine at Covent Garden*, Ballet Today, April-May 1947, Vol 1 No 5, p7

26 Mary Clarke, *The Sleeping Beauty Again*, July 1947 Vol 1 No 6, p31

Hat became the first live transmissions from the Royal Opera house.

Over the summer, Somes and Leslie Edwards went off for a welcome holiday in Villefranche, then a quaint little fishing village on the Riviera, as yet undiscovered by tourists, with what was said to be the most beautiful sea view in Europe. They went over to Monte Carlo to see the traditional Farandole danced through the streets, meeting up with a tired Moira Shearer and a surprisingly affable Massine, who were on location filming *The Red Shoes*. The celebrations for Prince Louis II jubilee, with processions, floodlighting and superb fireworks, were fun, but Somes preferred the quieter Villefranche, enjoying lavish meals (patisserie and ices got ecstatic mention in postcards home) under a clear moon and stars with fishing boats bobbing in the bay. They stayed nearly three weeks before Somes returned home to his obligatory holiday with his parents; Budleigh Salterton wasn't quite the same. So began his life-long love of the Riviera – which he was to visit in very different circumstances in later years.

*****

In September and October 1947 the company undertook its longest European tour, taking in Brussels, Prague, Warsaw, Poznan, Malmo and Oslo. Sadler's Wells Ballet was now a major cultural ambassador in the British Council's policy of showing Britain to the world. Initial reaction to the company still tended to be astonishment that a nation never considered artistic nor creative could not only achieve such a level of execution so quickly, but also create '... no milk-and-water imitation of Continental standards, but something completely national and forceful – even, to the stranger, slightly brutal ...'[27] This interested European audiences far more than 'antiquated mummery' (as one critic described *Swan Lake*), or visiting Russian companies' weighty, realistic productions and showpiece pas de deux. In theatre-conscious Eastern Europe, where ballet was regarded as an adjunct to opera, it was a revelation that the classical vocabulary could be used to reflect the contemporary world.

For Somes, who was much admired on the continent, these tours were very positive. In Brussels, he danced Hamlet for the first time to general approval. De Valois told him he was 'magnificent'! – altho' I *personally* thought it pretty stinking.'[28] The favourable impression was confirmed when he performed the role in London: 'a youthful prince, bewildered and pained by the corruption around him' wrote Clarke, 'but I am doubtful whether, even in a sleep of death, he would have had such a singularly nasty dream.'[29]

27 Constant Lambert, *Slightly Brutal*, unidentified pc, nd

28 MS to ES, September 12(?) 1947

29 Mary Clarke, *Sadler's Wells Ballet at Covent Garden Ballet Today*, January 1948, Vol I No 9 p6

Anticipation in Eastern Europe was intense. In Prague, Warsaw and Posnàn seat prices were doubled, yet tickets sold out within a few hours and a flourishing black market developed.

The coverage in Prague exceeded that given to any other visiting company.[30] '... opening night was a sensation! ... they just *wouldn't* stop clapping, – we had to come back & back, – long after all the lights were out, & de V had to come on & make a speech. Everyone says its surpassed their wildest hopes, – & I must say, I've never known us have quite such an ovation anywhere. It's all a great relief as we'd heard so much abt. the Soviet ballet & were apprehensive. 'Lac' went splendidly ...& 'Dante' was *very* moving, & of course they adored 'Rake'. The Co. all danced exceptionally well.' He was pleased that the British Ambassador reported their success to the Foreign Office – 'so that should boost us a bit.'[31]

Interest in *Hamlet* and *Miracle in the Gorbals* was intense and, in Helpmann's absence, Somes upheld their reputation. '... Hamlet when they eventually *did* stop (applauding), – they started up *again* after about 2 mins, & I had come back from my room to take another curtain!!'[32]

The past met them on Warsaw station in the person of de Valois' colleagues from Diaghilev's Ballets Russes, Leon Woizikowsky and Marian Winter, who was to act as their interpreter. Woizikowski gave class and coached Turner and Somes in *Three-Cornered Hat*, in which many had considered him Massine's equal: '*very* interesting as his version was obviously more authentic than Massine's who had obviously "watered it down" as he got older ...' observed Somes.[33]

Warsaw put Allied bombing of Germany into perspective: '... *never* have I seen anything to *compare* with the complete & utter devastation,' wrote Somes, '– it is absolutely *unbelievable*, & worst of all is the Ghetto ... literally not a building left ... the insurrection in 1944 ... must have been *too* ghastly to imagine from some of the stories *we* heard.'[34] Somehow an extra matinee in aid of the city's rebuilding was slotted in. Accommodating the 65-strong company was a huge logistical problem and de Valois paid tribute to the stimulating and inspiring 'spirit of a people who can find time and inclination, in the midst of reconstruction problems of a size of which we had not dreamt, to welcome a company of foreign artists so generously, and with such imaginative forethought.'[35] An even greater problem was finding

---

30 In Britain, paper shortages restricted critics to 150 or 200 words; Czech coverage ran into feet.

31 MS to ES undated

32 MS to ES undated

33 MS to ES 14(?) October 1947

34 MS to ES 14(?) October 1947

35 Ninette de Valois, *British Ballet in Poland*, *Sunday Times*, nd 1947

enough musicians for the orchestra, as so many had died in concentration camps. Yet food was abundant and Somes was hugely cheered by the luxury of two eggs every day.

The British Council had brought off a major coup in arranging performances in the state theatres in Brussels, Prague and Warsaw, but the Swedish and Danish State Theatres refused to allow an upstart company to perform on their hallowed ground, so King Gustav had to travel to Malmo to see the only Swedish performances. Entertaining got even grander – 'Press conference at 4, cocktail party followed by Anglo-Swedish dinner followed by a *ball* in our honour!! & tomorrow a big party on the stage at night & lunch given by the French Ambassador!! ... The Swedes are a bit patronising & we are being 'grand' back, – I don't really like them, – they're too rich & smug.'[36] Somes countered by praising Polish generosity and warmth despite their suffering, but had to do a volte face after the opening: '... once we had performed the Swedes "came round" & couldn't do enough for us! They say it had never been known for any Co. to have such applause & acclamation, & they were mad for us to go to Stockholm, & were trying to arrange it for the last 3 days ... The Danish Ballet came all the way from Copenhagen & many from Stockholm where they ran a special train!! & they were all absolutely *thrilled* & said they didn't want to attempt to dance again after seeing us!!'[37] Swedish audiences traditionally applauded through a performance but not at the end; now they refused to leave.

In Oslo the opening was attended by King Haakon and the entire diplomatic corps. Success bred confidence: everyone was dancing superlatively well and Somes repeated his success in *Hamlet* and *Miracle in the Gorbals*. Again it was the backhanded compliment as *Ballet* reported: 'The many dancers who came to watch rehearsals said that it was a complete revelation to them and they had no idea that England could produce a company of such importance. Ashton concluded by comparing the impact of their visit to the first visit of the Ballets Russes to Paris in 1909.'[38] Norway had no national ballet, and, to help raise interest, Ashton, Somes, Fonteyn, May, Grey, Hart and Turner gave a demonstration for teachers and students.

The later successes in America have obscured the Sadler's Wells Ballet's impact in Europe. It was through its post-war tours in Germany, France, Italy, Holland and Eastern Europe – mostly nations with long ballet traditions and a lively interest in theatre – that the company became of international standing. Most hailed the company not just as a dance machine, though they acknowledged the achievement of establishing dance to such a high degree

---

36 MS to ES nd

37 MS to ES nd

38 R(ichard) B(uckle) and P(eter) W(illiams), *Sadler's Wells Abroad, Ballet,* November 1947, p42

in such a short time, but they also recognised the growth of something new and particularly British in both de Valois and Helpmann's dramatic works and Ashton's emotional use of dance. For much of Europe, the classical vocabulary seemed incapable of expressing the new world and they were excited by the way the Sadler's Wells Ballet were stretching the possibilities of the classical technique.

Back in London, a bombshell awaited them: Lambert resigned as Music Director to devote himself to composition, leaving a professional and personal gap that would never be adequately filled for de Valois, Fonteyn, Ashton and Somes. Helpmann, too, was absent during the Autumn tour and opening weeks at Covent Garden, filming *The Red Shoes*. He spent the next few years juggling dance, theatre and film, which was unsettling for everyone, especially Fonteyn, and frustrating for Somes, now certainly heir-in-waiting, but he always acknowledged that Bobby was, and always had been, the star.

Somes did, however, partner Fonteyn in *Giselle* on the opening night on 12 November. He was only too aware of resentment from Helpmann's fans, but Fonteyn's serene imperturbability helped him through. He lifted her performance too: 'Margot danced as she never danced before,' de Valois wrote to Joy Newton '& Somes was excellent & had a wonderfully good press.'[39] The ovation was for both, but Somes got the lion's share of the reviews, his excellent Act II solo being particularly singled out.

At this point, he was more comfortable as the lover of Act I than the distraught romantic of Act II but, in time, his Albrecht developed into a fully rounded character. He approached the role as an essay in period style, within which Albrecht was a virile foil to Giselle's femininity and fragility, a man whose heedless amatory escapade sets off a tragic chain of events.

Having performed the distraught Albrecht, Somes did a quick change into the Cossack Chief in *La Boutique fantasque*. In the 1940s and 1950s *Giselle* was not considered a full evening's entertainment and was programmed with a short, often contrasting ballet, thus giving the audience full value for money and the dancers more performances.

November brought the return of Massine to mount *Mam'zelle Angot*, a major reworking of his ballet originally created for Ballet Theatre in 1943. 'With so much grimness in the world,' he declared, 'the time is ripe for a really comic ballet to cheer audiences up.'[40] André Derain's designs were delicious, though producing eighty costumes with rationing still in force was a major headache and mothers and sisters of the wardrobe staff were all dragooned into knitting maroon and white striped stockings.

Massine created a high-spirited romp about Mlle Angot (Fonteyn) forsaking

39 Ninette de Valois to Joy Newton, 14 November 1947, Royal Ballet School Archives
40 Anon, *High-spirited*, unknown publication, 26 November 1947

her barber fiancé (Grant) for a handsome Caricaturist (Somes), who is in love with an Aristocrat (Shearer). There were fourteen curtain calls at the 26 November premiere. Manchester titled her review 'A cheer for Mam'zelle Angot': a loud cheer indeed for the first scene, a miniature masterpiece of narrative and dance construction; the highlight was a perfectly orchestrated romantic pas de deux for Angot and the Caricaturist, counterpointed by a comic pas de quatre for the suffering Barber supported by Butcher, Tailor and Bootmaker, against a background crowd, yet at no time was the clarity of the stage picture compromised (well, not after de Valois stopped Massine egging on the Barber's comforters because they were upstaging the pas de deux). Scene two merited a half-hearted cheer as the plot got more complicated – try expressing the relationship 'old school friend' in mime. Scene three became almost incomprehensible as any remaining plot was swamped by much sound and fury, carnival figures, unrelenting jollity and flailing mass movement, all desperately trying to conceal that the ballet had nowhere to go; Brahms likened it to a kaleidoscope before the pieces fall into place.

Whatever its shortcomings, the dancers performed with all the bubbling fun that had eluded them in *La Boutique fantasque*. Somes had his showiest part since *Horoscope*, dancing with 'a flashing kingfisher quality at one with his elegant blue costume,' which streamlined his figure, the white stock softening his chin, which he still had a habit of tilting upwards.[41] He invested the caddish character with a smooth, arrogant charm, displaying real bravura in the showy first solo, based on beats and *tours en l'air* ending with *grands pirouettes a la seconde*; the difficult pas de deux with Shearer was performed with great ease and tact. Purists, however, were horrified: 'vulgar ... with acrobatic lifts – pure Broadway ...' cried Winifred Edwards.[42] Cyril Beaumont protested at the excessive use of lifts which 'is threatening to cast a blight on contemporary choreography'; in scene two, he declared, Massine achieved 'a degree of acrobatism more appropriate to a circus performer than to an exponent of the classical ballet'.[43]

The pace never slackened. Somes frequently partnered Shearer at this time and was her regular Prince in *The Sleeping Beauty*. He also made an impact with Grey in *Checkmate*, bringing, for Clarke, 'a musical sensitivity that simplifies the awkward duel, and almost lends distinction to the Red Knight's solo'.[44]

---

41 P. W. Manchester, *A Cheer for Mam'zelle Angot*, *Ballet Today*, January 1948, Vol I No 9, p6, 30

42 Winifred Edwards, Theatre Diary, Book II 22 July – 21 April 1949, mss Theatre and Performance Collections V&A

43 Cyril W. Beaumont, *'Checkmate' and 'Mam'zelle Angot'*, *Ballet*, January 1948, pp7-15

44 Mary Clarke, *Sadler's Wells Ballet at Covent Garden*, *Ballet Today*, January 1948, Vol I No 9, p4

8 Prince Florimund in *The Sleeping Beauty*. Photograph by Edward Mandinian.

After *Mam'zelle Angot*, work began on Ashton's *Scènes de ballet*, to Stravinsky's astringent score, premiered on 11 February 1948. The choreography reflected the austerity of the music: Ashton brought books of Euclid's geometry to rehearsals and let the dancers work out the mechanics before transforming it into pure abstraction, the choreography marrying crystalline clarity to urbane elegance and classical ballet's stark beauty to the music's wit, elegance and crisp sophistication.

Fonteyn and Somes were the fulcrum of a company ballet, he in the pivotal position of five men. Ashton created a ballet that worked from any viewpoint: a single pose was picked up and reflected from a different angle or with a minute variation by another dancer across and around the stage. Those used to Ashton's overt romanticism were bewildered; there was booing on the first night and critics were split not only for and against but between those who thought the leads were uncomfortable and those who thought they danced magnificently

'People uninterested in ballet except as a consolation will find ... *Scènes de Ballet* chilling, meaningless and quite heartless,' wrote Philip Hope-Wallace. 'But it will much excite those who are interested in choreography ... a delighted comment on the whole business of the grand ballet divertissement ... a much-needed stimulant and corrective for the Sadler's Wells repertory which is dangerously clogged with self-satisfaction, sentimental reminiscence and second-rate artisticness.'[45] Beryl de Zoete in *The New Statesman* was also pro: '... as one listens and watches, the correspondences of musical and plastic space shape themselves before one into a geometric, dispassionate harmony which is indeed something new and strange and altogether admirable ...'[46] In time, Somes developed a mix of virile solemnity and technical precision which suited the role, but Fonteyn never succeeded in fusing the style with her own natural elegance and soon relinquished the ballet.

Scènes de ballet was in the repertory when the company went back to Holland in March 1948. Audiences, which at the Hague included twenty-seven Ambassadors, stood on their seats to applaud and refused to leave. Memories of 1940 came flooding back as the flower petals showered down. Somes joined the pilgrimage to the Hague hotel in which they had been trapped, where they learned that their abandoned clothes had been sold for food on the black market. The press was rapturous and people stopped Somes in the street to congratulate him. An extra matinée had to be arranged: '2 S/V's & Dante's in 1 day is more than enough!' wrote Somes to his mother. '...

---

45 Philip Hope-Wallace, *Scènes de Ballet*, unidentified publication, February 1948

46 Beryl de Zoete, *"Scènes de Ballet," at Covent Garden, The New Statesman and Nation*, 21 February 1948

this touring is all very exciting in it's way, – but *terribly* wearing ... one can't keep it up for long.'[47]

A new mentor now entered Somes' life with the appointment of Latvian-born Harjis Plucis as ballet master. 'He adored Harjis Plucis' recalled Antoinette Sibley, '(and Plucis) *worshipped* (Fonteyn and Somes) and taught them most of what they knew.'[48] Although Clover Roope described him as 'a soft, pudgy teddy bear',[49] Plucis was a ruthless taskmaster who profoundly influenced Somes' own approach to teaching and rehearsing. They masked their deep affection by bandying what would now be considered politically incorrect insults. Fonteyn and Somes had started working together with Volkova and now, under Plucis's unrelenting regime, they explored and refined their classical roles, reexamining character and situation, ceaselessly striving for perfection. Somes worked constantly on honing his partnering skills, including strengthening his hands with exercise balls, resulting in a vice-like grip that was so important in executing Ashton's dead weight floating lifts, which would prove so incredibly hard for later generations (especially visiting guest artists) to master.

In 1948, Somes at 31 and Fonteyn at 29 were entering their prime years. They worked with Plucis, Volkova and alone, repeating details over and over until they became second nature. Expressing feeling had never been a problem for her, but, with her personal life now something of an emotional wasteland, she had become hasty and mechanical, resulting in performances which some found cold. She had lost her youthful spontaneity and instinctive reactions to Helpmann, for whom no two performances were alike (he hated spending unnecessary time on rehearsals and rumour had it that he, and therefore Fonteyn, had never rehearsed Act IV of *Swan Lake* after they first danced it in 1937). Now Somes' and Plucis' analytical approach forced her to take stock and reexamine her interpretations, making the hitherto unconscious conscious; both she and Somes rooted their performances in the character and situation, not just the technical problems of a role, and Somes' more considered approach was crucial to her development in the classics. It would take time for her to adjust, but they had always had a chemistry together and her complete confidence in him was a great boost to his performances.

With Helpmann acting *King John* at Stratford-upon-Avon, a landmark in Somes' development and the burgeoning partnership came on 13 April 1948 when he danced Prince Siegfried with Fonteyn in the full evening *Swan*

---

47 MS to ES, c19 March 1948

48 Interview with author

49 Interview with author

Lake for the first time.[50] 'Somes makes a most noble & manly Prince & his performance in Act III was as good as anything I have seen him do' wrote Bradley; '&, perhaps, as good as any performance I have seen in that act. He seems to have found a new confidence & may end by becoming, what English ballet very much needs, an outstanding classical dancer.'[51] For Clarke, he 'gave a performance of remarkable completeness in which mime, dancing and partnering were all part of a real characterisation',[52] a fusion that became a hallmark of his mature performances. Beaumont, however, felt the partnership had some way to go: 'I detect no spark ... no emotional contact born of a situation that each feels intensely by virtue of his and her powers of imagination.'[53] He was a lone voice amid the audience's cheers that went on and on.

Maybe Somes was fired up by Fonteyn, who, Winifred Edwards recorded in her diary 'appeared to transcend the physical and to have in truth become an enchanted being floating across the stage, entirely without trace of effort. The pas de deux was a poem of movement and lyric grace. Somes was quite transported and mimed with real feeling.'[54]

The performance was not without problems. With Lambert gone, the orchestral playing was slovenly, but, while the rest of the company 'suffered from the prevalent laxity',[55] Fonteyn and Somes serenely adjusted. Their innate musicality could always adapt to the most erratic musical tempi.

They never stopped working on their roles. Bradley, who saw dancers many times in the same parts, recorded their progress and the minute changes that helped build their characterisations: by 1950, 'Somes ... has never danced this role better. He had thrown off the hesitations and weakness ... & danced with great ease & an extraordinary elevation. He lived the part, too & was throughout a true *danseur noble*',[56] who could also be 'downright harrowing'.[57] He even merited the headline – *Michael Steps Out* in the *Evening*

---

50 De Valois had further revised the production with input from Harjis Plucis. Changes included restoring the Pas de Trois to Act I after its wartime posting to Act III and introducing Peasant Boys into Act I. Later, Elvin suggested other alterations, based on versions she had danced in Russia.

51 Lionel Bradley, ballet diaries, 13 April 1948, unpublished mss, Theatre and Performance Collections, Victoria and Albert Museum

52 Mary Clarke, *The Sadler's Wells Ballet*, A&C Black, London, 1955, p224

53 Cyril W. Beaumont, *'Swan Lake' at Covent Garden, Some Problems of Presentation*, Ballet, June 1948, pp49-55

54 Winifred Edwards, Theatre Diary, Book II 22 July 1947-21 April 1949, unpublished mss, Theatre & Performance Collections V&A

55 Anon, *Sadler's Wells Ballet: "Lac des cygnes"*, The Times, nd April 1948

56 Lionel Bradley, ballet diaries, 16 March 1950, unpublished mss, Theatre and Performance Collections, Victoria and Albert Museum

57 Mary Clarke, *Here's Richness!*, Ballet Today, June 1950, p4

News. Winifred Edwards, too, was impressed: '... I have never seen him dance so well. At the end of the coda the whole house burst into cheers & thunders of applause. The last Act was most moving and both of them sustained the emotional climax beautifully.'[58] Now Beaumont felt Fonteyn and Somes 'are true partners in the creation of a work of art, and not, as sometimes happens, an Odette and a Siegfried dancing with no more than formal reference to each other'.[59]

Fonteyn and Somes seamlessly blended characterisation, dance and mime into an adult romantic fantasy. The male-female contrast was central to their performance: his virile Siegfried anchored the ballet in reality, a foil to Odette/Odile's femininity and other-worldliness. Their sheer dance quality in Act III caused most excitement – Manchester described the *pas de deux* as 'almost insolent in its control and timing',[60] while for American critic John Martin, Somes' variation was 'the suddenly released joy of a young man who has just fallen in love'[61] – but their quiet ecstasy in Act II came to be equally valued.

In a key moment, as Siegfried calmed Odette's fear and she succumbed to love: her head drooped onto his shoulder and she nestled in his protecting arms as he gently rocked her to and fro, creating a moment of extraordinary intimacy. The characters' dependence on each other fuelled the pas de deux, not the performance of a showpiece, although Somes' one-handed control of her pirouettes was, in its way, as technically stunning as his Act III jetés.

Somes was not given to written analysis of his roles, but he did leave his impressions of Siegfried which, by implication, also explain some of his approaches to other characters. He saw the role in accordance with the traditions handed down through Sergeyev: 'Very much a "Fairy Tale" Prince who had to be made believable through a lot of conventional mime. This was achievable in those days, which were more courteous, courtly & restrained ...' There was no need for deep analysis: 'Siegfried must be essentially romantic in the most simple way, but virile in his movement & stature, and, of course, most importantly, a tender & excellent partner, willing to take second place to the ballerina without becoming nauseatingly self-effacing ... the whole story should not be subject to over-scrutiny, being mainly something on which to hang what *can* be (& alas!, – so often is *not*) a beautiful combination of dancing, scenery, costume and above all, unsurpassable music, which in the hands & bodies of great artists will overcome the need for analysis of its

---

58 Winifred Edwards, Theatre Diary. Book III 25 April 1949 -, mss Theatre Theatre and Performance Collections, V&A

59 C. W. Beaumont, unidentified publication

60 P. W. Manchester, Editorial comment, *Ballet Today*, July 1950, Vol 3 No 25 p3

61 John Martin, *First 'Swan Lake' of the Season Performed by Margot Fonteyn, The New York Times*, nd 1957

parts and psychological motivations, – so beloved of today ... Above all the performer must absorb the character into his own, and believe in what he is trying to portray on the stage, – how else can any audience be expected to come to terms with it,' adding 'I have yet to see "Swan Lake" in modern dress, – & hope not to!!'[62]

Beaumont's reservations about the early Fonteyn-Somes partnership were borne out when Markova and Dolin guested in June 1948: their rapport was now almost telepathic. Their masterly *Giselle* was frenziedly acclaimed. Dolin's Albrecht was still an example, 'an aristocrat to the finger-tips and one of the most exciting performances given by a male dancer in London for many a long day,' wrote Eric Johns. 'They have given the younger generation a taste of that magic, style and authority which belonged to the Russian Ballet in its palmiest days ...' [63]

They were less successful in *The Sleeping Beauty*. Winifred Edwards found Dolin's partnering magnificent, but his interpretation 'bombastic and rather vulgar'; she was relieved to find Somes 'very dignified and in character ...'[64] when he partnered Fonteyn as an ecstatically received Aurora on her return from Paris, where she had triumphantly created Agathe in Roland Petit's *Les Demoiselles de la nuit*. 'Suddenly', wrote Edwards, 'our lovely child has become a great classical ballerina – reposed, poised, sure of herself, and using her exquisite technique simply as her instrument – her means of expression – to serve her artistry.'[65] She had been cocooned in the company since childhood, dominated by her mother and her naturally passive nature overshadowed by Helpmann. Acclaim abroad and an affair with Petit were steps in her flowering; reassessing performances with Somes was another.

Massine's first creation for the company, to Haydn's *Clock Symphony*, brought another legendary name to work with the new generation – designer Christian Bérard. Bérard perfectly understood Massine and a stage designer's role: '"His choreography is wonderful"' he told de Valois, '"– but why everyone with the fidgets. I tell him stop fidgeting & let us look at what is beautiful ... I watch the choreography for the 3 men – & I alter the costume to *one* design because the choreography is so good & my 3 designs be more fidgets."'[66]

After his success as the Caricaturist, Somes might have expected another rewarding role from Massine, but Grant was the clockmaker who wins the

---

62 MS to Mr Labuschagre, 20 April 1989

63 E(ric) J(ohns), *Markova-Dolin Season, Theatre World*, August 1948

64 Winifred Edwards, Theatre Diary, Book II, 22 July 47 – 21 Ap 1949, unpublished mss Theatre and Performance Collections V&A

65 Winifred Edwards, Theatre Diary, Book II, 22 July 47 – 21 Ap 1949, unpublished mss Theatre and Performance Collections V&A

66 Ninette de Valois to Joy Newton, 22 June 1948, Royal Ballet School Archives

Princess and Somes was one of two Genies of the Lightning. In rehearsal Massine was like a burning flame, but the fire of inspiration was lacking: *Clock Symphony* was a plethora of fidgets. It was well received at its premiere on 25 June, but the dancers hated it.

Somes' progress that season even impressed critic Audrey Williamson, hitherto no great admirer: 'Your dancing (as Blue Bird and the Red Knight) seemed to me ... to show a steadiness, line, finish and attack I have, frankly, felt it lacked before,' she wrote to Somes. '... I think you danced magnificently ... and I have a very acute sense of words and never use that one lightly.'[67] Nevertheless, he felt he could no longer do Blue Bird justice and, at his own request, relinquished another role.

*****

At the Edinburgh Festival that autumn, Somes made his debut in *The Three-Cornered Hat* with Palma Nye as the Miller's Wife. The jury remains obstinately hung: Leo Kersley just wanted to forget it and his contemporary Michael Boulton remembered him doing it 'not very well', but Kathrine Sorley Walker, normally no Somes fan, remembered him as good and Farron thought he had the makings of a fine performance. He never performed the role often enough to master it, and perhaps it needed a charismatic extrovert rather than Somes' strong, but introspective, stage presence.

From Edinburgh the company went back to Paris and Germany. 'They were all delighted with us in Paris,' Somes wrote to his mother, '... I think I had a big personal success too, – & got applauded in the middle of my solo in 'Lac'.'[68] In Germany, he received a letter written 'in the name of a great number of young German artists' to thank him 'for his magnificant and intelligent dancing, especially for that clean atmosphere of beauty, decent passion and of eternity you have spread in "scenes de ballet". We'll never forget it ...'[69] It was signed 'Hans Werner Henze (composer).' Somes was impressed by how efficiently the Germans were coping, despite '... miles & miles of utter destruction. All they have been able to do is shove it all off the roads ... Where the people live is a mystery ... It can never be put right ... The miracle is ... [Cologne] Cathedral, – a huge great place standing alone amidst all this ruin.'[70]

Only a month separated Ashton's two ballets that autumn, the *Don Juan* designed by Edward Burra that he and Somes had planned in the War, and

---

67 Audrey Williamson to MS, 16 June 1948

68 MS to ES p 7 October 1948

69 Hans Werner Henze to MS, 16 October 1948

70 MS to ES undated

9 The Prince in *Cinderella* with Fonteyn as Cinderella.
Cover *Dance and Dancers* January 1953.

the three-act *Cinderella*, using Prokofiev's score. De Valois needed bigger productions to fill the Opera House stage and provide more roles for the enlarged company, besides responding to the audience's growing appetite for full-evening works.

The Prince to Fonteyn's Cinderella would be created on Somes, with

Helpmann and Ashton playing the Stepsisters. However, when Fonteyn strained a ligament on the opening night of *Don Juan*, Shearer, basking in the success of *The Red Shoes* following its release that summer, moved up to first cast Cinderella.

The ballet was rapturously received on 23 December 1948. Somes confessed to Cyril Beaumont that it had been a 'nerve-racking occasion', but Ashton felt it had worked and 'that is the only reward one asks'.[71]

Act I reflected Fonteyn's lyrical fluidity, but her injury meant that parts of Act II were created on Shearer, whose sharper, faster style Ashton used to suggest Cinderella's transformation. The heart of the ballet lay in the delicate poetry between Cinderella and her Prince, their meeting at the ball and their solos, 'bright and lovely – like youthful talk, the girl's more original, the boy's more amiable'.[72] Prokofiev's pas de deux music didn't lend itself to grand passion, but for Edwin Denby, Ashton created something very English, elegant, simple and deeply felt, 'civilised and innocent, a tone which is personal to (him)'.[73] In Somes' solo, Beaumont discerned Ashton's tribute to Cecchetti.

Partly for financial reasons, partly because he didn't care for the music, Ashton cut the Prince's round-the-world search for Cinderella, reducing Somes' role to 'a Covent Garden *porteur*', as one wit remarked, and fewer dancing opportunities for everyone.[74] The Act III pas de deux was something of an anti-climax and the ballet rather fizzled out. Alexander Grant as the Jester had the most spectacular dancing, but everyone was upstaged by Ashton and Helpmann as the Stepsisters, no caricatures, but believable characters with heart: 'Helpmann's interpretation has the heady quality of a fruity port;' wrote Beaumont 'Ashton's the dryness of a pale sherry. It is to be hoped, however, that the present balance will remain undisturbed by that tendency to exaggerate which so often follows repeated performances of a humour role.'[75] Well, he could hope. Ashton and Helpmann shared a dressing room with Somes and tended to stay in character throughout the intervals, with Somes trying to keep the peace. In fact, he was quite capable of holding his own: Michael Boulton recalled Somes being 'highly amusing. He and Bobby in the dressing rooms ... it was a riot. Bobby and he would send

---

71 MS to Cyril W. Beaumont, 26 December 1948, C. W. Beaumont Collection, Theatre and Performance Collections, V&A

72 Edwin Denby, *Ashton's "Cinderella", Ballet and Opera*, February 1949, p31

73 Edwin Denby, *Ashton's "Cinderella", Ballet and Opera*, February 1949, p31

74 The porters at the fruit and vegetable market, which surrounded the Opera House until it moved to Nine Elms in 1974, were famous for carrying numerous stacked baskets on their heads.

75 Cyril W. Beaumont, *Ashton's "Cinderella", Ballet and Opera*, February 1949, p6-26

each other up and then they'd score a few points (off each other).'[76]

Somes' Prince was well received; though Coton felt that 'half his potentialities were not exploited'.[77] This was no cardboard cypher: Percival recalled him as debonair and 'so good-humoured and courteous, even to the ill-mannered Ugly Sisters'.[78] Especially prized was Dolin's tribute: '... how fine your performance was. How greatly you have improved in every way ... Now (my affection) is truly coupled with genuine admiration. The whole ballet was pretty magnificent but you gave it a truly Princely air. Bravo.'[79]

Fonteyn first danced Cinderella in February 1949. Somes predicted her success: 'She is rightly acclaimed,' he recorded in his diary. 'Super perf. especially in pas de deux ... It's lovely to dance with her,' and dancing with her always raised his game. Although he would not become her sole partner yet, *Cinderella* cemented their partnership and they made Ashton's beautiful ballroom pas de deux, his first in the Petipa grand manner, their own, the youthful white heat of *Horoscope* replaced with a warmer romantic love. The 'air walking' came as climax to an enchaînement, with Cinderella skimming the ground, her legs swinging in opposition through a short arc, which, for Beaumont, had 'the effect of a gentle sigh'.[80]

Cinderella enshrined Somes as Ashton's ideal prince and often he never saw beyond that. He came to rely on Somes and Fonteyn, his perfect instruments, whose understanding of his choreography made his life easier and whose presence in his ballets could almost guarantee a favourable reception. An editorial eye became ever more essential.

Somes showed that his range extended beyond Princes when he tackled Satan in de Valois masterpiece *Job*, mostly at morning performances for schools, noting proudly in his diary that he managed the spectacular fall down the staircase 'without bruises'. He also had an input into the revival of *Apparitions*, worrying as much as if he were dancing the lead.

Cinderella was taken to the Florence Festival in May 1949 at the request of the organisers. It was a huge hit, the Italians, with their own pantomime traditions, particularly appreciating the Stepsisters. *Symphonic Variations*, too, was a great success. En route to Florence, the company managed a stopoff in Milan to see La Scala and its museum, where Somes was awed at seeing the Rossini and Verdi artefacts and scores. He managed to get into a gala performance of *Orfeo*, attended by Princess Margaret and was amazed when she recognised him and gave him a smile. The Princess was something of a

---

76 Interview with author

77 A. V. Coton, *Dance News*, February 1949

78 John Percival, *Danseur Noble, Dance and Dancers*, April 1959, pp18-19

79 Anton Dolin to MS, January 18 1948

80 Cyril W. Beaumont, *Ashton's "Cinderella", Ballet and Opera*, February 1949, p20

fan, often singling him out to dance with her at company social occasions, to his acute embarrassment.

From Florence, Somes, Shearer, Grant and Anne Heaton, with Jean Gilbert as pianist, went on to give performances and demonstrations in Ankara, where, at the invitation of the Turkish government, de Valois had established a school, run by Joy Newton. Although tired after a long season and tour, they rehearsed items not in the regular repertory, including the pas de deux from *The Fairy Queen* and Somes even learned Harlequin in *Carnaval* and John Cranko's jolly *Tritsch-Trastch*, as well as dancing excerpts from *Les Sylphides*, *The Rake's Progress*, *Cinderella*, *Mam'zelle Angot*, *Les Patineurs* and *Swan Lake*. Performing was made more difficult because of the altitude and oxygen had to be laid on to enable them to get through. Photographers followed them everywhere and there was the usual plethora of official receptions with the Turkish president, Consuls and Ambassadors.

At the end of May 1949, Somes, Fonteyn and Turner appeared in a television programme of excerpts from Ashton ballets, some of which would never be seen again – *The Lord of Burleigh* pas de trois, extracts from *The Fairy Queen*, *Rio Grande*, *The Wise Virgins*, *Le Baiser de la fée* and Somes danced his 'Leo' solo from *Horoscope* for the last time.

Somehow, he still found time for theatre and films – almost once a week in early 1949. His tastes were eclectic – plays from Olivier's *Richard III* to *Dark of the Moon* ('well produced by Peter Brook'); he greatly admired Eric Portman in Terence Rattigan's *The Browning Version* and enjoyed popular films like *Passport to Pimlico* and art films like the French *Carmen* and *A Yank in Rome*; however, he was cool about Ashton's *Le Rêve de Léonor*, created for Les Ballets de Paris. Most of his free time, however, was spent indulging his passion for music, broadcast and recorded, deliberately seeking out the unfamiliar.

8

New York

American impresario Sol Hurok had long lived on the richest artistic diet, presenting the world's greatest musicians, singers and dancers, and by the 1940s he was sated, especially with dance. Then he was captivated by the Sadler's Wells Ballet's *The Sleeping Beauty* and Fonteyn's Aurora, 'the radiant gaiety of all the fairy tale heroines of the world's literature compressed into one'.[1] His impresario's soul awoke to the immense box office potential and he told de Valois that her company was ready for America.

A New York season at the Metropolitan Opera House was fixed for autumn 1949, followed by a five-week tour. Hurok's staff were distinctly nervous about an unknown company at a time when ballet in American was in a lull: neither American Ballet Theatre nor Ballet Russe de Monte Carlo were doing good business; New York City Ballet was just establishing itself. Sadler's Wells Ballet meant nothing in America, so Hurok needed all his considerable astuteness in selling them. Believing that people accept what they are told, he presented the company as extraordinary: advertisements extolled choreographers, designers and composers (alive and dead) and tickets went on sale an unprecedented four months in advance. Just three weeks after booking opened the only way to get a ticket, advised *New York Times* dance critic John Martin, 'was to spot somebody who had one, entice him up a dark alley and shoot him'.[2] Even so, Hurok was always nervous about 'thicket' sales and used to hover around the box office watching the crowds, his eyes seeming 'to click like cash register signs behind his glasses'.[3]

However, Hurok had reservations about the standard of male dancing and suggested bringing in André Eglevsky, but de Valois, having supported her men this far, refused to renege on them now: the modern repertory would show them to advantage and the classics needed few virtuosi. Hurok vetoed her plan to open with a triple bill, arguing that the full *Sleeping Beauty* was unknown in New York and would not invite comparisons with the American repertory.

That summer the English press was filled with pictures of the girls acting

---

1 Sol Hurok, *Sol Hurok Presents*, Hermitage House, New York, 1953, p211

2 John Martin, *Britain's Royal Ballet: Our Favourite International Relation*, The Royal Ballet souvenir book, 1963

3 Margot Fonteyn, *Autobiography* p111

as ambassadors for British fashion; manufacturers enthusiastically provided dresses, coats and accessories for every occasion, which, as clothes rationing was still in force, saved them from having to appear at functions in dowdy, much-worn utility clothes. The men got a beret apiece.

With *Hamlet, Miracle in the Gorbals, Apparitions, Checkmate* and *Job* already prepared, an August season put the final polish on the rest of the New York repertory – *Symphonic Variations, Cinderella, The Sleeping Beauty, Swan Lake* and *A Wedding Bouquet*. Somes was on top form: 'Mr. Somes gave the performance of a decade as Siegfried,'[4] wrote Coton, and Buckle's comment '(his) romantic frenzies are really moving'[5] suggest he was loosening up. The production had been revised and Somes now danced the 'correct' solo, rather than one choreographed to the 1877 'Odile' variation which had been used hitherto. He spent hours rehearsing with Fonteyn, especially the Rose Adagio, playing all the princes; according to legend, she would take her attitude balance, he would leave the room, and come back to find her still rock solid. In New York he would partner Fonteyn and Shearer in *Cinderella*, Fonteyn in *Swan Lake* and appear in *Symphonic Variations*, as Guy in *A Wedding Bouquet*, a Messenger in *Job* and as Shearer's First Rose Adagio Prince.

Even amid the flurry of preparations, de Valois was thinking beyond America. Always planning new directions for her dancers, she decided that Somes should try his hand at choreography; that he had no choreographic ambition was irrelevant. Reluctantly, he agreed to produce something for the Sadler's Wells Theatre Ballet in spring 1950.

On 3 October, crowds of well-wishers waved the company off from Covent Garden, the men suppressing their envy as they chivalrously carried the women's suitcases, bulging with free finery. The company travelled in two planes, the girls flying charter, the men and de Valois on a scheduled flight: 'Not very good planning,' observed Alexander Grant. 'Things were rather dicey with airplanes in those days. If anything had happened, wouldn't have left much of a company would it?'[6] Flying was a new experience and many were apprehensive: 'Poor old Constant is sitting ahead of me,' Somes wrote to Ethel. 'He's had a lot to drink & is pretty far gone. I think he did it on purpose, because he's afraid of his ear ...'[7] New York was reached in hops via Prestwick, Gander in Iceland and Newfoundland, arriving at each in time for breakfast, which Somes, with the dancer's usual concentration on food, recorded with relish.

Hurok and a barrage of cameras met the company in New York. '...

---

4 A. V. Coton, *International Variety in Dancing, Sunday Times*, 21 August 1949

5 Richard Buckle, *Ballet Commentary, Ballet*, November 1949, p 5.

6 Interview with author

7 MS to ES undated

10 Arriving in America: de Valois, Fonteyn, Shearer, Ashton, Somes and conductor Robert Irving.

strangely (it) seems more foreign & difficult in so many ways than Continental cities' Somes wrote home. '... it's all at such a pitch ... shops *packed* with such things as we've *long* forgotten ... (Broadway) just defies description. The thousands of signs & lights, – Piccadilly is literally like a damp match ... I shall have had quite enough by the end of a month.'[8] He was considerably cheered by the Metropolitan Opera House ('very old & not as pretty as the Garden but bigger & very lovely all the same'), the excellent orchestra and the big, light rehearsal room, a far cry from those gloomy London basements. Like Covent Garden the Met's setting contrasted with its grandeur, being in the centre of the rag trade district, so instead of avoiding fruit and veg, the dancers dodged rails of dresses.

Sunday 9 October – 'The most terrific night in the history of S. Wells' as Somes recorded in his diary – dawned as a combination of fog and humidity that intensified into the hottest night of the summer. Outside the Met, touts

8   MS to ES 6 October 1949

offered tickets at $80 apiece; inside the stifling, unairconditioned theatre, American and British flags hung from the Diamond Horseshoe. Flowers and telegrams swamped backstage: '... great *batches* from all over the World. All our friends in London, – all the theatrical Co, & from over here too ... everyone to do with theatres & dancing wherever we've been ...'[9] The company had become a symbol of Britain; Buckle envisaged that Fonteyn at the beginning of the Rose Adagio 'supports the honour and glory of our nation and empire on the point of one beautiful foot'.[10]

Out front, Hurok's aide, Martin Feinstein described the audience as a mix of 'the dyed-in-the-leotard balletomanes who had advance word about the quality of the company ... the first-nighters who were there because it was the first big opening of the season and it gave them a chance to parade their new clothes ... and ... the curious attracted by the name Moira Shearer,'[11] then at the height of her *Red Shoes* fame. The dancers were more intimidated by de Valois' colleagues from her Diaghilev years – Balanchine, Vera Nemchinova, Anatole Oboukhov and Pierre Vladimirov, who had been Prince Desire in Diaghilev's 1921 *Sleeping Princess*; Alexandra Danilova and Frederic Franklin flew in from their own tour in Salt Lake City; Lincoln Kirstein, Vera Zorina, Maria Tallchief and Tanaquil LeClerq were there and Ballet Theatre friends Nora Kaye, Jerome Robbins and John Kriza. For John Martin, the audience 'vibrated with an indefinable exhilaration',[12] but backstage, Feinstein told Hurok, 'They're so frightened, I'm not sure they'll be able to stay up on point.'[13] De Valois' advice was 'Be yourselves.' Somes, who was not on that night, squeezed into the packed standing room. Tension mounted as the curtain was held eleven minutes before Lambert stepped onto the conductor's podium.

It was love from the first note of Tchaikovsky's score, conducted by Lambert at the height of his powers; it intensified as the curtain rose on Messel's opalescent set and with every variation. By the end of the Prologue the audience was shouting and cheering – 'and there was poor Margot,' recalled Alexander Grant, 'never even made her entrance yet – can you imagine the nerves? She was very calm – I've never seen her so "on" as she was that night. She had this wonderful thing of being able to rise to a challenge ... (then) she was at her very best.'[14]

She was so confident that, legend has it, she missed one Rose Adagio Prince

9   MS to ES 9 October 1949

10 Richard Buckle, Ballet Commentary, *Ballet*, November 1949, p 5.

11 Feinstein, Martin, *The Royal Ballet Twenty-five Years Ago*, Royal Ballet Souvenir, 1963

12 John Martin, *Britain's Royal Ballet; Our Favourite International Relation*, Royal Ballet souvenir booklet, 1963 (no pagination)

13 Feinstein, Martin, *The Royal Ballet Twenty-five Years Ago*, Royal Ballet Souvenir, 1963.

14 Interview with author

altogether. There were the inevitable near-disasters – the knitting-women's wool came on with the garlands, tangling around the dancers' legs, hats came adrift and there was a heart-stopping moment when it seemed that one of the transformation scenes would succumb to the traditional technical difficulties – but Lambert never faltered, while Helpmann's sure theatrical sense covered any tension.

Even Somes was impressed. 'Well, – I can only say I've never seen Margot & the whole Co. rise to the occasion & dance so magnificently. Margot was "out of this World" ... the applause increased & increased until I thought the show wld. never end. They cheered & clapped even when people came on & after each step & in the middle of the dances. At the end of the Rose Adagio & pas-de-deux, – there was an absolute furore ...'[15] Somes spent the intervals collecting comments – '"marvellous" – & "we've never seen ballet before" & "surely this is the finest Co. ever" & "how can our American Cos ever show their faces again" etc. etc.'[16]

At the end, 'Fonteyn's final ovation was like a hundred cannons firing a thousand charges.'[17] As curtain followed curtain, she stubbornly refused to take a solo call, maintaining that it was the company's night. Ashton changed out of his Carabosse costume so was not recognised when he took his calls and de Valois' disarming admission that 'we were terrified of you' was inaudible beyond the first few rows.

Backstage, 'Nemchinova, Obhukov (sic), Vladimirov, Zorina, Balanchine, etc. ... were all in tears, & Danilova said they cld. never thank Ninette enough for at last showing them over here what real dancing was. Naturally she was overwhelmed ...' As for Fonteyn 'she was simply treated like a goddess ... it was clear to *all* who was the *star*!!'[18] Somes was not anti-Shearer, but felt that *Red Shoes* hysteria precluded reasoned judgement.

It was past midnight when the company fought their way through cheering crowds and were given a police motor cycle escort, sirens screaming and ignoring all red lights ('just like on the films'), to Mayor O'Dwyer's reception at Gracie Mansion. 'When we got there the people all cheered & clapped ... & then they played the anthems & we sat down to champagne supper in the open night by the river on a lawn and *very* select Co. Newsreel flashing all the time ...'[19] At 2.30 am Fonteyn said 'Where do we go from here?' Somes, never a night owl, went to bed.

Euphoria continued as press reports flooded in: 'the notices almost without

15 MS to ES 24 October 1949

16 MS to ES 24 October 1949

17 George George, Ballet Commentary, *Ballet*, November 1949 pp5-6

18 MS to ES 24 October 1949

19 MS to ES 24 October 1949

exception have been terrific & unprecedented they say ... I was so pleased for Ninette ...'[20] It was not just Fonteyn but the *company* that impressed everyone – a unified ensemble with its own unique style built on a classical foundation, in contrast to what Martin saw as America's own experience – 'transient, opportunistic and derivative', still tacked together from the fringes of Diaghilev, 'the canapés and the meringues of today's – and unhappily, yesterday's – snack bar'.[21] Sadler's Wells Ballet's classics were not virtuoso fireworks interspersed with ensembles and semaphore, but convincing entities, in which the principals were part of the whole.

Kirstein struck a carping note, finding *The Sleeping Beauty* 'prim rather than precise ... underdone, underdanced, and overmimed'[22] and Lambert's conducting as crucial, whipping up 'applause, purely by sound; when nothing was really happening from a dancer he seduced everyone into somehow imagining that she was divine': Fonteyn he thought 'unawakened ... she seems to breathe through a haze behind which there may be a brilliant presence, but it is not yet brilliantly announced ...'[23] New York was another step in Fonteyn's awakening in which Somes would also play his part.

New York first saw Somes in *Symphonic Variations* on 12 October. Although it had its admirers, '... on the whole S.V. hasn't been *the* success here as I thought it wldn't ...' he wrote to Ethel, 'alto' it got most applause & individual people were high in their praise ... But I think they've seen too many abstract ballets.'[24] It was some consolation that Jean's playing was admired and audiences outside New York were more enthusiastic.

The furore over *The Sleeping Beauty* has gone down in history, obscuring the excitement created by the full-length *Swan Lake* on 20 October; American audiences were (over) familiar with Act II but the complete ballet was unknown. Now Kirstein had no reservations: '... superbly done ... Fonteyn was exquisite: ... Somes ... behaves with real nobility ... The corps was marvellous, and the ovation COLOSSAL. It was deserved, every bit of it.'[25] Their second performance went even better with a scintillating Somes winning an even greater ovation. The reception was so great that it made the evening news back home and Somes was gratified to hear that he had been named alongside Fonteyn ('Mum says at last someone mentions *me* a bit!!').

'I think it's gone the best here' he proudly recorded. 'Nemchinova was very

---

20 MS to ES 24 October 1949

21 John Martin, *Britain's Royal Ballet; Our Favourite International Relation*, The Royal Ballet souvenir book, 1963

22 Lincoln Kirstein to Richard Buckle, quoted *Ballet*, November 1951, p 12.

23 Lincoln Kirstein to Richard Buckle, quoted *Ballet*, December 1951, pp 19-20.

24 MS to ES p24 October 1949

25 Lincoln Kirstein to Richard Buckle, 21 October 1949, quoted *Ballet* December 1951, p20

sweet & thrilled with us both.'[26] Another admirer was Léon Bakst's nephew, André Velmar: 'my greatest admiration for your great dancing and the beauty that you reveal ... Never have I seen such divine gestures, movement and line, in dancing as you convey ... not since Diaghileff has any company shown such efficiency in the coordination of the arts and fine organisation.'[27]

Except for Ashton and Helpmann, *Cinderella* had a mixed reception, as did the modern ballets: *A Wedding Bouquet* was the surprise hit and *Façade* and *The Rake's Progress* were popular, *Symphonic Variations* hardly registered, *Hamlet* was admired but *Miracle in the Gorbals* and *Apparitions* were politely damned and, as de Valois had foreseen, *Job* was incomprehensible. The praise accorded the corps de ballet puzzled Somes who, while appreciating their work, always had the image of the Rockettes in his mind; the fact was that, in America, ensemble dancers were recruited on short contracts and so never had the chance to achieve Sadler's Wells Ballet's unity and integration into a production. Although the general level of male dancing was considered weak, '... everyone says *I've* been a great success, – but Bobby *hasn't* really, & lots of people say they wished I'd been doing S.P. & they wanted to see more of *me*.'[28]

In fact, Somes was on most nights, yet somehow he squeezed in an orgy of theatre-going, sightseeing, shopping, formal receptions, parties and lunch with friends. He was hugely impressed (and it took a lot to impress Somes that much) by Alfred Drake and Harold Lang in *Kiss Me Kate* ('it's the same standard as 'Oklahoma', – only *better* really, & so slickly done.'[29]) and Mary Martin got him into her hit show *South Pacific*; the Rockettes surpassed his memories – ('I've never seen such precision ... dancing like one, & keeping incredible formations'[30]). He saw *The Madwoman of Chaillot* with Martita Hunt, *Mr Roberts* with Henry Fonda (another company fan), a 'wonderful' ice show and Ethel Merman in cabaret. He adored Harlem. He spotted Garbo in a store. John Kriza drove him to see West Point and the New England fall colours. Nothing, however, matched the thrill of escorting Shearer to a Toscannini rehearsal, including Berlioz, after which the legendary conductor presented Shearer with his baton.

American School of Ballet and Ballet Arts invited the company to take classes at any time, enabling them to work with several Ballets Russes teachers, including Balanchine, Nemchinova, Doubrovska, Oboukhov, Leonide Lazovsky and Margaret Craske.

---

26 MS to ES p 2 November 1949
27 André Velmar to MS, mss letter 29 October 1949
28 MS to ES p 9 November 1949
29 MS to ES p 9 October 1949
30 MS to ES p 9 October 1949

Memorable parties included Lucia Chase's, mainly because food was kept back for the company (at most parties, by the time the starving dancers arrived, the guests had swept through the food like a plague of locusts, the most efficient scavengers being the wealthiest steel-elbowed socialites). Basil Rathbone's guests included the legendary Mary Pickford. '... more praise and adulations' at Kirstein's, where Somes was thrilled to meet Balanchine, '... & when I told him I had to do a ballet was *so* sweet & helpful & I felt very thrilled as *he* is really the greatest of the lot, & yet he wldn't talk to anyone else ...'[31] Somes' transparent devotion to dance and its traditions inspired trust from the most legendary names.

If New York's love affair with the company increased, for Somes some of the gloss wore off as first night nerves abated, the contrasts with deprivations in England became more pronounced and his craving for privacy resurfaced. 'Everyone has had colds owing to the humidity ... I can't say I really like it here ... it's *too* much of a rush & too artificial & almost wicked I feel. The food is fantastic but one even gets sick of that! ... it's alright to see, – but it's *so* noisy & *never rests*!! ... They seem to dislike the British so much tho' & I get furious with them ... we have social engagements by the dozen to cope with ... The people are very; kind & generous, but tend to be a bit overbearing & boring, especially when you are tired.'[32] There were also different working methods to get used to, especially the two hour time limit for daily stage rehearsal, which meant careful organisation of rehearsal time for the full evening ballets.

Punctuated by shouts of 'Come back', the last night reception was even greater than the first. Afterwards, in an unprecedented tribute, the Met stage staff threw a party: 'They said they'd never had such a lovely Co. & wanted to show their appreciation & this hadn't happened in 20 years.'[33] 'Ballet will never be the same in New York henceforth,' wrote Murray N. Friedman. 'Having seen what magnificent artistic direction has been able to accomplish with a company handicapped as Sadler's Wells has been, the public will insist on comparable standards for our own companies.'[34]

The ensuing five week tour passed in a blur of performances, receptions and early-morning train calls; the Sadler's Wells Ballet now had to get used to tightly scheduled one or two-night stands with only placing calls and a warm-up before each performance. First stop was Washington, which had no theatre, so performances were fitted into Constitution Hall: '... dreadful, – no scenery – tiny stage & curtains ½ way up which were drawn across by 2 men!

31 MS to ES p 24 October 1949

32 MS to ES p 24 October 1949

33 MS to ES p 9 November 1949

34 Murray N. Friedman, *The American View of Sadler's Wells, Ballet Today*, November-December 1949, pp15-16

& no d(ressing) room accommodation ... all the papers apologised & said it was disgraceful to expect our distinguished Co. to appear there ...'[35] The stage was lethal and Fonteyn fell on her first entrance before an audience that included President Truman and the entire diplomatic corps.[36] In two days they squeezed in three performances (Somes dancing *Symphonic Variations* and *Swan Lake Act III* both evenings) and two receptions which went on into the early hours.

In Richmond, they performed at the cavernous Mosque Theatre, seating 3,800. In Philadelphia they were met with flags and a large banner proclaiming 'Welcome Sadler's Wells Britain's gift to America', but they arrived only two hours before the first performance with no time for even a class to acclimatise themselves to another ice-like stage. Already there were concerns about how standards could be maintained under such conditions. On the brighter side, between performances and a huge reception before goggling crowds at Strawbridge & Clothier's department store, Somes fitted in a Philadelphia Orchestra concert conducted by Eugene Ormondy. At 1.30 am it was back aboard the train.

Chicago had planned a triumphal welcome, with a pipe band, dancers and police escort – but *en route* their Ballet Special coaches had been switched from the Chicago Express to a freight train, which meant they arrived six hours late; band and dancers had dispersed, but the coaches still warranted the police escort through the empty, rain-washed streets. The Civic Opera House was part of a 48-floor skyscraper and it was not possible to have lighting rehearsals during the day because all available electricity was required for the television theatre and offices. The opening, however, was a triumph, followed by the now inevitable reception and plethora of invitations, while Chevrolet Dodge provided a fleet of limousines for sightseeing. It was in Chicago that they became The Incomparable Ballet.

As Fonteyn and Somes danced *Swan Lake* in East Lansing, crowds stood outside to hear the music, the full score being as unfamiliar in America as the full ballet. Then, with winter setting in, there was the luxury of ten days in Toronto (free Coca-Cola and a visit to Niagara Falls): with a rare two nights off in a row, Somes went to see the Calgary Stampeders and the film *That Forsyte Woman*. Then on to Ottawa, 'off sleeper, do show, (reportedly 75,000 were turned away) attend big Government reception and straight back onto sleeper for Montreal',[37] where the tour ended on 11 December.

Everywhere the same story – capacity houses and thousands turned away. Even before they left New York, Hurok had been talking about a coast-to-

---

35 MS to ES p 9 November 1949

36 'You are not the first to have slipped up in Washington,' Sir Stafford Cripps assured them on their return to London.

37 MS to ES p 23 November 1949

coast tour, desperate not to disappoint those thousands and all the other cities clamouring for a visit.

American success would be the icing on the cake of the Sadler's Wells Ballet's international reputation. From cultural flag-waving in post-war Europe, the Sadler's Wells Ballet became dollar-earning superstar and British and European touring were cut back in favour of American riches. Whereas Europe enthusiastically responded to the native, dramatic ballets, rejecting the 19th century repertory as old-fashioned and irrelevant, in America, Sadler's Wells Ballet meant the classics. Reports of their success fuelled the demands for more performances in London, at the expense of the modern works which gave the men more opportunities. Had regular continental tours continued, European modern dance influences, already seen in de Valois' choreography, might have co-existed alongside American in British dance. What, too, about the provincial audiences so painstakingly built up during the War? Eventually, the Sadler's Wells Theatre Ballet had to fill the gap, then take on the classics and, like its successor the Touring Company, spend their lives living down complaints that they weren't from Covent Garden and where was Fonteyn?

The tour held another significance for Somes: he was now taking 'most of the classes'.[38]

---

38 Copy letters notebook 1949

9

Interlude and Across America

The American reception put new life into the company, although it was not immediately apparent as the exhausted dancers returned to Covent Garden in *Cinderella* on Boxing Day. Ashton made some changes to the Act II pas de deux, adjusting it to Fonteyn as opposed to Shearer on who it had originally been set, and created a new, though no more effective, adagio in Act III; the Sisters, too, had some new business, but they always did. Somes was 'a superb Prince in appearance and dancing' recorded Lionel Bradley. The audience was lacklustre, 'applauding mildly in musquash', as Buckle observed, although they did wake up at the end: Fonteyn made her first speech from the stage but Ashton took five minutes to persuade de Valois to say something: famously she snapped 'Ladies and Gentlemen it takes more than one to make a ballet company', and rang down the curtain.

America had given Somes' confidence a boost: he was back on form and beyond, partnering more surely, dancing well and his youthful, sulky looks had matured into 1950s glamour. He had learned to relax and gained in fluidity. He was now ranked Senior Principal, alongside Helpmann and Turner. Helpmann was relinquishing some roles and cutting down on performances, but he was still the leading dancer and Fonteyn's partner, and Somes could only wait.

His immediate concern after America was *Summer Interlude*, his choreographic debut for Sadler's Wells Theatre Ballet. Characteristically, he refused to take a fee in recognition of all he owed the Sadler's Wells organisation. Typically, he was simultaneously learning the lead in Balanchine's *Ballet Imperial*, scheduled for its first performance the week after *Summer Interlude*'s premiere.

On a Fedorovitch-designed sunlit beach, the Village Boy and Village Girl (lyrical) encounter a bathing party of city visitors (sophisticated); a 'city' girl flirts with the boy, but when the bathers lend the peasant girl a swimsuit, she attracts one of the men and goes off with him, leaving the dejected boy alone; his hopes rise on hearing someone returning, but it is only the man collecting the girl's shawl as the curtain falls. The music was Ancient Airs and Dances, Ottorino Respighi's modern arrangement of Renaissance lute pieces.

Somes selected his dancers shrewdly: having partnered Elaine Fifield in *Swan Lake Act II*, he knew that being pigeonholed as a classical dancer made her tense, and so confounded expectations by casting her as the heartless city girl; the Village Girl was the serene Patricia Miller, who subtly conveyed how the sophisticated swimsuit changed her character; Pirmin Trecu's remarkable *gamin* stage presence was perfect for the Village Boy, as was David Blair's brash self-confidence for the leading city bather. Hardly surprisingly, Somes used the men to advantage, especially in the solos.

There were fifteen curtain calls after the premiere on 28 March. 'I hope you have had just as much pleasure teaching us as we have had learning it' Miller wrote to Somes,[1] and their pleasure spilled over the footlights: 'Everyone danced as if they love it and it was evident how much they loved their choreographer,' wrote Beryl de Zoete, adding 'There was a beautiful variety in its simplicity.'[2]

Summer Interlude was astonishingly self-assured. *Dancing Times* noted how much the ballet reflected Somes' own qualities, 'that same understanding of flowing movement, well placed lines and excellent elevation' although the ominous word 'acrobatic' was also invoked.[3] Buckle was impressed: 'The patterns are clear, the movements are graceful and not evidently derivative, and the dancers glide, spin, and fly through the summer air with untroubled animal elegance.'[4] Although some lifts were considered too elaborate for the music, Bradley recorded that none was 'ugly & none indecent' and one was 'possibly' original.[5] *The Daily Worker's* LM noted how everything was expressed in dance, 'an all too rare achievement, which sets Mr. Somes apart as a choreographer of major promise'.[6] 'Charming' was the most used adjective, followed by 'light,' 'gay' and 'romantic'. The general feeling was that it would have been a good ballet from an experienced choreographer, let alone a beginner.

Particularly notable was the marriage of movement and music. '... you have used (the music) so well' wrote Manchester, 'that the discrepancy in period almost turns itself into a virtue and makes a "conceit" of it.'[7] Especially gratifying was composer Howard Ferguson's reaction: 'It is so astonishingly rare to find choreography that really fits & belongs to music, & that gives the impression of growing out of it. Yours does all of this & is utterly delightful into the bargain. More, please!'[8] John Lanchbery, who conducted later

1   Patricia Miller to MS nd

2   Beryl de Zoete to MS, nd

3   Anon, *Dancing Times*, May 1950, p468-469

4   Richard Buckle, *Ballet, Observer*, 2 April 1950

5   Lionel Bradley, ballet diaries, 28 March 1950, unpublished mss, Theatre and Performance Collections , Victoria and Albert Museum

6   L. M. *Day on sands in ballet, Daily Worker*, 29 March 1950

7   P. W. Manchester to MS nd

8   Howard Ferguson to MS nd

11 *Summer Interlude*: Pirmin Trecu as A Country Boy, Patricia Miller as A Country Girl, David Blair as a Bather. Photograph by Roger Wood.

revivals, remarked on Somes' impressive musicianship in rehearsals and remembered how delightfully the music counterpointed the modern theme.

'What does it feel like to be exposed as a rank imposter gaining sympathy under false pretenses while all the time you had that darling ballet up your sleeve?' demanded Manchester. '... you must surely know it is absolutely delightful – clean and fresh, beautifully unmessy and most ingeniously put together. Whatever agonies you went through, and I do know they were real, I hope you felt last night that it *was* worth while. I sat in that audience and could feel them simply breathing it in and loving every moment ... I'm sure you are still in the "never again" stage, though you must also unless you are sub-human, be feeling elation.'[9] Fedorovitch too wanted more: 'I enjoyed

9   P. W. Manchester to MS nd

working with you immensely as from the start I had great faith in you – but I must admit that you surpassed my expectations. You must know by now that you have done an excellent work – also ... that this (is) only a beginning. I have been already thinking of a "subject" for you!'[10] Above all, Balanchine had been in the audience, applauding enthusiastically and was overheard to say 'Jolly good' to Kirstein.

Others agreed. *Summer Interlude* hadn't even reached the stage before Somes was offered other projects, including Purcell's *Dido and Aeneas*, Sadler's Wells Opera's showcase for the Festival of Britain, and *Ile des Sirènes* for Fonteyn's concert group. Somes, however, was not won over by the success: after the first night, 'drinking champagne out of a tumbler backstage, (he) said cautiously: "I still like dancing best,"'[11] and disappointed the Wells and Fonteyn. He did, however, recommend Alfred Rodrigues, thus launching his colleague's career as a choreographer in ballet, revue and musicals: Rodrigues never knew of Somes' suggestion until after his death.

Summer Interlude was a useful programme builder, performed a respectable 71 times in four years, but it did not bear repeated viewings. Peter Wright declared it charming, but 'it didn't have any real choreographic personal signature, and I think he realised it'.[12] 'He wasn't really a talented choreographer,' de Valois admitted, 'and he was much more aware of what other people should be doing than what he was doing himself.'[13] Somes was rather a superb editor, a sounding board for Ashton.

How Somes combined creating his first ballet with working on *Ballet Imperial* remains a mystery. Balanchine had only three weeks to extensively revise and set the ballet, originally created for American Ballet Caravan in 1941. He found the dancers' silence and discipline intimidating, though it was probably nothing more than intense concentration as they struggled with an unfamiliar style and insufficient time.

Premiered on 5 April, *Ballet Imperial* was a paean to the aristocratic ideals embodied in 19th century classical ballet. The male lead was the ideal danseur noble, the man-prince in service of the ballerina-princess; Balanchine exploited Somes' innate regal authority, sure sense of style in the courtly walks and partnering skills (not least of which was partnering three different ballerinas in the lead – Fonteyn, Shearer and Elvin). Originally in the second movement, the ballerina and her partner performed a classical pas de deux for two lovers, incorporating mime passages hinting at misunderstandings; Balanchine now eliminated the mime and embodied the suggestion of heartbreak into the formality of the choreography.

---

10 Sophie Fedorovitch to MS nd

11 Mary Steel, *Mchael takes 15 curtains*, *Daily Express*, 29 June 1950

12 Interview with author

13 Interview with author

Balanchine's demands were very different from Ashton's and came as something of a shock to the dancers. Somes' memory was of Balanchine's 'long leaps, high arabesques and little or no demi-plié, also most things done at double speed!' and he was 'thrilled' by the arrangement of the Tchaikovsky piano concerto cadenzas.[14]

Buckle described the sequence for Somes and ten girls, '... like two wings ... attached to his shoulders ... who seem less like his fellow human beings than like symptoms of some inner trouble that assails him in waves'.[15] Left alone, he slowly walked off, in Kirstein's words, '... simply, yet with authority, across a stage emptied of all other movement ... holding his scene, a mimic duchy, by the mastery of his own moral conception of the lively symbol of the Prince'.[16] No one else made that exit so simply, certainly and naturally, the impassive, noble exterior masking the inner conflicting emotions, and it always elicited a round of applause. Like Nijinsky's leap in *Le Spectre de la rose* and Fonteyn poised in the Rose Adagio, the walk became a key image in the audience's perception of Somes, until he came to dread the words 'I always remember you in ...'[17]

Three days later, on 8 April, Vaslav Nijinsky died in London. At his funeral on 14 April, Somes was a pallbearer alongside Ashton, Cyril Beaumont, Lifar, Dolin and Richard Buckle. At the end of the month, he and Fonteyn made their first guest appearance together, dancing one performance of *Aurora's Wedding* with the Royal Danish Ballet in Copenhagen and receiving as much press coverage as all the English papers devoted to ballet in a year. This established their practice as guests, fitting into an existing production, often with very little rehearsal; they never just turned up and did a star turn at the expense of the whole.

On 15 May 1950, a gala at Sadler's Wells marked the company's twenty-first anniversary. *A Wedding Bouquet* united thirteen members of the original cast, including de Valois as Webster and Somes as Guy. There were some memory lapses, although surprisingly not from Lambert, who delivered a narration that 'was a wonder in itself, not least that he got through it at all after drinking a bottle of champagne during its progress & being heaven-knows how-well-primed beforehand'.[18]

---

14 Buckle, Richard, *George Balanchine: Ballet Master*, Hamish Hamilton, London, 1988, p182

15 Richard Buckle, *George Balanchine: Ballet Master*, Hamish Hamilton, London, 1988, p130

16 Lincoln Kirstein, *Ballet*, May 1950, p26

17 When *Ballet Imperial* was revived in 1973 Balanchine tried to make it 'plotless', dressing it in leotards and wisps of chiffon and renaming it *Piano Concerto No 2*. The ballet defiantly refused to co-operate.

18 Lionel Bradley, ballet diaries, 15 May 1950, unpublished mss, Theatre and Performance Collections, Victoria and Albert Museum

Harold Turner retired at the end of the season. Some eight years older than Somes, Turner's virtuoso technique was at the mercy of the years and after the war there were fewer ballets to which he was suited. Somes felt that later generations often forgot how brilliant Turner was and his great contribution to the company, not just as a dancer but in his subsequent career as an influential and much loved teacher in the School. At 41 Helpmann, too, must have known that he couldn't go on much longer. De Valois, whose fondness for him never clouded her judgement, knew it was hard for him to face giving up, but running parallel dancing and acting careers was unsettling for everyone; she also felt he had become an adverse influence on Fonteyn, and his relationship with Ashton had so deteriorated that they hardly spoke.

* * * * *

By now, invitations were pouring in for the Sadler's Wells Ballet to dance abroad, including Spain, Egypt, Turkey and Australia, but America had prior claim. Hurok started publicising the 1950-51 coast-to-coast tour six months in advance, before either dancers or repertory were finalised, so posters just read 'The Fabulous Sadler's Wells Ballet the greatest theatrical attraction of the century.' So immediate was the demand that Hurok nearly got reported to the Commissioner of Licenses by those who failed to get tickets and refused to believe that performances were sold out.

Hurok had considerable say in the repertory. *Swan Lake, Sleeping Beauty* and *Giselle* dominated, accounting for nineteen of twenty-four performances in New York; after the low-key reception for *Symphonic Variations*, he was reluctant to include *Scènes de ballet*, so triple bills were made up from works already seen in New York – *A Wedding Bouquet, Façade* and *Checkmate* – plus *Les Patineurs, Dante Sonata, The Rake's Progress* and de Valois' latest ballet *Don Quixote*. Somes was critical, not because of his roles – although five months of the classics, *A Wedding Bouquet, Dante Sonata* and the occasional *Façade* was hardly stimulating – but because he thought they didn't make strong programmes. However, New York would be significant for him: with Helpmann still filming *The Tales of Hoffmann*, he would partner Fonteyn in *Swan Lake* on the opening night.

British manufacturers were anxious to repeat the successful 1949 export drive and this time the men also benefitted, with raincoats, suits, shoes, bedroom slippers, six white shirts, socks (tartan were favourite), ties, trilby hats, handkerchiefs, then-novel folding umbrellas and two pairs of gloves, including white chamois for evenings. Somes was featured in *The Evening News*, trying on a stylish overcoat and contributed touring tips: 'like many of the men ... he washes and mends his own socks. Before going to bed he spreads his wet handkerchiefs smoothly over the dressing-table mirror.

12 Pamela May and Somes in a publicity shot promoting British fashions for the 1951-2 American coast-to-coast tour.

"In the morning they are as good as if they have been ironed,"'[19] He and May were photographed walking down Regent Street in their Aquascutum raincoats '... these two fabulous personages who bring with Royal Command and Fairy Blessing the best that Britain has to offer.'[20]

Somes bid farewell to his parents and his proud new acquisitions, his

19 Gwen Robyns, *On Their Toes With The Fashion*, *Evening News*, 7 July 1950
20 Publicity photograph caption

spaniel Tigger and first car (his *Who's Who* entry now listed hobbies as 'Music and motoring'). Sister Laura Theresa from the nearby Convent, where Lilian Baylis used to pray, promised to keep an eye on Ethel and sent him a text, 'Serve God and be cheerful!', which 'so voices Lilian Baylis's ideal for the stage & what she desired for Sadler's Wells that I feel it will appeal to you'.

New York greeted them with another heat wave. The atmosphere before *Swan Lake* on 10 September was intense and Fonteyn was uncharacteristically nervous, afraid that they couldn't live up to audiences' idealised memories. The curtain went up in silence; Somes' entrance got the first good hand and Fonteyn's triggered such an ovation that she started to dance through the applause; the dancers watching from the wings were transfixed, some in tears. By Act III the heat was unbearable and Fonteyn was tiring, yet she and Somes upped their performance level, whipping the audience into near hysteria until 'The *coda* became such a frenzy of dance and applause ... it was like living in a storm.' wrote dancer Ray Powell. '... It made me go cold down my spine.'[21]

Arthur Todd, veteran of 15 years of New York openings, confessed that he had never been so moved, hailing Somes as 'a virile and commanding Prince ... if slightly less than sensational, in the *pas de deux* ...'[22] Fonteyn had no reservations: 'Michael was really wonderful and has had a great success,' she wrote to his parents. 'He looks terribly well and happy. I hope he will stay like that and not be too exhausted by the very hard work he is doing.'[23]

His success continued with *The Sleeping Beauty* – 'a handsome and believable Prince and bears himself accordingly'[24] – but *Giselle*, which New York knew from Markova and Dolin's legendary performances, was not well received; after five *Beautys* in three days, the first night was flat. Somes was not surprised: the production had hardly changed since the 1930s, and, he complained, lacked drama and atmosphere. However, the *New Yorker*'s anonymous critic thought well of his Albrecht '... a lightheaded, gullible fellow, to be sure, but no namby-pamby either'.[25]

The modern British ballets had a rough ride. While Ashton's *Wedding Bouquet* and *Façade* repeated their 1949 success and *Les Patineurs* captivated audiences, *Dante Sonata* was not liked, nor de Valois' *Don Quixote*.

Somes shared Fonteyn's triumphs only until Helpmann arrived, though he remained an off-stage bulwark against her growing number of admirers. One took them to Harry Winston's to see the Hope diamond and the Star

21 Ray Powell, *Dance and Dancers Abroad USA, Dance and Dancers*, November 1950 p23

22 Arthur Todd, *Again, A Triumph, Ballet Today*, November 1950 p5

23 MF to ES 16 September 1950

24 Arthur Todd, *Again, A Triumph, Ballet Today*, November 1950, p5

25 Anon, *Ballets From Britain, New Yorker*, Oct 1950

of the East; when he started calculating whether selling a city block would cover the cost, Fonteyn and Somes slipped nervously away.

At the beginning of October the company embarked on the coast-to-coast tour. Somes' frequent letters home charted their zig-zag progress – four months of mostly one to three night stands performing a repertory of nine ballets with *The Sleeping Beauty* performed in the few cities with theatres large enough to take such a big production and cast. In cities without a theatre (and there were many) performances had to be given in vast sports centres or municipal auditoria, where the company regularly played to audiences of 6,000: these rectangular spaces were divided into back to back arenas, the second space often used the same night for another entertainment, or even wrestling. Stages were wide and flat with horrendous surfaces, including concrete, and often slippery, having been highly polished for the Roller Skating Vanities, who seemed to precede the company throughout the Mid-West. Technically most were badly equipped on and backstage; dressing rooms were inadequate to non-existent and the dancers often dressed in passages or behind screens, making up in available light and just hoping they would look right on stage. Conditions were a nightmare for the stage staff, coping with inadequate equipment and constantly adapting the scenery, built for the generous spaces of Covent Garden, for different venues, which caused lasting damage to the backcloths. The Wardrobe had to cope in cramped conditions (often shared with the orchestra and sometimes the dancers), with no washing machines or steamers (although steam from a boiling kettle could be pressed into service) and costumes often had to be packed straight after a performance, when they were soaked in sweat. The audience did not fare much better; seats were arranged on the flat floor with banked galleries to back and sides, the side seating at 90 degrees to the stage.

Travel was by rail on The Ballet Special – six double-berthed sleeping cars, six baggage and scenery cars and two dining cars, and on long hauls a lounge coach with bar. It sounds glamorous, but each hotel stop-over involved unloading everything as different coaches were used for the next leg and more than once personal luggage got left behind. Specials were classed as freight and could be diverted, held up for scheduled services and generally shunted around. Apparently, this was not allowed for in the already tight schedule and even a short delay left barely enough time for setting and lighting the ballets, let alone warming up or placing calls. Sometimes there was a lunchtime and/or evening reception, which didn't always provide enough food, leaving the dancers looking for somewhere to eat in the early hours. Stage calls or travelling ate into the few free days.

With so many different temperaments squeezed together in such a confined space, organising the sleeping cars called for delicate diplomacy, but the management subtly grouped friends and like minds together, so the partying night owls did not disturb those who valued peace and quiet. Even so, travelling was not without dramas: romances, serious and fickle, 'erupted and evolved in complicated patterns' Fonteyn recalled. 'Dramatic eternal triangles inevitably formed, bringing bliss to one compartment and tears to the next.'[26] Some became addicted to the new card game Canasta, which had only been introduced into the United States two years before, although the orchestra stuck to incessant high-staked card games. Somes was constantly on call as, not to be deprived of his 'cuppa', he travelled his own spirit stove, dispensing innumerable brews to the tea-starved dancers, while Richard Ellis came into his own at parties, with his knowledge of how to mix any drink ever invented.

It was not a particularly arduous tour for Somes and he was buoyed up by his success, but tight scheduling, long journeys and unsatisfactory venues soon took their toll: everyone was quickly exhausted and casualties mounted: 'we are still alive if only just kicking!! ... we are all so tired we only want to go home to bed, as we don't really rest on the train'.[27] They saw little of each city outside the theatre, and, with much of the travelling at night, hardly more of the country, so Somes' parents gleaned more about America from the postcards he sent home from each stop. With union rules limiting rehearsals to two hours a day (anything over incurred large overtime payments), there was time for sightseeing, but, except on the few longer stop-overs, the dancers were usually too exhausted to take advantage of it. On the longer stays local organisations and private individuals were generous with their hospitality, organising parties and often taking small groups for drives into the local countryside.

First stop was Philadelphia, where Charlie Chaplin arranged a special showing of his film *City Lights*,[28] then Pittsburgh's Syria Mosque, with its wide proscenium, shallow stage and large square auditorium. In Atlanta, at the Municipal Auditorium, Somes saw for the first time the separate entrances marked Black and White: the space was so huge that the scenery trucks drove directly into the auditorium to unload; even the classics were diminished and *The Rake's Progress* was completely lost. Everyone loved New Orleans, where between two performances the company tried to pack in as much sightseeing, visiting the famous clubs and eating as much as possible. Houston became a favourite, boasting of one of the most enthusiastic audiences in the South, and luxurious accommodation at the Shamrock Hotel where, with temperatures in the eighties, the dancers practically lived

---

26 Margot Fonteyn, *Autobiography*, Hamish Hamilton, London, 1989, p116

27 MS to ES p 16 October 1950

28 As they danced *Giselle* designed by James Bailey, conducted by Robert Irving, at the theatre next door Hurok was presenting Katharine Hepburn in *As You Like It*, designed by James Bailey with music by Robert Irving. .

in the swimming pool, resulting in some rather pink swans.

Touring bound the company together, if only because being incarcerated allowed everyone to have a good moan. Somes was not alone in feeling they were being exploited by Hurok for his own benefit and by Covent Garden to underpin the opera, and was incensed to learn that profits for just two weeks was $80,000 when '... the dancers, who after all, – make the show, – get the thinnest time of all. (Webster) will come over here, – for no apparent reason, – & charge up a fabulous expense acc. ... usual successful houses & rave critics everywhere, – so there's nothing to tell abt. the performances, except we're all pretty sick of the present rep ...'[29] They were beginning to feel very cut off.

After a journey from Houston to the West Coast lasting two days and two nights, they were reunited with Hurok and de Valois in Los Angeles. Hurok had initiated a vast publicity campaign and the company's reputation had already preceded them from New York, so everyone was on their mettle. As Somes was not appearing on the opening night on 19 October, he mingled with the crowds as all Hollywood converged on the 6,800 seater Shrine Auditorium to see Fonteyn and Helpmann in *The Sleeping Beauty*. Today, his description reads like any Oscar night, but then Hollywood had rarely seen such an occasion: '... great cars were arriving directed by swarms of police, with loudspeakers & watched by literally hundreds of people all cordoned off. In the road were two *huge* portable searchlights sweeping the sky, with the Union Jack & Stars & Stripes ... they say there has never been such a gathering, – even here ... Claudette Colbert, Gene Tierney, Greer Garson, C.(lark) Gable, Danny Kaye, Charlie Chaplin, Ronald Colman, Laurence Olivier, Vivien Leigh, Joseph Cotton, Esther Williams, Van Johnson, Loretta Young, Sojna Heine, Ava Gardner, (Ezio) Pinza, ... I sat in a corner seat next to Ida Lupino & C. Gable & his wife!! ... most of them looked pretty faded & artificial ...'[30] De Valois crisply put straight anyone overawed at the thought of an audience of Hollywood legends: 'What nonsense,' she snapped, 'they're only a lot of old pros who've made it.' Among the 'old pros' was one of Diaghilev's first stars – the great Adolph Bolm. The reception was predictable: '... they say it's the greatest company in the World & have never seen its like here before – which is saying a lot for Hollywood!!'[31] Even de Valois admitted that they had been a 'wild' success. At subsequent performances Hurok ordered curtain calls be curtailed before performances ran into overtime.

The Hollywood community had planned a post-show party for selected dancers, but de Valois made herself extremely unpopular after decreeing that official parties should include the whole company, not just principals. Hurok

---

29 MS to ES p 5 December 1950

30 MS to ES 10 October 1950. Somes didn't mention Cary Grant (who arrived thirty five minutes late), Betty Hutton, Cyd Charisse, Tony Martin

31 MS to ES October 10 1950

therefore arranged a post-show party at the Ambassador's Hotel, where the company was staying, attended by all the dancers and selected movie stars. Charlie Chaplin acted as master of ceremonies and ballroom dancing contest judge – winners Herbert Hughes (the company's non-dancing General Manager) and Pauline Wadsworth, while Kenneth MacMillan triumphed in the Charleston with Greta Hamby. Chaplin responded by hosting an exclusive dinner, including Somes, at which Charlie and Ashton ended up performing together. Fred Astaire came to the party given by Robert Zeller, the company's American conductor. Gene Kelly and Eugene Loring, although filming all day, went to every performance.

Despite the company's success and Hollywood encounters, which included meeting Doris Day on a tour of Warner Bros studios, Somes didn't warm to Los Angeles and would have agreed with de Valois's description as '... Satan's idea of a nice night club. For vulgarity, snobbery, unreality &, underneath it all sheer human unhappiness – it should beat any spot on earth.'[32] The twelve-day season didn't allow much rest or sightseeing, being used to catch up with classes and rehearsals, when all Somes longed to do was to go to the beach and 'dip my toes in the Pacific'.[33]

After so many unsatisfactory auditoria, it was bliss to arrive in San Francisco and the luxury of the War Memorial Opera House with its carpeted principal dressing rooms and en-suite bathrooms. Audiences, however, were less satisfactory; whereas the Los Angeles 'pros' had understood and appreciated the professionalism of the company, in San Francisco audiences were more 'society', a harder audience to reach; their less hysterically appreciative response was easier to take than their bad behaviour, coming in late through every act. However, it became Somes' favourite American city and every visit he would go to the top of the Mark Hopkins Hotel, to drink in the spectacular sunsets across the bay.

San Francisco marked the end of a chapter. Helpmann suddenly resigned after what de Valois described as 'monkeying with his contract' and 'a dirty trick or two ... I have refused to quarrel with him', she wrote to Newton, 'because I am fond of the old rogue & he is now going down the ladder & I can't kick him – He'll bob up again ...'[34] He gave his last performance in the *Aurora pas de deux* with Fonteyn on 11 November 1950. It was so sudden that the first Leslie Edwards knew was when he was invited to a small dinner at which he, Helpmann, de Valois, Ashton, Fonteyn, Somes and May buried any differences, laughed a lot, and said goodbye. Somes was sorry to see him go and could hardly imagine the company without him. There was no sense

32 NdeV to Joy Newton nd
33 MS to ES October 10 1950
34 NdeV to Joy Newton, nd

of euphoria in his letters at having at last achieved his goal – his elevation to leading male dancer and Fonteyn's partner seems to have been assumed, and apparently no one suggested an increased salary nor that he receive Helpmann's expense allowance.

Having rehearsed the company into the ground, de Valois returned to London to revive *The Prospect Before Us* for the Theatre Ballet, leaving Ashton in charge. Ahead lay five weeks of between one and three-night stands of either a triple bill or *Swan Lake*. '... we just spend our time packing up & getting into new places & hotels, & settling into theatres, – then off again, & it's very wearisome'.[35]

After two nights in sunny Sacramento they embarked for Denver and, within an hour of leaving, autumn changed to the snows of winter. The journey took two days and nights, travelling on 'rest' days. The huge Denver Auditorium was a new low, with only a single washbasin and a stage marked out for basketball. The altitude caused nose bleeds 'but we managed somehow'.[36] The post-first night reception (insufficient food and square dancing demonstration) was so depressing that the company organised its own fancy-dress party to celebrate the tour's half-way point. '... the best party we've had ... the kids really got themselves up in some wonderful gets-ups they had made out of bits of paper & odd things. Freddy put on a tutu & Swan Lake headdress & did all the Swan Queen's part, & everyone did imitations of Ninette & everyone in the Co! It was great fun, & we all had a good laugh, which cheered us up.'[37] Among the 'wonderful get-ups' were Nadia Nerina as a tea bag (Orange Pekoe), Christine du Boulay as a Schiaparelli perfume bottle, Kenneth MacMillan as a much-labelled travelling bag while Pauline Clayden, mummified in bandages, was Prospect Before Us. Somes played safe in jeans and check shirt as a cowboy.

The next stretch was dire, with no stop-overs and sometimes two performances on a one-night stand. Memphis wasn't even one-night; they got off the train, gave a performance and got back on the train nine hours later. Freight engines were now pulling the train, which meant a less smooth ride, and even heavy sleepers began experiencing disturbed nights. 'Denver – matinee – onto train – Lincoln – 1 show in University Theatre, changing in the gym – on to Des Moines that night, same routine – onto train to Omaha (substitution for Kansas City because of some 'mess-up') – from Omaha to Kansas City at 7 in morning – turned out of sleepers in freezing cold and change onto ordinary train for Tulsa arriving 4.30 23rd – Completely worn out by 4 successive nights on the train & nowhere to rest in the day ... packing

---

35 MS to ES p 15 November 1950
36 MS to ES p 20 November 1950
37 MS to ES p 20 November 1950

& unpacking & nowhere to bath etc, – it was pretty grim!'[38] Especially grim was Lincoln where it soon became clear why no ballet company had ever played there before: the stage was slippery, there were no dressing rooms, mirrors or proper lights for making up and no weights to brace the scenery, so stage hands had to support the more dangerous wing flats. Total power to light the stage was only a few hundred amps, enough for only ten of the 750 watt spots, while two lighting batons in the auditorium consisted of 14 lamps of 250 watts, nowhere near capacity to light a large stage, even allowing for the additional lighting board carried by the company (lighting the Covent Garden stage used, on average, 2,000,000 watts).

'... [I]t's all just one blur, & I couldn't distinguish Lincoln from Des Moines or Omaha ... I'm afraid the performances got pretty ragged, – it is imposs. to keep any standard, – the conditions are too severe, & some of the stages pretty rough, or like ice!'[39] Although people stopped them in the street, in stores, on buses to say how wonderful the performances were, Somes felt the compliments were undeserved as they weren't being seen at their best. His regard for American companies, who endured such conditions all the time, increased daily.

Thanksgiving coincided with a free day in Tulsa, when everywhere was shut, but at least there was the chance to have a bath – the first since Denver – and a night in a proper bed. Temperatures fluctuated wildly – snow in Denver, blizzard in Kansas, 80° in Dallas. Unable to carry enough clothes to cope with such extremes, many went down with colds and flu, but Somes remained stubbornly healthy and went on for the indisposed. Injuries increased and May and Larsen had already returned home. '... somehow one gets past caring and just goes on,' reported Powell.[40]

In St Louis, the vast Kiel Auditorium was another 'back-to-back': Sadler's Wells' part seated 4,000 while behind an iron-curtain a circus performed to 10,000. 'We could hear their orchestra most of the time, & we used to slip thro' ... & watch the acts between ballets, & *they* used to do the same, & we got to know them quite well. There was a terrific high-wire act & trapeze people, elephants & jugglers ... (a) man & his sister ... were shot out of a cannon simultaneously 2'ce daily!!'[41] (the company longed for the firing of the cannon to coincide with Somes-Siegfried's jeté landings). From the stage, Somes could see in the wings two red-nosed clowns, a midget and two girls in tights and spangles, watching spellbound behind the waiting swans. The dancers got to try out their own balancing skills on the less elevated rail

---

38 MS to ES p 24 November 1950
39 MS to ES p 24 November 1950
40 Ray Powell, *Sadler's Wells Across U.S.A.*, *Dance and Dancers*, February 1951, pp20-21
41 MS to ES p 5 December 1950

tracks en route to Bloomington when the engine developed a 'hot box' and had to rest for a few hours.

Ear muffs and snow hats were de rigeur as winter descended in Lafayette, where the frozen locks on the scenery trucks had to be dynamited open. The Christmas lights in Detroit were cheering and Somes loved the elaborate animated window displays in the big stores, otherwise it was the familiar 'Opened with Lac usual terrific reception and they say never so much enthusiasm for anything in this city', in spite of considerable anti-British feeling, due to Britain's withdrawal from Korea. The British and Canadian consuls were grateful for the boost to British prestige at such a difficult time, although Somes was not exactly diplomatic: '… it makes me mad, – what do they expect us to do? – just because, for *once* the Americans have been "bitten first", – when before they have always come in at the end, & then said they had won the War. I've told several of them so too!!'[42]

The largest venue on the tour was Cleveland, a huge cold space, where they played to 19,000 over the two nights. The stage was only visible from half the seats, the front rows could only see waist up and the music had to be amplified, but the audience, many of whom had travelled hundreds of miles to be there, was enchanted.

Somes was enjoying dancing with Fonteyn to general acclaim and receiving excellent notices. Hurok sometimes slotted in extra performances or altered the repertory, bolstering the triple bills with the *Aurora* or *Swan Lake* pas de deux. Now they proved their true leadership of the drained company by raising their own performances. 'Watching such work is a help to the rest of us' reported Powell after a particularly notable *Swan Lake* in Memphis.[43]

In his memoirs, Hurok records the company's success, the ecstatic audiences and breaking records everywhere, but Somes saw the hidden toll: 'I suppose we'll get slated when we get back as we have nothing new to offer right away, – & all our old things are really looking so tatty now, after being dragged abt. these thousands of miles, in & out of all these trains in all weathers. … The Co. will be pretty dead by the time we get back, & just *must* have a week or 2's rest.'[44]

A relieved company reached Chicago on 18 December for a two-week season. Resentment rose as Webster postponed his visit and Hurok cancelled the promised Christmas party, although Webster did agree to pay for another. 'Freddy is President of the Party Committee & is seeing that Webster will really have a good bill to pay for us!! … but how we'd all rather be home!!'[45]

---

42 MS to ES p 5 December 1950

43 Ray Powell, *Sadlers' Wells Across USA*, Dance and Dancers, February 1951, p20

44 MS to ES p 13 December 1950

45 MS to ES p 9 December 1950

Chicago was another hot-bed of anti-British feeling, but the first night was a triumph and even Somes thought it was an excellent performance. There were more functions than usual, including a pre-Christmas lunch at Marshall Fields department store with pudding flown in from England. Somes loved the extravagant lights and stores bursting with luxuries; he was so transfixed by the toy trains that Jean considered buying him one for Christmas, until they found that it wouldn't run on English current.

Somes went to Midnight Mass on Christmas Eve and the company party was held on Christmas evening: '... after we all stuffed ourselves silly, – they brought on the Cabaret which Rodrigues had got together with Anne Negus & Gillian [Lynne] & a few of the boys, Leslie etc, & it *was* good! They did funny skits on all the tour, & on the 3 conductors, Irving, – Hollingsworth & Zeller ... & made up verses to the ballet music & impersonated Ninette & Freddy etc! ... they cracked at Webster & Hurok... we saw a film that Alec Grant has been taking with his cine camera ... I came out very well ...' Clayden organised silly games and Robert Irving acted as Father Christmas, but the hit of the party was 'The Swans that Stayed Behind in Kansas City' performed by Leslie Edwards, Ray Powell and Kenneth MacMillan in jeans and swan headdresses. Then came 'dancing & general jollity until abt. 2 A.M. – & we gradually broke up & went to various people's rooms & had cups of tea, & then to bed!!'[46]

Hurok eventually gave a small party, to which Somes reluctantly went; he 'said "he'd never been so happy to manage anyone as this Co – in all his experience" (I bet he hasn't!!).'[47] Enthusiastic packed houses, an excellent press and record box office countered homesickness and helped restore sagging enthusiasm and Fonteyn and Somes, according to their peers, gave their best *Giselle* yet; Somes proudly noted that his applause equalled hers.

New Year's Day brought the news that de Valois had become Dame Ninette in the New Year Honours list. The company celebrated on the day-long haul through beautiful country from Chicago to Winnipeg. Somes was pleased – despite finding her difficult on a day-to-day basis and his often trenchant criticism, he admired and revered her achievements. During the 1950s she was often unwell, undergoing several operations, and Somes' letters were as full of anxiety about her as complaints.

In Winnipeg the atmosphere was exhilarating after the confinement of the train. Temperatures dropped and the company gleefully swooped on the post-Christmas sales for wind-proof clothes. The night they left temperatures dropped to 32° below zero and the storage batteries froze, leaving the train with only candle light and little heating, adding to the misery of dilapidated sleeping cars and rough track. Somehow, no one had realised the implications

---

46 MS to ES 26 December 1950
47 MS to ES 26 December 1950

of crossing the US/Canada border twice in four days, with consequent delays as Customs made sure that every member of the company and their personal possessions leaving Canada exactly matched the company and personal possessions entering Canada four days before. Then, already late, they had to detour around a wrecked train. They arrived in Boston nine hours late after a journey lasting three nights and two days, leaving Stage Manager Louis Yudkin only a few hours to set and light *The Sleeping Beauty* (which needed twelve hours). Such challenges put the company on its mettle, and the performance on 8 January was voted one of the best on the whole tour.

The combination of cold and long distances between venues made the last leg seem endless. Everyone was so tired that Snap superseded Canasta as the preferred game. Somes was increasingly concerned: '... we have so many down ... they can hardly get the shows on, & *then* only with a lot of old 'crocks'! *I'm* alright & perfectly fit, but some of the poor girls, who *are* in everything, have just abt. "had it"! ... the Co. is dead-beat ...'[48]

Every New York balletomane travelled to White Plains for Fonteyn and Somes in *Swan Lake* on 15 January, the last performance in America. Ahead lay eight or nine shows a week in Canada but the end was in sight.

In Toronto eight performances in five days did not daunt the hospitable locals, who simply arranged for their parties to start in the early hours of the morning. Here and in Ottawa, people besieged the sold-out theatres, offering anything to get in, scant compensation for Montreal, where the St Denis Theatre was the worst yet '... so small back-stage, – it was almost impossible to get the show on. Most of the girls were stuck under the stage with the orchestra & the wardrobe, & an open sewer with water running thro' it!! I really thought they wld strike ... all so filthy, – it was the last straw ... Webster & Hurok were here to greet us, & so they came in for a packet of trouble ...'[49] Webster was given a strongly-worded letter of complaints: ' ... I think even *he*'ll find it a job to smarm his way round it. ... everyone (wants) at least 2 weeks rest on returning ... the Co. are certainly in no fit state to open at C.G. for quite a while.'[50]

In Ottawa social functions were back to back and the dancers had to be forced to attend: '... it never ceases, & one just gets dizzy & *no* time to oneself at all. But they're *all* so mad keen, – & have been waiting for us *so* long, – we just have to go ... we are treated like Gods everywhere ... I wonder if we will be in England?!!'[51]

Two days in Quebec, a few more parties and it was over. 'How thankful

---

48 MS to ES p 24 January 1951
49 MS to ES p 24 January 1951
50 MS to ES p 24 January 1951
51 MS to ES p 24 January 1951

everyone is', Somes wrote home. 'I really don't think they cld. do another *day!*'[52] In a burst of high spirits, toboggan races were organised, Fonteyn, Edwards, Irving and Franklin White beating off strong opposition from Somes, Jean, Plucis and Peter Clegg. At the farewell party, given by Hurok, Ray Powell's spontaneous toast to Fonteyn elicited the biggest cheer of the tour but, typically, she reminded them that a ballerina couldn't exist without a perfect setting.

Leaving the company and staff partying all the way to Montreal airport, Somes and Fonteyn went back to New York to appear on the prestigious Ed Sullivan show. They travelled with the orchestra and stage crew and it was an emotional journey: '... they'd all enjoyed it so much, & adore Margot, & said it was the finest Co & grandest people they'd ever worked with, & most of them were almost in tears, & kept saying goodbye over & over again!! ... those poor things are out of a job now ... & life is pretty tough for musicians over here.'[53]

Somes didn't want to stay on, but a Sullivan invitation was considered an honour and unmatchable publicity. '... I really can't forfeit my position as her partner just now when Bobby's gone & I've come into my own ... (Margot) has no ties at home it seems & doesn't seem to care when she gets back ... *I* desperately *want* to get back ...',[54] he wrote to his mother who was now crying that he didn't want to come home, never read her letters and never wrote to her ('I *always* do – & tell you everything, – usually 6 times *over!*'[55]). He was furious when the *Daily Telegraph* reported that they had been in New York sight-seeing.

Five months, 32 cities, 21,000 miles, broken records everywhere and $2½m gross ($25.6m): that year in Britain only the Cunard Line earned more and that was over twelve months. The Opera House's share was $500,000 ($5.12m), of which $340,000 ($3.4m) disappeared in rehearsal, production, maintenance and travelling expenses, taxes, salaries, the orchestra, insurance and royalties. The hidden costs of wear and tear on the dancers and productions couldn't be assessed. The success was too good an opportunity to miss for Hurok and the Royal Opera House. The next tour would be undertaken by the Theatre Ballet, but after that the Sadler's Wells Ballet toured America biannually in the 1950s at the expense of appearances in Europe and outside London.

'In addition,' Somes added morosely, 'I have to rehearse people as well as dance, (& for no more money!).'[56]

---

52 MS to ES 28 January 1951
53 MS to ES 31 January 1951
54 MS to ES 30 December 1950
55 MS to ES p 9 December 1950
56 MS to ES letters notebook 1951

10

Ambition Achieved

On their return to Covent Garden from America in February 1951, the Sadler's Wells Ballet was welcomed home in *The Sleeping Beauty* in the presence of Princess Elizabeth, and the Government gave a formal dinner in recognition of their achievements. 'I'm glad they seem to be making a little more of our homecoming this time,' Somes recorded drily.[1]

Although there were laments for Helpmann (who never gave a farewell performance in London), everyone agreed that Somes had raised his performance level. At 33 he had achieved his ambition – leading the company at Covent Garden, partnering Fonteyn. '... [S]ince his return from the American tour,' observed Peter Williams, 'he seems to have found an added quality to his nobility which makes him unquestionably the outstanding *danseur noble* in this country ...'[2] Clive Barnes, too, noted more fire: 'His body is still a bit stiff in movement ... (but) it is only a little more assertion (which is coming) and a little more fluidity of movement that are needed to make him truly outstanding.'[3] His youthful sulky looks had matured into archetypal 1950s glamour; he was more relaxed and had a new authority and confidence. His security lay in his rapport with Fonteyn, his partnering skills and his steady development as artist and stylist, setting an example not only in dancing, but in stage-craft and presentation. He knew how to maximise his talents and, though others surpassed him in specific areas, overall he was the outstanding male dancer in the company.

Somes' importance lay both in his influence on Fonteyn and setting standards in presentation, partnering and consistency; his work ethic, loyalty, devotion to the Sadler's Wells Ballet and, beyond that, to dance itself set the benchmark. His uncompromising masculinity was a counter to those who still equated male dancers with effeminacy, though old prejudices died hard and a concerned BBC, nervous of men in tights when men's tights were hardly sheer, insisted that *two* pairs were worn for any television appearance. Over the next few years there grew up around him a promising group of young men, who could hold their own with any company, including Field,

---

1   MS to ES, p4 January 1951
2   Peter Williams, *Sadler's Wells at Covent Garden, Dance and Dancers*, May 1951, p19
3   Clive Barnes, *Sadler's Wells at Covent Garden, Dance and Dancers*, June 1951, p18

Hart, Grant, Shaw, MacMillan, Blair, Philip Chatfield, Bryan Ashbridge and Desmond Doyle, but determination, hard work and intelligence kept Somes at the top for the next decade.

After the 1950-51 American tour, Fonteyn and Somes began working on *The Sleeping Beauty* as they had on *Swan Lake*, reassessing and exploring the choreography and characters. Florimund is usually described as a thankless role, but Somes showed the full possibilities of the character, demonstrating that the Prince 'has many subtleties that make something more than the flat cardboard lover we often see. He has true nobility of bearing and he partners wonderfully without losing any of his personality.'[4] In the grand pas de deux, he and Fonteyn 'brought their partnership ... to such perfection that the spectator is left in a daze, wondering whether it all really happened. The spectacular fish-dives and the subsequent triumphant lift on to the shoulder, in a curious unconventional way, appear to proclaim that a love, lain dormant for 100 years, has at last been magnificently consummated.'[5] Musically and visually harmonious, they projected love serenely triumphant and fulfilled, with a depth of private feeling underlying the public expression. Somes also had the advantage of dancing a good variation and his performance set the standard for the upcoming generation.

Somes' fears about the long-term effects of the American tour were justified as dancer after dancer went down. '... (they) crawled through the motions' observed Manchester, 'as though their one idea was to keep upright somehow until the fall of the curtain.'[6] He had been right to worry about the scenery too – a broken *Sleeping Beauty* column here, creased and flaking backcloths there, culminating in the spectacular collapse of the *Patineurs* set during a performance.

Somes and Fonteyn remained unaffected, standing in for ill and injured colleagues while working on Ashton's *Daphnis and Chloë*, based on Longus' novel charting the sexual awakening of goatherd Daphnis and shepherdess Chloë; he wins a dance competition over his rival, Dorkon (the prize a kiss from Chloë) and is seduced by Lykanion, while Chloë is abducted by pirates but rescued by the god Pan who reunites her with Daphnis. Ravel's score had been commissioned by Diaghilev and choreographed by Fokine in 1912 for Karsavina and Nijinsky. Less drama than poetic evocation, the lovers were passive, although Ashton did hot up Lykanion/Elvin's seduction of Daphnis/ Somes, played down by Fokine, as lusty goatherds were hardly Nijinsky's forte. Ashton rejected the classical vision of Isadora Duncan, believing that myths and gods were still a living force in Greece, and chose as designer

4   Peter Williams, *Right ballet, right occasion, Sadler's Wells at Covent Garden, Dance and Dancers*, April 1954, p27

5   Peter Williams, *Sadler's Wells at Covent Garden, Dance and Dancers*, July 1953, p18

6   P. W. Manchester, *The Rest of the season, Ballet Today*, April 1951, p4

13 Daphnis in *Daphnis and Chloë*. Photograph by Roger Wood.

14 Daphnis in *Daphnis and Chloë*: with John Field (on floor) as Dorkon.
Photograph by Roger Wood.

the Greek-based British painter John Craxton, whose designs were at once modern and timeless, capturing the colour, light and austere geometry of the Greek landscape.

Fonteyn remembered the ballet's creation as effortless: 'Each of my variations seemed to be worked out, with a brilliant off-hand casualness on Fred's part, in less than an hour, often in half that time.'[7] Although involved in the creation of so many Ashton ballets, Somes could never fathom how he did it: 'All I can say is that he has a tremendously perceptive ear and capability of seeing the broad line of the music and its infinite shades of colour, and these are indispensable to its choreographic creation ... Many were the arguments – no two people hear the same things it seems – but we admitted he was invariably right.'[8] Somes was one of a small group on whom Ashton worked out the corps de ballet steps, experimenting with different rhythmic accents to find the most satisfying aural-visual balance, adding to elements of Greek folk dance frieze positions in profile 'with everything turned in (a godsend to some dancers I won't name!)'. Ashton's rhythmic response to the score was so intricate that even Somes was in danger of getting lost and sometimes had to count.

Ashton took the pose of Daphnis standing with arms draped over the crook held across his shoulders from images of Nijinsky in Fokine's version.[9] The solo was deceptively difficult (Anthony Dowell summed it up feelingly as 'tough'[10]) and needed a sure lyricism to avoid looking laboured; it was full of pirouettes, the signature double tours and effortless jumps, often from a standing position, with feet twitching.

Ashton's understanding of Fonteyn and Somes' lyricism, instinctive sense of line and extraordinary response to music lay at the heart of the climactic pas de deux as the reunited lovers danced with growing ecstasy: a 'gentle pas-de-deux of apparent relief and love,' wrote Somes. 'She tucks her head into his shoulder and he swings her in ever-faster circles and slow, slight lifts just off the floor, making her seem weightless. She merely moves her legs but does not jump, all the weight being carried from start to finish of the lift by her partner.' As she lay across his knee, gazing into his eyes as he rocked her gently, the 32-year-old Fonteyn and 33-year-old Somes movingly conveyed the tenderness and ecstasy of adolescent love. They hadn't looked so beautiful since *Horoscope*.

Though the reception on 5 April 1951was tumultuous, reactions were

---

7   Keith Money, *The Art of Margot Fonteyn*, Michael Joseph, London, 1965, unpaginated

8   All Somes quotes from Michael Somes, *Music for Dancing – the Part it Plays with special reference to 'Daphnis and Chloë'*, RAD London Music Course, 7 May 1961

9   Beaumont, stickler for accuracy, told Somes that, as Daphnis was a goatherd, not a shepherd, it should be a wand, not a crook.

10 Interview with author

extreme, the atmosphere in the interval was venomous and reviews ranged from cool to frozen. Somes seemed unhappy, although some sensed that it would become one of his best parts and in time his performance developed an appropriate faun-like quality. Maybe he disliked playing another passive role: in his view '(Daphnis) easily lost the dance competition anyway, and throughout seemed to me to be a bit of a "drip"!' There was nothing for the character to overcome, not even, as Buckle complained, 'a forest of thorns or an angry old owl'.[11] It seemed almost perverse to cast him yet again as an inactive figure, expressed in a lyrical, limpid classicism, but the character was written into the music and Daphnis did exploit one of Somes' less acknowledged qualities – a sense of innocence, one of his 'potty-peasant-heroes ... who must have an aura of exaltation & goodness about them to make them possible'.[12] Somes himself so often referred to his 'rough exterior' and his volatility features so often in people's memories of him, that this equally characteristic quality has been overlooked. 'He has dignified reserve and simple nobility of interpretation after the best tradition of male dancers, a tradition dear to my heart,' wrote Karsavina.[13]

'Daphnis was a throwback,' declared Kersley. 'Suddenly there was the freshness ... you had all the steps that were like pre-war Michael. He was stiffer than before but ... it was our Michael again,'[14] the forcefulness of *Horoscope* transformed into lyrical strength, anger into a quiet intensity. Technique was subsumed into interpretation: '... exquisitely phrased to the music; each section is given the right emphasis and each step is executed with a clean finish which makes the outline of the dance clear-cut and distinct; yet the principal impression, is, rightly, of the young goatherd dancing to win a kiss from Chloë'.[15]

Daphnis and Chloë showed the men's continuing improvement. Grant was most obviously spectacular as Bryaxis, 'with his agitated movements and sadistic pleasure as he taunts Chloe'; Field was excellent as Daphnis' rival, the oafish Dorkon. Men and girls were equal in the ensembles, and despite adverse criticism of Craxton's costumes, it was a relief to see men in shirts and trousers: as *Dance and Dancers* observed, '... there are few more distressing spectacles than bow-legged Britons capering in chalmys, chitons, and sandals'.[16]

Ironically, as Britain dragged itself out of the post-war depression, the

---

11 Richard Buckle, *Modern Greek*, Observer, 8 April 1951
12 Ann Thouger to MS, 28 October 1961
13 Tamara Karsavina, *Four Opinions on Daphnis and Chloë*, Ballet, June 1951,
14 Interview with author
15 John Percival, *Danseur Noble*, Dance and Dancers, April 1959, pp18-19
16 Editorial, *Dance and Dancers*, May 1951, p4

Sadler's Wells Ballet, which had been on the up during the Age of Austerity, hit its first real low in the 1951-52 season. 'The epithets hurled at it are the price paid for excessive praise in the recent past,' suggested Alexander Bland,[17] though as Peter Williams pointed out 'Sadler's Wells is lucky that in its twenty-two years this is the first sticky patch.'[18] There were rumours that de Valois had had enough, that the company was breaking up.

The American tours had left less time for creating new works or maintaining the repertory and the company, especially the corps de ballet, was debilitated. Many dancers had left and their replacements needed time to integrate. After the publicity given to the success of the classics in New York there was pressure for more performances in London, and audiences grew increasingly resistant to new works and triple bills. This meant a diet of Princes for Somes; he would have welcomed working with a new generation of choreographers, like John Cranko, but they were working with the younger dancers. He could, however, still expect to be cast in Ashton's ballets, which in 1951 meant *Tiresias*, set to Lambert's first major score since *Horoscope*, which was given a royal premiere on 9 July.

Lambert had originally proposed a 35-minute satirical treatment of the Greek myth, but delivered a long, brooding tragedy which, Mary Clarke recalled, 'seemed to go on for a week and a day'.[19] Grant, who was understudying Somes, remembered, '(the score) didn't really work and I think Ashton was devastated by that'.[20] With Lambert's health deteriorating, no one had the heart to tackle him about it.

Tiresias changes sex when he strikes first a female and then a male copulating snake, thus experiencing love as both man (Somes) and woman (Fonteyn), so, when Hera and Zeus stretch mime to its limits in disputing which sex derives most pleasure from love, they consult the aged Tiresias. He finds for Zeus and woman and a furious Hera strikes him blind, but Zeus grants him the compensating gift of prophecy. Lambert submitted his programme synopsis with the note: 'I have done my best to make the point of the story clear to the gallery while keeping it concealed from Royalty. A very difficult task ...', but easier than making the points clear balletically.[21]

Dressed in white tights, feathered headdress, gold armbands and a gold chain over his bare torso, the young Tiresias sported amid Minoan maidens in leaps, acrobatics, handsprings and back somersaults, but, with so much

---

17 Alexander Bland, *Ashton's 'Tiresias'*, *Ballet*, October 1951, pp6-14

18 Peter Williams, *Sadler's Wells Ballet at Covent Garden*, *Dance and Dancers*, September 1951, p18

19 Interview with author

20 Interview with author

21 Constant Lambert to Michael Wood, quoted Haltrecht, Montague, *The Quiet Showman, Sir David Webster and the Royal Opera House*, Collins, London, 1975, p18

music, the choreography declined into interminable posturing, biceps-flexing and perambulations, athletic prowess which, wrote Barnes, 'would hardly have won third prize at a prep school sports';[22] Clarke sensed Somes was almost embarrassed by all the 'futile little jumps and hops'.[23] The main solo, a vigorous dance of triumph, came after twenty minutes by which time his energy was flagging; Beaumont thought it 'well composed and stirring to watch', with an aggressive virility reminiscent of Lifar's choreography;[24] others settled for 'uninspired,' 'pedestrian,' 'monotonous.'

The scene 2 pas de deux for Fonteyn and John Field, however, was one of Ashton's best, radiating an atypical eroticism with the underlying undercurrent that Tiresias' transformation was physical, not psychological. In the final scene, Somes as the blinded Tiresias achieved an awe-inspiring dignity, despite any suggestion of venerable age being negated by his still-bare youthful torso. There was little scope for development: Tiresias was young and athletic in the first scene and old in the third.

Tiresias fuelled frustrations about the company. *Dance and Dancers* was not alone in asking 'Is there not anyone strong enough to cry "halt" before a spectacle that ... was old-fashioned at a time when the Vic-Wells ballet was in its first flush of creation?'[25] Rambert, Fedorovitch, Chappell and Osbert Sitwell leapt to its defence. Not all music critics were hostile: Evan Senior thought it the finest ballet score since *Petrouchka*, 'reinforcing the emotional and psychological tension of the choreography'.[26] Philip Hope-Wallace was also positive: 'What a relief to have a *new* score – and of this order. Admirable for dancing, it is only too long and does not apparently give Ashton the big climaxes he needs to sustain our interest in the story.'[27] Richard Johnson, however, laid the blame squarely on Lambert: 'Ritualistic passages of the utmost banality and dull dances ... (an) arid score ... not worthy of (him).'[28] When Sitwell told Buckle that these comments would upset Lambert, Buckle replied that his *Observer* review would be worse.

Buckle attacked the whole organisation: 'Ninette de Valois is too busy to supervise every detail of production; Frederick Ashton is too easily reconciled to compromise.' *Tiresias* was obviously doomed from the start and de Valois should have forbidden it. '... she is a woman of taste and imagination, as well as of common sense', but should renounce administration, committees and

---

22 Clive Barnes, *Tiresias, Choreography, Dance and Dancers*, September 1951, pp13-14

23 Mary Clarke, *Three Revivals – One Welcome, Ballet Today*, April 1952, p15

24 Cyril W. Beaumont, *Tiresias, Sunday Times*, 15 July 1951

25 Editorial, *Dance and Dancers*, September 1951, p4

26 Evan Senior, *Tiresias, Music, Dance and Dancers*, September 1951, p14

27 Philip Hope-Wallace, *Time and Tide*, 14 July 1951

28 Richard Johnson, *New Statesman*, quoted *Ballet* November 1951, p14

'crusading abroad' and concentrate on planning new works and scrupulous supervision of productions.[29] He continued his attack in *Ballet*: 'The chief danger for an institution once it becomes state-subsidised is complacency; and the Sadler's Wells Ballet has been getting complacent. Criticism is a wholesome tonic for this ill.'[30]

The company was certainly unsettled. On the August regional tour, Ashton was in charge but avoided de Valois on her unannounced flying visits: 'I had only been telling him off for his lack of interest, & responsibility in the Co.' Somes wrote to his mother. '... he said the usual old thing that de V never puts in him charge etc & never lets him have any credit. That may be true, but in his own interest, he ought to do so much more. – He's just bone lazy that's all ... She asked (me) how things were going & I told her st(raight) in my opinion performances were disgraceful & that the whole Co. was falling to pieces, & it was time she gave it a little more time. Of course, she didn't believe me, – she only believes what she wants to hear, & also I think she really *likes* to feel the Co. can't do without her ... between them all the whole thing *will* go down the drain before long ... there's no direction at all, & the dissension in the Co, – everyone out for themselves goes right thro' ... I've never been so fed up with the whole lot of them & had such a rotten tour & seen the thing reach such a low point of disillusionment ... Half the Co look half-starved & I'm sure that's why they're always breaking down & getting ill ... so far I've been on every performance.'[31]

On 21 August, Lambert died, destroyed by long-term alcoholism exacerbated by diabetes. His death was a devastating blow. Somes, whose musical development owed so much to him, felt the loss keenly. Ashton lost his long-term collaborator and friend. Lambert's taste and extensive knowledge had been crucial to the company's development and de Valois had relied on his keen eye for detail to maintain performance standards. Fonteyn lost the lover who had done more for her, personally and professionally, than she would ever admit; she poured her emotions into Tiresias, dancing with a fierce intensity until a strained foot gave way and she was off for several months.

Lambert's death seemed to jerk the administration into action. Ashton became Associate Director in mid-1952 and he and de Valois began overhauling the over-worked repertory while a new intake revitalised the corps de ballet. *The Sleeping Beauty* was refurbished: Ashton created a magical vision scene solo 'after Petipa' for Aurora and de Valois later choreographed a variation for the Prince, built around *entrechats* and *double tours*, but slightly

---

29 Richard Buckle, *Sadler's Wells*, Observer, 29 July 1951

30 Richard Buckle, *Constant Lambert, an inquest*, Ballet, November 1951, pp13-15

31 MS to ES p16 August 1951

amended for Somes, Hart or Field. In 1954, this was replaced with a new variation by 'Frederick Ashton after Marius Petipa', which suited Somes perfectly.

With the company under attack at home, foreign tours were much-needed morale-boosters. In April 1952, Somes and Fonteyn went in advance of the company to Lisbon, where their reception was manic: '... I've never known such a list of parties, dinners, luncheons, teas & every other function imaginable ... which doesn't leave us a spare minute the whole day! ... (we were) treated like celebrities & fussed over ... met by a battery of ... B(ritish) Council, Govt. & cameramen, – all very embarrassing ... people from all the dominions & Consulates Embassies & Portuguese ... Terrific dinner ... but we were dropping with fatigue. Finally we had to go to the Theatre where we were met by the Director etc with great ceremony & shown all over it!' One problem immediately became apparent: the San Carlos theatre was beautiful, but a disconcerting notice read 'Dancers are reminded not to touch or even breathe on the scenery, owing to the difficulties presented by the steep stage.' The rake was so formidable that, at first, Somes had difficulty even standing up. '... Altho' it was past 1 by then crowds of people were ushering us round like visiting Royalty ...we cld have asked for, – (& got) the Moon! – Such a change from C.G! ... we staggered home & in our rooms were great bunches of flowers & a great list of instructions & packet of invitations.'[32] For all he professed to be irritated by and blasé about the celebrity treatment, he enjoyed being recognised in the street and treated like a star.

Their groundwork prepared the way for the company's success – *Swan Lake*, *Symphonic Variations* and *Checkmate* were audience favourites and even Somes admitted that the standard was 'quite good'. The downer was the late nights; with performances starting at 10pm, it could be 5am before he got to bed.

The celebrity treatment continued in June when Somes accompanied Fonteyn to Paris for their first international gala, in aid of the restoration of Fontainbleau. They had to encore *The Sleeping Beauty* pas de deux and, as undoubted stars of the evening, were mobbed by photographers as they were received by President Auriol. A dry reference to 'the dance she led me when we were here!!!' implies that the visit was not all champagne and cheering.[33] More than once when guesting, Somes had cause to refer to Fonteyn's 'muleishness' and having to 'drag her thro' a performance.

Recognising that Somes' career was at a critical point, de Valois sent him back to Volinine. He spent three weeks taking daily classes (other pupils varied from Paris Opéra stars Alexander Kalioujny and Janine Charrat to

32 MS to ES, 11 April 1951

33 MS to ES p 29 June 1951

'ghastly ... I don't feel so bad beside them'), private lessons and listening to the old man reminisce about Pavlova. 'He works the classes round me as a 'star' pupil & makes great fuss of me & says *he* cld. do wonders for me if he had me for a mth or 2!!'[34] Volinine's exercises were just what he needed to loosen up and fine tune his elevation and ballon.

Autumn was spent working on Ashton's *Sylvia*, his seventh ballet taken from Greek mythology and literature. Lydia Kyasht, who had danced the title role in a version at the Empire in 1911, came to rehearsals, as did her Aminta, the celebrated English *travesti* Carlotta Mossetti. Whatever prejudices still existed around male dancers, at least the idea of a *travesti* now seemed absurd.

Sylvia opened the 1952-53 season on 3 September. To Delibes' delectable score, Ashton conjured up a pastiche Second Empire ballet, set in Robin and Christopher Ironside's sumptuous, exquisitely detailed designs, with stage transformations, lighting tricks, traps and a ship on stage, all of which audiences adored.

Essentially the plot boiled down to the shepherd Aminta loves Sylvia, nymph of Diana (devoted to chastity and chase); Sylvia scorns Aminta; Eros shoots Sylvia with dart of love; Sylvia loves Aminta; Sylvia abducted; gods restore Sylvia to Aminta; divertissement.

Ashton created a pastiche of late 19th century French ballet, married to Fokine's principles of the expressive body and integrated corps de ballet, but the thin plot meant padding was inevitable and though there was some variety in the ensembles and dramatic climaxes, they were too delicately differentiated to create much theatrical excitement. Sylvia's abduction recalled Chloë's and Aminta was even more passive than Daphnis, the role having been originally devised for a *travesti* dancer when the ballet was created at the Paris Opéra in 1876. While Sylvia allowed Fonteyn to display a range of dramatic skills – the proud, chaste huntress who melts into love, the feigned seductress, and woman in love – characterwise, Ashton asked Somes to do a lot with very little. Aminta was, fumed Barnes, '... a deplorable hero! A Peeping Tom with poor eyesight, he has all of Daphnis's uselessness with none of his charm. It is greatly to Michael Somes' credit that he was able to some extent to colour the small area of paste-board allotted to him ... If only this Aminta had been permitted to have searched for Sylvia with half the vigour with which he danced, the intervention of Eros would have been uncalled for.'[35]

Somes was dancing with a new buoyancy, confidence and unexpected panache, which Ashton exploited in some of his best male choreography.

---

34 MS to ES p 29 June 1951

35 Clive Barnes, *Sadler's Wells at Covent Garden, Fonteyn's abilities inspired creation, Dance and Dancers*, June 1955, p22

There was what Bradley described as 'a vivid solo of expectation'[36] in Act I and a magnificently showy variation in Act III based on *cabrioles* and jumps. Volinine's influence extended into the choreography, Beaumont recognising elements of the Act III solo as in 'the Volinine manner'.[37]

The culminating pas de deux in Act III was breathtaking from the moment that Somes entered holding Fonteyn aloft by one beautiful ankle. The effect was of a 'love lyric with enchanting seconds of startling juxtapositions and an enraptured air of youth', classical magnificence married to Ashton's humanity, tenderness and rapture, as when Aminta drew her head back and simply placed his cheek against hers 'a gesture which, done by Fonteyn and Somes in particular, is one of the most moving in recent *pas de deux*'.[38] *Ballet Annual* called it 'one of the great performances of contemporary ballet'.[39]

Ashton was showered with flowers during the eighteen-minute ovation and thirty curtain calls on 3 September, but reviews were cool. *Sylvia* was stretched thinner than strudel pastry, even when Ashton later reduced it to one act.

For once, de Valois did not indulge Ashton's 'second-cast' phobia: Elvin, Grey, Nadia Nerina and later Svetlana Beriosova gave Fonteyn a run for her money while Field and Philip Chatfield were notable Amintas without quite achieving Somes' romantic ardour or mastery of the choreography. The difficulty of fleshing out such roles, where stagecraft and personality were needed as much as technique, only became clear when later casts took over from Somes.

Among the Muses in the Act III divertissement, a pretty blonde dancing Erotic Poetry caught the critics' attention. Her name was Deirdre Dixon.

At the end of September the company paid a brief visit to Berlin, never a ballet city. Audiences were distinctly sticky, but Fonteyn and Somes won them round with a *Giselle* that reduced Mary Wigman, doyenne of German modern dance, to tears.

Soon after, Fonteyn contracted diphtheria, and the revival of *Apparitions* went ahead on 17 November with Somes, second cast since 1936, partnering Anne Heaton as Woman in Balldress. His Poet had a refreshing vigour but lacked Gothic-drama passion; he simply looked too healthy for a drug-taking decadent.

Misfortune continued. In January 1953, only eighteen months after Lambert's death, Sophie Fedorovitch was found dead in her flat from a

36 Lionel Bradley, ballet diaries, 12 September 1952, unpublished mss, Theatre and Performance Collections, Victoria and Albert Museum

37 Cyril W. Beaumont, *Four Opinions on Ashton's 'Sylvia'*, *Ballet*, October 1952, p10

38 Clive Barnes, *Sylvia, Choreography*, *Dance and Dancers*, November 1952, p13

39 *Ballet Annual 1954*, Adam & Charles Black, London, 1953, p11

gas leak. Ashton lost 'not only my dearest friend but my greatest artistic collaborator and adviser'.[40] It was a bleak time: 'I think then he realised that he was getting to be more on his own,' wrote Somes, 'and that is a very difficult moment of truth for a lot of artists.'[41] Ashton now relied more on his dancers, Somes foremost among them.

Somes also kept an eye on the slowly recovering Fonteyn, being '... very sweet and useful "partnering" me around the flat!'[42] After several false announcements and doom-laden rumours, she returned on 18 March 1953 in *Apparitions*. At the end, she stood in a sea of flowers as the audience, swollen by the company and Opera House staff, went wild – the great dancer was becoming public icon.

In response, Somes again raised his game. '... Michael seems to improve literally by leaps and bounds,' Fonteyn wrote to his parents. 'I hear nothing but praise for all his performances from people in the company and in the audiences. I am so happy for him.'[43] To Somes she wrote: 'Mishkie darling, ... I can't tell you how happy I am to see you dancing so excitingly and having so much command of the stage. Everyone is impressed with you and it is wonderful for me to have your help and support. With very much love, always Sarah.'[44]

Somes was now the hardest-working dancer in the company and his schedule in the 1950s is witness to his artistry, skill and sheer stamina. In the 1952-3 season alone he danced fifteen *Giselles* to Fonteyn's four and partnered three different Auroras in five performances (Fonteyn did not dance full-length ballets on consecutive evenings). In under two weeks in March 1953, he partnered Rowena Jackson in *Swan Lake* (13th), Shearer in *Swan Lake* (14th); Markova in *Giselle* (16th), Fonteyn in *Apparitions* (18th), Shearer in a gala *Swan Lake* before Marshal Tito of Yugoslavia (19th) and Markova in *Swan Lake Act II* (20th). Following more *Swan Lakes* with Jackson and Markova and *Apparitions*, he gave his final performance in *Ballet Imperial* on 25 March, dancing *Apparitions* on the same night. Over the years he partnered both experienced ballerinas and steered newcomers through their debuts before relinquishing them to other partners, among them Nerina in *Cinderella* and *The Firebird*, Elvin in *The Sleeping Beauty*, *Giselle* and *The Firebird*, Pauline Clayden in *Daphnis and Chloë*, Elaine Fifield in *Swan Lake Act II*, Anya Linden in *The Firebird* and Jackson in *The Sleeping Beauty*; he

---

40 *Sophie Fedorovitch. Tributes and attributes. Aspects of her art and personality by some of her fellow artists and friends.* Compiled by Simon Fleet, 1955

41 Zoe Dominic and John Selwyn Gilbert, *Frederick Ashton and His Ballets*, George G Harrap & Co Ltd., London, 1971, p126

42 MF to ES, nd

43 MF to Ethel and Edwin Somes, March 23 1953

44 MF to MS, 23 March 1952

still performed *Tiresias*, and *Scènes de ballet* after Fonteyn relinquished them besides ballets created without her, like the later *Rinaldo and Armida*, *Antigone* and *The Miraculous Mandarin*. Sometimes, when he and Fonteyn were guesting outside London, he would go back between guest performances, or appear in a charity matinee with Fonteyn and partner another ballerina the same evening at Covent Garden.

Markova returned in March 1953 without Dolin. If Somes was nervous at the prospect of partnering her in *Giselle*, her greatest role, he didn't show it and she declared that their first performance together was perfect. Dolin always complained that she never helped in the lifts, claiming it would shatter the illusion and it was his job to make her seem weightless; she had no complaints about Somes who '... seems to be restraining her from taking wing, rather than raising her into the air'.[45] '... [B]oth of them seemed to glow with happiness' wrote Bradley '& the earlier pas de deux was like the mating dance of a bird of paradise.'[46]

Ironically, Somes got more attention than when he danced with Fonteyn. 'It would be impossible to speak too highly of Michael Somes both as cavalier and *danseur noble*,' wrote Haskell. 'He has been consistently underrated because of that very *noblesse*. The public has been used to the *premier danseur* with the "manners of a tenor" ... I can think of few dancers – Skibine and Youskevitch are exceptions – who can convince one as Somes does, that they belong to the balletic Almanach de Gotha.'[47] Dolin could not contain his admiration: 'Michael Somes, though never effacing himself, never obtruded too much, but nevertheless gave a great performance ... a performance worthy of (Markova).'[48]

Somes was simultaneously rehearsing Ashton's contribution to the Coronation festivities. *Homage to the Queen*, premiered on 2 June, was an extended divertissement in which the Queens of Earth (Nerina), Fire (Grey), Water (Elvin) and Air (Fonteyn), their Consorts (Rassine, Field, Hart and Somes respectively) and entourages paid homage to Elizabeth II. The highlight was Fonteyn and Somes in the Air pas deux, which owed not a little to *The Fairy Queen*'s Spirits of the Air. They seemed 'propelled as if blown by a zephyr, like thistle-down on a summer's day,' wrote Williams. 'The masterly pattern of the choreography gives the impression of being aimless, yet the effect is wonderfully contrived. I love the way it never seems to finish and

45 Anon, *Sunday Times*, 22 March 1953

46 Lionel Bradley, ballet diaries, 16 March 1953, unpublished mss, Theatre and Performance Collections, Victoria and Albert Museum

47 Arnold L. Haskell, *Markova in "Giselle"*, London Musical Events, May 1953, p53

48 Anton Dolin, *Markova, Her Life and Art*, W H Allen, London, 1953, p283

15 *Giselle* with Alicia Markova. Photograph by G B L Wilson.

one feels that they are going to be wafted back again.'[49] The effect depended on Somes, as Fonteyn rarely touched the ground, although even he found it difficult to maintain the illusion of airy nothingness when running with her draped across his shoulders.

Later in June, Markova and Somes appeared in Eastbourne and Brighton, performing extracts from *Les Sylphides*, *The Sleeping Beauty*, *The Nutcracker* (a first for Somes), and various solos, including Aminta's. They were so successful that a friend suggested that they should team up, tour the world and '"rake in the sheckles"!!' If Markova and Somes didn't, Fonteyn and Somes would.

Somes continued to develop. 'This year ... has seen the modest Michael Somes established beyond a doubt as a *danseur noble* in the grand manner,' recorded the *Ballet Annual* for 1954. 'His success will do much to overcome the prejudice against male dancers.'[50] At last, it was agreed, the company had a true *danseur noble*. 'Somes must cease to look surprised at his own virtuosity,' chided Barnes. 'That he is now an equal partner with Fonteyn may possibly come as much as a pleasant shock to him as it does to us, but

49 Peter Williams, *Right ballet, right occasion, Sadler's Wells at Covent Garden, Dance and Dancers*, April 1954, p28

50 Arnold L. Haskell, *Outstanding Events of the Year, Ballet Annual 1954*, Adam & Charles Black, London, 1953, p4

we, as an audience, can be permitted the luxury of amazement; he, as an artist, cannot.'[51] '... [W]e are now seeing the fine dancer we always knew him to be,' wrote Williams. 'He lacks the showy brilliance of a French or Russian dancer, but he has the quiet good taste (which) we expect from the best of British male dancers.'[52]

Even as they wrote, a new generation was knocking at the door, for whom self-effacement was not on the agenda. In 1953, the extrovert David Blair transferred from the Theatre Ballet to Covent Garden. A season in London by the Royal Danish Ballet, with their superbly trained men, also made audiences thoughtful.

Somes knew how much, or if, acclaim was justified. He valued the praise of peers and colleagues; he mistrusted most critics (Beaumont and sometimes Buckle were exceptions); he disliked uninformed fan gush and kept his distance, even leaving after performances by a side door, claiming that the Stage Door crowds were there for Fonteyn.

---

51 Clive Barnes, *Sadler's Wells at Covent Garden, Sylvias, tempered and untempered, Dance and Dancers*, June 1954, p22

52 Peter Williams, *Sadler's Wells at Covent Garden, More surprises from Somes, Dance and Dancers*, May 1954, p23

11

The Partnership

If Somes' position and success were linked to Fonteyn, her development into an international star in the 1950s owed much to his skill and the steadfast reliability of his support. *Dance and Dancers* stressed the importance of a partner who could 'match her femininity with virility';[1] with Somes, suggested Barnes, she became 'freer, more eloquent, and, most of all, more technically at ease'.[2] She had never enjoyed solos, needing to direct her emotions to someone who would feed back to her. 'I'm sure he taught Margot a great deal,' commented Barbara Fewster. '... in being a star, remembering that she was a star in the days perhaps before she really had confidence.'[3] It is difficult to remember now that her partnership with Helpmann had always been seen, by the company as well as the audience, as Helpmann-Fonteyn; Somes helped build her self-assurance as she stepped out of Helpmann's shadow, when she needed complementary support and consolidation, not challenges.

Somes was rooted in a tradition of a rare, then highly prized, breed, the danseur noble, which demanded effacing the self to reflect everything back onto the ballerina.

In fact, this gave a partner great power, for he can make or break a pas de deux, and a great partner can make an average dancer look like a star. This does not mean that he just faded into the background; his strong stage presence was no less a foil to Fonteyn than his partnering.

Fonteyn and Somes had looks, glamour and that extra indefinable chemistry generated between all great partnerships, which is god-given, not learned. The merest gesture of one found a reflection in the other as their bodies fell naturally into glorious sculptural symmetry. He was the 'perfect foil to Fonteyn's gentle, simple aristocracy',[4] his uncompromising masculinity making her look fragile and feminine. From their earliest years together, photographs bear witness to their instinctive sense of line, two bodies in perfect harmony, every limb and space between the bodies breathtaking.

1   *Dance and Dancers*, April 1958, p5
2   Clive Barnes, *Nureyev*, Helene Obolensky Enterprises Inc, New York, 1982,
3   Interview with author
4   Arnold Haskell quoted Hugh Fisher, *Michael Somes*, A & C Black, 1955, p7

From the rise of the ballerina in the 1830s, the male dancer lost prestige in Europe, but in Russia his role was transformed in the early 20th century by Michel Fokine. He only demanded traditional partnering in ballets which deliberately looked back, like *Les Sylphides* or *The Firebird* and Diaghilev's male stars, including Nijinsky and Massine, while rooted in classicism, did not perform the 19th century ballets which required conventional classical partnering; thus, by the time Diaghilev mounted *The Sleeping Princess* in 1921, so few men were skilled partners that he had to poach Anatole Wilzak and Pierre Vladimiroff from the Maryinsky to perform the Prince. It was from them that the young Anton Dolin absorbed the elements of partnering, and it was Dolin who had set the standard in 1930s England.

Dolin stressed that the male dancer must subdue his personality to that of his partner, becoming 'a firm pillar of support. She is the performance. I am ... showing you her perfections.'[5] Somes, too, believed that his function was to make it appear 'as though she were doing things by herself' which were impossible',[6] and presenting her to the audience as the most beautiful and desirable woman in the world: 'my function was very much to put myself in the background. I projected her, and the greater her success, the more credit, I felt, came to me,'[7] although he was aware that this might become 'nauseatingly self-effacing'.[8] He found this completely satisfying, an attitude with which the great Balanchine dancer Edward Villella concurred: 'Looking after a woman onstage, projecting the sense of caring, of giving something to a woman, is a wonderful, masculine feeling, and it became one of the great sensations of my life.'[9]

Somes learned much from Dolin, who knew all the technical skills – how to make the ballerina easier to support by changing hands from side waist to front in long carrying lifts; remembering to check her shoes (new shoes meant she would turn more quickly); how to take the strain from her; when to allow a second of rest ('She will be – or anyhow she ought to be – grateful.). And the dictum: '"two (turns) and clean" are better than "three with a shove".'

Dolin could have been describing Somes when he wrote: 'Stand firmly on your two legs. Forget the fifth position or any other. Just be natural. Don't try to take up dancing position. Just be the gallant, man cavalier. Leave the poses to the ballerina,' and let his manly strength contrast with her femininity, lightness and grace. Somes described his role as that of a dynamo, the energetic force translating basic movement into theatrical energy.

For Karsavina, the ideal partnership required an 'inner cohesion between

5   All Dolin quotes from Anton Dolin, *Supported Adagio, Dancing Times*, April 1935 p10-11

6   Meredith Daneman, *Margot Fonteyn*, Viking, London, 2004 p285

7   John Gruen, *The Private World of Ballet*, Penguin Books, London, 1976, p165

8   MS to Mr Labuschagre, 20 April 1989

9   Edward Villella, *Prodigal Son*, Simon & Shuster, New York, 1992 p

16 Harjis Plucis rehearsing Fonteyn and Somes. Photograph by John Hart.

the two',[10] the *mental* union that Dolin saw as paramount. 'You have to *want* to work as one,' insisted Barbara Fewster. '(To have) a sixth sense of how to deal instead of your own body with somebody else's at the same time. (Somes) was a very good partner, he knew the technical side as far as we knew then, but he also had a sympatica when he was partnering somebody, which other people often don't have. I think he had a natural instinct to be a partner.'[11] Peter Wright said he saw that instinct only in Dolin and Somes. Antoinette Sibley recognised him as 'the most phenomenal partner. You literally did nothing – oh, I mean nothing. He would take you through the ballet. All you had to deal with were the acting and the musicality – he did the rest for you. I have never known anyone like that.'[12]

For de Valois, musicality lay at the heart of a great partnership: 'A sense of rhythm, generally and actually intelligence',[13] to which Haskell added 'a knowledge of the ballerina's musical reactions, phrasing, and a dramatic sense that calls for the greatest discipline and restraint'.[14] Musicality was the

10 Tamara Karsavina, *Diaghilev – and Other Partners Dancing Times*, January 1967, p196.
11 Interview with author
12 Meredith Daneman, *Margot Fonteyn*, Viking, London, 2004. p372
13 Interview with author
14 Arnold Haskell quoted Hugh Fisher, *Michael Somes*, A & C Black, 1955, p7

defining quality of the Fonteyn-Somes partnership, an integral part of their instinctive communications which made it difficult for her to dance some of 'their' ballets with anyone else.

Although hearing music slightly differently, they easily adjusted to each other as well as to some conductors' bizarre tempi. Musically their performances were right from the start. They did not merely dance to the music, rather it infused the whole body, music and choreography indissolubly linked. So great was this rapport and so securely rehearsed were they that Somes said he could partner her blindfold. Her musicality meant that he knew exactly where she was going to be from second to second and he could anticipate her every need. 'It was a different kind of partnering in those days,' he later recalled. 'If I had any sort of quality (and I know what I could and couldn't do), it came out in the way we matched our musicality and our complete confidence in each other. I knew instinctively when she was in trouble, so we could prevent any mishaps.'[15] He enjoyed the physicality of dancing with her, the feeling that they were one body and the enjoyment of their skill, breathing through each other, as Sibley described it.

'(It) sounds such a dreadful term,' admitted Leslie Edwards, 'but in partnering reliability is almost the keynote of any ballerina being safe and sound.'[16] Philip Chatfield enumerated 'absolute selflessness .. which was certainly Michael to a T. Strength, determination and perfect timing',[17] while de Valois identified a quality of 'dedication rather than unselfishness'.[18] In this he differed from many of his contemporaries in Europe, who gave only perfunctory attention to their ballerinas, saving themselves for their solos.

'I suppose basically it was a sexual thing,' surmised Mary Clarke. '... Margot herself said that when she danced with Massine in *Tricorne* what an extraordinary difference it made.'[19] Fonteyn-Somes was a romantic relationship in which pas de deux were not flashy virtuosity but love duets, integral to the action. His obvious commitment and admiration enhanced her poised serenity. Sibley was passionate about his role: 'No ballerina can achieve what (Fonteyn) achieved without someone like Somes behind her ... Whatever she did later with Rudolf was magic as well – but you *cannot* take away from Somes what he was to that partnership. And people try to do it *all* the time ... Because he was such a partner – a generous man staying in the background – people took advantage of that, particularly when Rudolf

---

15 Jann Parry, *Homage to Fonteyn*, Observer, 13 August 1980
16 Interview with author
17 Letter to author
18 Interview with author
19 Interview with author

17 Somes with Fonteyn and Ashton.

came on the scene.'[20] 'It wasn't about making yourself evident and obvious,' explained Anthony Dowell, 'It was the true cavalier – manners and great aristocracy, that's why Fonteyn always looked so glorious.'[21]

Their curtain calls expressed that relationship: she always acknowledged him, but he stood an inch or two behind her: admirer Ann Orledge recalled the pleasure in watching him 'receiving an ovation, and how you seem to pass it silently on to the ballerina as though you yourself had done nothing'.[22]

Much that Somes did was technically difficult but not obviously spectacular like one-handed high lifts. His speciality, which often went unnoticed so perfect his execution, was partnering one-handed, preserved in his television performances, Paul Czinner's film of *Swan Lake* Act II or any recording of *Marguerite and Armand* – 'A bit of a trick' admitted Wayne Eagling, but hugely impressive,[23] especially in pirouettes: one hand by his side, the other held a few inches from her waist, both move in at the last possible microsecond to stop her in perfect position to the audience, a stark contrast to the paddling round that became the norm.

Another specialty was timing: '... where the end of the music is coming up, and it's accelerating, and you'd think she's never going to make it in time, never going to finish on the beat ... All those (finishes) in the Aurora,' Sibley recalled, 'it was just magic. But that's *him*, that's *not* Margot ... you step out, you make the most of it, but ... you can't stop the action, you can't get there on that beat because you are totally in his hands. And those lifts where you just reach it in time, like those amazing runs in *Ondine* – it's absolute timing between you both, but you are relying on the chap to get you there.'[24]

Few understood that many of the ballerina's highly praised and applauded effects were entirely due to expert partnering. Somes once apprehended a critic who had written about 'the pas de deux danced by Margot Fonteyn ...' and demanded 'When was a pas de deux only danced by one person.' Maybe he played the perfect partner too well, his rare gifts being scathingly reduced to 'not dropping Fonteyn'. One historian of the male dancer, deceived by the self-effacement, actually declared that Somes played no part in Fonteyn's development,[25] while another declared him 'invisible' and, while admitting this was expected of the *danseur noble*, concluded that 'it has meant that Somes holds a minor place in the Fonteyn legend'.[26]

---

20 Interview with author
21 Interview with author
22 Ann Orledge to MS, nd
23 Interview with author
24 Interview with author
25 Ramsay Burt, *The Male Dancer: Bodies, Spectacle, Sexualities*, 2007
26 Peter Stoneley, *A Queer History of the Ballet*, Routledge, 2006, p134

Nor should his part in the development of Ashton's choreography be underestimated. As individuals and as a partnership, he and Fonteyn were fundamental to the creation and development of his ballets, particularly the pas deux – 'a remarkably extensive anatomy of the nature of love, which they interpret with a touching delicacy and compassion'.[27] These are as much about Somes as Fonteyn – the deceptively simple dead-weight lift, Ashton's hallmark walking on air, was possible because of the great strength that he developed in shoulders, forearms, wrists and hands, which gave his ballerinas such a sense of security. He described how he tried to make it look as though she was floating: she would extend her legs and arms just after the moment of being lifted and bring them down just after the moment of touching the ground.

Michael Boulton recalled their qualities: 'Great dignity and they understood what they were doing – they understood the ballets and everything – just very good. Fonteyn was sheer beauty on the eye, and Michael was just perfect for her. You look at any old photos – it's all there.'[28]

It was a partnership that would define the company for the 1950s.

27 John Perceval, *Margot Fonteyn's Partner, Dance and Dancers,* March 1959, pp16-17
28 Interview with author

12

America, America

Throughout the 1950s and 1960s, Sadler's Wells Ballet toured America every other year for between four and a half and five months. Most tours followed the 1950-51 pattern and engendered the same feelings – exhausting slog, cities which all came to look the same – train, eat, hotel, theatre, reception. By the third tour in 1953-54, acclaim was no compensation for the stresses and, after 1950, there weren't even fashion promotions as a perk: '... I never look further ahead than the next place, & hardly know where it is next ... One even gets bored with the food, – they *all* overeat to a degree.'[1] '... I really have *no* feelings abt. it over here this time, – the novelty has gone, & it's just a job of work to be done & finished with as soon as poss. ... I have a drawing room to myself ... so I'm quite undisturbed, altho' I can never really sleep on the trains.'[2] Somes had an additional gripe because, in addition to the heavy performance schedule, he, Hart and Field were all taking classes and rehearsals, and he also substituted for de Valois when she was away lecturing or suffering a migraine attack – all taken for granted and unpaid. Any enjoyment was usually subsumed in sheer exhaustion and frustration at trying to maintain standards under trying conditions.

Realistic planning could have reduced the stresses of tight scheduling and late arrivals – outside New York, there were often two performances a day and rarely a clear twenty four hours. Matters weren't helped by Hurok, who would shoehorn in extra performances or ask for changes to the repertory according to how a work was received, which was unsettling for the dancers and meant that new works often didn't get a showing.

After the 1953-54 tour, de Valois put her foot down; four to five month tours were still the norm but with fewer dates, although it took fifteen years of constant complaints about bad routing and a schedule that left the dancers crying with exhaustion before one night stands were dropped, they were given one day off each week and no longer had to perform on the day they arrived in a town. In the 1960s tours dropped to three months or less with longer stays in major cities.

New York's love affair with the Company grew throughout the 1950s.

---

1   MS to ES p 10 October 1953
2   MS to ES p 19 October 1953

Somes recorded a 'terrific' reception in 1950, growing to 'colossal' in 1953. The acclaim in 1955 was even greater, despite the exceptional heat that New York seemed to reserve for Sadler's Wells Ballet openings: 'The notices, without exception, were *marvellous* ... several people said they considered it 2ce the Co it was when we first came ... I must say I'm surprised, as I didn't think we'd get away with it again ... I got a lot of praise, & the usual adulation.'[3] It was even hotter in 1957: 'I think it's a great tribute to the Co. that anyone comes to see us at all in this terrific humid heat!' Somes wrote. ' ... There's *no* air-conditioning at the Met at all being an old building due for demolishing they don't spend any money on it, & it's normally closed during the summer & Autumn ... we literally are in one continual bath of sweat, & most of us are taking salt pills to counteract it ...'[4]

The company was rarely out of American papers or off the radio; in restaurants, to be a Sadler's Wells dancer meant at least a drink on the house. In time, having used all available extreme vocabulary, critics were reduced to 'The same old triumph only more so.'[5] There were seasons of vague disappointment as the company became more familiar and the number of visiting companies increased, but The Royal Ballet was, as Clive Barnes wrote in 1974, '... one of those companies ... where it doesn't matter much what they dance as long as they dance'.[6] Somes found it strange that they could be such personalities in America and yet, after those first seasons, the British press ignored their success, only devoting a paragraph to the New York opening, though usually mentioning him as well as Fonteyn.

Familiarity bred indifference. A decade after the furore of 1949, they flew cramped tourist class, there was no Hurok or photographers to greet them, only Hurok's publicity manager, the American company manager and Oscar, the baggage-man. By 1964, even they had gone and everyone manhandled their own luggage on public transport. Touring by train became increasingly uncomfortable but, once planes took over in the late 1960s, the Ballet Special became a nostalgic memory, the worst forgotten.

From the first tours Somes fretted about how the company and the new works would be received and then, as the tour progressed, about the wear and tear on dancers and productions. At first, the company's modern works, apart from *Façade* and *A Wedding Bouquet*, were often dismissed in New York, so Somes was pleasantly surprised in 1955 when *Daphnis and Chloë* became their most admired modern work, Todd declaring it the most moving ballet seen in New York in living memory, and Daphnis was hailed as Somes' most

---

3   MS to ES nd September 1955

4   MS to ES 16 September 1957

5   Lillian Moore, The Sitter Out, *Dancing Times*, October 1957, p9

6   quoted Judith Cook, *Mixed Metaphors*, *Guardian*, 15 May 1974

18 *Swan Lake* with Fonteyn.
Photograph by Maurice Seymour.

rewarding role to date. *Tiresias* was a surprise success and Somes' fears that 'they'll pick some holes' in *Sylvia* proved groundless as, stunned by the sumptuousness of the designs and dancing, audiences and critics willingly overlooked the stretched narrative and passive characters; that Aminta was thought a rewarding role, confirms how Somes could flesh out the thinnest character. Chicago, however, a law unto itself, greeted *Sylvia* with the thinnest applause and some even wondered if it was an expensive joke. San Francisco was unique in disliking *La Fille mal gardée*. *The Firebird* was generally dismissed as a period piece except by the Ballets Russes old guard, who '... were full of praise for our 'Firebird' & 'Sylphides' & said it was the first time they'd seen them as they really were in Diaghilev's time'.[7] *Homage to the Queen* was frenziedly received and was a big success on tour, *Rinaldo and Armida*, won ardent individual supporters; *La Péri* was welcomed as a vehicle for Fonteyn and Somes (Chigago again dissenting), but *Ondine* suffered in being introduced to New York in 1960 alongside *La Fille mal gardée*. In 1961,

7   MS to ES p 13 October 1955

Somes was delighted that there was so much interest in the new works that Kenneth MacMillan's *Le Baiser de la fée* and John Cranko's *Antigone* replaced *Swan Lake* for one performance.

Somes appeared more than any other principal: one day he did *Rinaldo and Armida* and *Daphnis and Chloë* matinée and evening and another multiple was *Tiresias, Firebird* and *Rinaldo and Armida*, (giving the lie to him being just a one-dimensional partner). Dancing and teaching now left little energy for theatre-going and usually he just went back to the hotel and watched late-night television, something unknown in 1950s England.

Many of his letters record 'I got a lot of praise, & the usual adulation', especially in New York. John Martin on the *New York Times* was especially perceptive of his talents: in 1953, he 'told me himself how wonderful I had been & he's hard to please & Kirstein ... said to Fred I was the greatest male dancer in the World today. – All nonsense of course!! – but it's nice to know some appreciate it. I've had the most success of the men ... I've had dozens of letters comparing me with the great of the past, Nijinski etc.'[8] Fonteyn confirmed that his success was 'one of the pleasant surprises of the Co's visit ... he's dancing wonderfully!'[9] while de Valois told his parents that 'He has been dancing beautifully & his work has received great appreciation.'[10]

His best showcase was *Swan Lake*. In 1957 he and Fonteyn headed what many considered the company's greatest performance in New York: their Act III had the audience shouting with excitement and there were twenty-one calls, eight with the house lights up. For Martin, Somes 'contributed notably to its perfection. His variation was danced with the suddenly released joy of a young man who has just fallen in love, and his dramatic conviction was as strong a support for Miss Fonteyn as was his excellent physical support as her technical partner. A wonderful job.'[11]

Somes, however, had his own standards and was unaffected by praise. As P. W. Manchester dryly observed after seeing Brian Shaw's Blue Bird: 'I think that Shaw would have danced better if his initial leaps had not brought forth a storm of clapping. It was noticeable that the more experienced Michael Somes was not to be "drawn" by a similar demonstration.'[12] Most prized were tributes from Russian dancers and teachers, like Wilzak, who said Somes reminded them of the Maryinsky. In 1955, Nemchinova gave a party attended by all her Russian colleagues: '... they were so sweet, & so full of

---

8   MS to ES p 7 October 1953

9   Copy letters notebook, nd

10 NdeV to ES 21 October 1953

11 John Martin, *First 'Swan Lake' of the Season Performed by Margot Fonteyn, The New York Times*, 1957

12 P. W. Manchester, *Sadler's Wells Ballet, New York Reception, The Stage*, 24 September 1953

praise for us all. It was a lovely evening ... old-fashioned Russian, – caviare, peroshki & vodka flowing like water! ... They all made speeches & even I got up & said "thank you" etc!! ... it must have been the vodka ... Nemchinova wept as usual on my shoulder!'[13]

In the early 1950s, socialising was exhausting as civic authorities vied to outdo each other; '... one seems to spend all one's free time meeting people one will never see again, & trying to be polite & answering silly questions, – the same thing over & over again ...'[14] Somes, Ashton, Fonteyn and Nerina, were once sent to a civic reception with 'well over 100 women!! – whipped around for 2 hrs from 1 group to another, – natter, natter, natter all the time!!'[15] Even worse for Somes were occasions like Los Angeles in 1953 when the hugely successful opening night was followed by a ball '& Margot & I were introduced from a platform, – as "these great dancers of the World's greatest Ballet Co," – you can imagine what a fool I felt standing there being applauded & photographed ...'[16] When his birthday fell during a tour, he liked to celebrate quietly with a few friends, so in 1953 he was very disconcerted to be greeted at an official party with a becandled coffee ice cream cake, everyone singing Happy Birthday and a kiss from Ava Gardner.

Gradually, official functions diminished. By the 1960s there was more time to see friends, like conductor Robert Irving, who became Music Director of New York City Ballet in 1958, or former company dancers living in America – Catherine Boulton and Jean Gilbert had married Americans, while Richard Ellis and Christine du Boulay were now running a successful school in Chicago – and Somes always made time in his increasingly busy schedule to see Nemchinova and Olga Spessiva. Fonteyn often included him in her private socialising with star friends, like Danny Kaye and John Wayne.

Venues varied considerably. Before the Kennedy Center opened in 1971, Washington had no theatre, and the company once appeared in America's capital in an ice stadium. Somes dreaded Toronto's Maple Leaf Gardens ice hockey stadium, capacity 12,500, '... a "fit up" stage at one end & no atmosphere at all ... no proper dressing-rooms etc & awkward stage, – but it was a good performance & the audience were spell-bound altho' I doubt if many could see much sitting on the side right high up in tiers ...';[17] it was a relief when the 3,200 seater O'Keefe Centre opened in 1960, although Hurok still favoured Maple Leaf Gardens because of its greater capacity. *Swan Lake* and *The Sleeping Beauty* all but disappeared in Winnipeg's vast

---

13 MS to ES p 13 October 1955
14 MS to ES 14 November 1953
15 MS to ES 14 November 1953
16 MS to ES 9 December 1953
17 MS to ES nd

City Auditorium, while San Diego's stage was so small that it was actually dangerous. Sometimes it was impossible to hang scenery, while ice hockey arenas in Montreal and Boston had no dressing rooms or scene storage. In the Hollywood Bowl, the sound took so long to reach the back of the huge auditorium that the dancers seemed out of time and the stage was so hard that one boy broke his ankle.

Real antagonism broke out in 1956 when, towards the end of the tour, David Webster committed the company to a televised *The Sleeping Beauty*, partly, Somes felt, to compensate Hurok for lower profits from the shorter tour. Returning to New York and learning a new hour-long television version was intolerable at the end of an exhausting tour, when rehearsals for London had already increased. Although the transmission was seen by between 30 million (*Dancing Times*) and 40 million (*Dance and Dancers*), that did not outweigh the extra stress.

1957 was a new low. '... it was a disgrace to send us here', Somes wrote from Boston '& proved that *all* they think abt. is the *money* they get in & to *hell* with the artists or even the quality of the performance. From an audience point of view it is *worse* than Croydon by far – shallow stage & a lot of people can't see properly ... All the boys have to dress in a building *next* door, – actually *on* the stage of *another* small disused theatre & walk down a filthy alley *in the open* down some fire-escape dangerous iron steps – in all abt. 100 yards to get to the stage door & into the theatre ... & the girls are all packed into 8 tiny rooms. Of course in the pouring rain the alley was like a river, & they put duck-boards down & bought us galoshes to put over our shoes & built a sort of tent canopy to stop us getting soaked as we slithered along in semi-darkness, shivering in dressing-gowns. At the end of the performance I had to wait while the public queued out from the seats & finally fight my way thro' them in dressing-gown & costume to get back ... *So* much for "Royal Ballet", & all the baloney they talk.'[18] There was a fracas when the scenery, stored in a garage opposite the theatre, was dumped in the street because Hurok hadn't paid the storage fees, 'all in the *pouring* rain, – ruining what's *left* of it, – then it all had to be set up & folded back to fit this *hideous* place'.[19] In Philadelphia there was no hot water, so after *Sylvia* everyone had to stay in body make-up until they got back to the hotel.

'From a staging point of view,' he wrote to his mother, 'the tour has been *so* badly arranged. The stage staff can't get *into* the theatre at *any* place on the day of arrival because there is always either a film or concert on ... they have to get in & set up the show for the perf. on the *same* day, – & naturally it's not enough time to do it properly & it's a shambles. It has a demoralising

18 MS to ES p 9 October 1957
19 MS to ES p 9 October 1957

effect right thro' the Co. ... the houses were *packed*! ... but they often criticised the general way in which things are presented – & *no* wonder!!'[20] Even as late as 1960, few theatres were fully equipped with permanent trained staff and, as union rules forbade the English stage staff handling equipment, they usually had to direct untrained American crews.

Audiences and critics appreciated how the dancers worked as a unit, paying attention to the smallest detail, and keeping performances fresh. Somes, however, while recognising how hard the company worked under trying conditions, had his own high standards and was incensed that no one oversaw day-to-day production details on tour. 'Ninette floats in & out, as she feels, – & doesn't really see, – or doesn't *wish* to see any of these things ... I never speak to her, – it's better that way, because I couldn't contain myself. That fat slob Ashton has done literally *nothing* except the 1ˢᵗ perfs of his rôles in N.Y. taken 1 or 2 ½ hearted rehearsals & goes off most week-ends, – so we *never* see him ...'[21] Hurok or Webster only appeared at prestige dates like Los Angeles or Chicago.

Increasingly, the dancers felt the discrepancy between what they earned for Hurok and the Royal Opera House and what they were paid: '... you can imagine the money *some*body is making!' was a continual gripe.[22] At one point, Somes' American dresser was earning more than he was. His complaints were not only for himself: on the 1955-56 tour he was enraged that the corps de ballet's New York daily allowance was only $5.50 and angry at the increase – 50c a day; Somes recognised how hard they worked, often under the worst conditions (only one tap in their dressing-quarters in Washington in 1965) and that they had the least time off. Their only reward was knowing how highly they were valued by both their mentors and the public.

Tour profits diminished throughout the 1950s – from $2½m gross in 1950 to $14,000 ($130,363) in 1959, which was felt insufficient return when weighed against the strain on dancers and productions. However, over thirty years of touring, Somes did see some improvements, notably the building of new theatres in the major cities and the system of dancers being pre-booked into luxury hotels being replaced by *per diem* payments, allowing individuals to choose their own levels of accommodation; Somes favoured smaller, quieter hotels, while many dancers put themselves on such frugal living ('It's amazing how long you could make one tea bag last' recalled one dancer) that their savings enabled them to buy country cottages back in England.

---

20 MS to ES p 14 October 1957
21 MS to ES p 14 October 1957
22 MS to ES nd

13

International Stars

Hardly was the Fonteyn-Somes partnership established than it looked as though it might be over. On the 1953 American tour Roberto Arias, who Fonteyn had met in pre-War Cambridge, came back into her life and announced that he was leaving his wife and family to marry her, which may account for Somes' reports that she was dancing better than ever. One thing Arias purportedly decided was that the erotic *Tiresias* was unsuitable for his future wife and she should never dance it again. Then she suddenly decided to relinquish *Symphonic Variations*. 'I think Freddy was a bit upset ...' wrote Somes, '& cried when the last perf. was over, saying it was awful that he'd never see her do it again. I've been trying to persuade her, – but I don't think she will somehow, – she seems too wrapped up in her new life, & I very much doubt if she'll do anything very much for a great deal longer, which is a pity.'[1] She last danced *Symphonic Variations* in 1963.

For the present, however, life got more hectic as invitations poured in to guest abroad, gathering speed throughout the decade and peaking in the late 1950s. Some were fleeting stop-overs, performing show-stopping pas de deux in international galas, or longer visits, dancing the classics with a resident company, often taking in several venues. Fonteyn and Somes became adept at fitting into widely-differing productions, whether appearing with young companies, as in Japan, or long-established, as in Sweden, and their high standards and work ethic were an inspiration to dancers everywhere. Their achievements are even more impressive when it is remembered that the most strenuous guesting began when they were in their late 30s and that he was beginning to suffer aches and pains that indicated the onset of rheumatism.

Stars they may have been, but glamour was usually tempered by far from ideal conditions and sheer hard work. In summer 1953 over 4,000 people saw them at the Granada Festival, dancing pas de deux from *Swan Lake* Act II and *Sylvia* in the magical setting of the Alhambra gardens at night. The romantic setting did not extend backstage: 'The conditions ... were terrible of course, – bad stage, non-existent lights, open air etc, ... *we* felt we were awful, – but they seemed to think it was marvellous & the notices next day were

1 MS to ES July 1954

fantastic ...'[2] After the performance, a Spanish Duchess invited them to her home (which had belonged to Manuel de Falla), where they were entertained until dawn by a troupe of Spanish gypsies. Photographs of them in *The Sleeping Beauty* set in the Alhambra made the cover of *Picture Post*, Britain's most prestigious illustrated magazine.

In the early days of international air travel before long-haul, non-stop flights, guesting could be fraught: London to Tokyo could take 43 hours, Japan to New Zealand three days. However, it didn't pay to be too sanguine about the reliability of short flights, and optimistic planning did not always allow for unexpected delays, sometimes resulting in a dash from airport to theatre with less than ideal time to prepare for a performance.

In June 1954 they danced *Swan Lake* at Covent Garden and left immediately after the performance for an RAF base from where they flew overnight to Belgrade; the flight was terrifying and sleep was impossible. They were greeted on arrival by the entire Yugoslav National Ballet, whisked off to the theatre and expected to rehearse. Fitting into an unfamiliar *Swan Lake* in the short time available was a severe test of professionalism, but the reception, in a city not notable for welcoming foreign artists, was one of the most phenomenal in their partnership. Even Somes dropped his usual reserve: after a hysterically-received Act III, the audience gathered to shout their appreciation beneath their dressing-room windows and Fonteyn found a beaming Somes throwing flowers to the ecstatic crowd below.

While in Belgrade, he learned a Yugoslav folk dance complete with axes (ceremonial), which he performed when they returned to the Granada Festival in June, this time with a small group – Ashton, Grant, Clayden, April Olrich, Anya Linden, Brian Shaw and Michael Boulton – which allowed a more substantial repertory, including *Symphonic Variations*.

International galas could be a nightmare – too many stars with different demands and no overall control: '... the usual muddle' Somes wrote to Ethel from Monte Carlo in 1960, '... far too many people, & too long a programme as usual ... there was no piano & the lights all went out ½ way thro' & it will be quite a struggle to get what we *are* going to do done anyway.' Neither he nor Fonteyn liked ripping a piece from its context, so Ashton, adapted the *Cinderella* and *Sylvia* pas de deux as stand-alone concert pieces, showcasing their lyrical artistry in contrast to the traditional gala fireworks favoured by other artists. Appearing alongside other world renowned stars, Fonteyn and Somes were often the most acclaimed and audiences and critics, unused to the true danseur noble, were quick to see the contrast between Somes and those more interested in their own solo than their partner.

Guest appearances were considered important for international relations

---

2 MS to ES, p 5 July 1953

and reports from British Consuls, diplomats, British Council and Foreign Office representatives, praising their performance and social skills, followed them back to London. Reports make clear that Somes was a recognised personality in his own right, charming audiences, dancers and administrators alike, though not mentioning that he left behind dozens of love-lorn corps de ballet girls.

There were common factors to every visit. Tickets, at inflated prices sold out within hours; dozens of photographers and journalists met them at the airport, and, however jet-lagged, they had to appear fresh and intelligent at the mandatory press conference. As representatives of Britain, they were on show the whole time and fulfilling public engagements, almost like minor royalty, added to the strain of performing – in New Zealand, some women even curtsied to them, while in South Africa their dressers were bribed for souvenirs from their costumes. Official lunches, cocktail parties, dinners, meetings with teachers and students and charity appearances had to be fitted around class and learning new versions of the classics, often with inadequate rehearsal time, while coping with stages ranging from the sublime to the horrendous. Somes' desire for early nights was usually thwarted by organised dinners or impromptu suppers after which Fonteyn would invite everyone back to their hotel until the early hours. They used the social functions '... to urge those in authority who willingly come & applaud us, to look after their *own*', knowing from experience that only 'the seal of success from abroad, seems to enliven that sense of pride & respect for one's own product' that led to official support which would provide the stability for local companies to develop.[3]

Autumn 1954 found them nearer to home, performing in Edinburgh. The Festival was dedicated to Diaghilev on the 25th anniversary of his death. The Sadler's Wells Ballet's contribution was Fokine's *The Firebird*, revived by Serge Grigoriev, Diaghilev's legendary *répétiteur* of phenomenal memory, and his wife, Lubov Tchernicheva, who had danced the Tsarevna for Diaghilev; she was still performing many of her Diaghilev roles when Somes saw her with the De Basil Ballets Russes in the 1930s. Somes was Ivan Tsarevitch, who, with the help of Fonteyn's magic Firebird, defeats the magician Kostchei, frees the maidens he has enchanted and marries the most beautiful.

Rehearsing them was Tamara Karsavina, who had created the title role in 1910. Somes partnered her as she demonstrated the Firebird's capture ('Not like *Swan Lake*. You're a wild bird'); she was nearly seventy and slightly lame, so he approached her gingerly, but she was so strong that he had to fight against her. During rehearsals, she paid Somes his most cherished compliment: when Fonteyn was slow to trust him she chivvied 'Come along,

---

3 MS British Council lecture 1961 nd

19 *The Firebird*: Tamara Karsavina rehearsing Fonteyn and Somes.

20 *The Firebird*: as Ivan Tsarevitch with Fonteyn as the Firebird.
Photograph by Houston Rogers.

you have the finest partner in the world, I only had Nijinsky.'[4] He often repeated the story with almost incredulous pleasure, provoking the reaction 'does he really think he was better than Nijinsky?' Well, once asked 'Was Nijinsky a good partner?' Karsavina replied 'Not as good as he was dancer. I loved him, but I was never sure he would be just in the right place. One night he forgot me entirely ... He was at one end of the stage and I was at the other. I was starting a fall, relying on his support. It did not come. So I fell right on to the stage and rolled towards the footlights.'[5]

Often, having learned one thing from the Grigorievs, Karsavina would say they had not remembered it correctly and change it, only to have them change it back again. Nor did Grigoriev and Tchernicheva always agree on details. The experience might explain Somes' reluctance to consult too many of an original cast when he came to revive ballets.

Diaghilev's spirit hovered over the first night on 23 August: on the podium was his conductor, Ernst Ansermet, in the audience were his dancers and many who had seen the ballet in the 1920s and 1930s. All agreed it was the company's most successful Diaghilev revival. After a champagne supper, Richard Buckle showed the company round his groundbreaking Diaghilev Exhibition, which Somes hugely enjoyed. Few then realised just how much had survived and to see it all together for the first time was overwhelming, revealing to a new public Diaghilev's huge influence on 20th century ballet, theatre and art; it spawned myriad Ballets Russes exhibitions and opened up a new area of academic studies.

The Firebird was liberating for Somes, a blow to the 'Fonteyn's partner' cliché. Ivan showed how good an actor he could be, every moment concentrated and true. Despite the title, Ivan is the heart of the ballet, on stage throughout, linking the real and magic worlds in a role which requires a wide range of skills – a partner of strength, stamina and immense expertise in the long, hard pas de deux, a command of lyrical folk style with the Tsarevna, convincing acting and the authority to dominate the static finale. His problems may be solved for him, but, unlike Daphnis and Aminta, he shows spirit – hunting, wooing the Tsarevna and defying Kostchei and his entourage. The first meeting with Svetlana Beriosova's Tsarevna, had a charming gaucheness melting into a gentle rapport and the long kiss held the audience spellbound.

Everybody was amazed that an Englishman could be so *Russian*, embodying folklore's innocent peasant prince who triumphs through honest simplicity. The character was there as soon as his head came over the wall, expectant, innocent and manly, 'the naïve hero, who triumphs through

---

4 Karsavina had danced *The Firebird* with Adolph Bolm, but Nijinsky was her usual partner.

5 *Ballet, Evening Standard*, 15 November 1954

21 *The Firebird*: as Ivan Tsarevitch with Nadia Nerina as the Firebird.
Photograph by Houston Rogers.

bluntness, honesty and simplicity'.[6] For Beaumont 'his deliberate gait in profile brought to mind Russian icon art', heavy, almost lurching, stylised yet utterly truthful.[7] 'His Tsarevitch is a rough and gauche princeling, out of the remote days of legend' wrote John Martin, '... he never makes a move that is not both fully enkindled from within and beautiful to look at.'[8] Every second was sustained, filled and real. There was not an extraneous move nor an unmotivated one. Moments of humour were equally part of the character – indeed *The Firebird* reminded people that Somes *had* a sense of humour – the wry bow as he started to removed his hat to greet Kostchei, the taunting of the enchanter before he broke the egg containing his soul – performed with style and wit and integrated seamlessly into the character.

In the long finale, Somes dominated the crowded stage by stillness, the only movement a slow raising of his hand in beneditction as the curtain fell. 'The peasant prince became the essence of majesty – hero, lover and prince triumphant. His grave nobility matched perfectly the exaltation of the music. He became the music.'[9] For many, it was his greatest performance and he remains without peer. He danced the ballet frequently, with Elvin, Nerina and Linden as well as Fonteyn, and lovingly taught it to later generations. Nerina remembered him as 'without peer ... when he grabbed hold of you, you really felt you had to fly away from him in fright ... His performances were always exciting, and he always excited me.'[10]

A minor, but important, skill for Ivan is surreptitiously ridding the stage of any stray fruit from the dancing area after the maidens' dance with the golden apples. Somes became so adept that fans would wait to see how and when he would cope.

From Edinburgh the company went to Europe and the Paris Opéra, one of the remaining bastions to be stormed if the company was to be acknowledged as truly world class. The full-length *Sleeping Beauty*, being performed for the first time in Paris, failed to impress the critics – Paris still valued novelty and chic above authenticity, although they admired *Swan Lake* for its romantic drama, the corps de ballet's discipline and Somes' 'cold assurance'.[11] *Homage to the Queen* was considered too British, although Somes' partnering was admired; *Le Figaro* slated *Daphnis and Chloë*, except for Fonteyn, and others condemned its modern treatment. A mix of damnation and respect greeted *Tiresias*. Only *Mam'zelle Angot* was enthusiastically received for its score and

6 Clive Barnes, *The Firebird, Dance & Dancers*, May 1963, p26

7 Cyril W. Beaumont, *Dance and Dancers*, March 1962, p20

8 John Martin, *Ballet: First 'Firebird', New York Times*, 25 September 1957

9 John Martin, *Ballet: First 'Firebird', New York Times*, 25 September 1957

10 Nadia Nerina, *The Men in my Dances* , *London Life*, nd

11 Quoted Marie-Francoise Christout, *The Wells through French eyes, Dance and Dancers*, December 1954, pp14, 27

design (both French) and its joie de vivre. All English design was damned. The company's very existence was grudgingly admitted a considerable achievement, but with the underlying implication that this upstart was now being judged in ballet's birthplace by those who really understood what ballet should be.

Somes' letters tell a different story. At a lunch given by millionaire Louis Weiller: ' ... they were all raving abt. the Ballet & Margot & I in particular, & saying how stupid the critics were in France. But of course, – the London papers will get hold of it & *we* can't say anything or they'll think we are just "sour grapes."' *Swan Lake* was accorded 'a great success ... terrific reception, like they say they've never had here before. So if the Press damn that it will really be too obvious they are just being jealous. We have heard that the critics were *told* they must take a line *against* us ... & altho' the place is *packed every* night & queuing all day for seats, & the reception's good, – they've been absolutely stinking abt. us ... the wardrobe & stage-staff have a *terrible time*. They set the 3rd scene of Tiresias instead of the 2nd! ... last night they were all *drunk* as it was pay night! Our wardrobe-mistress was in tears & cldn't get them to wash or iron anything.'[12]

With de Valois attending so many official functions and with no one else available, Somes had to take on a lot of classes and rehearsals. From the early American tours, he had usually filled in when de Valois, Plucis or Rodrigues weren't available, which annoyed him when it was expected rather than officially acknowledged.

On to Milan, another sold-out triumph, although Somes was furious at the low musical standards: the La Scala orchestra felt that ballet was beneath them and were so bad that *Tiresias* had to be replaced. Touring was a nightmare for the company conductors, sometimes faced with a different orchestra at every performance and musicians incapable of playing scores like *Scènes de ballet*.

In Rome the rave reviews were their best ever in Europe although Somes didn't think the performances that good and was horrified when he saw *The Sleeping Beauty* from out front: '... *appalling, –* so drab & tired & *ragged, –* I can't see where all this precision we're supposed to have comes in.' The highlight was the rare honour of an audience with Pope Pius XII, who said 'that he wld. *like* to [meet the company] as apparently he had read the press notices ... He spoke ... abt. Art music poetry & movement being ... a 'reflection of God' ... he spoke to everyone a few words & gave us each a medal ... wonderful eyes & hands, & marvellous face & bearing ...'[13]

Naples was equally successful, but in Genoa, audience enthusiasm was no

---

12 MS to ES October 1954
13 MS to ES October 1954

22 Publicising Ballet for Athletes with Olympic high jumper Dorothy Tyson.

compensation for the theatre: 'a dump – still half destroyed by the War, – & no *cold* water even, leave alone hot!! & filthy dirty & smelly.'[14]

Back home, Somes became involved with the Whip and Carrot Club, an association fostering 'jumping' sports, which had approached the RAD to see if ballet might help in training high jumpers (the name came from the saying 'There is a time for the coach to use the whip and a time to dangle the carrot). The consultative group assembled in 1955 included Fonteyn, Idzikowski, Harold Turner, Claude Newman, Alexander Grant, Errol Addison and former New Zealand junior high jump champion Bryan Ashbridge.

14 MS to ES 6 November 1954

The distinguished cricketer, C. B. Fry commented 'If I had my way I'd send every boy to Sadler's Wells for a fortnight's ballet dancing before I'd have him in the nets. Teach him how to move; how to get his hips over his feet. Where your hips are, there your poise is also ...'[15] Dolin dryly commented that he hoped results would be two way and that the athletes might teach British male dancers 'to have more guts and stamina.'[16] Soon gymnastics became part of The Royal Ballet School boys' curriculum. Somes went on to serve on the committee and became a spokesman for the cause, discussing it on television in America and Canada, with film comparing dance and athletics. Over time, athletes found a significant reduction in their injury rate and most improved on their previous best performances.

The initiative was a sign of increased respect for the male dancer. Somes also participated in Hulton's Boys and Girls Exhibition at Olympia, organised by Marcus Morris, editor of the comics *Eagle* and *Girl*, where children met role models from all walks of life. When a set of tumblers engraved with dancers was marketed, representations of Somes, Ashton and Field were included alongside Fonteyn, Grey and Beriosova. Nothing earth shattering, but neither would have happened a decade before.

The same year Ashton created three ballets, *Variations on a Theme of Purcell*, *Madame Chrysanthème* and *Rinaldo and Armida*, all showcasing younger dancers but with the insurance of Grant in the first two and Somes in the last. *Rinaldo and Armida*, to a score commissioned from Malcolm Arnold, had been intended for Fonteyn, but, wanting to reduce her performances following her engagement to Arias, she withdrew and was replaced by Beriosova. De Valois was not displeased, confiding to Joy Newton: 'It will be the making of (Ashton). He is startled out of his complacency & insistence of (Fonteyn) in every work – sometimes just to make sure of its success. It is time that our admirable young dancers were developed by him & encouraged as they were in the old days. The situation was getting dangerous & disheartening for all concerned – rather like the Markova period at the end!'[17]

Rinaldo and Armida was premiered on 6 January 1955. The enchantress Armida compels men to fall in love with her; the price of her love is their death, but when she returns Rinaldo's love, she dies in his arms. It was essentially a three-part pas de deux with interruptions – Rinaldo falling in love, Armida's thawing emotions and her eventual surrender. The mounting passion was expressed in a recurring lift when Rinaldo faced Armida and held up his arms: the first time she jumped at him and sank to the ground, the second she clung to his neck and at the climactic third rose onto his shoulder. There were

15 *Ballet gives athletic poise, Curtain Up, Dance and Dancers*, August 1955 p17

16 *Ballet gives athletic poise, Curtain Up, Dance and Dancers*, August 1955 p17

17 NdeV to Joy Newton, 2 July 1954

beautiful passages in the subtly supported pointe work and significant use of the hands – hands searching for contact or Armida holding Rinaldo in a vice-like grip. Where Beriosova-Armida melted from sphinx-like enchantress to woman in love, Somes-Rinaldo was a single emotion, with terror tacked on at the end, but somehow he developed a believable character. He loved the ballet and working with Beriosova and the strong interplay between them was one of the ballet's highlights.

The reception was split between coolly dismissive and strongly supportive. Barnes became its champion: 'a tiny understated masterpiece ... (The) simple *pas de deux* of the destructive power of love is exquisitely carried out, with a most marvellous economy of art. Like a direct, lyric poem, the ballet wastes nothing ...'[18] It survived for several years, mainly as a vehicle for Beriosova.

1955 brought the first book devoted to Somes. Cyril Swinson (writing as Hugh Fisher) produced a picture book with introduction by Arnold Haskell and extended captions, giving an insightful analysis of Somes' career and speculating on his future. The well-chosen photographs reflected his energy, line and masculine presence; they were also a timely reminder of how Somes was more than 'just' a partner, showing not only how different he *looked* in each ballet – Greek youth in *Daphnis and Chloë*, Russian prince in *Firebird*, fairy tale prince in *Cinderella*, romantic hero in *Rinaldo and Armida*, Cretan athlete in *Tiresias* – but how the body language reflected each character.

Meanwhile, Fonteyn was preparing for her new life. Somes found her tearing out the inscriptions from all the books Lambert had given her – '... like ripping out a heart,' he told Wendy Ellis.[19] '[Margot] is quite changed;' de Valois wrote to Newton, 'more conservative, & more concerned with the art of "living" rather than drifting in a no man's land which left her a very lonely person.'[20]

The night before her wedding, on 6 February 1955, she danced Chloë and in the finale Somes bore her on his shoulder through the dancers amid a shower of rose petals, confetti and streamers. Backstage was gridlock: 'Stage hands, usherettes, dancers in dressing gowns ... squeezed round the ballerina, to wring her hands, to snatch a kiss, to pour out their good wishes for her future happiness. The popularity of Dr. Arias with every member of the company – his simple courtesy, his discerning taste – contributed not a little to the general enthusiasm.'[21] Somes might not have concurred, nor some of Fonteyn's close friends.

The next day, she flew to Paris with her intimate circle – Ashton, Edwards, de Valois, Somes and Jean Gilbert. They weren't scheduled to be at the

18 Clive Barnes, *Crime and passion*, *Dance and Dancers*, November 1959, p26

19 Wendy Ellis to Meredith Daneman, *Margot Fonteyn*, Viking, London, 2004, p211

20 NdeV to Joy Newton, 2 July 1954

21 Elizabeth Corathiel, *Margot Fonteyn*, *Ballet Today*, April 1957 p10

wedding itself as the Panamanian Consulate had room only for close family, but Ashton rebelled and they made for the Consulate, where they found no private ceremony but a media circus amid which the bride could hardly hear when to make her vows. After the honeymoon, she held a reception on the Covent Garden stage for the company and entire Opera House staff, plumped up with the occasional film star, like Errol Flynn and various society celebrities. She wore her wedding dress and danced with as many of the male guests as possible. Somes presented her with the company's gift of a silver salver. Marriage and new 'romantic' elevation to diplomat's wife, changed Fonteyn, both personally and in relation to the company. From now on, she would be *the* ballet star, a household name, a media icon, a public idol. She had shifted into the stratosphere.

Life became somewhat unsettling for Somes as he pondered on what his future boded if (or as he thought, when) she gave up dancing. Arias now accompanied her on their guest appearances abroad and though Somes was not excluded, inevitably their friendship shifted into another key. Life became unpredictable: '... things get changed, & Margot alters her plans – & I quite expect there'll be another change in plans tomorrow, if the Great Man so decides ...'[22]

In March on their way to guest in *The Firebird* in Milan, they stopped in Paris for lunch at Maxim's with whaling friends of Arias ('not a very prepossessing lot' commented Somes) followed by a visit to the House of Dior, which opened especially for Fonteyn – Arias had just been appointed as Panamanian Ambassador to the Court of St James and Fonteyn needed an appropriate dress to wear when he presented his credentials. Personal was beginning to intrude on professional.

In April, Fonteyn and Somes danced *Swan Lake* and *The Sleeping Beauty* in Helsinki and *The Sleeping Beauty* in Stockholm. Helsinki Opera Ballet had produced the full length *Swan Lake* in 1922 and by 1953 was on a fourth production, by Mary Skeaping. L. Nyholm praised Somes 'a dancer worthy of this great ballerina (his grands jetés were something of a sensation), and he is a fine actor; he was even able to give life to the I Act dull mime scene ... an unforgettable artistic experience.'[23] The second performance was 'one of those rare evenings when ... one is tempted to say, electric waves are moving between the Ballerina and the audience ... they danced with such an artistry and intensity as one does only seldom, or perhaps they do it always?'[24]

Having learned Helsinki's *Sleeping Beauty*, they moved on to a different production with the Swedish National Ballet. Their performances were

22 MS to ES p8 March 1954

23 L. Nyholm, *Queen of all Swan Queens*, *Dancing Times*, June 1955, pp573

24 L. Nyholm, *Queen of all Swan Queens*, *Dancing Times*, June 1955, pp573

hailed as the most remarkable guest appearances in Stockholm since the war and there were requests for a return visit even before they left. Between 1955 and 1960, they adapted to versions of *Swan Lake* (full or Act II) in Helsinki, Stockholm, Oslo, Belgrade and Warsaw, *The Sleeping Beauty* in Copenhagen, Helsinki, Stockholm, *Giselle* in Helsinki, Japan, Argentina, Uruguay, Chile, Brazil.

Back in London, Somes appeared without Fonteyn at the prestigious annual Night of 100 Stars at the Palladium, in aid of the Actor's Orphanage, partnering Hermione Baddeley in her 1939 revue number *The Creaking Princess*, a take-off of the Vic-Wells' *The Sleeping Princess*. 'A masterpiece of sharply-observed mistiming' opined the *Daily Telegraph*,[25] while *The Times* thought it a 'devastating ... impression of decay'.[26] Considering that they were up against Laurence Olivier, John Mills and Danny Kaye singing Noël Coward's *Three Juvenile Delinquents*, and Marlene Dietrich in top hat, white tie and tails singing *Knocked 'em in the Old Kent Road*, being mentioned at all was a tribute. Baddeley so enjoyed performing with Somes that she was still talking about it when they met again in New York in 1963.

Change on the professional front coincided with change on the personal. Somes' relationship with Jean Gilbert had ended amicably and his eye had been caught by Deirdre Dixon, the pretty white-blond Erotic Poetry in *Sylvia*. His letters from the American tour in autumn 1955 were full of plans for them to set up home together: 'You know we both wld. like you to be near around,' he wrote to his parents, '- for as you say, – you cld. pop in & out & it wld altogether be nice for us. ... Margot seems well – but is getting a little tired I think, – I don't think *she* will do many more tours of this sort, – I can tell she wld. really rather be home being an Ambassadress.'[27] If Fonteyn was tiring there were few outward signs. She even resumed *Les Sylphides*, but Somes stuck to his resolution not to dance it again and she was partnered by Rassine or Blair.

The first half of 1956 was a breathless scramble through company celebrations and anniversaries with charity galas and guest appearances fitted around scheduled performances. *The* rumour for the company's 25th anniversary season was that Ashton would revive *Horoscope*.

The year started with Fonteyn's appointment as Dame in the New Year Honour's List. Somes partnered her on 2 January in *Swan Lake* when she received a huge ovation from her devoted London public.[28] On 6 January they danced the Act II *Swan Lake* pas de deux at a gala to mark the 25th

25 *Daily Telegraph*, 24 June 1955

26 HB, *The Times*, 25 June 1955

27 MS to ES, 17 September 1955.

28 Appearing on the Covent Garden stage for the first time that evening, as a Swan was Antoinette Sibley.

anniversary of the reopening of Sadler's Wells, showing 'what magic can be wrought, even on a bare curtained stage, by artists of their quality'.[29] On 12 January they danced *Cinderella* and the next day flew to Monte Carlo to guest with Festival Ballet (now English National Ballet), dancing in *Swan Lake* Act II and the *Sylvia* pas de deux; their luxury digs were on Onassis's yacht, *Christina*. On 14 January they danced *Swan Lake* Act II, after which Onassis threw a party at the Casino, which broke up about 3am. After the matinée on 15 January (*Sylvia* pas de deux with Winston Churchill in the audience), Princess Antoinette of Monaco threw a party, and in the evening Onassis threw a dinner party, which broke up at 2am. Although affecting world-weariness, Somes secretly enjoyed all the celebrity junkets. On 16 January they returned to London, where, on the 18th, they danced *Cinderella* and on the 20th he guided Rowena Jackson through her first Odette-Odile before returning with Fonteyn to Monte Carlo on 22 January for a Red Cross benefit gala, but they were back in London the following day to dance the Air pas de deux at a midnight gala commemorating the 25th anniversary of Pavlova's death.

Squeezed into the to-ing and fro-ing were rehearsals for Ashton's first new ballet of the season, premiered on 15 February. Disliking adapting pas de deux for guest appearances, Fonteyn had asked him for a suitable small ballet, 'Something that would be colourful, exotic, original and yet true to classical standards.'[30] He suggested Paul Dukas' *La Péri*, which meant that, in accordance with Dukas' wishes, permission to use the score depended on the male dancer not actually dancing, reducing Somes' role to little more than mobile scenery.

Iskender (Alexander the Great in Persian mythology) steals the flower of immortality from the guardian Péri, but is torn between his desire for her and everlasting life; he chooses desire, returns the flower and dies as she mounts to heaven. The opening, with Somes-Iskender caught in cross-spotlights on the dark, starlit stage, was, for Barnes, 'outstandingly effective – the symbol of Man eternally groping for immortality under the cold, watchful stars'.[31] However, mystery disappeared when the lights came up: Ivon Hitchins' backcloth, a study in angry reds and browns, was little more than one of the distinguished artists blow-up paintings and sat uncomfortably with the star glamour of André Levasseur's barbarically rich costumes. Somes looked magnificent in an exquisitely embroideried bright blue tunic with yellow and green sleeves, and a shimmering earth-coloured cloak, scattered with gems and embroidered pink tulips. Fifteen tailors, milliners and embroiderers

29 The Sitter Out, *Dancing Times*, February 1956, p288

30 Elizabeth Corathiel interview with Frederick Ashton, *How a Ballet is Born*, *Ballet Today*, April 1956, Vol 9, No 4, p10

31 Clive Barnes, *La Péri, Choreography*, *Dance and Dancers*, April 1956, p7

worked on the costume for four days, augmented by a further fifteen on the fifth, before it was finished. Fonteyn was resplendent in shades ranging from orange to pale peach. Both dancers adored their costumes, which had the requisite glamour for guest appearances.

The choreography reflected the hypnotic Westernized-Orient of the voluptuous score, only a hand movement here or neck-jerk there diverting from the classical framework. In one memorable sequence, Iskander held the flower away from the Péri as she reached longingly towards it in a series of unusual lifts, slides, twists and slowly stretching arabesques; otherwise there was overmuch running about and, fatally, it was impossible to convey Iskander's longings for immortality. Fonteyn was exotic, limpid and elegant but sensuous she was not: Somes' customary noble bearing came to his rescue. Elizabeth Frank's conclusion was 'Highly ornamental trivia'[32] while one American critic dismissed it as a 'piece of junk in the 1911 manner'.[33] In fact, large theatres overwhelmed *La Péri* and it came into its own when performed, as intended, as a guest artist showpiece, especially in the compact Monte Carlo Salle Garnier.

During the week of 20 February, to celebrate the 10th anniversary of the Opera House reopening, the Sadler's Wells Ballet showed how far it had come by mounting a week of *Sleeping Beauty*s with six Auroras, and four Princes: Somes partnered Fonteyn and Beriosova with inspiring certainty, while Blair partnered Elvin and Fifield, Chatfield Grey and Rassine Nerina. The Sadler's Wells Ballet might not always reach the highs of some companies (nor the lows), but it certainly had depth.

On 29 February Somes accompanied Fonteyn to Oslo to appear with the Norwegian Ballet in *Swan Lake* Act II and *Sylvia* pas de deux plus the Miller's Dance from *Le Tricorne*'s for Somes and Ashton's new *Entrée de Madame Butterfly* for Fonteyn. Watching them rehearse, the Norwegian Opera Society singers were so moved that their own rehearsal had to be abandoned because they couldn't remember what they had to do. Louise Browne later reported that, while no one was surprised by Fonteyn's skills as a cultural ambassador, 'I must also pay tribute to the charm and friendliness of Michael Somes which captivated all the Norwegians who met him.'[34] Her impressions were confirmed by Jonas Brunvoll, Director of the Norwegian Opera Society, who wrote to Company Manager Michael Wood that Somes became 'very, very popular. What a splendid partner and a charming person.' He may have disliked such occasions, but Somes was a professional to his fingertips.

April was almost as hectic. On 4 April, he appeared in *Symphonic Variations*

---

32 Elizabeth Frank, *Margot Fonteyn*, Chatto & Windus, London, 1958, p100

33 Quoted George Jackson, *The Royal Ballet*, Ballet Today, March 1958, p17

34 Louise Browne, *Oslo Revisited*, Dancing Times, April 1956, p379

before Mr Malenkov, the Soviet Minister of Power Stations. On 12 April it was back to Helsinki, for four performances of *Swan Lake* and *The Sleeping Beauty*. On 15 April, they flew to Monte Carlo, to appear at the wedding celebrations of Prince Rainier and Grace Kelly, again staying on the *Christina*.

The church wedding on 19 April was marked with a performance in the beautiful Monte Carlo Salle Garnier, redolent with memories of the Diaghilev Ballet. Diaghilev's last star, Serge Lifar appeared alongside a galaxy of international stars, including Yvette Chauviré, Nina Vyroubova, Toni Lander, Fleming Flindt and John Gilpin. Fonteyn and Somes danced the Aurora pas de deux with their customary 'effortless ease and faultless technique', reported J. R. Farrington.[35] The programme was repeated for the general public the next night in the open-air Stade Louis II in arctic conditions. Once again, praise for Somes' fully rounded Princes and selfless partnering was an implicit comment on some other male dancers.

A week later, back at Covent Garden, Somes appeared in *Swan Lake* Act II before the Soviet leaders, Nicolai Bulganin and Nikitina Khruschev, after which the Soviet Embassy sent every girl four bottles of Russian perfume and a 2lb box of chocolates, and every man two bottles of vintage Georgian wine and 500 Russian cigarettes (Somes still smoked, threatening to give up with each tax rise). With no language barrier, ballet was a useful Government tool and in the 1950s most state visits included a gala at the Opera House and over the years Somes appeared before the Presidents of France including General de Gaulle, Finland, Peru, the Shahanshah of Iran and numerous Heads of State.

A revival of *Horoscope* proved to be wishful thinking, and Ashton's new work for the 25th anniversary gala, scheduled for 5 May, was *Birthday Offering*, set to Glazunov's *The Seasons*:[36] the programme would be completed by *The Rake's Progress* and *Façade*, both with Helpmann as guest star.

Birthday Offering showcased seven ballerinas and their partners, Fonteyn and Somes, Grey and Chatfield, Elvin and Blair, Nerina and Grant, Beriosova and Ashbridge, Jackson and Doyle, Fifield and Shaw. It had a real sense of occasion, the grandeur and aristocracy of the classical school tempered by English lyricism – Ashton's gift to the company which had become infused into its style.

Following seven solos for the seven ballerinas, came the men's Mazurka, in which Ashton matched Glazunov's triumphant music with rapidly shifting patterns and broad jumps, conveying a forceful masculinity and culminating in Somes executing a series of his signature fast double tours en l'air, flanked by pirouetting Blair and Doyle while the other men spun in circles round

---

35 J. R. Farrington, *Monte Carlo, Ballet Today*, June 1956, p10

36 The ballet was originally announced as *Fricassée* although, as it was for seven couples, the staff inevitably called it *Seven Brides for Seven Brothers*

them: '... seven male dancers that any company would be proud to possess' extolled Haskell.[37] Even Barnes was proud: 'dancing with a combined verve and brilliance ... one felt that English male dancing had irrevocably got somewhere, and that in future lilies will be reserved for bouquets.'[38]

The climax was another of Ashton's ravishing creations for Fonteyn and Somes, a formal yet luminously tender classical pas de deux in which he deliberately avoided any big lifts, although the walking on air was there, in skimming, supported bourées, and a gloriously simple moment when Somes ran past Fonteyn, tipping her hand and setting her spinning.

The costumes, by André Levasseur, had the requisite grandeur, reviving the knee length bell-shaped tutu of the late 19th century for the ballerinas; unfortunately, the matching men's costumes looked fussy, with leg-of-mutton sleeves and a swag across the front neck, finished in floating 'tails' from the shoulders; it says a great deal for the men's discipline that scissors were never surreptitiously wielded. Somes, as usual, got away with it, but some of his colleagues looked a little uncomfortable.

At the end of the evening, de Valois stood surrounded by the whole company and ballet staff and spoke again about the company's success being due to many, not one, and even reminded her audience that Sadler's Wells Ballet did not stand alone in establishing British ballet – citing Rambert and Festival Ballet. Unable to name everyone she used a few names to stand for the many. She acknowledged that for many years the question 'What are you going to do about the male dancers?' was 'an honest and genuine problem we had to face ...' and used as symbols of those 'who made it possible to prove that this could be done' Dolin, Helpmann, Turner and Somes.[39]

That Somes was now a personality in his own right was confirmed when he hosted a television programme on 29 April celebrating ten years since the reopening of the Opera House. He gave a short history of the theatre and escorted cameras around the Royal Box ante-rooms, Edward VII's smoking room, the scene docks, wardrobe and canteen and introduced excerpts from *The Magic Flute* before dancing with Fonteyn in an Ashton-adapted *Sleeping Beauty* Act III. Viewers found him natural and informative, 'So if you ever decided to change your job!!!' suggested the BBC's Ian Atkins, reporting the positive feedback.[40]

Shortly before the end of the season in June, Somes and Deirdre were involved in a car crash. He was driving and unhurt but she suffered head and

37 Anon (Arnold L Haskell), *The Sadler's Wells Ballet Birthday Offering, Ballet Annual 11*, Adam & Charles Black, London, 1956, p39

38 Clive Barnes, *Birthday Offering, Dancing, Dance and Dancers*, July 1956, p20

39 Ninette de Valois, *Speech, Ballet Annual 1957*, Adam & Charles Black, London, 1956, p42

40 Ian Atkins to MS, 28 May 1956

23 *The Miraculous Mandarin:* as the Mandarin with Elaine Fifield as the Girl.
Photograph by Houston Rogers.

leg injuries. Whether the crash was his fault or not, Somes felt responsible. After she recovered, they were quietly married on 7 July at the Church of the Most Holy Redeemer in Islington before family and a few close friends. Although they tried to keep it secret, several papers ferreted it out, resulting in headlines like 'Michael Somes Marries almost in Secret' and photographs of bride and groom leaving the church surrounded by the shoppers and stallholders of Exmouth Market. She was 22 and he was 39.

After a four-week honeymoon in the South of France, Somes and Deirdre settled down in Lloyd Square, the flat furnished with then unfashionable Victoriana. He had an eye for the perfect finishing touches, be they fingerplates, tiles or light fittings, and a gift for the practical – decorating, repairing gilt carving, hand-cutting a mosaic-tiled floor, with meticulous attention to detail. Islington was still years from gentrification, but 'it has a restrained, effortless distinction about it. That is like Michael Somes the man ... There is a strong feeling for the past and for a rather Victorian restraint in all (his) taste ... his love is for elegance and graciousness.'[41] The downside, for Deirdre, was that Ethel was only across the square and still expected to see her son every day.

Professionally, too, 1956 was a time of new beginnings as Alfred Rodrigues, seeing beyond the self-effacing cavalier and Ashton's ideal prince, cast Somes in the title role of *The Miraculous Mandarin*, to Béla Bartók's eponymous score. It was his first non-Ashton created role since *Ballet Imperial* and a world away from anything he had done before.

A prostitute lures rich victims to her rooms where they are robbed by her pimp and his thugs; when the Mandarin succumbs to her advances, he survives smothering, stabbing and hanging, only dying when the girl, overcome with compassion, embraces him. In Bartók's native Hungary, the subject was so unpalatable that all visual representations had been banned, a fact that did not go unnoticed by the British press. 'I loathe 'chi-chi' in ballet.' Rodrigues declared. 'Only the truth – even if it is not pretty – will serve.'[42] Elaine Fifield was the Girl, Pirmin Trecu and Ray Powell hoodlums and Grant the pimp who 'had the joy of trying to kill Michael ... It was rather amusing really. He never complained.'[43]

From years of working in the company, Rodrigues knew that Somes had the acting skills, authority and integrity to anchor the ballet. His Mandarin was a mysterious, macabre figure, with slate-blue skin, dragon-decorated torso, high forehead and a skull-cap, which drew attention to the heavily made-up eyes; exotic jewellery encircled his neck and arms and rings emphasised his hands as they twisted in controlled anguish. Character and emotion were subtly conveyed with minimum facial expression, 'Oriental' gestures and a technically difficult pas de deux full of novel holds and lifts. While Somes did not spare a particle of the horror, he and the cast heroically avoided tipping the Grand Guignol violence into laughter. The choreography was not without merit but it failed to reflect the passion which 'rages in the music, consumes him and keeps him alive'.[44]

41 Anna Christophersen, *The Quiet Dancer*, *The Sketch*, 28 January 1959, p59

42 Alfred Rodrigues, *Ballet Today*, November 1956, p10

43 Interview with author

44 Peter Brinson, *The Miraculous Mandarin*, *Dancing Times*, November 1956, p20

Reactions after the 27 August premiere at the Edinburgh Festival were extreme: reviews branded the ballet sexy, obscene, sadistic and revolting. 'Nerve-Wracking Ballet of the Underworld' quavered the *Press & Journal*; '*That* ballet left them stunned' shrieked the *Daily Mail*. Under the headline 'I Watch a Horror Comic', Noël Goodwin in the *Daily Express* almost qualified as 'disgusted Tunbridge Wells': 'In the name of art and entertainment the Sadler's Wells Ballet tonight presented ... the most brutal and obscene ballet it has ever been my misfortune to see. And this at the Edinburgh Festival ...'[45] Haskell leapt to the defence arguing that, to be taken seriously, ballet should deal with a wide range of emotions and subjects, and that the test was not the subject-matter but its treatment. The questions raised by *The Miraculous Mandarin* were almost more important than its quality: in the age of John Osborne and Kingsley Amis, could ballet embrace the new mood and contemporary themes or only deal with shocking subjects if cushioned by romantic mist, like *Giselle*? The only consensus was that the Mandarin was one of Somes' best creations. 'Trust *me*' he lamented, 'to have good notices in a ballet which is sure not to last or be liked!'[46]

Some thought that the ballet would be too shocking for the delicate sensibilities of Covent Garden audiences, and indeed, at the first London performance, a stunned silence lasted for several curtain calls before the applause mingled with hisses began. Audience comments recorded by the *Daily Mail* ranged from 'for Soho, not a Royal Opera House' to 'why should British taxpayers fund violence in the theatre when you can get it in reality outside.' 'I have danced in many more suggestive ballets than this one' responded Somes, without specifying what they were, though he warned that it was 'not the sort of ballet to bring young children to'.[47]

The controversy ensured Somes publicity at a time when he was becoming increasingly familiar to the general public; he usually appeared in photographs with Fonteyn, not always behind her, and popular women's magazines started to publish articles on male dancers: *She* singled out 'the active leadership of ex-Army/P.T. instructor Michael Somes' under whom 'we have a growing team of sturdy young men who are proving themselves not only fit partners for our bevy of beautiful British ballerinas, but stars in their own right as well.'[48]

However, in her anniversary speech, de Valois had said that the way forward was to 'sit up and remember what we still have got to do'.[49] A sharp

---

45 Noel Goodwin, *I Watch a Horror Comic*, Daily Express, 18 August 1956

46 MS copy letters notebook 1956

47 Anon, *London can judge for itself now*, Daily Mail, 4 September 1956

48 R(?) Leslie, *Ballet for the Boys?*, She, August 1957, p43

49 *Ninette de Valois' Speech*, Ballet Annual 1957, Adam & Charles Black, London, 1956, p40

reminder came in October 1956 with the first London visit of the Bolshoi Ballet, fulfilling Somes' prediction in 1944, that '... they would find the difference when the Soviets etc, come over, & people *really* see what dancing *is*.'[50]

Although the Sadler's Wells Ballet were performing in outer London, Somes and many of the company were at the opening night and he managed to get to as many rehearsals as possible. The Bolshoi Ballet was a revelation, a company honed in a school with a tradition measured in centuries not years. They were powerful, compelling, strong in characterisation, with mature dancers bringing weight to the mime roles. *The Fountain of Bakhchisarai* and *Romeo and Juliet* were thrilling in scale, with full-blooded characters and vivid crowd scenes: if not as choreographically sophisticated as European ballets, they were refreshingly lacking in nymphs and shepherds. However, the dancers lacked the stimulation of working on new works in different styles, and were eager to hear about Fokine's revolutionary ballets, which had passed Russia by. If they were criticised as old-fashioned, especially in design and construction, in fact, they foreshadowed the resurgence of neo-realism in Zefferelli and Visconti's opera productions.

Galina Ulanova created a furore: a middle-aged woman, neither conventionally beautiful nor physically perfect, she transformed into a heartbreaking Giselle and a passionate Juliet. The Bolshoi men were powerful and compelling, with exciting young dancers, led by Nicolai Fadeyechev and, though not helped by the costumes with 'modesty trunks' under their tunics, their training shone through.

Somes only caught part of the Bolshoi season, as he and Fonteyn left on 11 October for South Africa. When plans for the visit were mooted, Arias proposed, without consulting anyone, that Somes produce *Le Tricorne* and *Swan Lake* Act II for a specially recruited company: Somes had assumed that there was an existing company which knew the ballets, and, anyway, mounting *Tricorne* without reference to Massine was out of the question, so he sensibly suggested engaging Festival Ballet, as both ballets were already in their repertory. In the end, Dudley Davies staged *Swan Lake* for CAPAB (Cape Performing Arts Board), using Benesh Notation, then in its early days as a professionally viable dance notation: Somes confirmed the accuracy of the reconstruction.

To fill out a short programme, Somes agreed to dance the Blue Bird pas de deux with Patricia Miller, his Village Girl from *Summer Interlude* who was now settled in South Africa with her husband, Dudley Davies. Presumably this was the only *pas de deux* that they both knew: why else would Somes have chosen to dance something he had relinquished a decade before because he

---

50 MS to FA, nd

felt he couldn't do it justice? He did point out to the Festival organisers that it was a great concession on his part considering his fee. There never seemed any question of Fonteyn filling in.

The £200 tickets for their performances sold out long before any other Festival performances and newspapers were full of pleas for seats. They flew to Johannesburg on 11 October, to be greeted by the inevitable frenzy. They were welcomed by the Lord Mayor and a children's choir; their car was surrounded as they drove to the hotel, where more crowds awaited them. Their dressers were bribed for old shoes and bits from the costumes. Four performances of *Swan Lake* were given, one on a raft moored on Zoo Lake for an audience of 6,000.[51] They visited the Hope Training Home for disabled children (where Somes deliberately concentrated on one of the boys who was especially interested in ballet) and attended African dance demonstrations and exhibitions.[52] Somes hated what they saw of apartheid and they enraged the white population by giving a special performance for a black audience, although it had to be given under rehearsal conditions.

On their return, they topped the bill on Sunday Night at the London Palladium, the most popular programme on television, which included ballet if dancers had scored a particular success at home or abroad, publicising their achievements to an audience of up to 20 million. They danced the *Birthday Offering* pas de deux, and if the editor incorporated camera tricks, like superimposition, and close-ups were used indiscriminately, it was a small price to pay for the exposure.

By now, preparations were advanced for the Sadler's Wells Ballet's exchange visit to Russia: scenery and costumes were on their way, souvenir programmes had been printed, the pre-publicity was in place. Somes expressed the hope that he would be able to meet his idol Chabukiani, 'for to me he symbolises the ideal male dancer'. He was concerned, however, that the size of the Bolshoi meant that the 'smaller' ballets were not being taken, so that the Russians were not being given a true picture of the repertory. But he looked forward to the benefits of exchanges between Russians and English dancers: 'There must be lots of things that we do differently, and this is where this exchange is so important ... From the ensuing discussion and examination of these ideas, both will be able to draw greater benefit from a common pool of experience.'[53]

Then, on 4 November, Russian tanks rolled into Budapest to quash the Hungarian government's introduction of democracy, freedom of speech and religion and plans to leave the Warsaw Pact. The insurrection was put down

---

51 In the corps de ballet was student Deanne Bergsma.

52 During the visit, Fonteyn appeared in an advertisement for Albany cigarettes ('with the wonder Aylon filter') 'the cigarette Dame Margot Fonteyn would offer you'.

53 Michael Somes, publicity handout

with the utmost brutality and, given the depth of public feeling throughout Europe and the West, there was no option but to cancel the Sadler's Wells Ballet visit. A London season was hastily organised, but *Cinderella* and *Sylvia* seemed lightweight after *Romeo and Juliet*; MacMillan added some Soviet-style jetés to his Step-Sister, but otherwise there were pleas for everyone to loosen up and take a higher arabesque.

New Year 1957 found Fonteyn and Somes back in Milan, appearing in Alfred Rodrigues' production of *Casse Noisette*, designed by James Bailey, with a Kingdom of Sweets that he described as Fabergé realised in icing sugar. Karsavina taught them the pas de deux which she had performed at the Maryinsky, more love duet in the Bournonville-French style than the alternative Ivanov fireworks: '... purest gold' declared *Dancing Times*, 'and seems to have about it the lustre of the Maryinsky. It is gracious and poetic, rich in style, wonderfully musical.'[54] Fonteyn and Somes admired Rodrigues' production, and recommended it to de Valois, but Ashton didn't share their enthusiasm.[55]

They returned in time for the announcement that the Sadler's Wells Ballet had been granted a Royal Charter, becoming The Royal Ballet, under which umbrella was included the former Sadler's Wells Theatre Ballet and the School. Rumours of the company becoming 'Royal' had been circulating for a number of years, drawing the comment from Hurok that if 'everybody without exception wanted to see the fabulous Sadler's Wells Ballet' twice as many people would want to see the Royal Sadler's Wells Ballet.[56]

The *Nutcracker* pas de deux became another gala choice for Fonteyn and Somes. In February they danced it the Arts Theatre in Cambridge giving three performances to celebrate its 21st anniversary, between which Somes was also dancing *The Firebird* with Nerina at Covent Garden.

In March Somes was invited to become a Director of the newly-formed Western Theatre Ballet, based in Bristol, but, faced with his commitments in The Royal Ballet and his increasing appearances abroad, he was reluctant to serve in a non-participatory role, although he did offer to help in an advisory capacity. He had already turned down an invitation to become Hon President of Glasgow Ballet Club, although possibly with less reluctance.

At the end of April, having filmed *Birthday Offering* for *Off Season*, a film aimed at attracting overseas visitors to London, the company left for New York to dance *Cinderella* for NBC television. Transmitted in both black and

---

54 The Sitter Out, *Dancing Times*, May 1958, p358

55 In the 1950s, only Festival Ballet performed *The Nutcracker* in Britain and depended on its drawing power at Christmas to help them survive. There was an unspoken agreement that Sadler's Wells Ballet with *Cinderella* and *The Sleeping Beauty* in the repertory, would not compete.

56 Sol Hurok quoted in *Sales value of a word, curtain up!*, *Dance and Dancers*, July 1953, p14

white and colour, it was expected to attract an audience of twenty six million, the largest ever for a single performance. The reception was mixed, mostly because of the close-ups and restless camera work and because the black and white was very blurred while the colour looked enchanting. Ashton and MacMillan 'occasionally seemed carried away by the glorious fun of clowning in close-up' complained Lillian Moore, although she thought Fonteyn more marvellous than ever while a regal Somes gave 'impeccable support'.[57] Both dancers had upped their performance level, perhaps in response to the Bolshoi. Clive Barnes reported her acting and dancing superbly, while 'the radiant Somes is partnering and dancing in the grand manner.'[58] Perhaps, he suggested, the cancelled Russian trip was a blessing as if they continued in this way they could achieve a triumph in Moscow that might have been beyond them a year earlier. Somes, however, was nearing 40, and it was not surprising if some critics noted that he was beginning to look rather stiff and unyielding.

He was not involved in Grigoriev and Tchernicheva's mounting of *Petrushka*, but was nonetheless in people's minds when it was premiered in March. Mary Clarke, commenting that dancers needed more detail and weight in crowd scenes, explained: 'The coachmen do not need to *be* six foot huskies, but the must *look* like strong, muscular working men on the stage. With one or two honourable exceptions, the present cast look like ballet boys in beards. If only Michael Somes had led this group, the effect could have been utterly different.'[59]

However, with all his other commitments he was was simply no longer available for the smaller roles in a repertory ballet. Invitations were flowing in from ever further afield. From 20 May to 22 June 1957, Somes, Fonteyn, Rowena Jackson and Bryan Ashbridge were in Australia, guesting with the Borovansky Ballet. The schedule was sixteen performances in fifteen days in Sydney, sixteen performances in eleven days in Melbourne, a free matinee for a thousand ballet students and disabled children, plus public appearances, including at the Benefit Race Meeting at Randwick in Sydney and Melbourne Cup day. Fonteyn and Somes danced either *Swan Lake* Act II or the Rose Adagio and *Casse Noisette* pas de deux, not ideal given their dislike of concert programmes, but complete ballets were impossible given the punishing schedule.

For months beforehand, the Australian press was full of the visit. Fifteen hundred people queued during one of the coldest nights of the year to buy tickets, while in Melbourne agents opened at midnight to cope with

---

57 Lillian Moore, *Cinderella on American T.V., Dancing Times*, June 1957, p391

58 Clive Barnes, *The Royal Ballet at Covent Garden, Dance and Dancers*, May 1957, p35

59 Mary Clarke, *The Royal Ballet in 'Petrushka', Dancing Times*, May 1957, p355

24 Farewell to Melbourne, 1957.

the waiting crowd, some of whom had queued for thirty-four hours. An exceptional barrage of photographers and reporters and a two hour press conference greeted the quartet on their arrival in Sydney.

The opening on 25 May, was the most diamond-studded occasion since the 1934 Royal visit, the hysteria even surpassing the 1947 Old Vic tour with Laurence Olivier and Vivien Leigh. Over the season, more people flew to Sydney to see them than had flown to Melbourne for the 1956 Olympic Games. Fonteyn created a traffic jam as nearby stores ceased business when she simply went out to tea, there were reports of people curtseying to them, and in Melbourne a little girl refused to wash her face after Somes painted her eyebrows with his make-up brush: 'all my friends think I am so lucky, and I have been treated like a princess'.[60] They gave up one of their free days to visit the Margaret Reid Orthopaedic Hospital, where Fonteyn was presented with a Koala tea cosy and Somes 'brought screams of laughter from the children as he put the tea cosy on his head and did an impromptu dance'.[61] With male dancers still regarded with deep suspicion and derision in Australia, Somes and Ashbridge took every opportunity to suggest the adoption of ballet as a sport and promote its benefits in sports training in general, prompting a gratifying burst of publicity, including several cartoons, one showing a

---

60 Faye Black to MS, nd

61 Somes press cuttings, unidentified publication, June 1957. Remember Billy Connolly's dictum 'Never trust a man who, left alone in a room with a tea cosy, doesn't try it on.' How much more trust a man who puts it on *in public*.

disgruntled team of rugby players in tutus captioned 'And remember, mugs – no gouging in the entrechats'.

Audiences were enthralled, although critics were not unanimous. RR in *The Sydney Herald* thought Somes' Siegfried had 'little of the essential princely bearing and courtliness,' although in *The Sleeping Beauty*, his '... Prince Desire (sic) was ever her watchful protective, lovingly gentle partner.'[62] Overall, the visit provided a huge boost for ballet in Australia, but it was not without friction; the laid-back Australian dancers found the guests formal and aloof, especially as Fonteyn insisted on being addressed as 'Dame Margot', although she relaxed once the strain of the opening night was over. For the first time, she and Somes defied a director when, before the long overnight train journey from Sydney to Melbourne, Borovansky ordered a full dress rehearsal of a programme they had already danced a dozen times. They also had to ask him to stop giving instructions to the corps de ballet during performances, although it was a habit Somes adopted in later years. Throughout the tour Somes' knee was giving him trouble, and his dressing room mirror was marked up with the remaining number of performances and he gleefully ticked one off each night.

The visit was financially rewarding (Fonteyn's fee was reputedly the highest ever paid to a ballet dancer), although, when the rival managers went to court over their profits, Somes was not pleased to learn that their fees were minuscule compared with the income they had generated.

Money was again an issue on the American tour in the autumn of 1957, Somes still feeling that that the company was being run into the ground for profits that none of them shared. Fonteyn, he thought, was exhausting herself chasing Arias instead of concentrating on her work. And *still* nobody was keeping an eye on day to day production details and standards, with de Valois back in London overseeing the Touring Company's Opera House season and Ashton away most weekends.

Though concerned about his own performances, Somes was always aware of the *company*, reporting in his letters on how the *company* was doing – or how he thought they were doing. Only perfection was good enough. Nothing escaped his notice and he was particularly critical about the choice of repertory, especially on long tours, which, he felt, needed ballets that stimulated dancers and audiences, not endless repetition of box-office favourites. He saw the importance of detail, as well as the big picture.

1957 had been a good year for the male dancers. They, and particularly Somes, were winning a higher profile but he felt they should be accorded the same attention and recognition as the ballerina. A. V. Coton, however, noted that, with Elvin, Fifield and Grey having left, there was near ballerina-

---

62 Quoted Estelle Herf, *The Australian Tour 1957, Ballet Today*, November 1957, pp12-13

starvation at Covent Garden, whereas the rate of development among male dancers made them equal of women 'a state of affairs not frequently met with in any ballet company over a very long stretch of years'.[63] But they still needed the ballets to show off their new prowess.

De Valois went even further when she wrote in the *Ballet Annual*: 'The standards of performance at the moment, and the new and exciting element of competition (which is the best incentive to drive our men forward) convince me that the days of our female caretaker government in English Ballet are drawing to a close ... It is my belief, that the time is now approaching when the men will once again assume their rightful place of leadership in our ballet.'[64] She argued that men had always been the thinkers, creators, teachers and administrators in ballet, while women were the interpreters and provided glamour, a view pounced on by ardent feminists, but in the 1950s it was understandable if ballet was to be accepted as a viable career for men.

De Valois had a habit of deciding what was best for someone without consulting them, springing it on them as a pleasant or unpleasant surprise, as she had with Somes and *Summer Interlude.* In 1956, John Field was transformed almost overnight from dancer into Director of the Sadler's Wells Theatre Ballet without any consultation beforehand. John Hart was now Ballet Master with a brief to tackle corps de ballet standards. De Valois was always 'as "nice as pie" to me,' Somes admitted, 'but I get so bored with her eternal egotism & theories about this & that & she always fastens on *me.* Freddy keeps out of her way ...'[65] She needed someone to talk at, but references in Somes' letters imply that she had plans for him too.

Speculation about de Valois' successor had begun as early as 1954, when Caryl Brahms reported that the 'popular theory' for the post-de Valois company was Fonteyn and Ashton co-heading 'a benevolent committee' of Somes, Webster and conductor Robert Irving.[66] 'I felt very embarrassed' Somes wrote to his mother, 'but of course [de Valois] laughed abt. it, – [Brahms] also said we'd make a mess of it! (which must have pleased her!).'[67] By the mid 1950s, commentators noted his increasing involvement in administration and were speculating on his future. In nominating him as the company's hardest-working dancer, *Dance and Dancers* cited his unacknowledged involvement in the administrative side and commented: 'We should not be at all surprised if one day his role in the company became a much more important one than that of principal dancer.'[68] Mary Clarke noted that he

63 A. V. Coton *London Ballet Month, Ballet Today,* June 1957, p6

64 Ninette de Valois, *English Male Dancing, Ballet Annual 11,* 1957, p96

65 MS to ES October ?20 1957

66 Caryl Brahms, *A Change of Dynasty, Ballet Today,* October 1954, p9

67 MS to ES p 9 October 1954

68 *Dance and Dancers,* unknown date

was showing a gift for administration[69] and Hugh Fisher suggested that his post-dancing years would be as important as his performing.[70]

At the Ballet Sub Committee on 11 June 1958, de Valois proposed that Somes be prepared for 'extra work in the theatre, in a position like that of John Field' and that he should be appointed an assistant director; she needed another aide, particularly on American tours, and 'as it would take time for Somes to accustom himself to this kind of work, and to find how his abilities could best be used, it was not too early to make the appointment.'[71] The sticking point was Fonteyn and her increasing guest appearances: in 1958 and 1959 Somes would spend as much time guesting with her as with the company.

They went back to Ankara in May 1958 for two performances of *Swan Lake* Act II and *Casse Noisette* pas de deux with the Turkish State Ballet and School as part of British Week. The visit was a nightmare, but their patience, hard work, professionalism and sheer stamina on and off stage was typical. Problems began with Somes and Fonteyn's mother being booked from Istanbul to Ankara but not Fonteyn, who had to get the next plane. Once she arrived, after greetings by the official reception committee, they were whisked off to a theatre exhibition, laid a wreath on Ataturk's tomb and lunched at the British Embassy.

The tight social timetable allowed for only one and a half hours' rehearsal. It was a shambles. The conductor was uncooperative, his tempi beyond erratic; the inexperienced corps de ballet 'gallumphed all over the place impeding Odette and her Prince at every turn'.[72] The next day, they were afraid to move in case they got in the way, but Fonteyn simply said that she and Somes could work around them, so long as they knew where the mistakes were *likely* to be made. They drew small chalk circles around the worst parts of the stage, arranged to work in the afternoon on *Casse Noisette* pas de deux, with which they had not been satisfied, thanked everyone and went for lunch with the Iranian Ambassador. Between rehearsals and the two performances they also fitted in a British Embassy reception, followed by a buffet dinner with the British Council representative, lunch at the British Embassy, tea at the Arts Lovers' Club, a Music Society cocktail party and supper with Mr and Mrs Mithat Fenman (as Beatrice Appleyard she had been one of de Valois' original six dancers at Sadler's Wells in 1931 and a stalwart of the early years), lunch with the Turco British Association and, attended a tea party at the Conservatoire. The next morning, they caught the 7am flight

---

69 Mary Clarke, *The Sadler's Wells Ballet*, A&C Black, London, 1955, p300

70 Hugh Fisher, *Michael Somes*, A&C Black, London, 1955, p7

71 Ballet Sub Committee 11 June 1958 BSC(59) 6th meeting. Item 13

72 Naomi Benari, *Vagabonds and Strolling Dancers, The Lives and Times of Molly Lake and Travis Kemp*, Dance Books, London, 1990, p174

for London, leaving behind memories of their charm, unfailing courtesy and meticulous care in packing their costumes.

Deirdre's career was now moving forward. De Valois considered her primarily as a character dancer, the natural successor to Julia Farron, and such dancers mature slowly. She was beginning to attract attention in solos, notably as a precise and musical Fairy of the Golden Vine. Her intensity could degenerate into over-acting – as Clive Barnes remarked, there was 'something rather engaging in the way Dixon always gives everything she has got, but not infrequently – and this is particularly true of her *corps* performances – either she has got too much or the others have got too little.'[73]

In August, Deirdre had her biggest break to date when she created a leading role in Kenneth MacMillan's *Agon*. She and Ronald Hynd introduced the various episodes (some thought them Bordello-keepers-come-Greek Chorus, others the uncaring Fates) her dancing subtly combining ironic touches of humour with underlying menace. Alhough *Agon* survived only a few performances, critics and audience had taken note.

The Royal Ballet operated on a strict hierarchical system. 'We were the untouchables at the bottom – one didn't speak unless one was spoken to,' recalled Monica Mason, who joined the company in 1958. 'But I could see that Michael was a very approachable, human person ... and he loved the company and he loved the younger dancers ...' He and Deirdre were '*wonderful* to the new people' inviting a group to supper 'because they just wanted to get to know us and they were both absolutely charming, so sweet ... I thought, I'm sure this is unusual, I'm not sure that everybody in the company will do this, and they didn't. I think Michael liked to get to know everybody in the company and I think that must have been probably how he always was and went on to be so that his involvement was with young people.'[74]

Another young dancer making her mark was Antoinette Sibley, first as the Fairy of the Crystal Fountain and then, at the end of the season, in Blue Bird pas de deux with Graham Usher. Somes coached Usher and Jill Gregory Sibley, but Somes took their final rehearsals together. He could not resist flirting with the pretty nineteen-year-old, which was difficult for both Dixon and Sibley, who had always been friends; Sibley remembers that it went no further 'but ... you were aware there was always the possibility that it could ...'[75] Monica Mason summed it up as 'really naughty'.

At the end of the London season, Robert Irving left to become Music Director of New York City Ballet. Somes had admired his work and wrote him 'a lovely & emphatic letter as well as giving me that delicious Russian box,

73 Clive Barnes, *The Royal Ballet (I) at Covent Garden, last season's debuts, Dance and Dancers*, September 1958, p28

74 Interview with author

75 Interview with author

which I love more than anything else I have been given. I shall really miss you almost the most, because you have always stood not only for the best in artistry but the highest integrity and sincerity: and I am sure I shall never work with anybody who surpasses you in these qualities. I hope to see you in the *highest* positions before long ...'[76]

That autumn Somes was working on Ashton's *Ondine*: Palemon (Somes) deserts fiancée Berta (Farron) and marries the water nymph Ondine (Fonteyn); when she is reclaimed by Tirrenio, Lord of the Mediterranean Sea (Grant), Palemon marries Berta, but when Ondine returns, he begs forgiveness, knowing her kiss will be fatal. Ashton's first choice as composer was William Walton, who was reluctant to commit himself and suggested Hans Werner Henze, Somes' 1948 German fan who was also a great admirer of Ashton, especially *Scènes de ballet*. For the first time, Ashton had to work to a tape recording and the constant stopping and starting exacerbated the tensions of creation and the extremely complex score, with intricate cross-rhythms and phrasing, was not of a kind to inspire his lyrical invention; it did not always evoke the flow and surge of water and the dancers felt it didn't always reflect the scenario, leading to long arguments between Fonteyn, Somes and Farron. Grant remembered a lot of sitting around while Ashton worked on the long scenes for Ondine and Palemon: 'Michael wasn't happy, and Ashton would just sit there and wait and say "I want this" and they had to work it out and it took *ages*."'[77] When Somes recalled how Ashton could create a beautiful effect from his seemingly impossible visions he added 'But not always.' *Ondine*'s creation seemed full of 'not always' mornings.

Inspired by the sea, Ashton's choreography flowed unbroken, melding dance and mime, passing from solo to pas de deux with hardly a break. The ballet is a restatement of Fonteyn, capturing her qualities so perfectly that future generations can discern from the ballet her very essence. So much was it perceived as 'her' ballet that some hardly acknowledged Somes, even writing as though she performed the pas de deux on her own, yet the heart of the ballet lies in those pas de deux, which owe so much to his particular skills. The first developed from Palemon pressing Ondine's hand to his heart; she was afraid, for water nymphs don't have hearts, and the pas de deux followed naturally from his attempts to reassure her. 'Of all the many *pas de deux* Ashton has created for Fonteyn and Somes, this is perhaps the truest and purest,' wrote Barnes.[78] Ondine caressing Palemon's hair, was breathtaking in its simple truth.

The second scene, set in Lila de Nobili's dreamlike gauze forest, was virtually

---

76 Robert Irving to MS, undated

77 Interview with author

78 Clive Barnes, *Ondine, Production and Choreography, Dance and Dancers*, December 1958, pp9-13

an extended love duet with the corps de ballet swirling and submerging the lovers like waves and forming groups inspired by fountains and waterfalls. The poignant Act III duet of passion and farewell was Ashton's last great creation for his ideal cast. Somes made everything look easy, but they were full of tension lifts, which future casts found very difficult. His only solo came in Act I, expressing solitude and sorrow through the slow pirouettes and arabesques that had been so effective in *Sylvia*; a variation was later added in Act III, but it was long, difficult to sustain and contributed nothing to the character.

Overall, Palemon was an ungrateful role. Somes played him as the ideal Romantic hero, intense in ardour, moving in remorse, but Ashton had given no rational motivation for his fluctuating emotions. His virile movement and naturalness helped give the ballet some reality, but Palemon could have been the fulcrum, embodying the Romantic dilemma between woman as spirit and woman as flesh. Berta, however, was a cypher, a plot necessity, the conventional wronged woman who hardly had a scene with Palemon. It was left to Tirrenio, swirling a wonderful cloak, to 'rage through the ballet with the magnificent air of controlling its destiny'.[79] When young choreographers were turning to contemporary themes, could even Ashton go on drawing on the myths and style of another age? He was working within his comfort zone, knowing that Fonteyn and Somes would always deliver and, indeed, there were twenty-five calls on the first night on 27 October. Reviews were ecstatic for Fonteyn, otherwise respectfully guarded.

The pas de deux from *Ondine* was the highlight of a gala organised by Fonteyn in aid of the Royal Academy of Dancing, of which she was President. The galas became an annual event on the London ballet scene, featuring established stars and introducing younger dancers. Usually attended by the Queen Mother or Princess Margaret, they were equally notable for the audience's amazing millinery.

At the end of November, Fonteyn and Somes were due to dance *Giselle* in Munich, where Alan Carter was now in charge of the ballet. Just before leaving London, Somes received a letter from 10 Downing Street, saying that he was to be recommended for a CBE in the New Year Honours List and asking if this 'would be agreeable to you'. It was a significant honour for Somes was the first male dancer to be nominated – a fitting tribute to his achievements. Although traditionally such honours remain secret until their announcement, he told Fonteyn and Carter, and they celebrated with a quiet drink in a country inn. *Giselle* was met with a 20 minute ovation.

With scheduled flights now established throughout Europe, guesting plans were becoming almost too optimistic. On 3 December, they were scheduled

---

79　Clive Barnes, *Ondine, Dancing, Dance and Dancers*, December 1958, p13 to leave Munich in the morning and Somes was programmed for *Rinaldo and Armida* with Beriosova and *The Firebird* with Fonteyn that evening at Covent Garden. However, fog delayed their take off and Somes did not arrive back in time for *Rinaldo and Armida*; as he was the only one who knew the role, *Swan Lake* Act II had to be substituted, although he and Fonteyn did just make it in time for *The Firebird.*

Over Christmas, Somes and Fonteyn appeared in a television transmission of *The Nutcracker* arranged for television by Peter Wright, the first time Somes had ever appeared in the full ballet. In a blonde wig, he still looked the traditional handsome Prince, but effects that came easily a few years before were now obviously costing him more effort. However, at the 10th anniversary performances of *Cinderella* Clive Barnes still thought him dancing 'with characteristic verve'.

On 1 January, the day his CBE was announced, Somes was singled out in all the papers and on the radio news; telegrams and congratulations flooded in and he was filmed arriving at Covent Garden that evening to partner Beriosova in *Cinderella*. He made his entrance to a huge, warm ovation, '... a heart-catching moment,' reported Barnes, 'to hear and participate in this public demonstration to a man who has done so much to raise the standard of male dancing in the national ballet'.[80] At the end, he was presented with a laurel wreath and the company ran from the stage to make him take a solo call and pelted him with roses from the wings. Afterwards, he gave a select party, making a speech in which he remembered 'all who also deserved it'.

'I was amazed' Somes told *Dance and Dancers*, 'though I don't feel that in any way I deserve it ... I am very glad to think that it also means recognition for the male dancers in our company.'[81] They felt so too: 'We feel that we have all been honoured,' one of the youngest told de Valois.[82] The bitchy ballet gossip was that he got it for never dropping Fonteyn. Somes was often underrated by everyone except his colleagues.

A spate of interviews and articles followed and, when he guested in Monte Carlo with Fonteyn the following week, he was toasted by Onassis and his distinguished guests. For once he openly enjoyed the fuss. Always looking for new challenges, he and Fonteyn had hoped to perform a new pas de deux by Kenneth MacMillan based on the Orpheus legend, to Milhaud music with designs by Nicholas Georgiadis, but unfortunately MacMillan couldn't fit it into his schedule, so they performed a pas de deux from *Ondine* in a set designed by Levasseur.

In February came a new challenge when Fonteyn and Somes became

---

80 Clive Barnes, *The Royal Ballet (I) at Covent Garden, Cinderella revival, Dance and Dancers,* February 1959, pp30-31

81 *Curtain Up!, Dance and Dancers,* February 1959, p22

82 *Michael Somes, C.B.E., Dancing Times,* February 1959, p229

25 Arriving in Japan, 1959.

the first British dancers to appear in Japan, performing *Swan Lake* and *The Sleeping Beauty* with the Masahide Komaki Company. Komaki had trained in Manchuria and in 1946 formed a company from the only twenty-seven dancers in Japan; by 1959 he could have selected from two thousand. Although some of his dancers had studied with Preobrajenska and Antony Tudor, most of the few Japanese teachers got their technical knowledge from books. As traditional in Japanese theatre, the dancers gave their services in return for training, expenses and food, with occasionally a little money when rehearsing and performing.

Fonteyn was stranded in Biarritz with 'flu, so Somes had to endure the nightmare forty-three hour journey alone and the reception in Tokyo: '... there were literally hundreds of photographers & all the officials lined up! There they were laying out a great red carpet & white ropes, for me to walk thro'!! – I *did* feel a fool! ... I had to ... stand on the steps of the plane & be photographed ... Then the B(ritish). C(ouncil). rep greeted me & his wife & Komaki & Embassy people & goodness knows who! I was wafted thro the Customs & V.I.P.d up to the reception hall & *there* – the whole Japanese ballet etc. all in their traditional kimonos etc. were waiting!! They all clapped & cheered ... I had to be photographed & make a statement for the Press etc & eventually with relief was whisked off in a big car! Thankfully, they had been forewarned abt. Margot & were very nice abt. it ... Tokyo is *hideous* ... dark heavy, gloomy & forbidding ... I never want to go on these long trips anymore.'[83] He had to go through it all again when Fonteyn arrived, even

83 MS to ES 21 February 1959

26 *The Sleeping Beauty* with the Masahide Komaki Company, Japan 1959.

speaking for her as, in Japan, women did not speak in public.

Komaki's productions were totally unfamiliar so adapting was difficult and time consuming. There was much else to get used to. Japanese stages were mostly wide, but unnervingly shallow; dressing rooms were unisex with tables and mirrors designed to be used kneeling on the floor. Equally disconcerting was Japanese food, then unknown in Europe. Leslie Milligan of the British Embassy remembered Somes 'seated in front of a large Japanese dish, gazing with pale face at a vast quantity of what my mother would have called 'with wash', with a few dubiously anatomical bits floating about ...'[84] Their translator, Ayako Ogawa, who danced the Lilac Fairy, had studied at The Royal Ballet School and had a trick of putting Western names into Japanese characters and then translating them back – by which process Michael Somes became 'Crazy dancing horse' and Margot Fonteyn 'Everytime you dance you soar up into heaven'.

They opened in Tokyo on 24 February moving on to Nagoya, Osaka and Kyoto, finishing back in Tokyo on 11 March. Everywhere they were treated as important celebrities – reception after reception, radio and newspaper interviews, massive press coverage and the Union Jack flying outside their Osaka hotel. Yomuiro newspapers, who were sponsoring the tour, looked after every detail and covered them in luxury. It was a triumph, the famously

84 Leslie Milligan to MS 30 March 1959

undemonstrative Japanese even applauding in the middle of the pas de deux and solos and shouting 'Nihon Ichi', a cry more usually heard at football matches.

The two guest stars became very close to the company. '... these are not amateur enterprises in presentation,' Somes reported, 'and standards, considering the conditions, are remarkably high.'[85] He recognised the Japanese dancers' natural facility, which had taken them a long way in a short time, but worried they had to take other jobs to survive.

Lincoln Kirstein was in Japan and wrote Somes one of his periodic fan letters: 'I wanted to say again what a beautiful performance you gave last night. It was transparent that every little girl in the company pinned you with rays of love; your encouragement and sweetness with them made an unforgettable performance.'[86]

Thousands were turned away from the last performance, attended by the British Ambassador and several Japanese Princes and Princesses. Most of the company were in tears, especially the love-lorn girls; they gave Somes a pair of cuff links to add to his already extensive collection, and every dancer brought some little gift – which moved him greatly, knowing how poor they were. Yomuiro newspapers presented him with an 8mm movie camera and a superb photographic record of the visit.

They left on 13 March, and, despite the flight being at 7am, the whole company 'waved & cried & sang us away!! ... *quite* fantastic – the *most ever*!!'[87] General opinion was that two British dancers had had more impact than previous visits by the Bolshoi and New York City Ballet; the British Council felt that they had done more for British prestige in a few days than they could do in years: 'I hope that you will take not a little of the credit unto yourself.' Milligan wrote to Somes. 'I thought that your attitude throughout a 'difficult' tour from your point of view – was so exactly right ... I have had a very touching and in many ways moving letter from Komaki, which shows how much he owes to you both.'[88]

Into the 1970s, Somes would advise and help Japanese dancers to train in London.

While he was in Japan, he missed another important milestone in Deirdre's career, when she was one of the three leading couples in Ashton's *La Valse* at the Royal Ballet Benevolent Fund gala on 10 March. Following her success in *Agon*, she was now dancing leading solo roles and Somes could be optimistic about her future.

---

85 MS British Council lecture, 1961

86 Lincoln Kirstein to MS nd

87 MS to ES 25 March 1959

88 Leslie Milligan to MS 30 March 1959

From Japan he and Fonteyn embarked on a three-day flight to New Zealand to dance *Giselle* and *Swan Lake* with the Royal Ballet 'second' company. Although Somes could be dismissive of the touring section, he thought they were dancing '*very well* indeed,' adding dryly, 'being free from all the restrictions & miseries of the poor people at C. Garden. It makes such a difference – they are much happier, & consequently, work so much better ...'[89]

New Zealand rarely saw world class performers and there was intense interest in their performances. In Christchurch on 19 March, their entrances in *Giselle* were greeted with two minutes' applause and there was a huge ovation at the end. Police held back the crowds as they left the theatre. At their second performance on 21 March the audience 'went quite mad ... they had cordons of police holding back the crowd ... & they had to drive the car into the Scene Dock to get us out!! They showered the stage with rose petals & threw streamers etc. They then all ran back to the hotel which was just around the corner, & did it all over again.'[90]

Somes had his first sight of Somes Island as they flew into Wellington – a tiny jewel embraced by the huge harbour. *Swan Lake* was a triumph and the next day he and Fonteyn processed through the streets with the Mayor and mace bearer, to a reception attended by Prime Minster Walter Nash. From Wellington, they went on to dance *Giselle* in Auckland; en route, during a brief stop in Masterton, over a thousand gathered outside their hotel and they had to make a balcony appearance to acknowledge the crowd.

For once time dragged, as they were not dancing every night and they had time for private sightseeing, or as private as celebrity allowed: when they went to visit a sheep station Somes was very touched when workers at the local butter-factory came in specially to give them a demonstration. 'Outside, the whole village had got to hear of our visit & were all lined up "gawping"! ... They drove us home & on the way they stopped in a little town as a crowd had gathered outside the local Woolworth's as they had heard (from the engine-driver on our train out)!, – that we were going through, & they wanted to see us!! So we had to stop, & speak to them, & they were *so* thrilled!!'[91]

In Wellington, local historians confirmed Somes Island's connection to Joseph Somes, and only now his astonished descendent learned that one of Samuel Somes' ships was the Samuel and Sarah. The island was currently a quarantine station and access restricted, but an exception was made on 1 April; accompanied by the Minister of Agriculture, his wife, high officials and photographers, Somes was whisked across to the unspoiled, steep-cliffed island, magically sited in one of the world's most beautiful harbours. The caretaker's wife produced a wonderful home-made lunch, which Somes

89 MS to ES p 20 March 1959
90 MS to ES 25 March 1959
91 MS to ES (28) March 1959

enjoyed more than any official function, before reluctantly dashing back for a dance teachers meeting.

The tour was financially rewarding, bringing Somes about £940 (£15,400) after tax and expenses in New Zealand, as well as £833 (£13,600) plus 'Yen loot' in Japan. This was considerably above his London salary, which was, of course, in abeyance while he was guesting away from the company. Overall, however, it was not an easy tour – the stresses of travel, social events, public commitments and adapting to so many different productions were beginning to tell; letters home were full of complaints about his developing arthritis and increasingly troublesome knee; his virility, simplicity of approach and superb sense of style remained and his partnering was as magnificent as ever, but lifting was becoming a strain and solos took more effort, detracting from his phrasing. Neither he nor Fonteyn could be taken for young lovers, but expert stagecraft compensated for youthful ardour.

On 9 April, Fonteyn and Somes travelled from New Zealand to San Francisco, where she waved him off to London and joined Arias on his launch, the Nola. What followed made headlines around the world and nearly created an international incident. After the holiday, Arias sailed away and Fonteyn returned to Panama, where she was arrested and jailed amid rumours that her husband was running arms to use against the Panamanian Government and stories of a sunken launch loaded with guns and ammunition. The British Ambassador secured her release and she returned to London to a media frenzy. With Arias in sanctuary in the Brazilian Embassy in Panama City, she was the picture of innocence as she protested her ignorance of any plot against anyone. Events became more surreal as the press speculated on the involvement of John Wayne, Errol Flynn, a 'mystery' woman and claims of impounded letters implicating Fonteyn in the plot.

Unusually Somes went into print in a front page interview. 'I do not believe in ... Margot ('the Rebel'). I never shall ... I frankly believe that her husband's political career in Panama has always been a mystery to her ... You cannot share the life we have shared in ballet together for all these years and still keep secrets from each other.' Fonteyn, he declared, had only two loyalties, career and husband, and her loyalty to the latter was so great that, if he committed murder, she would stick by him.[92] His intuition was correct.[93]

On 8 May, Somes and Deirdre went to Buckingham Palace for the investiture; he was surprised and gratified when the Queen told him how

---

92 Interview with Joan Powe, unidentified press cutting, 24 April 1959, Vivien Matthews scrapbooks, Theatre and Performance Collections V&A

93 Recently released papers show that, although Fonteyn knew what was going on, she had no realistic understanding of the situation; Somes was right – she had no comprehension of politics, except in relation to her husband.

much she had enjoyed the gala for the Shahanshah of Iran the previous evening at which Somes had danced Act II of *Cinderella* with Beriosova.

Hardly had Fonteyn arrived back from Panama than she and Somes left to guest in *Swan Lake* with the Polish National Ballet in Warsaw. Somes reluctantly agreed only after being told that it was a top priority request from the Foreign Office. On the way to Heathrow on 16 May, he called into the new company rehearsal rooms at the Royal Ballet School in Barons Court to see Deirdre; he missed her but managed to speak to her from the airport.

Warsaw was a nightmare. They arrived at the theatre to find no ballet master and no conductor. The next day they started at 10am '& have been going ever since, with no food, except for ½ hr. break till now – 7! The worst thing is we find the version *absolutely* & *completely* different, – not *one* step the same, & at times it looked hopeless for us to ever *try* & learn how to fit in ... but it's almost impossible in the short time with the language problem. We haven't the faintest idea *what* we're doing & how we are going to manage tomorrow at the orch. rehearsal ... Margot is her usual vague self!! & doesn't seem too concerned ...'[94] Unusually, they had to make notes and Somes was so worried that he got up in the night to run through them.

Whatever the problems, the first performance on 20 May was a 'fabulous success ... It was simply terrific & we had to repeat the coda in Act III. They tore the place down, & they say they've never heard an ovation like it before, & that we've done more good than anything for years for British prestige! ... How we did it, I'll never know! – No one else cld possibly have even attempted it!!'[95] The next day they toured the new opera house and school 'which is fabulous, – makes ours look like a village shop!! & as for the new Opera being built, – that is quite fantastic. It took 2 hrs. to just go over *part* of it ... marvellous rehearsal rooms – d. rooms restaurants, laundry rooms terraces foyers, – scene docks ... '[96] and followed this with a visit to two Polish folk dance companies. Their second performance on 22 May went as well as the first: '...They want us to do an extra performance on Sat night, but I really don't think we'll have the strength ... but they say the people of Warsaw love us so that they threaten to tear down the Opera if we don't!! ... longing to get home – this has been quite a 'do' & Mrs H(ookham). drives me nuts!! ... Never again!! ... We have never had to work so hard & I've never gone on the stage with such trepidation.'[97] Fonteyn, knowing she could rely on Somes, remained calm throughout.

Back in London, Deirdre was working on a Sunday Ballet Club

94 MS to ES 16 May 1959

95 MS to ES 20 May 1959

96 Covent Garden was then years away from a basic overhaul, and decades from building new facilities

97 MS to ES 20 May 1959

27 After receiving the CBE at Buckingham Palace with Deirdre.

performance. One evening she confessed to Antoinette Sibley that she had a terrible headache that wouldn't go away. '... the song at the time was "Stay as sweet as you are, don't let a thing ever change you."' remembers Sibley: 'She started singing it (and) said "You should remember that always, just stay as sweet as you are, whatever happens to you." It was so weird because I never saw her again.'[98]

---

98 Interview with author

Somes was at a dinner party in Warsaw when he received a telegram telling him that Deirdre was in hospital.[99] He returned on 23 May to find her critically ill with a cerebral abscess and meningitis. She briefly rallied, but on 27 May slipped into unconsciousness and died at 2.30 am the following morning. She was 25.

Although meningitis is viral in origin, a cerebral abscess can be the result of a head injury and Somes was convinced that her death was connected to the injuries received in the car crash before their marriage and he felt responsible. It was announced that he would not be appearing for a while and Blair partnered Fonteyn on Sunday Night at the London Palladium on 31 May, yet on the evening of Deirdre's funeral he danced Palemon. He was the only dancer who knew the role, so without him the performance would have to be cancelled; he felt he could not disappoint Fonteyn's public and maybe performing Palemon's betrayal and loss was cathartic. The rest of the season was a great strain and Estelle Herf noted, 'watching him with Fonteyn one became conscious of the common bond of sadness between them ...'[100]

Keeping busy helped hold memories at bay and gradually he was able to talk about his loss to friends, like Company Manager Michael Wood. He could not bear to go back to their home in Lloyd Square and hated going back to the Riviera, which held so many memories, but had to when Fonteyn was guesting.

In mid-June, Fonteyn arranged performances of *Giselle* in Brazil as a thank you for giving sanctuary to her husband in their Panama City Embassy. She and Somes later returned for a Red Cross gala and a short tour with a twelve-strong company – 'the kind of tour that is marvellous to do when one is young' she remembered. She was 40, Somes nearly 42.

Recognising his deteriorating technique, Somes would happily have given up, but he and Fonteyn had a pact that they would go together and if she wanted to guest, he could not refuse. She was often accompanied by 'the tribe' – her husband, her mother, occasionally brother Felix and wife Phoebe or friends – which Somes found wearing and left him feeling very isolated. Every time her career seemed to peak, she simply moved onto a higher level. Others were technically stronger, but, despite problems with her left foot, she was dancing better than ever. Talk about farewells and retirement usually ended with her airily saying that she would probably decide almost on the day.

The Opera House decided that firm action was required, and announced that henceforward Fonteyn would become a guest artist with The Royal Ballet. This recognised her increasing periods away from her home company,

---

99 There were thirteen at the dinner: Somes would never again sit down at a table for thirteen.

100 Estelle Herf, *Editor's Log, Ballet Today*, July 1959, p3

and that 'it is also right that Dame Margot's time should be completely at her own disposal, and not subject to the demands and policy of the Royal Ballet.' Prices were raised for her performances resulting in audiences that 'had something of the sleek and glassy look of the people who customarily turn up for La Callas' reported Clive Barnes.[101]

Changing her status, did not immediately change the fact that Somes went where she went, but it was a sign that she could no longer rely on him always being available as plans for his long-term future were coming to a head.

As the season closed, Michael Wood wrote to Somes about de Valois' plans. 'I am sorry it is only "half a cake" just now – but the whole cake will come in a far shorter time than Ninette thinks. No one of her temperament takes kindly to a division of labour or authority – but she neither wants to stop it nor eventually can. It is your problem and to some extent mine to make it painless & unnoticeable ... come back ready & fit both for the frustrations and also the eventual fun & pleasure of creating something both out of what you have already made yourself and also *on* what Ninette herself has already built. There is so much to do – & very very few to do it.' He concluded with a wish 'to see you where you are going to be'.[102]

De Valois' immediate plans included a remedy for Somes' deep depression following Deirdre's death. Believing in the therapeutic effect of work, she scheduled him to rehearse 20-year-old Antoinette Sibley and Pirmin Trecu in *Ballet Imperial* for the season opening in autumn 1959.

Like many ballet-besotted girls, the 9-year-old Sibley at the Cone-Ripman School had mooned over photographs of Somes and she and her friend Sally Judd decided they would marry Somes and Festival Ballet (now English National Ballet) star, John Gilpin, respectively.[103] When she moved to Sadler's Wells School, however, the students went mostly to matinées at Sadler's Wells, 'so our heroes and heroines weren't Margot Fonteyn and Michael Somes, they were Beriosova, Fifield, MacMillan, Cranko.'[104] She first set foot on the Covent Garden stage on 2 January 1956 as a last-minute substitute Swan.

Ballet Imperial rehearsals were fraught: '... it was his new career, so he was trying to prove himself too ... he needed it to be good for Madam ... he was an *utter* perfectionist and this ballet meant so much to him ... it was really frightening because I just decided I'm not up to this, I must get out of this, I'm a disaster, every single day.' Every rehearsal she was in tears. 'Some people said it was cruel and didn't like it. It was very, very depressing and

101	Clive Barnes, *Fonteyn assoluta, Dance and Dancers,* August 1959, p16

102	Michael Wood to MS 23 June 1959

103	Both achieved their ambitions

104	Interview with author

debilitating ... but in the end and after *years* of working with him you knew that ... the only reason he was pushing you was he knew you could do it.'[105]

She could. The performance on 25 August was '... a *huge* success and thanks have to go 98% to Somes through all the tears, through everything.'[106] De Valois now made a huge leap of faith and scheduled her as Odette-Odile with the Touring Company on 26 September. She had ten days to learn the role, make her debut as the Bride in *La Fête étrange* and her company debut as Swanilda in *Coppélia*. 'Because it's a bit tight,' de Valois told her with magnificent understatement, 'Michael Somes is going to work with you and do the first performance with you.' 'By now this is Alice in Wonderland ... I knew it was all wrong – me with Michael Somes ... the premier danseur noble, this icon ...'[107] Daily, Sibley did her own warm up, worked with Somes from 9am to 10.15am, then joined company class and rehearsals; de Valois' only concession was to allow her the Friday evening before her debut matinée off. The performance was so successful that, the following week, she replaced an indisposed Nadia Nerina on tour, partnered by Bryan Ashbridge.

Early in the morning of 24 October, Somes phoned Sibley to say she was on in *Swan Lake* that night at Covent Garden. Thinking he was referring to her scheduled performance in the Pas de trois, she thought no more about it until he rang again to say that Fonteyn had offered her some of her own rehearsal time. He had to spell it out: 'Nadia's off and you're doing Odette-Odile.' Sibley went through rehearsals in a daze, and Fonteyn sitting in to help did nothing to calm her nerves.

Word quickly spread among the ballet audience, and that night the Opera House buzzed with expectation. Sibley more than fulfilled everyone's hopes. Her performance was fresh, youthful yet authoritative and her musical phrasing exquisite, but she admitted that Somes got her through – 'I might have been doing *Beauty* for all I knew.'[108] 'Somes, standing in the background with proud reticence, was superb.' wrote Barnes. 'I have never admired him more.'[109] That night he made an exception to his leaving-by-the-side-door rule and accompanied his protegée through the stage door, his pride in her achievement there for all to see.

'The overnight star' was jam for the media and the performance made radio and television news and pictures in every newspaper. The following weekend, Sibley and Somes topped the bill on Sunday Night at the London Palladium, and all England knew about her. Then the fairy tale spilled over

---

105 Interview with author

106 Interview with author

107 Interview with author

108 Interview with author

109 Clive Barnes, *Sibley in full-length Rôle*, *Dance and Dancers*, December 1959, p29

28 Somes coaching Antoinette Sibley for her first *Swan Lake* in 1959.

29 Somes teaching at the Royal Ballet School in the late 1950s.

into real life: '... of course I fell hook, line and sinker in love – doing *Swan Lake* which is such a soulful, *huge* passion of the heart and with this man – that was it!'[110]

'Remember,' Sibley told Barbara Newman, '... every girl was affected by him ... everybody was a little bit in love with Michael. He was the top dancer, the most handsome man – he was like Rock Hudson, Paul Newman, his looks were like a film star ... he had been through the most huge ordeal himself with Deirdre dying – but he was wonderful to me.'[111] They were together for the next decade. He thought her supremely talented and his admiration and belief gave her confidence. 'The best *répétiteur* in the world she ever had was Michael Somes,' declared de Valois. '... naturally she was ambitious, and most artists like the old Svengali idea; they're always looking for someone who will bring them out, they have an instinct for the person who will do it for them ...'[112]

In the meantime, however, lest the ballyhoo get out of proportion and expectations become unreasonable, de Valois sent Sibley to join the Touring Company's tour in South Africa, where she could develop out of the limelight. When she returned, her career would be in Somes' hands.

On 29 October, five days after Sibley's *Swan Lake*, Somes created Creon in *Antigone*, John Cranko's most ambitious ballet to date. Set to a dramatic score commissioned from Mikis Theodorakis and danced in a striking, timeless setting by Mexican painter Rufino Tamayo, which suggested the requisite mystery and terror, *Antigone* centered on the contest for the Theban crown between Creon and Antigone's brothers Polynices and Etiocles; after the brothers' deaths in battle, Creon orders that Polynices remain unburied and when Antigone defies him, he orders her buried alive and she commits suicide. Creon is left alone, having achieved the crown but at the cost of alienating his people. Cramming everything into forty minutes resulted in a lack of focus: '... where' asked Alexander Bland, 'was the sound of fate, the great pile-driver, pounding home its blows?'[113]

On the plus side, the characters were not conventional ballet heroes and heroines, although the dancers had to work in broad outlines. Blair (bullish) and Gary Burne (hysterical) were the warring brothers, Beriosova made a lyrically poignant Antigone with Donald MacLeary gravely sensitive as her lover Haemon. Creon, alone had scope for development and Somes relished the subtle, scheming politician who, as Buckle observed, could 'freeze the

---

110 Interview with author
111 Barbara Newman, *Antoinette Sibley*, Hutchinson, London, 1986, p113
112 Interview with author
113 Alexander Bland, *Theban Mix-up*, *Observer*, 25 October 1959

back row of the gallery by raising a finger.'[114] He invested his gestures with an underlying hint of menace and treachery and, at the end, alone in empty triumph clutching the blood-stained crown, he achieved an epic grandeur.

Audiences received *Antigone* warmly. Critics were split, but all praised Somes: '... an exceptionally strong piece of mature acting in the Bolshoi manner,' wrote Haskell. 'Somes is constantly developing, the noble young prince will give life to the great character rôles, the tenor become a *basso robusto*.'[115] In New York, Cranko was accused of trespassing on Martha Graham's preserves, although she was observed standing and applauding with tears running down her face.

From political manipulator, Somes returned to romantic lover for the RAD Gala matinee on 26 November. Karsavina, who had danced Raymonda in St. Petersburg, had long wanted Ashton to choreograph the full ballet, but he thought the story weak; *Raymonda scène d'amour* for Fonteyn as Raymonda and Somes as Jean de Brienne as he leaves for the Crusades was his toe in the water. The result was Ashtonian Petipaesque, with a typical dying fall when the lovers sank into a last embrace, Raymonda put Jean's cloak around his shoulders and held it as he walked away until it fell from her grasp. It was a restatement of a remarkable partnership and their skill in creating atmosphere and emotion even in the shortest works. Somes' warrior-lover epitomised romantic chivalry, though not helped by an unflattering pudding basin wig and a Leslie-Hurry designed tabard worn for his entrance and exit. He was moved when Karsavina told him how 'lovely' she had found it. It was the last choreography Ashton created for him and Fonteyn.

While Ashton had always seen Somes as a romantic, idealised figure, the younger choreographers valued his dramatic talents, as seen in the roles created for him by Rodrigues and Cranko. Now Kenneth MacMillan wanted him to create the Husband in *The Invitation*, which he was choreographing for The Royal Ballet Touring Company. While admiring MacMillan's work, Somes resisted all blandishments, as he disliked the idea of performing the climactic rape scene.

There were other signs that he was moving on, like his part in the creation of *Song of the Earth*.

In 1959, MacMillan proposed a ballet to Mahler's *Das Lied von der Erde*. The Ballet Sub-Committee thought that it could be a major artistic event and worth consideration, if the considerable problems could be resolved; these included finding conductors and singers who could fit into a repertory schedule and the high costs of singers, orchestra rehearsal and performing rights.

---

114 Richard Buckle, *Putting on the Agony*, *Sunday Times*, 25 October 1959

115 Arnold L. Haskell, *Royal Ballet at the Royal Opera House "Antigone"*, Ballet Annual 1961 p17

Musicians, who revered Mahler's masterpiece, would probably be horrified, and trouble was also possible from Mahler's widow, Alma, one of those designated by Pierre Boulez as the 'unmerry widows', notoriously over-protective of their deceased husbands' works. Somes was asked to sound out the likely response. He consulted Adrian Boult, who contacted Mahler's pupil, legendary conductor Bruno Walter: Walter thought the idea almost sacrilegious and was adamant that he could not approve 'no matter with what reverence the task would be approached ... such an enterprise would be entirely alien to the composer's intention.'[116] Boult therefore advised that, while Alma Mahler, her daughter Anna and Walter were alive, it would 'not be right' to go ahead. 'It may be that later on one might consider it.' he wrote to Somes. 'I am not sure, for somehow I feel that the human voice linked with a stage interpretation would hardly work, but I should be most interested to hear all about it some time, though of course I am not a Ballet expert.'[117] MacMillan created *Le Baiser de la fée* instead.[118]

The bond with Fonteyn was loosening as Somes shed some of his most personal roles. 29 October would have been a poignant evening if anyone had known that it was their last *Sylvia* together; on 11 November they danced their final *Swan Lake* and 9 December, he bid farewell to *Symphonic Variations* and *Daphnis and Chloë*. Not that he was performing less in the roles he had retained, and indeed still often went beyond the call of duty. In December, for a hastily arranged midnight performance in aid of the victims of the Fréjus dam collapse in France, he and Fonteyn chose the perfect gala piece, the *Birthday Offering* pas de deux, although it meant extra rehearsals as it was not in the repertory. Somes had already partnered Anya Linden in her Firebird debut earlier that evening.[119]

Over Christmas, he starred with Fonteyn in Margaret Dale's television adaptation of *The Sleeping Beauty*, with Sibley doubling a Prologue fairy and Princess Florine to Brian Shaw's Blue Bird. Shot mainly in profile, Somes was wonderfully melancholic in the vision scene, scrambled through some effective briars to reach the enchanted palace and in the awakening close up looked exactly what any right-minded Princess would like to wake up to after a hundred years. However, Dale's assistant Peter Wright, remembered him being extremely tired because he was working so hard at Covent Garden, and

---

116 Bruno Walter to Adrian Boult, 13 November 1959

117 Adrian Boult to MS, 26 November 1959

118 When MacMillan resubmitted the idea in 1964, the proposal was rejected out of hand. He created *Song of the Earth* for Stuttgart Ballet in 1964 and it was taken into the Royal Ballet repertory in 1966.

119 It was the kind of gala that would be impossible to arrange even at long notice today. Almost every star then appearing in the West End took part: Ralph Richardson, Laurence Olivier, Vivien Leigh, Paul Scofield, Joyce Grenfell, Leslie Caron, Jayne Mansfirld, the Crazy Gang, Charlton Heston, Peggy Ashcroft, Paul Robeson, Zizi Jeanmaire and Roland Petit.

30 International guesting in Monte Carlo at a gala marking Diaghilev anniversaries: left-right: Serge Lifar, Fonteyn and Somes in costume for *The Firebird*, Princess Grace of Monaco.

it certainly showed in his solo, although his partnering was as impeccable as ever.

New Year 1960 saw Fonteyn and Somes back in Monte Carlo for a gala celebrating fifty years since the Diaghilev Ballet's debut and thirty years since his death. Fonteyn was accompanied by her mother, Felix, Phoebe, niece Lavinia and friend Dalal Achcar – which exacerbated Somes' sense of isolation. Everywhere reminded him of Deirdre: 'It was very strange going down the familiar road, & of course I could see the Diodato & all the places we used to go to. The sea & the rocks looked so lovely... I remembered how we used to bathe off those very rocks, & how Deirdre once cut her leg on them & always had the scar till she died.'[120] Rehearsals were pretty haphazard, with so many stars with different demands and nobody particularly in charge. The gala, attended by Prince Rainier and Princess Grace brought out so much chinchilla that one wit suggested it must be another homage to Diaghilev. In a very mixed programme Fonteyn and Somes's *Firebird* pas de deux was

120 MS to ES p 29 December 1959

deemed a triumph and they repeated their success at the subsequent Ballet de Noël, dancing *The Nutcracker* and *Raymonda*.

Much surviving film comes from Somes' later years, when physical problems were increasing and his technique was in decline. A surer test of his talent is Paul Czinner's film *The Royal Ballet*, released in January 1960, which preserves his performances in *Swan Lake* Act II, *Ondine*, and his unrivalled Ivan in *The Firebird*. The film had been shot in January 1959, from 9am to 1am over one night mid-week and two Sundays, with one camera on a 65' platform over the stalls and orchestra pit and ten others around the auditorium. To overcome Fonteyn's dislike of filming's stop-start, Czinner divided the shooting schedule into ten minute takes, half an hour apart. He allowed the dance to breathe and used few closeups, an exception being Somes' subtle byplay in *The Firebird*. Even film critics who disliked, or knew nothing about, ballet were won over either by Czinner's presentation or by the performances. Ironically, they gave Somes more attention than the dance critics; Caroline Lejeune fleetingly mentioned Fonteyn but 'could hardly take my eyes off Michael Somes, who appears in all three ballets, powerfully and modestly. How on earth, I thought, would a *prima ballerina assoluta* manage without support like this?'[121]

On 28 January 1960, Ashton broke free of his dependency on Fonteyn and Somes, creating *La Fille mal gardée* for Nerina, Blair, Grant and Stanley Holden. Somes' first night gift came with the message: 'Just to wish you everything I can for your Masterwork ... I sincerely think it is the best thing you have done to date, – which is saying a lot!' The ballet was a total triumph and put Blair, with his virtuoso technique and ebullient personality, in a class of his own among younger male dancers.

It should not be forgotten that, throughout these hectic years, Somes was rehearsing and teaching alongside performing. From the late 1950s, besides company classes and coaching, he also taught at the School and worked with the students once annual public performances began in 1959. Lamenting later training that ignored the dramatic and emotional aspects of dance, Peter Wright recalled Somes teaching senior students: 'He'd say "Go and pick up that rose, smell it and let us know you can smell the perfume" – things like that.'[122] Embarrassing, but Somes knew that conviction was a lesson they had to learn: as he wrote '... ballet is *so* near the absurd mark, – especially the ones *we* do, – that if *we* find it difficult to believe in them, what abt. the audience.'[123]

Despite his increasing responsibilities and shedding some roles, there were

121 Caroline Lejeune, *Observer*, 10? January 1960
122 Interview with author
123 MS to ES p14 October 1957

few other signs of slowing down. He danced *Sylvia* pas de deux with Fonteyn at a gala in Bruges on 16 January 1960 and on 11 February they were in Milan, dancing *La Péri* and *Cinderella* pas de deux in a marathon programme which included two Balanchine ballets and a Massine premiere. Balanchine spent a lot of time with Somes, talking about his wife, Tanaquil Leclerc, whose glorious career had been ended by polio. Between performances, Fonteyn and Somes had to go to Rome for a showing of the *Ondine* film at the British Embassy and then to London for the dress rehearsal and first night of *Giselle* in the presence of the President of Peru before going back to complete their contract in Milan.

On 21 March, Somes was on the popular radio programme *Desert Island Discs*. His seven records included his favourite Berlioz ('Un bal' from *Symphonie Fantastique*), *Love Me a Little Today*, a revue number which Hilda Gaunt often played for class, and *Beim Schlafengehen* (*Upon Going to Sleep*) from Strauss's *Four Last Songs* in memory of Deirdre. His book was *Theatre Street* and the luxury a telescope 'so I can look at the stars and perhaps feel a little less lonely'. His unassuming manner, charm and emotional tribute to Deirdre won him a spate of fan letters.

Ashton's *Raymonda* pas de deux was on the programme at the Royal Ballet Benevolent Fund gala on 1 March, when Princess Margaret made her first public appearance with her fiancé Antony Armstrong-Jones. On 4 May Somes went to Buckingham Palace for the pre-wedding reception, and on 6 May was a guest in Westminster Abbey at the wedding. What do you give a Princess for a wedding present? For Somes music was, as usual, the only possible gift, in this case Verdi's *Macbeth*: presumably he had sounded out the recipients in advance.

On 13 April came another milestone, when Fonteyn and Somes led the company in *Cinderella*, the first full-length ballet to be transmitted on British television. Ashton worked with director, Mark Stuart on the adaptation, increasing the importance of the Jester from the start, revealing the seasons through the flames of the kitchen fire and each fairy bringing part of Cinderella's ball dress – Spring a coronet and Autumn two leaves transformed into slippers. Both leads came over well, but Mary Clarke, while admitting that the dancing was of the highest standard, complained that television highlighted things one could avoid in the theatre, like the 'gormless expressions' of those dressing the stage.

In May it was off again to Finland for a gala and four performances linked to the visit of Royal Navy ships to Helsinki, and yet another version of *Giselle*, this time by Leonid Lavrovsky, director of the acclaimed Bolshoi production. Somes had to cope with an uncharacteristically nervous Fonteyn, because Maya Plisetskaya was rumoured to be out front; having 'stumbled through the evening', they learned that she hadn't arrived in time.

31 Rehearsal for the television production of *Cinderella*: Fonteyn and Somes with director Mark Stuart.

In June they returned to South America, dancing *Giselle, La Péri, Raymonda* and *Sylvia* pas de deux in Argentina, Uruguay, Chile and Brazil. Having danced one *Giselle* in London and another in Finland, they now adapted to productions in Buenos Aires, and, for one night only, in Montevideo, and intense concentration was needed to avoid confusing the different versions. Press conferences, official lunches, post-show receptions, often not finishing until 3am, were fitted around long, tiring rehearsals which sometimes went on until midnight. There were the usual delayed flights and long journeys, often ending with a performance on the same day.

Somes always found late nights intolerable and, unlike Fonteyn, he could neither sleep nor cat nap on long journeys.

By now, 'exceptional reception' had become a cliché in Somes' letters home, but they really did get more and more extreme. In Buenos Aires the calls went on and on and they couldn't leave by the stage door for fear of being mobbed by near-hysterical girls screaming for Somes. In Montevideo, the great De Basil Ballets Russes dancer Yurek Shabelevsky was maître de ballet '& had made quite a good job of the small Co ... it's rather small & impoverished, & it's touching to see how absolutely thrilled they are to have us here even just for *one* performance, as they don't perform very often & don't have much money ... I shouldn't think there'll be anything left of us by the time we've done this little lot … we have Chile to cope with & then Brazil!! … I'm just plugging along, trying to get through all this somehow. Margot's leg seems alright, – but she gets *very* tired …'[124] Back in Buenos Aires, the demand was so great that they agreed to give an extra performance: '& it has nearly killed us … working all the time & what time we've had has been *packed* with social engagements … It just isn't worth it .. it really only suits Margot who naturally wants to get in with all these S(outh).A(merican). people… for *me* it's just Hell.'[125]

Amid the frenzied activity, Somes still kept an eye on upcoming talent. He was at the dress rehearsal of *Swan Lake* for the 1960 Royal Ballet School matinée when de Valois told one of the Pas de six boys that if he couldn't do the required turns to the right, he would be replaced. Somes sought out a devastated Anthony Dowell in the supers dressing room ('I mean, Health and Safety would have blown up if they'd seen it,' remembered Dowell), told him gently to pull himself together, took him into a nearby tiny practice room 'and he just pulled it to pieces – and found what was going wrong – try this, try that, spotting, the level of spotting,' until they had resolved the technical problem of making a naturally left turning dancer turn to the right. 'After that … if he saw me around the building … he'd take me into the room – 'Look at my hand' and up we'd go. He *cared*. He saw a talented person and he salvaged it.'[126] Sibley, still in South Africa, first heard about Dowell from Somes' letters.

Giselle featured large in 1960. That autumn, The Royal Ballet production, which had hardly changed since the 1930s, was at last overhauled. In consultation with Karsavina, the Queen of the Vintage and Berthe's miming of the wili legend were restored to Act I and Ashton created a charming new girl's variation in the Peasant pas de deux; Albrecht had more dancing and his actions were clarified, including reaching for the missing sword in the confrontation with Hilarion; Hilarion became less of a stereotype and the hitherto all-female village acquired six boys. Act II was influenced by the Lavrovsky production, which Somes had danced in Finland.

'… [I]t woudn't have been done at all if *I* hadn't pushed it along,' Somes wrote to Ethel, '& got Karsavina & went into all the music, etc. Never mind, – it came off, & that's the main thing'[127] and acknowledgment came from those who really counted: 'Yesterday at the rehearsal I was on the point of tears,' Karsavina wrote to him. 'Yours and Margot's performance moved me profoundly. It is you I am grateful to for understanding and remembering

---

124　MS to ES 12 June 1960
125　MS to ES 12 June 1960
126　Interview with author
127　MS to ES 3 October 1960

faithfully all that I tried to put back into Giselle, the Ballet dearest to me.'[128]

When the production was unveiled in New York on 30 September, the reception for Fonteyn and Somes almost surpassed that for the 1949 *Sleeping Beauty*. '... they all say I never danced better' Somes wrote home. ' ... *everyone* was terrific ... After the 1ˢᵗ Act Mad Scene the tension in the house was fantastic, & the whole production *felt* so much better than it ever has been ... in the 2ⁿᵈ Act ... I got terrific applause *during* & at the end of my solo ... at the end, – they just roared & roared away, & apparently we had abt. *20* calls ... De V & Freddy were thrilled & came round to congratulate me, – something *very* rare for *her*! – Jean (Gilbert) & Antoinette who were in front say they've never seen a perf. like it ... easily the best we'd done ... The notices have been terrific – for all of us & the production & I'm so pleased for Karsavina.'[129] Somes' input went publicly uncredited, although recognised by a select lunch party.

Even that first night reception paled before the final performance on 29 January 1961 when, for Arthur Todd, Fonteyn and Somes 'gave a performance of such soaring perfection that it will never be forgotten by those that witnessed it. For this observer, this evening was one of the six most majestic moments of ballet in the last quarter of a century.'[130]

The reception was all the more remarkable as it had been touch and go whether Somes would get on at all; he had been suffering severe rheumatism in his leg and only decided to risk appearing on the day of the performance. Treatment left him nearly free of pain for the first time in years, although he was warned that he was storing up trouble if he did not slow down.

Somes' Albrecht became overshadowed by the legendary Fonteyn/Nureyev performances, but in the 1950s Barnes was not alone in thinking it 'among the finest portrayals of the part in our time,'[131] while Todd in 1960 called it 'the most rounded interpretation of the rôle yet seen' in New York.[132] John Lanchbery, who saw myriad dancers over a long period from the conductor's podium, considered Somes' Albrecht one of the greatest he had seen.

Fonteyn and Somes dashed from New York to London for the 1960 RAD gala. Despite only having a few days, they actually considered reviving the ballroom scene from *Apparitions*, but it proved too much even for their stamina. They also threw in two performances of *Cinderella* during the Touring Company's Covent Garden season before returning to America.

Despite the acclaim, Somes knew that his dancing days were nearly over. In April 1961 he and Fonteyn danced *Giselle* with the Touring Company in

128　Tamara Karsavina to MS 31 August 1960

129　MS to ES 30 September 1960

130　Arthur Todd, *The Royal Ballet Triumphs Again*, Dance and Dancers, March 1961, p29

131　Clive Barnes, *Fonteyn assoluta*, Dance and Dancers, August 1959, p16

132　Arthur Todd, *The Royal Ballet in New York, Giselle*, Dance and Dancers, December 1960, p30

Tokyo and Osaka. They and conductor Emanuel Young watched a television recording of the performance. At the end, recalled Young, Somes said '"I'm handing in my resignation as a dancer ... If that's what people pay for they are being completely done out. I'm a ham actor ... I'm a stodgy dancer, I don't stay up in the air, I come down heavily and I'm not going to continue if that's what I look like." Michael's standards were so high and he didn't kid himself that he was God's gift to the world.'[133]

Pact or no pact, matters now came to a head. It was clear that Fonteyn, free of injury, was nowhere near retirement and The Royal Ballet could no longer wait: Somes told de Valois that he didn't want to entirely give up the stage and it was agreed that he would continue to appear in *The Firebird* and *Ondine* but relinquish his other roles with Fonteyn. Early in 1961, a press statement baldly announced that Fonteyn and Blair would dance *Swan Lake* Act II and III at the International Baalbek Festival in August, leaving rumour and speculation to flourish. Somes officially became assistant director although there was no public statement.

He had to be available for a final challenge. In June and July 1961, The Royal Ballet at last danced in Russia, taking *The Sleeping Beauty* back to its birthplace – the cradle of their own tradition.[134] Somes would also dance *The Firebird*, hitherto unseen in Russia, *Ondine*, *La Péri* and *Rinaldo and Armida*. It would be the icing on his dancing career.

Stocked up with bathroom plugs and soft lavatory paper for themselves and coffee and chocolate for gifts, the company flew out on 11 June. Those Kirov dancers not on tour in Paris met them in Leningrad, along with droves of photographers and interminable formal speeches about friendship. Somes loved Leningrad and the Kirov: smaller than Covent Garden, it was perfectly proportioned for ballet and the higher orchestra pit allowed the dancers to hear details of the score, whereas at Covent Garden the sound was projected under the stage or into the auditorium.

It was difficult to sleep in the perpetual daylight of the White Nights and the timetable was exhausting: 7am breakfast, bus to the theatre, 9am class, rehearsals until 5pm, back to the hotel for 'lunch' then back for the show, interspersed with organised visits to myriad museums and palaces. The company 'have risen to the occasion magnificently & danced their utmost,- & really brought it off,' Somes wrote home, '– but the strain is taking its toll. The food is not quite what we are used to, & all this sight-seeing en masse is very tiring, – yet there's *so* much to see.' He liked the whole company being together, eating at the same time and the same menu which saved him

---

133 Interview with author

134 The tour only went ahead after de Valois threatened to cancel Leningrad when the Russians, implying the company was not worthy of the Kirov, tried to change the venue to the Palace of Culture.

having to choose 'which I always find such a bother'. He was in a minority in liking the food, which was very plain, like veal and potatoes – Ashton could face little but yoghurt. A particular pleasure was visiting a home for retired actors and dancers 'which was wonderful ... many knew K(arsavina) ... they had lots of old photographs ... (and) were *very* sweet.'[135] He was less well disposed to the Soviet regime and, playing to the (probably true) cliché that every hotel room was bugged, voiced his criticisms whenever near a likely floral display or light fitting.

Russian dancers and teachers scrutinised every class and rehearsal and there was a free exchange of views. The general reaction was only too familiar – astonishment that a tradition, unique choreographic style and maturity could be achieved in only thirty years; for Zakharoff, 'this classicism appears to have a dramatic and poetic range and an essential inventiveness of choreography which make it quite unfamiliar and, indeed, wonderful to Russian eyes.' Mikhail Gabovich praised the 'Artistic, scenic expressiveness, concern for the inner content of the role, and artistic finish of the parts,' while Semeyonova recognised 'Your ballet has great soul.' Natalia Roslavleva was impressed by Somes' teaching (he was taking most of the mens' classes): 'his instructions are very clear and all of the enchaînements are built so as to develop good posture and line.'[136] One compliment came from an unlikely source: 'Look at those girls' Soviet Premier Khruschev remarked during *Ondine*, 'they might all be Russians.' 'We must have been working along the right lines during the last 30 years,' declared a relieved de Valois.[137]

Performing *The Sleeping Beauty* on the stage of its creation was a very emotional experience; de Valois was particularly struck by how the choreography perfectly related to the architecture. Although uncharacteristically nervous, Fonteyn was acclaimed (she thought the first night her worst performance ever), and Somes hailed as a true danseur noble. While his increasing lack of mobility could not be ignored – Monica Mason remembers thinking that he was finding the solo tough that night – his bearing, elegance and stage presence still marked him out and Roslavleva noted he was developing into a 'deep-thinking actor'.[138] Whatever the critics thought, two Russians who remembered pre-Revolutionary days, told de Valois, 'Tchaikovsky and Petipa should have been here tonight.' Sibley and Usher became audience favourites in the Blue Bird pas de deux, although Russian dancers were mystified when the men repeated the temps de poisson;

---

135 MS to ES 20? June 1961

136 Natalia Roslavleva, *A Rewarding Experience, The Royal Ballet in Moscow, Dancing Times*, September 1961, pp734-737

137 All quotes Nina Karasyova, *Ballet Today*, December 1961

138 Natalia Roslavleva, *A Rewarding Experience, The Royal Ballet in Moscow, Dancing Times*, September 1961, pp734-737

when Shaw said that was the choreography, they replied that they preferred to execute the steps once and more spectacularly, an attitude that horrified Somes and his peers, for whom choreography was paramount.

Ondine was eagerly awaited, a modern romantic full evening ballet being a new concept in Russia, where Soviet realism ruled. There were 15 minutes of applause on the first night. Opinion was divided, although it was the expected triumph for Fonteyn and Somes' performance did not go unnoticed. The Russians were not used to such subtle and intricate choreography and they admired how Ashton used all the music.

La Fille mal gardée was a great success; Somes was pleased at the positive reception for the men, particularly Blair as Colas, remarking dryly that they didn't get such attention back home. Everyone was struck by the youthfulness of the company – a reversal of the Bolshoi's London performances in 1956, when everyone had remarked on the strength of the company's older and character dancers.

Short ballets were rare in Russia and were not as extensively reviewed as the full evening works. Was the party line seen in Gabovich's praising *The Rake's Progress* but dismissing *Rinaldo and Armida* and *La Péri* as 'decadent impressionist poems'?[139] *The Firebird* had a mixed reception; some thought it outmoded, without realising Fokine's deliberate archaisms, some felt that the dancers did not fully understand the folk style while some, having read reviews of the 1910 production or Fokine's memoirs, picked holes in details. On 25 June *The Firebird* was televised with *La Péri*; Somes appeared in both ballets, partnering Nerina in the former and Fonteyn in the latter.

Contact with London was intermittent and it was from Georgina Parkinson's husband, Roy Round, that they heard the *Daily Express* had reported that Fonteyn thought Leningrad dreary: 'as if she wld. say such a thing to a journalist as a guest in *any* country,' fumed Somes. 'She was furious.'[140] In passing, Round mentioned that a Kirov dancer named Rudolf Nureyev had defected in Paris.

After Leningrad, Moscow exuded a sense of menace and Somes desisted from making critical remarks to the floral arrangements. Again, the company was under scrutiny: Asaf Messerer gave classes and, while acknowledging the English dancers' solid foundations, stressed deficiencies in épaulement and back. To Somes' joy, Chabukiani came to watch; his comment that each movement needed its own arms was welcomed by de Valois who said she was always telling them that.

The season ended with *The Sleeping Beauty* on 15 July. The gallery shouted themselves hoarse and ran out of flowers to throw, after which rhythmic

139 Natalia Roslavleva, *A Rewarding Experience, The Royal Ballet in Moscow, Dancing Times*, September 1961, pp734-737

140 MS to ES 20 June 1961

applause and shouts of 'bravo' continued for twenty five minutes as the company clapped back Soviet style, before Vassily Pakhomov, Director of the Bolshoi, presented special badges of honour to de Valois, Ashton, Fonteyn, Somes and Lanchbery.

And the curtain came down on Act one of Somes' career.

14

Assistant Director

Asked in 1975 if he missed being in the spotlight, Somes replied: 'Of course I do ... I'd love to turn the clock back,'[1] but admitted that dancing 'gave me up ... There is no point in doing (the classics) when other people can do them better ...' adding 'I really think I had a better dancing career than I deserved ...But I do not enjoy life better now. It can never be the same, watching others.'[2]

His departure did not go entirely unnoticed. *The End of a Ballet Partnership* in *The Times* 'brought tears to my eyes, for a thousand different reasons,' wrote Edith Russell-Roberts, 'but mostly because it was so typical, & so right that you so quietly stood back. Anybody else ... would have had a farewell performance & a blaze of publicity.'[3] *Dance and Dancers* recognised his importance in Fonteyn's development and in establishing a tradition of male dancing: '... in his style and bearing, his authority and nobility, his good looks and natural dignity, his unforced acting and always virile personality ... he has set a standard which his predecessors (sic) will not easily equal.'[4]

The grapevine gossip was that semi-retirement had been forced on Somes and galleryites pleaded with de Valois for the partnership with Fonteyn to continue. De Valois's reply was crisp and pragmatic: 'No dancer's career can remain stationary, and no management, with an interest and appreciation of the artist concerned, allows any situation to continue until it reaches a moment that spells nothing less than abrupt oblivion. [Somes'] special talents have been known to the management for a long time. The moment has now arrived for the development and encouragement of these gifts, and we are aware that they now require our serious consideration ... the preparation naturally calls for some reduction in his roles ...'[5]

So Somes relinquished Fonteyn to Blair. It could hardly be expected that she would immediately establish a rapport with a new partner as she had with Somes after Helpmann; not only had they danced together over the years but they also had a natural empathy and physical harmony. Fonteyn-Blair was an uneasy match, with his extrovert ebullience pitted against her romantic elegance, and the partnership never gelled. They were first seen together in

---

1 *Observer*, 13 April 1975

2 Unidentified incomplete press cutting, possibly *Woman's Journal,* April 1976

3 Edith Russell-Roberts to MS 26 October 1961

4 *Personality of the Month, Dance and Dancers*, October 1961, p5

5 NdeV to 'Galleryites', 11 October 1961

Giselle and *The Sleeping Beauty* and suddenly people began asking if she was really as good as they had thought. As Ashton always said, Fonteyn looked wonderful in the classics because Somes *made* her look good; how much she owed to him only became clear when he wasn't there. It must have been a difficult transition for both Fonteyn and Blair, especially as Somes was still partnering her in *Ondine* which was in the repertory at the same time.

The classics, however, were not exclusive to Fonteyn and Somes. Fonteyn later asserted that the ballets she created with a particular dancer were, 'like love affairs, and I was inflexible in my fidelity ... Fred made (*Daphnis and Chloë*) so personal to Michael and me that I danced it very little after Michael retired';[6] in fact, within weeks of his retirement, Somes was rehearsing her with Blair not only in *Daphnis and Chloë* but also *Symphonic Variations.* While no press were invited to the Fonteyn-Blair *Giselle*, it was perhaps tactless to invite them to see the new partnership in two of Somes' most personal roles: the result was, as Andrew Porter observed, that seeing Blair in Somes' roles 'we tend to think either: how little there is in these parts; or alternatively how good Somes was in them'.[7] That Somes appeared in both *Antigone* and *The Firebird* on the same evening that Blair made his debut with Fonteyn in *Symphonic Variations*, gave audience and critics food for thought: 'an epoch of British Ballet came to an end last night,' mused Clive Barnes, under the regrettable headline 'Margot's Mr. Somes Tip-Toes Out'. 'Such reticence may be commendable. Yet it seems unfortunate that Mr. Somes has left the limelight of the great classics without so much as a farewell performance.'[8] It was some consolation, although Edith understood what he was going through: 'So hateful & hurtful to have to watch – but you are so philosophical & right-thinking, I am sure you are facing it in the right spirit.'[9] That spirit was to be subject to many strains in the coming months.

It was not easy for Blair either. At times it seemed that he and Fonteyn were in different ballets, although he always danced brilliantly and partnered well, technically better than Somes, who had been finding lifts difficult for some time, but he lacked natural nobility and romantic style and often looked uneasy. They would need time to establish a rapport and, as things turned out, they never got the chance.

Throughout September, Somes was on hand suggesting, helping, supporting and criticising as Ashton created a solo to Scriabin's *Poème tragique* for Rudolf Nureyev's British debut at the annual RAD gala in November. Fonteyn and Somes danced the *Birthday Offering* pas de deux and

6 Margot Fonteyn, *Autobiography*, Hamish Hamilton, London, 1989, p126

7 Andrew Porter, *A Triple Bill, Financial Times*, 23 October 1961

8 Clive Barnes, *Margot's Mr. Somes Tip-Toes out ...*, *Daily Express*, 12 October 1961

9 Russell-Roberts to MS 26 October 1961

were photographed in the wings watching Nureyev dance 'as though a flame were burning him up inside'.[10] Then it was announced that Nureyev would dance *Giselle* with Fonteyn in February 1962.

That autumn de Valois finalised the new company structure. Ballet was now a viable performing career for men, but she wanted to show that there was still a career after dancing.[11] She was still firmly at the top with Ashton as Associate Director, but Somes and Hart now officially joined Field as Assistant Directors: Field directed the Touring Company; Hart took over administration of rehearsals, casting and performance scheduling ('... the way he ran that company' remembered Leslie Edwards. 'He knew what we were doing next year' – and probably the year after that); Somes was responsible for maintaining standards, directing rehearsals and developing the soloists and ballerinas; the Royal Ballet was beginning to live on its capital and there was an urgent need to bring on the next generation, especially the men, whose careers were no longer interrupted by National Service. However, until they came to maturity, Somes' semi-retirement left a gap in the classical male dancers which didn't seem to have been allowed for: several leading dancers had left and the Touring Company was not set up like the Theatre Ballet to develop young dancers for transfer.[12] Many roles had only two casts and once *La Fille mal gardée* had to be substituted for *Ondine* when MacLeary was injured and Somes was flying to New York for a television appearance in *The Firebird* with Fonteyn.

The changes were announced on 29 December 1961. Only Somes' appointment was reported by the BBC, fuelling speculation that, while alphabetically-listed Assistant Directors were obviously equal, some might be more equal than others.

Fonteyn considered making a formal farewell to her years with Somes at the next gala, but, enchanted with Nureyev, she danced with him instead. Somes was hurt but couldn't bring himself to remonstrate with her. Then he agreed to substitute for an injured Nureyev in *Swan Lake* Act II at the RAD Gala in December; it was the last time he and Fonteyn danced a classical pas de deux, but all the publicity centered on Nureyev's other replacement, Viktor Rona, and Somes didn't rate a mention, not even in the *Dancing Times* review. 'It was really, really upsetting for him,' Sibley recalled. 'All those years were like ... didn't mean a thing ... It was a *very* hard time, hard enough to give up the theatre anyway ... if (Fonteyn) had coped with (things) in a better way, it would have been easier for Michael.'[13]

10 Peter Williams, *Going Gala, The R.A.D. Matinee, Dance and Dancers*, December 1961 p18

11 Ninette de Valois, *English Male Dancing, Ballet Annual 1957*, Adam & Charles Black, London, 1956, p96

12 There was even a suggestion that Ballet Rambert should act as 'nursery' for The Royal Ballet

13 Interview with author

The media went into overdrive when Nureyev made his Royal Ballet debut on 21 February 1962 as Albrecht to Fonteyn's Giselle. She had begun to rethink her interpretation in her final performances with Somes and Nureyev's passionate Albrecht provided the final spur. Whereas Somes had projected the essence of a character, Nureyev was detailed, subtle and naturalistic, and drew the focus onto Albrecht, forcing Fonteyn to fight him for attention.

What Somes found especially galling was that Nureyev's every whim was indulged. He was allowed to relinquish the often unflattering wigs that Somes, who after all had a fine head of hair, had hated all his dancing life. When Somes had pleaded for a spotlight for Albrecht's entrance in Act II, he was told that it would break the mood. Sibley remembered Nureyev's rehearsal: '... in he comes and he stops "Where my light? I can no see. Why I come? Why I bother? I go." And Madam up there on the stage going "Light" ... and he got it all. After all those years.'[14]

Where Fonteyn-Somes had been calm, serene, elegant, noble and confidently secure, Fonteyn-Nureyev crackled with sexiness and danger of contrast, in age and style. If Fonteyn-Somes was like a long marriage, Fonteyn-Nureyev was a new love affair. Fonteyn-Somes was Hollywood 1950s, Fonteyn-Nureyev was rock and roll. Against Somes' virile self-effacement, reticence and gentlemanly good manners, Nureyev pitted unbridled energy, exotic charisma and sexy animal magnetism. The years with Somes had given Fonteyn confidence in her star status, and she would never be eclipsed by Nureyev but could establish another true partnership. Chameleon-like, she adapted to Nureyev and they became symbols of the 1960s.

Somes respected Nureyev's talent, if not always what he did with it. He enjoyed the way Nureyev sparked off Fonteyn and was pleased that she had a new phase to her career. He was the first to praise Nureyev's productions of *Raymonda Act III*, an amalgam of the best bits from the whole ballet, *The Kingdom of the Shades* from *La Bayadère* and an intelligent *Nutcracker*, all of which he often rehearsed. In later years Ashley Page recalled him saying 'This is one of the things that I learned from Rudolf' or 'One of those wonderful steps that Rudolf used to choreograph.'[15] However, genius did not excuse unprofessionalism. Nureyev was often late to class and rehearsals – he loved to make an entrance; photo-calls were unusable because he didn't make-up or kept his leg warmers on. Unmannerly disrespect never played well with Somes or with some of the younger dancers, who saw in this behaviour contempt for everyone else.

Somes certainly did not approve of Nureyev's partnering. He was always

14 Interview with author
15 Interview with author

impeccable with Fonteyn, but, as Dowell observed, '... a lot of ladies would have put up with a lot of bad handling just to be with him, where they almost had to do it themselves'.[16]

Somes had to ensure that younger dancers didn't copy Nureyev's idiosyncrasies without first learning the essentials: 'I had been watching Rudolf' recalled David Ashmole, 'And (Michael) said "Ashmole, you are only a cog within the wheel of this pas de deux – you stand there and look after them." It was the best way to start, as opposed to learning the tricks of the trade and not (caring) about your partner.'[17] In fact, most of the company were inured in the existing system and, while in awe of Nureyev's talent, at first regarded his shenanigans with mild disapproval.

Nureyev expected a production to mould itself around him, whereas Somes and Fonteyn had performed their own solos and pas de deux but otherwise fitted into an existing production; while Nureyev introducing a solo into *Swan Lake* Act I to establish the Prince's mood was acceptable, making significant changes to the Act II adagio, was, on a practical level, disconcerting for the corps de ballet. He abandoned the mime, arguing that Russian ballet, influenced by Stanislavsky, had rejected it. His attitude was not unfamiliar: when Violetta Elvin joined the company in 1946, she said to Fonteyn, 'In Russia ballerina often make other step if original not suit. We think more important make beautiful effect.'[18] Somes, however, believed in the supremacy of the choreographer and that the dancer's job was to make the ballet live within its conventions, not change things to make themselves look better or eliminate moves that they found difficult. Sometimes Somes stopped rehearsing dancers when they were partnered by Nureyev: 'I cannot bear to see him mutilating everything,' he told Monica Mason.[19]

It was vexing when de Valois (who had herself done quite a lot of tinkering over the years) told Somes that he had to accept the changes. She believed 'when (dancers of genius) do appear the theatre may have to submit to them ... I don't expect everyone to understand at the time and I do expect quite a lot of people to be upset.'[20] Especially upset was Blair whose career never recovered from the double blow of realising that Fonteyn-Blair was not a partnership made in heaven and being usurped by Nureyev. It didn't help that, according to Alan Carter, Blair was not in good shape at the time and remembered Somes 'giving him absolute hell in the Bournonville and thinking he needed it'.[21]

16 Interview with author

17 Interview with author

18 Margot Fonteyn, *Autobiography*, Hamish Hamilton, London, 1989, p109

19 Interview with author

20 *Madam talks to Alexander Bland, The Observer Weekend Review*, 15 September 1963

21 Interview with author

Somes later acknowledged that Fonteyn needed Nureyev's challenge and could even admit, somewhat ingenuously, that many didn't remember he had ever danced with her: 'I'm not saying that bitterly, because I'm terribly happy for Margot and for Nureyev ... Their great success is a marvellous thing. It doesn't mean anything to me any more: I mean, if you've had that kind of partnership, then you don't worry about other people also having it.'[22] Sibley felt for him "til I realised it simply wasn't the case at all. Michael wasn't in any way jealous, he's the most generous person ever ... '[23] '[H]e admired Rudolf *hugely* in the end – they had so much in common with their love of ballet – this passion for it. Helping everybody. Everything was for the ballet – well it was for themselves, particularly Rudolf, but it was also for the ballet, the performance, the production.'[24]

Nureyev was not the only guest artist. John Gilpin was contracted, but, frustrated by back problems and few performances, he returned to Festival Ballet, where he could dance every night. Performances by Erik Bruhn, Yvette Chauviré and Sonia Arova, meant fewer for the resident principals – Beriosova, Nerina, Anya Linden, Annette Page, Blair, MacLeary, Desmond Doyle and Ronald Hynd.

Bruhn was considered the greatest male dancer of his generation, combining superb technique and glamorous persona with an innate nobility which made him the perfect ballet prince. In spring 1962, he guested in *Giselle, Swan Lake, The Sleeping Beauty* and *Les Sylphides*, but, apart from *Giselle*, he disliked the Royal Ballet versions taught by Somes. Although he had never danced Florimund before, 'I took it upon myself to make some changes in the choreography, something that did not sit very well with Michael Somes, who taught me the role.'[25] Hardly surprising.

Thus Somes, beginning to establish his authority in a new career, was faced with guests who showed little respect for his revered traditions. His generation had unquestioningly accepted authority; he could not allow the challenge to spread in the company.

Nureyev certainly changed attitudes to male dancing, but that he provided a goad to British male dancers and did not obliterate them is a sign of how far they had come. He arrived when The Royal Ballet was already scrambling out of the trough of the late 1950s and the raising of overall standards had everything to do with Somes and the ballet staff's routine work. Ultimately, the company would benefit both from Nureyev's new vision of the male dancer and Somes' drive for perfection. A revitalised Fonteyn created other

22 John Gruen, *The Private World of Ballet*, Penguin Books, London, 1976, p166

23 Barbara Newman, *Antoinette Sibley*, Hutchinson, London, 1986, p121

24 Interview with author

25 John Gruen, *Erik Bruhn danseur noble*, The Viking Press, New York, p119

problems, as those who had come to maturity in her shadow, like Beriosova and Nerina, saw their careers stagnate and there were fears that another generation might also be overshadowed. Fortunately, Fonteyn, encouraged by Ashton, spent enough time away from the company for their talents to come to fruition, although it was galling that to the general public ballet meant Fonteyn-Nureyev. Somes was determined that Sibley, at least, should not go under.

Sibley's star was rising, her fair, English beauty gracing the pages of *Vogue* and *Vanity Fair*. She made her London debut as a radiant Aurora on 3 March 1962, revealing an unexpected authority and regal charm. 'A was very good' Somes confided to his diary – high praise. Her debut as the Girl in Ashton's *The Two Pigeons* he rated 'Very good indeed.' The ballet had been created by Lynn Seymour with Christopher Gable, but Ashton had conceived the male lead for the older Donald Britton: heaven forfend that in treating a May-December romance he had anyone particular in mind.[26]

Despite the acclaim in *Giselle*, Fonteyn and Nureyev were not yet indissoluble. In May she was again in Australia and New Zealand partnered by Blair with a concert group including Maryon Lane and Annette Page. 'Dearest Sam,' she wrote to Somes, '... Of course, everyone misses you very much, starting with me, and they are all terribly sad not to see you both on and off the stage. No one else quite replaces you and we all notice it ... The success this time in Australia was great in money and capacity audiences but not in crowds at the stage door and anywhere we went.'[27] It was nice to know he was missed, although perhaps he felt a little disquiet, when it was reported that she was asked by an unnamed company official not to do the current dance craze, theTwist (to which she was addicted), while in Australia, lest it create the 'wrong impression'. It was a sign of a new and different Fonteyn from the one he knew.

As Somes grew into his new role, he must have looked back on his performing years as positively leisurely. Only his teaching commitments tailed off during the 1960s; although his classes were praised by other teachers, his methods were not universally popular with the dancers; his special talents lay elsewhere.

Surviving jottings for talks reflect the complexity of his job and his aims: he described his role as 'nurse – office-boy, Mother Superior, professor, teaching & convincing ... interesting artist, not flog old ways. – fascinating because never perfection ... Choosing rep. difficulties. Meetings The Board!! ... Casting, rehearsing, change of rep. – hanging scenery, music, coaching,

---

26 The ballet was created on the Touring Company with Seymour and Gable but when first performed by the Covent Garden company the cast was Seymour with the older Alexander Grant.

27 MF to MS 5 May 1962

Fred's aide. Stage-calls – discipline, – choreographers (School of) Ballets of future ... *Rehearsals*. Of rep. Replacing for illness. Changing places & partners. principals separately. Then together. Splitting up during rehearsals. Pianists job. Later Conductor. Going back in rehearsals (names for musical cues). *Coaching* coaxing bullying ... *Planning* – Opera Co. Everything has to be *staged* ... Orchestra. ... Co-ordinated. Op[era]. singers from abroad. Conductors ... Plan 3 ballets for Season. Touring group. "Ballet for All" Principals go out & abroad. Balancing programme – Ideal for public entertainment & "leading on". Using everybody – what orch[estra] can play, what can be hung mat[inée]. availability of dancers, all on at once in everything.'[28]

His rehearsal schedule was formidable. He taught and rehearsed all the principals and major solo roles in *Cinderella*, *Swan Lake*, *The Sleeping Beauty*, *Giselle*, *Ondine*, *Scènes de ballet*, *The Firebird* and Ashton's new *Raymonda* pas de deux created for Beriosova and MacLeary. Over two days in autumn 1961 he took solo and full calls for *Daphnis and Chloë*, rehearsed John Gilpin in *Giselle*, taught *Ondine* to the second cast and rehearsed the Act III divertissement. By spring 1962 he was also rehearsing *La Fille mal gardée*, Ashton's *Persephone* and Bruhn's staging of Bournonville's *Napoli* pas de six and *Flower Festival at Genzano* pas de deux. He watched the creation of all new ballets, some of which he went on to rehearse, like MacMillan's *The Rite of Spring*. Jill Gregory, Gerd Larsen or Lorna Mossford rehearsed the corps de ballet, but Somes oversaw the final full calls. He was sometimes rehearsing from 11.30 until 5.30 and he was in the theatre for every ballet performance. Somes now filled the role suggested by Richard Buckle in 1950, for a 'Cecchetti in the house, whose eagle eye was marking every slight miscalculation, and who would come round afterwards to distribute his few terrible comments!'[29]

Fitted into his schedule were innumerable committees, functions, auditions, performances by and receptions for distinguished visitors; for the Royal Ballet School he was present at final auditions and on scholarship panels, oversaw test classes and assessments, judged choreographic competitions and took some rehearsals for the annual matinée; there were Ballet Sub-Committee and Board meetings. His potential influence was enormous.

Nor were his commitments limited to The Royal Ballet. He was an RAD consultant, adjudicating the Adeline Genée award, serving on the Scholarship committee, teaching and giving demonstrations; he revised the RAD Solo Seal syllabus, took close interest in the boys' classes, and kept an eye on Ballet for Athletes. He lectured to the Royal Ballet School, RAD and, although he felt that trade secrets and what went on off stage had nothing

---

28 British Council lecture nd
29 Richard Buckle, Ballet commentary, *Ballet*, April 1950 pp5-8

to do with the general public, the Friends of Covent Garden, ballet clubs and for the British Council. He was a Vice-Patron of the All England Sunshine Dancing Competition and, less onerously, President of Taunton Thespians in succession to Evelyn Waugh. In a desire to ensure accuracy, he made 'certain suggestions and corrections to the original drawings and text' of Dennis Knight's *Ballet*, a children's instant picture activity book, using Letraset rub down figures which do, indeed, display an admirable precision and attention to detail. Only the highest standards must be maintained, whatever the level.

He did, however, resist de Valois's attempts to get him involved in choreographic workshops, like the Sunday Ballet Club, and was, indeed, dismissive of their activities. Yet he suggested that the School introduce courses in the principles of choreography as well as a drama course and training for répétiteurs. His rough syllabus survives for a Choreographic Class, compulsory for senior students and optional for the Company; it concentrates on developing skills in moving groups, varying the numbers of dancers and the balance between male and female; there is an emphasis on floor patterns, exercises developed to different rhythms – waltz, mazurka, march – creating movements for different parts of the body according to the different musical rhythms and a stress on intermediate steps and overall musical shape. He understood the process even if he never wanted to choreograph himself. Dowell recalled that, when he was Director, Somes often recommended music he felt would be suitable for choreographers or for students attempting choreography.

In addition, in the early 1960s he was still giving 'performances of rare artistry and authority' in *Ondine*, *The Firebird*, *Antigone* and *Rinaldo and Armida*.[30] Then, in 1963, Ashton put the seal on the Fonteyn-Nureyev partnership with *Marguerite and Armand*. While he had seen Somes as idealised princes or shepherds, with nebulous heroines, for Nureyev Ashton created the full-blooded romantic hero of Alexandre Dumas's *La Dame aux camélias*: Somes was Armand's father, who persuades Marguerite to renounce his son for the sake of his family. Although Buckle saw an allegory – Somes symbolising disapproval at the excesses of Fonteyn and Nureyev – Somes publically declared that he took the role to show his acceptance of the partnership.

The dying Marguerite relives her affair with Armand in four passionate, impressionistic encounters. Anchoring the unconstrained emotions was Somes. Ashton's treatment of his role was inspired by a Kabuki troupe he had seen in Moscow: 'The way they just stand while the emotion builds up inside them and then suddenly alter the fold of a sleeve or something and that tells you everything ... (The father's role is) all tremendously compressed ... But I

---

30 Mary Clarke, *Royal Ballet at Covent Garden*, *Dancing Times*, December 1961, p151

would like it to be strong enough to kill.'[31] Somes' brief appearances, carrying the weight of an entire moral code but melting into gentle compassion, 'was touchingly human and lovely to see, like the sudden rays of the sun breaking through an overcast sky. It was the 'muted' performance brought to perfection,' which turned the ballet from a star vehicle into a human tragedy.[32] For teacher Prosso Pfister, the Father's first scene with Marguerite '... was one of the greatest pieces of dramatic acting that I think we'll ever see in this country in the dancing world. ... It was in his stance – acting with the entire body ...'[33] He also showed that, whatever Nureyev could do as a partner, he could do better, supporting Fonteyn one-handed – without putting down his stick. Scenery-chewing it wasn't, but it was as impressive as Nureyev's unrestrained passion.

A near-hysterical audience greeted the premiere on 12 March 1963. 'I don't like the ballet much, & I don't think it amounts to much either' Somes confessed, but he got his best notices in years.[34]

Ashton wanted the ballet to remain a 'souvenir' of Fonteyn and Nureyev. 'Nobody else could do it,' he declared. 'It would only be a bad copy which would have nothing to do with the original.'[35] Somes was equally integral; when it was revived in 2000, the question was not just 'Where are they going to get a Fonteyn, a Nureyev,' but 'Where are they going to find a Somes?'

American tours were now a routine chore. By 1963, the company flew tourist class and arrived without fanfare or even anyone to greet them, and even Ashton queued for the airport bus. For the first time, there were empty seats at the 17 April New York opening for Fonteyn and Blair in *The Sleeping Beauty*, but she was still rapturously received and Sibley, as Fairy of the Woodland Glades, was praised. Somes had advised against conservative scheduling: '... I *insisted* from the beginning that we shld. *never* have done all these S.B's [seven] in a row' he wrote home, ' ... what is the point of bringing in the new ballets so late for so few perfs? – If they are successful, as we hope, – then it won't do us any good ... They've had our "S.B." & we shldn't trade on it now.'[36] Out of 39 performances, 25 were the over-familiar classics and while critics found the new works – *The Invitation, The Two Pigeons, The Rite of Spring, Symphony* and *La Fête étrange* – tame and old fashioned, audiences were enthusiastic.

Marguerite and Armand was deliriously received. Somes was dared to

31 Alexander Bland, *Birth of a Ballet*, Observer, 10 March 1963

32 Gordon Anthony, *A Camera at the Ballet*, David & Charles, 1975, p91

33 Interview with author

34 MS to ES 7 June 1963

35 Hans-Theodor Wohlfahrt, *An Interview with Sir Frederick Ashton, Ballett-Journal/Das Tanzarchiv*, 1 December 1988

36 MS to ES p 19 April 1963

mingle with the audience in full costume and make-up. He did, but was most put out that no one turned a hair when a distinguished man dressed in the height of 1840s fashion appeared among them.

A diet of classics was not stimulating for audiences, dancers nor Somes: 'I have been rehearsing *all* day & sitting thro' the shows at night till I'm really dizzy!! I never want to see any of them again!!'[37] Despite his assertion that Petipa was the Busby Berkeley of the Maryinsky, and that the 'big three', especially *The Nutcracker*, survived mainly because of Tchaikovsky, he understood their merits and importance and fought for the Sergeyev versions, defending them from becoming a free-for-all reflection of individual dancers' egos and technical tricks. As a dancer he had had occasional nights off and free days, now, despite a painful knee, he was in the studio all day and at every performance, only making time to see Nemchinova and Olga Spessiva. He was furious that money was not available for adequate technical rehearsals; nothing aroused his wrath more than seeing performances where dancers were giving their all spoiled by inefficient technical crews or orchestras.

Another cause for anger was Nureyev and his effect on Fonteyn. He complained about his dressing room and rehearsals, but '(she) does nothing to help the situation, in fact, more often takes his side, & is herself demanding & difficult & so unlike what she used to be ...'[38] She too now came late to rehearsals, not dancing full out and 'messing about as usual!!', behaviour which came expensive in America where every minute of stage time had to be paid for.[39] Philip Chatfield recalled how, during the 1950s, Fonteyn and Somes were 'an example to us all ... They were top stars but behaved like ordinary warm, understanding people, with absolutely no side or delusions of grandeur.'[40] Somes could hardly reconcile that Fonteyn with this clichéd temperamental ballerina.

Equally distressing, was her disassociation from the company, only coming in to rehearse and perform, which affected the overall performance; according to one critic, 'it was almost as though (Fonteyn and Nureyev) were engaged in a concert tour of their own.'[41] Somes was exasperated. '... I can't speak to her now, – she is so selfish & thinks only of herself prompted by Tito, & nothing of the Co. ... I think we have taken quite a lot of money & done very well, – altho' as happened in London, Margot & Rudi get all the praise & publicity, yet the Co in everyone's opinion is better than ever & dancing

37 MS to ES p 29 April 1963
38 MS to ES p 29 April 1963
39 MS to ES p 21 April 1963
40 Philip Chatfield letter to author nd
41 Allen Hughes unpublished article

marvellously.'[42] Many knew that was largely due to Somes.

Whatever his criticisms and complaints, nothing overrode Somes' deep affection for Fonteyn and hers for him. They remained friends whose understanding was forged in the shared experiences of their youth. Somes later admitted: 'I suspect we were in love at some time. One usually falls in love with one's partners at some point. I mean, one gets so close.'[43] To the end they remained Sam and Sarah.

During the season, on 20 May 1963, Somes, Ashton, Fonteyn and Nureyev were secretly flown to Washington, where they toured the White House, including the family apartments, after which Mrs Kennedy entertained them to tea and introduced them to President Kennedy, who showed them over the rose garden. Nureyev couldn't resist trying out the President's chair in the Oval Office, while Somes purloined his own souvenir – the key from the nursery door.

The last night in New York roused audiences to an unprecedented demonstration – thirty-five curtain calls in a thirty-two minute ovation. The ensuing tour only took in nine, mostly short, dates. The train was new and not so comfortable. They were still subject to tight scheduling which often meant late arrivals. There were the inevitable nightmares: travelling from Toronto to Chicago they embarked at 4am, only to be delayed by a cloudburst, and then had to be bussed to Detroit while the train was floated in sections across a river; at Detroit station they hung about in thunderstorm and hurricane until 8am, when they resumed their journey, arriving in Chicago about 1.30 the following morning.

In Toronto, Nureyev was arrested for jay walking, lashed out and was handcuffed; Company Manager Michael Wood got him out of jail and smoothed things over, but the Canadian and British press had a field day. 'Nice publicity for the Royal Ballet', commented Somes. Nureyev being bailed out of scrapes and Fonteyn acting like an irresponsible teenager were hardly his idea of how to behave when The Royal Ballet was representing Britain abroad.

De Valois retired in summer 1963 and Ashton succeeded as Director. Her reputation was at a low ebb after accepting Massine's uninspired *Bal des voleurs* for the Touring Company against all advice, but she cannily knew that would help Ashton: 'I think I've timed it rather well' she said 'happily' to Mary Clarke.[44] Somes felt that she was 'fed-up & wants to get out without any fuss or farewells' but '... Freddy will have to pull *his* socks up & get down to it. Nothing has been decided, & it all seems chaotic, & *he* won't stir himself ... I

42 MS to ES p 31 May 1963

43 John Gruen, *The Private World of Ballet*, Penguin Books, London, 1976, p165

44 Interview with author

feel very well – but I am tired & very sick of the whole set-up ... I shld. think the next Season is going to be Hell!!'[45] Many who knew Somes, Field and Hart wondered if such different personalities could ever work together and rumours spread that de Valois was leaving the company in such a way that it would not survive her. In fact, The Royal Ballet was entering its golden years.

The Assistant Directors had been astutely selected to relieve Ashton of the burdens of discpline and administration, for which he did not have de Valois's flair. Somes and Hart ran the day-to-day London company, (although not without tensions as Hart would have liked more input into rehearsals, which Somes regarded as his province), leaving Ashton free to concentrate on choreography and artistic planning. As Sibley observed, 'everybody worked really happily; it was a good arrangement and they could all bully Fred ...'[46]

Ashton invited more consultation than de Valois, which suited his strongly-opinionated team. He worked out what he wanted to do and then invited their comments, including Lanchbery on the musical side, and the box office on repertory. Casting was worked out well in advance and major solo and character roles were cast alongside the principals on the throwaways; this was good for the dancers, who had a definite goal, and the regular audience, who, in those days of lower prices, could afford to follow the younger dancers as much as the principals. Ashton, Somes and Hart worked together on casting, so there was a breadth of opinion about dancers. The company was rich in young talent – Sibley, Seymour, Merle Park, Monica Mason, Deanne Bergsma, Georgina Parkinson, Vyvyan Lorrayne, Gable, Dowell, Michael Coleman – and Ashton cut back on Fonteyn-Nureyev performances in their favour. Sibley, however, felt that her relationship with Somes was having a negative effect on her career: 'He would not say anything to put me forward ... a lot of people were going "whisper, whisper – that's why she's so" ... and actually it was completely the opposite, but I was given hell ...'[47]

Somes was the most publicly prominent of the Assistant Directors and constantly tackled administrators and Board. Lord Drogheda was a frequent target: 'At the end of any Interview with him I came away deeply conscious of my inadequacy as chairman of Covent Garden. "How *can* you allow such and such to happen?" "*Why* does the ballet always have to put up with so and so?" Questions which usually hit some particular nail firmly into place ...'[48]

The first premiere under the new régime was Nureyev's mounting of the *Kingdom of the Shades* from Petipa's *La Bayadère* on 27 November. Before it was replaced with Natalia Makarova's full-length production in 1989, it

---

45 MS to ES p 1 July 1963

46 Interview with author

47 Interview with author

48 Lord Drogheda, *Double Harness*, Littlehampton Book Services Ltd, 1978, p296

was one of the glories of the Royal Ballet's classical repertory. Nureyev's assumption that he and Fonteyn would dance the leads, however, was met with 'open distaste' by Ashton, Somes and Hart, who felt that 'the company itself should become the star', and it did.[49] Fonteyn and Nureyev were jewels in the Royal Ballet crown, but a jewel only achieves full glory in the perfect setting and that Somes and his staff provided. As Nureyev later advised a company director, make 'your heart your corps de ballet, and you set your diamonds around it'.[50] Somes and his staff brought the soloists and corps de ballet to such a pitch of perfection that the superstars had to give not just their all, but their all plus.

Ashton inherited de Valois's plans for a new *Swan Lake*, on which Somes had been assigned to work with Helpmann. They went off to look at various European versions, though hopes of seeing the Stanislavsky Company's production in Moscow were thwarted by the Soviets, still incensed about Nureyev's defection. Somes spent a lot of time calming Helpmann's fears that de Valois would start interfering and Ashton's fears that Nureyev might have an unacceptable influence. Ashton choreographed a prologue showing Odette's bewitchment (later dropped), a pas de douze to the Act I waltz and a fireworks pas de quatre (with a fiendish solo for Sibley); Somes contributed much of the storm sequence to Ashton's new, lyrically beautiful, Act IV. There was the usual disagreement over the designer, de Valois voting for de Nobili, everyone else favouring Georges Wakehevitch; Sydney Nolan was suggested, then Beni Montresor became flavour of the month before Carl Toms was agreed on

When the production premiered on 12 December 1963 it was credited solely to Helpmann. It was *Giselle* all over again. Despite having a major input into the production, Somes refused to even have his name on the programme, although, as Ashton wrote to him, 'The whole thing would never have got on without all your hard work. You were the driving force & I am very grateful to you & to have you around gives me great confidence.'[51] Helpmann added a mss postscript to his typewritten thanks: 'Dear Boy. No one knows more than I do how much the success was due to you. I will always be more grateful than I can say.'[52]

Thanking Somes for his 'help & guidance', Carl Toms, admitted he had never been so frightened of anything.[53] Just what that help was can be surmised from David Walker's experience when he designed the 1977

49 Keith Money, *Fonteyn and Nureyev*, HarperCollins, 1994

50 Rudolph Nureyev to Derek Deane, *Summer of Dance*, *Harpers & Queen*, July 1991, p80,

51 FA to MS 16 December 1963

52 Robert Helpmann to MS 13 December 1963

53 Carl Toms to MS December 1963

production of *The Sleeping Beauty*. Faced with the ballet 'every designer dreads', Michael went to him and, 'very modestly, said "If you would be interested, I could take you through ..." None of them would have done that except Michael – they just wanted you to do it and they contribute nothing. Michael ... took me through the ballet from beginning to end – and also worked out some ideas which were logical and good because he was a very good man of the theatre ... it's a pity he didn't have the energy or the determination to do those things himself. He was very content to reproduce something for Fred and I think he liked to admire other people – he didn't want to be the person who was admired. Michael did it behind the scenes simply because he cared about the thing itself.'[54]

Such reluctance to have his work acknowledged means that the extent of Somes' contribution to The Royal Ballet has consistently been unappreciated, misunderstood and undervalued. He was very influential behind the scenes. As is clear from their wartime correspondence, he was closely involved in the evolution of many Ashton ballets, sometimes suggesting music, coaxing, cajoling, bullying when Ashton was stuck and countering his inclination to laziness. Like all the dancers, he suggested moves or would improvise if Ashton needed a kick-start, suggestions which were then polished and transformed. Another element in creation was Ashton's 'I dreamt last night' suggestions – usually countered by the dancers with the retort that they weren't humanly possible, then 'the long process of mechanics, trial and error, addition and subtraction, and invariably ... some beautiful effect, at first thought impossible, has been produced'.[55] If a score was commissioned, Somes was often present at the early meetings with the composer and on hand during its development. If later amendments were required, he would liaise with the composer, and thus in 1980 it was he, not Ashton, who discussed possible revisions to *Ondine* with Henze. But his extensive contributions, both to Ashton's work and other Royal Ballet productions, were never publicised.

In 1964 Ashton turned his attention to *The Dream*, based on *A Midsummer Night's Dream*, one of the company's contributions to the Shakespeare quartercentenary celebrations. Having decided on a 19th century setting and Mendelssohn's incidental music, he asked Somes, Hart and Lanchbery to produce scenarios: Somes and Lanchbery produced almost identical outlines, but in the end Ashton went with Lanchbery's version, which brought the lovers in later.

Hitherto, Ashton had resisted casting Sibley in his ballets, partly because she was de Valois's protegée, partly because he felt that she was just using

---

54 Interview with author

55 Michael Somes, *Working with Frederick Ashton*, Ballet Annual Fifteenth Issue, Adam & Charles Black, London, 1961, p

32 Somes' protégés Antoinette Sibley and Anthony Dowell in *The Dream*.
Photograph by Leslie E Spatt.

Somes to advance her career.[56] He now broke through his prejudices
spectacularly, casting her as Titania, no pretty Victorian fairy, but, as Sibley
described her, 'volatile and proud and angry and so ... womanly' with an
unexpected *farouche* quality.[57] 'Titania embodies the best of what she does:'
Somes declared, 'brilliance and softness, nobility and the quality of the fairy
queen, tongue-in-cheek humour in the donkey bits, which in my book adds

---

56 He even objected to her dancing his new *Giselle* peasant pas de deux, a role which she
coveted and for which, as proved when he eventually relented, she was magically suited.
57 Barbara Newman, *Antoinette Sibley*, Hutchinson, London, 1986, p129

up to charm – those things can be so dull and dreary without that.'[58]

As Oberon, Ashton cast Anthony Dowell, another Somes protégé. The chemistry with Sibley was potent and, under Somes' guidance, they developed into a great partnership which defined The Royal Ballet for the 1960s as Somes and Fonteyn had defined it for the 1950s.

Rehearsals coincided with tensions between Somes and Sibley. She was considering breaking with him because of the strains of working so closely together and because of disquiet over what was then considered an irregular liaison. Despite Somes' reluctance to marry again, at *The Dream* dress rehearsal Sibley proudly wore her Victorian engagement ring. 'I was going to leave him and then we got married instead. I mean, how crazy can you be at 24?'[59]

A small group of family and friends witnessed their marriage on 22 June 1964 at Milden in Suffolk; Edwards was best man. A fairy-tale unreality surrounded the romance: 'Michael used to say to me, "You'll expect them to play *Beauty* when we're coming down the aisle".' declared Sibley's friend, Sheila Bloom. 'And I always did.'[60]

Knowing the problems Deirdre had encountered with Ethel and her demands on her son's time, Sibley stipulated that they live a distance from his parents, so home became a charming house in Earls Court, near the company's rehearsal studios at the Royal Ballet School in Barons Court. The move coincided with Somes finally giving up smoking. Characteristically he simply decided one day to give up and did, but always kept a packet of cigarettes and matches prominently displayed; occasionally he would test himself by putting a cigarette in his mouth and lighting a match before putting it down.

Desperate to be the perfect wife, Sibley juggled her heavy work schedule with cooking breakfast, rushing from rehearsal to shop for dinner ('and I'm the most terrible cook there is'[61]) and getting the new home together; exhausted, she developed glandular fever, which kept her off stage until the following January. She became increasingly stressed, worrying that she couldn't look after her husband – 'not that he expected it, but *I* would have felt badly not being able to do it' – and about the effects of the illness and a long break on her career.[62] He was 'so sweet, he was rushing home from rehearsals to look after me', but inevitably he talked about work 'because after

58 Barbara Newman, *Antoinette Sibley*, Hutchinson, London, 1986, p129

59 Interview with author

60 Barbara Newman, *Antoinette Sibley*, Hutchinson, London, 1986, p138

61 Interview with author

62 Interview with author

all that's his life as it was mine'.[63] In her state any news was upsetting and she eventually went to stay with Winifred Edwards, who devotedly nursed her back to health. Sibley was 24, close to Deirdre's age when she died, and although hers was not a life and death situation, the effect on Somes must have been considerable, concerned for her and her career. .

Sibley always longed for the country and for her first outing after her illness Somes took her to see a derelict cottage near Thaxted in Essex set in countryside that reflected the private man – unspectacular, quintessentially English. Once renovated (thanks to increasingly generous American tour allowances), Somes slipped easily into local life, hobnobbing with villagers and farmers, many of whom had no idea what he did, with more enjoyment than the upper crust galas and tour receptions. It became the one place he could shed his professional life.

Somes' anxieties over Sibley coincided with Bronislava Nijinska's revival of her masterpiece *Les Biches*, created for Diaghilev in 1923. Ashton had learned his craft working in her company in the 1920s, absorbing her wit and elegance and mastery of the corps de ballet, observing how she built her works '... brick by brick, into the amazing structures that result in masterpieces like "Les Noces".'[64] He repaid the debt by ensuring the survival of her greatest ballets.

Somes worked with her as she set *Les Biches*. Rehearsals were extremely difficult as Nijinska was very deaf and spoke no English, only a little French, and mostly muttered in Polish or Russian as she worked from sheaves of notes in her personal notation. Discipline was draconian: men and women were segregated either side of the studio; concentration was absolute and her eagle eye missed nothing. Her husband, Nicholas Singaevsky, sat behind her and reported anyone who was smiling, talking or otherwise infringing their rules: if a dancer displeased her, he painstakingly recorded the miscreant's name in a little black book as Somes spelt it out for him. Marking was taboo. As the corps de ballet endlessly practised leaping over the sofa, Somes led away one girl after another as they became tearful, exhausted, injured or just fed up with trying to meet her standards. Because the Diaghilev dancers, on whom the ballet had been created, had smaller limbs than 1960s dancers, the movement emphasis changed; Vergie Derman recalled that Nijinska would ask a girl 'to extend an arm and then find that this had moved the girl's hand too far forward. She would push the hand back a little and then be cross that the elbow bent ...'[65] Yet she could convey the exact style with a few movements of arms or torso. Mason remembered as she reclined on

63 Interview with author

64 Frederick Ashton, *A Word about Choreography*, *Dancing Times*, May 1930, p124

65 Robert Clarson-Leach, *Ballet: Life as it really is in a dance company*, Robert Hale, London, 1986, p105

the sofa, '...beckoning, at the end of the Hostess's solo, the squat, ungainly woman became a seductive society woman. She loved showing that time and again.'[66] Similarly, when later reviving *Les Noces*, she demonstrated the movement as the Bride contemplatively cups her head in her hands and was transformed into a young girl.

Somes revered *Les Biches* and adored Nijinska, treating her with patience, courtesy and gentleness, somehow understanding her fractured French and her half-demonstrated movements while mediating between her and the company; when she became frustrated by her inability to explain or if somebody didn't immediately do something to her liking, he could calm her down. The moment she left the room, he rehearsed frenziedly so that everything was right when she returned. 'This,' she told him, 'is like working in Paradise.'

The effort was worth it. The understanding of Nijinska's style was so impressive that, after the first performance on 2 December 1964, everyone was asking 'What about *Les Noces*?' *Les Biches* had a European sophistication, but *Les Noces* was, to quote H. G. Wells, 'a rendering in sound and vision of the Russian peasant soul'[67] and, many thought, beyond the understanding of English dancers. De Valois, one of the 'Bridesmaids' in the 1920s, knew differently: 'The music is very difficult: but difficult music does not always worry English dancers as I have known it worry a Russian. In the old days it was the Poles and English in the ballet who held the musical fort.'[68] She had proposed reviving it in 1952, but the Ballet Advisory Panel demurred.

Les Noces went ahead in 1966. In retrospect, no one could explain how it ever got on, but everyone acknowledged that it would never have happened without Somes. 'It was just an amazing achievement,' recalled Monica Mason. 'His utter devotion and his ability to sort out from her mumblings ... she adored him ... She could tell from the moment she met Michael that here was a real pro and she really needed him and he rose to the challenge. But everybody who came in would trust Michael.'[69]

A major problem was establishing the dance phrases, which could start in the middle of one musical phrase and finish in the middle of another. Somes worked out how to count the complex rhythms with the pianists: 'Michael was used to this business of going backwards and forwards to the piano,' Mason explained, 'So she would say "De, dum tum tum tum tum tum, diddle de de de de, dum dum dum dum" And Somes would say to the pianist "Is that an 8 or is that a 12? How are you counting that? Are you counting two 8s

66 Interview with author

67 H G Wells letter to *The Times*, unprinted. Text distributed by Diaghilev at performances in 1926

68 Ninette de Valois, *Report on Competition No. 7, Ballet*, May 1948, Vol 5 No 5, p55

69 Interview with author

and a 6?" and Donald (Twiner) saying "Yes, I'm sure that's easiest two 8s and a 6" and we'd do it. Michael would go back and say "What about two 8s and a 12?" We'd count two 8s and a 12. It was literally going through like that.'[70]

Somes understood how frustrating this was for the dancers and tried to protect them whenever possible. Mason developed swollen knees from constant repetition and could not perform full out. Nijinska would not budge. No marking. For once, Somes failed to mollify her and spelt out 'm-o-n-i-c-a-m-a-s-o-n' for the little black book. There were no official breaks in the long rehearsals, but a code was worked out so that when a particular dancer made a 'T' sign everyone trooped out. Dowell remembered Somes' amusement before resuming the role of disapproving Director for Nijinska.

The first performance on 23 March 1966 showed that the supremely Russian work had been totally assimilated. Somes was pleased, with reservations: 'I know & am fully aware that 'Les Noces' would never have got on without you' wrote Ashton, '... of course we will all back you up over the orchestra!'[71] Lydia Sokolova, who had danced in the original production, sent her own tribute: 'Well, words fail me. Your wonderful coping with Les Noces, and with Bronja, who was difficult at the best of times, is nothing short of a miracle ... Without any doubt of all the old productions revived this one is the best ...'[72] She also added congratulations from Richard Buckle, who, when Somes wrote to thank him replied: '"Les Noces" was wonderful, and the curious thing is that I think it was a bit too well done. ... So I should like a few uncouth middle-aged people mixed up with the young ones, awkward lighting with shadows, and pianos and perhaps singers on the stage just to make things difficult. ... It is a serious and strange question whether works of art should be deliberately changed and slanted differently to give a new generation what they need – or expect – from them. This seems to me to have been done consciously or unconsciously with "Les Biches". It is delightful and it is what everyone wants it to be, but I bet it isn't a bit like it was originally – in atmosphere, I mean, not steps. ... I long to hear about it all.'[73]

The greatest tribute came from Nijinska herself when she left *Les Biches* and *Les Noces* in Somes' hands. Intermittently over the years he would receive letters from her, usually when she needed something. These he would proudly wave, tantalisingly, in front of audiences when talking about her and her work. They contained nothing that illuminated her choreography or philosophy; these mundane requests tempered with her affection and confidence, were a treasured symbol of her regard – Nijinsky's sister, trained

---

70 Interview with author

71 FA to MS nd

72 Lydia Sokolova to MS 23 March 1965

73 Richard Buckle to MS 3 May 1966

in St Petersburg, colleague of Diaghilev, master choreographer, put her trust in the boy from Taunton.

While working on *Les Biches* in 1964, Somes was also creating Lord Capulet in Kenneth MacMillan's *Romeo and Juliet* alongside Julia Farron as Lady Capulet. The title roles were created on Seymour and Gable, but MacMillan worked with multiple casts, including Fonteyn and Nureyev, Sibley and Dowell, Merle Park, Annette Page and Donald Macleary, all of whom had scheduled performances. The attempt to break the hierarchy did not work, neither David Webster, with one eye on the gala premiere, nor Hurok, planning the next American tour, saw any potential in 'a star is born'; Fonteyn and Nureyev *had* to open in London *and* New York. The decision was devastating for all the young dancers.[74]

Alongside the young talent, MacMillan made significant use of the company's first mature generation (hitherto Royal Ballet 'parents' were often younger than their 'children'). 'Kenneth used to despair of companies where ... (there were no dancers) who had stature and body and believability as an older person on the stage,' declared Deborah MacMillan, 'and Somes always had that – his Lord Capulet had a real gravure', giving his Juliets a strong force to rail against.[75] '... [T]he eloquence of his mime was fascinating.' wrote Gordon Anthony. 'He spoke with his hands; his dignified, calm but harsh natural dignity and stateliness was finally veiled with a gentle touch of remorse which I found more moving than a more explosive and less subtle performance would have been.'[76] Somes treasured a letter from Doris Niles Leslie written after he had relinquished the role: 'How Michel Fokine – my teacher would have enjoyed your performance ... how *empty* the Ball Scene was without you – an unbelievable void! The tremendous verve and elegance were not present ...'[77]

Romeo and Juliet became one of the most popular ballets in the repertory so Somes was on stage almost as often as in his prime dancing years. Over time, his Juliets got ever younger and his performance style increasingly old-fashioned, effectively emphasising the generation gap.

Leaving the Touring Company holding the fort at Covent Garden, the company embarked for America in spring 1965. The New York season was suffused with nostalgia as they were dancing at the Metropolitan Opera House for the last time before its demolition. Somes broke off a cherub's nose to add to his souvenirs. Classes were held in New York City Ballet's new studios in Lincoln Centre and several of Balanchine's dancers came to watch

74 Additional resentment came from Blair, who was creating Mercutio (a role in which he has rarely been equalled) but wanted to dance Romeo.

75 Interview with author

76 Gordon Anthony, *A Camera at the Ballet*, David and Charles, 1975, p91

77 Doris Niles Leslie to MS, 4 November 1983

Somes teach '& said they wished *I* gave *them* classes, – & what a wonderful teacher *I* was & raved on about it!!' Somes wrote to Ethel. They showed him over the building including the studio where Balanchine was working: 'He stopped the rehearsal & came right across to me, shook me by the hand & kissed me!! They said afterwards, they'd never known him do that to *anyone* in all the years they'd been with him!!'[78]

It was gratifying that success in New York did not depend solely on Fonteyn and Nureyev. *Romeo and Juliet* was rousingly acclaimed (especially Blair as Mercutio) and the new *Swan Lake* was a triumph, with praise for all the casts and the corps de ballet hailed as outstanding. Sibley's success was a constant source of pride; although his comment 'went *very* well' or 'v. good' seem flat, they were the highest praise from Somes. She became something of a cult, as, in Leighton Kerner's words, she 'sets her flashing feet in motion, bursts into a sunlit smile and cuts circles of lightning across the stage.'[79] Walter Terry praised her contrasts – speed and softness, staccato or legato and her bourées which 'shimmered like a pathway of pearls'.[80] To Somes great satisfaction, many said they preferred Sibley-Dowell to Fonteyn-Nureyev.

Although the New York season was sold out, the whole company, including directors, were on the ludicrous allowance of $7 a day: 'M[ichael] Wood said he thought it must be a mistake, – & I said it had *better* be Jack [Hart] told him st[raight]. that he would be on the plane home straight away if they didn't do something about it & he was not going to do *anything* until they had! ... We shouldn't have to be worried by things like that happening to us, when we have so much to think abt.'[81] After fifteen years, the old resentment still rankled – that Hurok and Opera House were maximising their profits at the expense of the company.

Tour planning was still unrealistic; after New York, there was never a clear twenty-four hours and often two performances a day; tight scheduling still ignored the possibility of late trains or bad weather (this time it was floods and hurricanes en route from Chicago to Los Angeles). Injuries were inevitable and there were hardly enough alternative casts to cope: 'It's *all* been *too* much of a strain, – & I always warned them this would happen. The Co. were half dead when they started the whole tour. I suppose we'll get by somehow, – but it's going to mean a lot of rehearsing & extra work for *me* ... It was ridiculous to try & run two major Seasons at the same time. There's just *not* enough people ...'[82]

---

78 MS to ES 18 April 1965

79 Leighton Kerner, *Woman's Wear Daily*, nd

80 Walter Terry, *World Journal Tribune*, nd,

81 MS to ES p 18 April 1965

82 MS to ES 2 June 1965. The Touring Company were concurrently performing at the Royal Opera House

Eventually Somes reached breaking point. He had, after consultation with Ashton, Hart and Peter Clegg, Ballet Master of the Opera Ballet, reassured a dancer that his job was safe and then found that contracts were not being renewed. Tired and exasperated, he offered his resignation to Ashton, who was in London mounting *Sylvia* on the Touring Company: 'I fail to see that there is any point in the 4 of us discussing *anything*, if contrary decisions are made subsequently. I am used to being made look a fool, – but I think it's very hard on the boy and says little for our muddled thinking.'[83] Ashton hastened to reassure him: 'I flatly refuse to accept any thoughts of your resignation ... It would be quite impossible for me to continue in my difficult task without your support, and although I may not say it often surely you must be aware of how much it means to me?'[84] Somes stayed. Ashton rejoined them in Los Angeles '... looking pretty harassed! – I don't think he got the help at home that he gets with us!!'[85]

There were, however, memorable highlights. At the Hollywood Bowl the company was asked to come on stage before the last act of *Swan Lake* and 'then they put all the lights out & on the count of *3* everyone in the audience lit a match, – 25,000 (sic) of them!! & chanted "Royal Ballet we *LOVE YOU!!*" – I must say it was *most* impressive ...'[86] However, in French-Canadian Montreal, the British could do nothing right, and audiences were so cool that even Nureyev didn't get back to take a call after his solo. In Detroit Sibley had a great success in *The Dream* and danced *Swan Lake* with Nureyev to great acclaim.

The final week took in five venues: '... pack & travel all the time ... Washington was an Ice Stadium & terrible d[ressing].rooms & no scenery!! We had no scenery in Baltimore either because the local Manager ran off with all the advance money, & Hurok had to cut down on expenses! [Theatres] all been hideous & the Co. are quite exhausted, – crying with exhaustion last night.'[87] For The Royal Ballet to be presented under conditions that did not allow them to give of their best was guaranteed to rouse Somes' wrath.

Yet Webster reported that it was the most successful of all the tours 'thanks to the Director ...'; Ashton told the Board that most of the credit was due to Somes and Hart. It was at last recognised that things must change: there would be no more one-night stands, a full free day each week and never again would the Company travel and perform on the same day.

Somes' work was publicly acknowledged in Frank Sullivan's prestigious

---

83 MS to FA 2 June 1965

84 FA to MS 3 June 1965

85 MS to ES p 30 June 1965

86 MS to ES p 1 July 1965. The official capacity of the Bowl is given as 17,500.

87 MS to ES p 24 May 1965

annual verse tribute to notables of the year in *The New Yorker*: '... *Joyeux Noël* to Jean Monnet, Michael Somes, Frances Macrae ...' alongside President Johnson, Grace Bumbry, Peter Shaffer, Groucho Marx, Irving Berlin, Ginger Rogers, Vidal Sassoon, Michael Caine, Christopher Isherwood, David Oistrakh,Tommy Steele and Arthur Hailey.

The story in Europe was somewhat different. Most European appearances were now undertaken by the touring section, which was cheaper for many of the venues in western Europe. Touring the Covent Garden company involved either an impresario prepared to undertake the financial risk, as in America, or prestige visits, like Russia, which attracted British Council subsidy; as British Council priorities were influenced by Whitehall, for whom Europe was low on the agenda at the time, they could not offer backing for the Covent Garden company unless the performances could be linked to trade fairs or special celebrations. It was a vicious circle – fewer visits meant unfamiliarity which meant smaller audiences which meant lower financial returns.

One of the few European tours was to Italy in1964, providing conductor Emanuel Young with a powerful memory that was typical of Somes. The company coaches had been delayed between Milan and Bologna and arrived at the Bologna hotel to find no staff to unload the dancers' personal luggage – about 150 cases – which was strapped to the roof of the coach. Young and Somes looked at each other and then Somes climbed onto the roof and handed the cases down to Young for the awaiting dancers. 'And Mike didn't turn a hair. This was a man who was Assistant Director ... going up and doing a porter's job, and not thinking he was being good about it. It was The Royal Ballet, it had to be done, these girls were going to dance that evening ... so why argue as to the rights and wrongs. Just do it. He was prepared to do the lowest possible job if it meant the good of The Royal Ballet.'[88]

If professionally Somes was riding high in the mid-1960s, his private life was increasingly under stress. His mother still expected to monopolise him. He spoke to her every day and wrote every few days when away; in London he saw her every weekend, even when there was a Saturday performance. Although Sibley '... tried to do it all right at first, bit by bit you knew you couldn't. You were so exhausted, you wanted to let your hair down and be with your husband or be by yourself.'[89]

As Sibley rose in the company she performed less, while Somes was rehearsing all day and in the theatre at every ballet performance. They mostly met in rehearsals, when he could reduce her to 'pulp' before building her up again in a relentless drive for perfection. With hindsight, Sibley could understand his methods, but at the time, '... if you're in love with somebody

---

88 Interview with author
89 Interview with author

as she was, deeply in love, you become more vulnerable and you can only be hurt'.[90] As pianist Donald Twiner observed, 'If it's someone you really care about you want desperately for them to do the best they can and if they falter or go by the wayside then [you] get up tight about it, and (Somes) did lose control,' often storming out of the studio.[91]

Sibley's experience was not unique: everyone got the same treatment as Somes pushed and pushed for more and more and it didn't always make it easier for a dancer to know that this was for their benefit. 'Once he got into the studio' declared Frank Freeman, 'that was his reason for being and he wanted the best and he wanted it to be as good as it could be and if that meant he was going to explode that's what he would do.'[92] In pushing to find a dancer's limits, he usually only used the brutal methods on those he felt could take it, although sometimes he misjudged a person's breaking point, but there were many, including Dowell and later David Ashmole, to whom he never raised his voice.

Dedicated and willing to give 100% plus, Sibley nevertheless came to want a life outside the theatre. For Somes there was nothing else: 'I've *never* known anybody with that utter passion for the dance. It was like an obsession with Somes and with Rudolf. They lived it, they died it, every single hour they breathed it. I couldn't live like that.'[93]

Stress manifested itself as skin problems, illness or injury which kept Sibley intermittently off stage throughout the 1960s. She had her first knee operation in autumn 1966, while the company was in Eastern Europe, but the anaesthetic poisoned her system. '... I am a little concerned at what I may hear tomorrow when I ring up' Somes wrote from Luxemburg, 'As I'm afraid they may have had to do more than we had hoped. ... Poor thing, she does seem to have been through it ...'[94] His feelings can only be imagined as once again he flew back from Eastern Europe to see a sick wife, and he could not be there for much of her long convalescence.

The tour was made no easier by what Somes saw as Fonteyn's decline: '... she really *has* slipped too far, & *I* think, is going to be an embarrassment to us' he wrote home. '... [I]f I thought that [Ashton's *Raymonda* pas de deux] had ever looked like that when *I* did it, – I *would* be ashamed, but people who saw it then assure me it *didn't*!! ... I just would not allow it to go on if I were Freddy. ... it really cannot be allowed to continue.'[95] With Nureyev unavailable, she

90 Sheila Bloom to Barbara Newman, *Antoinette Sibley*, Hutchinson, London, 1986, p168
91 Interview with author
92 Interview with author
93 Interview with author
94 MS to ES 17 September 1966
95 MS to ES 17 September 1966

was dissatisfied with her various partners and asked Somes to dance with her again. He was furious: 'She just doesn't think & couldn't care less abt. *them* or us. ... Then she wanted Firebird substituted by Lac Act II for the rest of the tour ... but of course we cannot do *that* ... She is a nuisance, & I bet she'll play up when Freddy's gone back ... adding almost wistfully 'We do miss Antoinette terribly. There is nobody remotely as good as *she* is ... & it really shows & everyone knows it.'[96]

The tour repertory was mostly the classics and *La Fille mal gardée*, and journalists asked why they weren't seeing any modern ballets: 'That makes me mad when I think how *I* pressed & pressed for us to do a modern rep that wld. show the Company off ...'[97] Somes could remember how Eastern Europe had admired the company's native works in the 1940s. No one was listening. It was New York and the seven *Sleeping Beauties* again.

Nor was life much happier in New York in 1967, when the company performed at the new Metropolitan Opera House in Lincoln Center. Functionalism had replaced the warmth of the old Met – Nureyev described it as 'just like a ballet supermarket. It's like a toy full of gadgets ... they forget people.'[98] There was an accident on the opening night when Beriosova's Cinderella coach overturned and everyone was anxious that the same might happen when Sibley made her New York debut in the role the next night. She had additional problems: her only stage call had been ruined by stage hands shifting scenery all around her, no kitchen set and no ballroom staircase to practice the difficult walk-down on pointe. Somes staged a spectacular rage on her behalf, but to no avail.

Ashton's *Jazz Calendar* was premiered in January 1968, based on the rhyme identifying the qualities associated with being born on each day of the week. Saturday, 'works hard for a living' was a ballet class, with a ferocious ballet master, who must have been based on Somes, driving the dancers one by one to exhaustion until Wayne Sleep (who had long suffered at Somes' hands) was last man standing.

Apparently, at this time, there were complaints about both Assistant Directors. Hart's aloof coldness and Somes' draconian rehearsal methods were, Ashton was told before the 1968 New York season, undermining company morale.[99] Inevitably, it was dancers who had difficulties with Somes who complained (no one was likely to run to the administration to say how much they liked working with him) but no one could deny that during this time the company had reached extraordinary levels of performance and

---

96 MS to ES 24 September 1966
97 MS to ES 24 September 1966
98 *Save the Met? Dance and Dancers*, June 1967, p31
99 Many, in fact, found Hart more intimidating than Somes.

commitment. For Michael Coleman, 'It was a whole era that I don't think could ever be bettered, when Somes was there, Margot was still around, Rudolf ... the best times, the best ballets, the best dancers – I should say best *performers* ...'[100] A company in depth, thinking, breathing as one. Fears of Fonteyn and Nureyev overshadowing The Royal Ballet had proved groundless. There were always those who only acknowledged the superstars, but for the majority, there was equal satisfaction in watching the up-and-coming soloists like Jennifer Penney, Ann Jenner, Lesley Collier and many younger dancers.

Yet, even as the company reached new heights, Somes' and Hart's futures were put in doubt as the question arose of Ashton's successor. The timing of the various decisions is difficult to establish – much was done without consultation or formal minutes and memories are unreliable about precise dates or the sequence of events. Georg Solti, Music Director of the Royal Opera, and David Webster were due to retire in 1970. When the company was in New York in spring 1967, *The Times* ran a leader stating that Ashton 'has said firmly that he intends to give up his position as director of the Royal Ballet before long.'[101] Ethel wrote to Somes that the *Evening Standard* too had reported Ashton's statement and had speculated on Cranko or Field as possible successors. 'If *they* come into it,' she wrote, 'I can well imagine that *you* won't like *that* ...'[102] On 6 June, Somes wrote back that '... Freddie ... has not as yet said anymore to me abt that School business, – only that *he* intends definitely to retire in 1970! I certainly won't stay after he goes, – so maybe I *shld.* think abt. going into the School, – but it's too early yet to think abt. – I'd like to get out of the *whole* thing.'[103] Ashton had often cried wolf, but this time it seems that Somes was taking him seriously.

According to Edward Thorpe's biography of Kenneth MacMillan, David Webster attended the first night of MacMillan's directorship in Berlin on 3 November 1966 and confidentially offered him the directorship, to take place in three years' time when Ashton was due to retire.[104] Apparently, this was done without reference to the Board. Others favoured John Field, citing his revitalisation of the Touring Company. Wester convinced Chairman Lord Drogheda that the question should not be formally discussed by the whole Board, as Ashton wanted to retire because of his dislike of the burdens of directorship, which he also felt were distracting him from choreography, and that de Valois favoured Field and MacMillan as joint directors. Matters were

---

100 Interview with author

101 Anon, *End of a Ballet Era*, The Times 27 May 1967

102 ES to MS p 14 May 1967

103 MS to ES p 6 June 1967

104 Thorpe, Edward, *Kenneth MacMillan, The Man and the Ballets*, Hamish Hamilton, London, 1985 , p94

further complicated when, in spring 1968, Field was offered Festival Ballet and Webster, apparently omitting to mention his 1966 conversation with MacMillan, hinted that he might lead The Royal Ballet.

Unfortunately, Field was not popular with the Covent Garden dancers: according to Edwards, for years de Valois extolled him as 'someone to remove many of the obstacles that had impeded the natural progress of our evolution as a company ...', which was hardly calculated to endear him to his fellow Assistant Directors.[105] Somes was not alone in feeling that the Touring Company success had been gained by distorting the classics, in that numbers, scenery and the orchestra had to be adapted for smaller stages. The two companies had little contact, referring to each other as Touring Trash and Resident Rubbish. Somes never had the ear of the Board; he spent no time politicking and indeed when he buttonholed Board members and Chairman Lord Drogheda or his successor Sir Claus Moser, it was usually to berate them about the ballet company playing second fiddle to the opera, or criticising orchestral standards. He left his work to speak for itself in a world where self-promotion is often a necessity.

Whatever impression he had given Somes in 1967 about wanting to retire, in spring 1968, a distressed Ashton told Lanchbery that he'd been 'sacked. Webster said "Fred, you've always said you wanted to retire when you were 65 ... Well, you're going to." When Ashton now said he didn't know if he was ready to retire, Webster told him it had been decided. When Ashton asked if he was going to be consulted about his successor, Webster said "I'm afraid not. You're going to be succeeded by John Field and Kenneth MacMillan reigning jointly."'[106] Ashton turned to Lanchbery and said 'What am I going to do about ... Jack and Michael'.[107]

It was left to Webster's deputy, John Tooley, to tell Somes and Hart the fait accompli, apparently making no suggestion as to how, or even if, they would fit in. Hart was extremely bitter and washed his hands of the company. Somes told Lanchbery, 'I felt like breaking down. All I could say to Tooley was "I don't feel any life without this company. It's my life and I'll come back in whatever capacity I can."'[108] Somes later stated unequivocally to the *Daily Mail*, 'I have virtually been given the sack. It happened some months ago and I have learnt since that I may be asked to stay on in some capacity, but I don't know what ... I don't know whether or not I want to stay.'[109] What really put him into the rage of all time was the incompetent handling of

105 Leslie Edwards, *In Good Company*, Dance Books, Alton, 2003, p189

106 John Lanchbery interview with author

107 John Lanchbery interview with author

108 John Lanchbery interview with author

109 Charles Greville, *A bit of bother at the Garden*, *Daily Mail*, 6 December 1968

33 *Façade*, Popular Song danced by Somes and Donald Britton for Friends of Covent Garden Christmas Party, 1967.

the succession. He expressed his disgust in a letter to Board member Lord Robbins and received a soothing diplomatic reply assuring him '... I hope and trust that of the various alternatives, each with its drawbacks, that which has been chosen will in the end prove the best for the future of the company ... please don't feel that you should *ever* have any inhibition in saying just what you think to ... Lionel Robbins.'[110]

With rumours circulating the company became increasingly unsettled, so Tooley asked the Board's permission, to formally announce Ashton's retirement and the MacMillan-Field succession. Ashton, he reiterated, had made no secret of his wanting to retire in 1970 and that he hoped MacMillan would succeed. If the press asked about Hart and Somes they should be told 'it

110 Lord Robbins to MS 29 December 1969

was hoped that they would continue to be associated with the Royal Ballet'.

If the powers that be didn't realise Somes' importance, Nureyev did, telling Tooley that whatever happened, Somes must stay if The Royal Ballet was to remain a great classical company. An estimated 75% of the dancers were also behind him and Hart.

Somes later told Wendy Ellis that, he had a highly emotional interview with Webster, during which he broke down and wept, telling Webster that he did not realise the consequences of retiring Ashton. Apparently, Webster, in New York for the company's American season, contacted Tooley to say he had revised his opinion about Ashton's retirement, but was told that the decision to make the announcement had been taken. Webster then announced the fait accompli to the company before the curtain rose on *Cinderella* on the opening night on 23 April 1968. Sibley, who was dancing the lead, recalled that '... the Company were to a man distraught. People were coming onto the stage crying, not knowing what they were doing ...'[111] The press release, excluding any reference to Somes and Hart, was issued on 26 April.[112]

But what had changed in the last decade that made Somes no longer a contender?

Apparently, he was offered the Directorship, although when is not clear. According to Sibley 'He always said no,' and Ellis says he was offered it before Field, but refused out of loyalty to Ashton. Somes later admitted that he would have hated being shackled by the responsibilities and administration; in the studio he could do what only he could do supremely well. As Assistant Director he frequently attended Ballet Sub-Committee meetings, and represented Ashton at Board Meetings if he could not go (or could not face going), but he had little patience for talk without action or endless meetings, planning and dealing with Board members whose reason for wanting a particular ballet revived was because it was the first one they saw with their wife. De Valois always felt that the company needed a choreographer at the top, so may never have seen Somes as sole Director, and she seems to have realised his distaste for administration when she proposed that he move over to the School. But whatever Somes felt, and however his ambitions changed, he could not help being hurt that his work in honing The Royal Ballet's high standards went unacknowledged and that, given his knowledge and

---

111 Interview with author

112 Webster's succession was handled no better. It was simply announced that the next General Administrator would be his second-in-command, John Tooley. Arnold Goodman, Chairman of the Arts Council, was furious that a publicly-funded body was appointing a successor from within without opening it up to public competition. When a Parliamentary Committee objected, Lords Drogheda and Robbins argued that Tooley was the best candidate and staff would be 'disappointed' if he did not succeed. Eventually a few selected names were 'invited' to apply for the General Administrator's job in phrasing that implied that they were unlikely to get it.

experience, he had no part in any consultations and everyone seemed to assume that he would just go on as before.

Tensions built up throughout the New York season. On the last night on 19 May, Sibley and Dowell danced Nureyev's *The Nutcracker* before an audience which included Maya Pliestskaya and the Bolshoi Ballet. Somes was hyper-tense, anxious the company should be at its best. Then the children playing the rats decided to have some last-night fun and instead of removing the top skirt of Sibley's dress, they ripped off the underskirt as well, leaving her apparently naked below her empire-line bodice. Through the long pas de deux: 'the entire choreography was with his arms through your legs – it couldn't have been ruder (or) more awful ... We did get through it somehow ...'[113] Somes was not impressed by resourcefulness, nor cared that it was not Sibley's fault and he vented his rage on her, reducing her to tears before the demanding second act. She recognised that he knew she could do nothing, 'but the sheer frustration and upset – that was obviously why he yelled and screamed and carried on, but for me that was absolutely the last straw.'[114] It was the end of their marriage.

Back in London, Somes returned to Islington while Sibley stayed in Earl's Court. Ronald Hynd took over her rehearsals.

Throughout autumn 1968, factions were forming and plots hatching.

Matters were not helped by a growing conviction at both the Arts Council and Covent Garden that maintaining a separate company on the road all year had become economically unfeasible and that the companies should merge; tours should be undertaken by a group performing small-scale works, leaving the whole company to tour large-scale productions to the few theatres big enough to take them. Provincial reaction was hostile: few Covent Garden principals were known outside London and many cities would be deprived of the classics and star dancers they knew and loved, like Doreen Wells and David Wall.

Amid all the unease, Ashton created *Enigma Variations*, music and theme matching his mood as his Directorship drew to its close. Like Elgar, Ashton had always relied on his friends and the ballet showed the importance of the 'friends pictured within' the variations to the creative artist, isolated by his genius. The cast included Grant, Shaw and Edwards and he paid tribute to Sibley as Dorabella and Dowell as Troyte; as others within the Elgar circle, Lorrayne and Robert Mead, Bergsma, Sleep, and Parkinson had rarely looked so good, and Beriosova was perfect as the gently caring Lady Elgar. Doyle was Jaeger-Nimrod, Elgar's closest friend and colleague, surely Ashton's tribute to Somes. Ashton was paralysed with nerves about choreographing the iconic

---

113 Interview with author
114 Interview with author

Nimrod, and it was Somes who gave him the way in. The variation evoked an autumn walk on which Elgar and Jaeger discussed the slow movements of Beethoven symphonies, so Somes proposed a walked 'conversation' which developed into a disagreement between Elgar and Jaeger, from this evolved a powerfully understated emotional trio as they were joined by Lady Elgar. Such disagreements were not unknown to Somes and Ashton, after which they sometimes stopped speaking adding spice to both their lives.

On 25 October 1968, Ashton sent a first night note to Somes: 'With my love and thanks for your most valuable help & enthusiasm over 'Enigma.' The Enigma really is who really did it, you or I?'[115]

John Lanchbery conducted the first performances, but for the 1973 revival, Adrian Boult was on the rostrum. Everyone was nervous, as Somes had a short fuse with guest conductors who were unsympathetic to the dancers' needs, often not attending enough rehearsals and giving a 'concert' performance.[116] Boult, however, commanded respect, not only through his links to Elgar but because he had conducted for Diaghilev and occasionally The Royal Ballet, besides his help over *Song of the Earth*. For him, 'Music in the theatre has a flavour that no concert hall can get near'[117] and he understood their differing demands. Also, like Somes, he believed that 'the highest standard was never good enough'.[118] They worked harmoniously over problems, especially the question of applause after 'Nimrod' and when to start the next variation: 'Concert silence = ballet applause often & I really believe it would convey Nimrod's effect better if we had quite a pause, & let Dorabella wait a bit longer before I start her. ... I *am* enjoying it all!'[119] They remained in touch, commiserating over back and knee problems. After his death, Lady Boult wrote to Somes that 'Our magical times at Covent Garden were a highlight of great happiness – *so* largely because of your care & coaching for him & your gentle kindness, to us both.'[120] An unrealised Boult-Somes plan was for Ashton to choreograph Elgar's *The Sanguine Fan*, and their last wish, also unfulfilled, was for Boult to conduct a revival of *Job*: 'When I read out your letter & the last paragraph but one ending "perhaps the Job family?" how I wish you could have seen the radiance spreading from ear to ear & chin to crown ....'[121]

---

115 FA to MS nd

116 One distinguished conductor contracted to conduct *Scènes de ballet*, sat through a rehearsal before asking, in Ashton's presence, 'Who is responsible for this ****?'

117 Sir Adrian Boult to MS 7 March 1975

118 Lady Boult to MS 10 March 1983

119 Sir Adrian Boult to MS March 7 1975

120 Lady Boult to MS 10 March 1983

121 Lady Boult to MS 30 November 1977

Peter Wright's experience on the new production of *The Sleeping Beauty* in 1968 was less pleasant. After twenty-two years the Oliver Messel-designed production was superseded by a version produced by Wright and designed by Lila de Nobili. Starting in the Sadler's Wells Theatre Ballet, Wright had taken charge of the Covent Garden Opera Ballet, moved into television production and then been Cranko's Ballet Master in Stuttgart before returning to The Royal Ballet in the mid-1960s, when Somes used to watch his classes and was generally encouraging. At first, Somes and Hart were cooperative over *The Sleeping Beauty*, galvanising Ashton into choreographing a new Garland dance, extra Jewel solo and a ravishing Awakening pas de deux, but as first night neared Somes began to resist the slightest alteration to what he regarded as the definitive version: he 'was very cross and terribly difficult and (he and Hart) nearly destroyed me ... shouting and screaming that I'd overstepped the mark and changed things that didn't need changing' until Ashton intervened and told Somes he'd gone too far.[122]

It was hardly surprising if Somes was short-tempered, his marriage break-up exacerbated by constant pain from his knee and worries about his future. The *Daily Express* caught up with the marriage breakup after Sibley ('the lovely dancer he groomed to ballerina stardom and then married') and Dowell danced the gala premiere of the new production, noting that Somes had been in the audience. 'Naturally I was there because of my position with the Royal Ballet,' he commented,[123] but his diary for February 1969 shows that he was still concerned: '1st Lac. A much better & shows her old form again at last. 22nd Lac. A unable to dance because of 'flu. Took her some flowers & champagne. 23rd Film 'Enigma' for Argo films. A unable to dance because of flu. Great shame.'

His low state is implied in diary entries for the New Year, recording the day to day irritations: 'January 10th Coppelia, otherwise usual dreary day. 15th Meeting abt NY & US tour. Now Margot wants SB as well as new ballet!! 29th Sub Comm meeting yesterday. Idiotic as usual!' Mixed in are darker notes, the deaths of close relatives, and, ominously, appointments with a succession of neurologists, reflecting growing concern about his mother's mental health.

Whatever his anxieties, Somes had to be with the company in America from April to July of 1969. In San Francisco his opinion of Fonteyn and Nureyev reached an all-time low when they were at a party which was raided by the drugs squad, resulting in screaming headlines around the world. 'Michael was going insane,' remembered Freeman. 'He was saying "I don't understand those two, how can they?" And he looked at us and said, "For

---

122 Interview with author
123 *Daily Express*, 19 December 1968

God's sake, what will your parents think?"'[124] an important point when the age of majority was still 21, so many of the corps de ballet were minors and their parents had to sign their contracts. How had the Fonteyn he knew become this stranger?

Fueling his apprehensions about the future were comments made by MacMillan in an interview about English male dancers. He saw a discrepancy between the standards of the girls and the men and stated that he would import foreign male dancers as the Royal Ballet men were not 'tough' enough. Vogue responded by commissioning a photograph of the current leading male dancers in 'heroic' poses. The male dancers were in transition from the older dancers like Grant, Shaw, MacLeary, Doyle and Hynd, to a younger generation, headed by Dowell and Coleman and David Wall in the Touring Company, but many younger men needed time to mature (and not all would stay the course), while there was a rich flowering among the girls – Sibley, Seymour, Park, Mason, Bergsma, Lorryane, Parkinson, Penny, Jenner and Collier.

Recognising what Somes was going through, Lincoln Kirsetin hastened 'to tell you how valuable you can be in the raising of a new generation ... Despair has its own rewards, and the chief one is to find out that it is self-indulgent in oneself and cruel to the people ... who love you ... You have half a lifetime ahead of you, with all sorts of fun from the service you will give. In spite of Fred's leaving, and things changing, there are always the incredible surprises of life, if only we allow them to happen, and not persist in our habit of well-anticipated gloom ... '[125]

Somes had cause for gloom. Back in London, a knee operation was only partially successful. Then his mother's health so deteriorated that she had to be admitted to a psychiatric hospital. For the next two years, he visited her every day between rehearsals and performances; from outside the hospital and along the corridor to her room, he could hear her incessantly calling 'Michael, Michael' but she could no longer recognise him. He stubbornly looked after his father, ignoring his aunt's eminently practical suggestion that Edwin might be happy in a religious house. Somes' strength and comfort was May, who had devotedly 'done' for him over the years and kept an eye on his parents whenever he was away.

Rumours of down-sizing both companies grew as the company returned to New York in spring 1970. Lanchbery remembered Webster jovially announcing before the opening on 21 April, "'I just want to scotch a silly rumour that's going round which is that quite a lot of you are going to be sacked. There's no plan to sack anybody. So just go out and give the wonderful

---

124 Interview with author
125 Lincoln Kirstein to MS nd

34 Ashton farewell gala finale: Fonteyn as Chloë with Somes as Daphnis.

performance that you've always given here." ... We all started to file out and Jack Hart said "... I think there will be cuts and changes and I advise a lot of you, to think what you will do if you did lose your job ... I've already made my plans."[126] Webster was furious.

Somes' immediate concern was the Ashton farewell tributes. The New York gala on 31 May opened with Fonteyn and Nureyev in the *Kingdom of the Shades*, showcasing the corps de ballet and acknowledging Ashton's debt to Petipa; Sibley and Dowell led *Symphonic Variations* and danced *The Dream* pas de deux after which came *Daphnis and Chloë* scene 3 and *Façade*. There were twenty-six minutes of curtain calls as New York said farewell 'vociferously, clamorously, and most of all affectionately'.[127]

In June, two years after complaining about the adverse effects of Somes and Hart's draconian rule, the Board at last 'resolved to record their appreciation of all that Mr John Hart and Mr Michael Somes had done for The Royal Ballet. Their time and their talent, unstintingly given, had played

126 Interview with author
127 Clive Barnes, *Tribute to Ashton, The Times*, 2 June 1970

a cardinal part in realising and maintaining the high standards which had been achieved, and in establishing the Royal Ballet's reputation as an international company second to none. Their work had been an outstanding contribution to the success of the recent visit to New York. The affection and respect in which they were held by the members of the company were no mean indication of their achievement.'[128] There was still no mention of their future.

The Royal Ballet's Ashton tribute at the Opera House was an evening of extraordinary devotion, love and magic which has passed into legend. Frank Freeman remembered the love surrounding Somes as, helped by numerous contemporaries, he reconstructed extracts from lost Ashton ballets, 'all to do with wanting the best not only out of individuals but the art form as a whole'.[129] Edwards researched accompanying images; his reward was a bill for £600 and a rebuke for extravagance, though for Webster's farewell, the Opera House had paid for singers to fly in from all over the world.

On 24 July Somes sent Ashton a gift with the note 'What can I say, except 'thank you' for all the glorious years we have spent together. You know, – (in spite of my rough exterior!), – how devoted I am to you in every way, – it has become part of my way of life, & the thought of being without it is desolation indeed. I only hope you will consider this performance as my humble & inadequate tribute to my dear friend & Master, & accept this tiny gift to remember it by. Love always, 'Mishki'.' In the auditorium, the audience opened their programmes to find a blank page: Ashton, sitting in the Grand Tier with Princess Margaret, was equally unenlightened.

The extraordinary retrospective included extracts from many 'lost' ballets – *Capriol Suite, Rio Grande, The Lord of Burleigh, Le Baiser de la fée, Don Juan, Apparitions, Nocturne,* in which Somes appeared briefly in Ashton's role of the Spectator, *The Judgement of Paris, Horoscope, Cupid and Psyche, Dante Sonata, The Wanderer, The Quest* and *Persephone,* alongside works still in the repertory – *Les Rendezvous, Les Patineurs,* Neapolitan Dance from *Swan Lake, Ondine, Homage to the Queen, Jazz Calendar, Giselle* Peasant pas de deux, *The Dream, Birthday Offering, Façade, Cinderella, Sylvia, Scènes de ballet, The Two Pigeons, Lament of the Waves, La Fille mal gardée, Monotones, Enigma Variations,* the *Sleeping Beauty* Awakening pas de deux, *Marguerite and Armand* and the complete *Symphonic Variations.* William Chappell wrote the linking narration, which was delivered by Helpmann. At the climax of the evening, Helpmann announced 'the finale from *Daphnis and Chloë*' and the atmosphere was electric as the audience awaited the lovers and then exploded as Fonteyn made her entrance with Somes. He had once written

---

128 Board minutes 23 June 1970
129 Interview with author

about this scene: 'This, I think I can honestly say, I have found one of the most exciting passages to dance in the whole of our repertoire. And one just *cannot* help being carried along with the gloriously exciting music and draining the last drop of energy for the last final twirl as the curtain descends.'[130] And carry everyone it did on a wave of nostalgia, the dancers affectionately gleeful that their mentor could hardly get through the fiendishly difficult choreography. On the last note, the stage blacked out, except for a lingering spot on a staggering Somes finishing his final twirl. As the company waltzed to *A Wedding Bouquet*, Ashton was brought backstage and, as Helpmann declaimed 'they incline to oblige only one, only one', he descended on the back stage lift to hysterical acclaim.

Congratulations, mixed with encouragement for the future, showered upon Somes. Ashton's sister, Edith, got straight to the point: 'all the love, & thought, & work that gone (sic) into the *wonderful* evening you gave Fred. A never to be forgotten evening, & all because all of you gave so much of yourselves ... Bless you & thank you from my heart – you dear, darling, loyal friend, & associate of Freds.'[131] 'You ... deserve a tribute yourself for having done it & thought it out with such loving care,' wrote Michael Wood. 'I hope the future both your own and the company's won't be as gloomy as you feel – one can only work for the company's enduring success.'[132] For Chappell, 'The only thing that absolutely maddened me was the fact that none of you got enough notice from the critics. Nor for that matter did I and so many of them wrote as tho' old Lady Helpmann had produced invented *and* written the whole thing ... Oh well, I suppose one should not be petty; and one great thing was to please Sir and I think Sir *was* pleased and surely at last satisfied with the praise heaped on him ... don't let the new regime get you too low. Just press on secure in the knowledge you have contributed a *great deal* to the R.B.'[133] – '... it was marvellous to see you so happy after such a great performance' wrote Ashton's nephew, Anthony Russell-Roberts. '... please allow yourself to be grafted wholeheartedly into the new regime. They are really going to need you.'[134] 'They' might need him, but there was still no sign that 'they' had acknowledged the fact.

---

130 Michael Somes, *Music for Dancing – the Part it Plays with special reference to "Daphnis and Chloë"*, RAD London Music Course, 7 May 1961
131 Edith Russell-Roberts to MS 25 July 1970
132 Michael Wood to MS July 27 1970
133 William Chappell to MS nd.
134 Anthony Russell-Roberts to MS nd July 1970

15

Eminence grise

'After the iron hand in the iron glove of de Valois there is bound to be something in the nature of a deluge, for a while,' predicted Caryl Brahms in 1954.[1] De Valois' careful planning postponed the deluge when she left in 1963, but in 1970 the same thought had not been put into the changeover and the Royal Ballet now had joint directors with conflicting areas of responsibility. Field assumed he would be overall director of the company, but found himself limited to administration, which he certainly didn't expect after a decade of autonomy in running the Touring Company. Neither he nor MacMillan showed much tact when Field announced to the company that, performance or not, Saturday class was now compulsory, adding 'So I'm afraid it's goodbye to those country cottages of yours.'[2] MacMillan, trying to lighten the atmosphere, quipped 'So if you've got something to say about casting or artistically, come and see me, but if it's the drains, then go and see John.'[3]

The drains were not what Field intended to deal with and only a few months later he resigned, leaving a vulnerable MacMillan to create new works while implementing the unpopular integration of the two companies and a new touring plan, having had no hand in forming either policy. For all the assurances about no downsizing, Hart's fears about cuts were proved right: thirty-five dancers were sacked, mostly from the former Touring section's corps de ballet, while several soloists and coryphées were demoted.[4] The reorganised company was top heavy, with fewer performances than ever for dancers who hadn't had many anyway, while those used to appearing every night on tour were bored.

Peter Wright was appointed Associate Director and became MacMillan's channel to the dancers.[5] Hart had already resigned. 'Thank you so very,

---

1 Caryl Brahms, *A Change of Dynasty*, *Ballet Today*, October 1954, p9

2 The Covent Garden company's country cottages, bought with savings from American tour allowances were, not unnaturally, a cause of resentment with the Touring Company, whose English touring payments allowed no savings whatsoever.

3 John Lanchbery, interview with author

4 Dancers to be dismissed were summoned to a meeting with the management by a 'yellow peril', the memo forms used for communication within the Opera House. They knew what it meant. The 'perils' were handed to them at the stage door, along with their Christmas cards.

5 Wright had been appointed to take over the Touring Company before the decision to combine the companies was taken.

very much for everything,' he wrote to Somes. 'Ann [Hart] has told me a little of what you have done for me – it is all very generous & I am truly very grateful. ... I will remember always & the friendship that grew out of our work has meant a great deal to me.'[6]

MacMillan's shyness, apparent indecision and insecurity masked the strength and inner toughness that he needed to function as Director and create while facing the prevailing animosity from a vociferous section of the public and some critics (mainly based on the premise that he wasn't Ashton); a lot of dissent was sown, in the company, the Board, Committees and the audience, ranging from spitefully petty to downright unbalanced –'terribly like Angela Brazil' remarked Deborah MacMillan, 'if you like her you don't like me.'[7] After de Valois, (autocratic and often arbitrary) and Ashton (liberal and possibly too accessible), MacMillan avoided dealing with the company en masse, communicating through his staff: 'There are others whose job [it is to rail at the company]', he explained disingenuously, 'Desmond Doyle, the ballet master, and Michael Somes.'[8] Although the atmosphere was hardly conducive to creation, he was under pressure to produce ballets for dancers he hardly knew. After creating the disastrous *Checkpoint* for the touring group, as his first ballet for Covent Garden he chose to extend his powerful *Anastasia*, produced in Berlin in 1967, into three acts. It was wildly controversial and there were boos on the opening night in July 1971. 'It sort of destroyed Kenneth' remembers Deborah MacMillan, who met him just after the *Anastasia* debacle; '(it) – set him off on completely the wrong foot – they were out to get him and he really couldn't redeem himself for years – such machinations and politicking.'[9] It took until *Manon* in 1974 for him to redeem himself in the eyes of audience and critics.

Whatever his personal feelings, Somes' loyalty to the company was absolute. He could have kept the title Assistant Director but felt he had been too closely identified with Ashton and he wanted 'no further share in making or endorsing policy. He wanted to do a job with well-defined limits, which he regarded as useful ... and ... a certain detachment, to advise, when and if the management asked for his advice, and generally to help maintain standards of performance.'[10] While this meant that he could avoid the hated meetings, he had no official voice, though that never stopped him apprehending Webster's successor, John Tooley, or various Board Members, especially on the eternal problems of inadequate stage time for the ballet, or the ongoing complaints about orchestral standards, about which he could be fearsome.

6 John Hart to MS 3 January 1971(?)

7 Interview with author

8 Robin Stringer *Keeping 130 Egos on their Toes, Daily Telegraph*, 8 March 1974

9 Interview with author

10 James Kennedy (Monahan), *Somes' Hindsight, Arts Guardian*, 1 February 1974

Deborah MacMillan's impression was that Somes 'was terribly, terribly loyal to Fred, and I think he was part of that group that saw Kenneth as a bit of an upstart, but I think there was a sneaking admiration for him and certain ballets he thought were terrific. I don't think he was manipulated by Fred to quite the same extent a lot of the others were. I think ... he had a respect for what Kenneth was trying to do, he saw that he was trying to push the art form forward and develop it ... He was a supporter, but also he detached himself because it was very much in camps ...'[11] Whatever his personal feelings, when MacMillan was ill before the premiere of *Triad* in 1972, Somes saw it through to the first night. MacMillan knew that he still had an important contribution to make and felt that he could have used his extensive knowledge and experience to develop his role, although apparently no one discussed with him how this might happen.

MacMillan established his own staff, notably Wright, Doyle and John Auld, with Peter Brownlee as Company Manager; Henry Legerton continued Hart's efficient advance planning. In October 1970, the programmes listed alphabetically three 'Principal Teachers and Répétiteurs' – Gerd Larsen, Brian Shaw and Michael Somes. In 1973, Somes' special position was recognised and he was designated Principal Répétiteur, primarily responsible for the Ashton repertory, the classics and certain MacMillan ballets.

Wright did all he could 'to get Somes involved in the right way with what was needed at the time for the company,' but, if anything went wrong, Somes blamed him. He dismissed Wright's experience with Stuttgart Ballet (which was certainly a very different world from The Royal Ballet), telling him 'You know absolutely nothing about being a Director, of course. I'd better tell you a few things ...' which he did, including priceless advice about planning balanced programmes, which he believed should entertain but also expose audiences to the unfamiliar – 'leading on' as he described it – mixing not just new and established works, but also ensuring a musical and visual variety. Somes was always generous in passing on his experience although 'he could be quite cruel when things weren't quite right,' declared Wright. 'It was good for me and for Kenneth too that he was there because he was niggling at us all the time. I think at the beginning he resented that I was still part of Touring Trash and he resented my presence ... he used to scream at me and say "The trouble is, everyone is frightened of you but they love me" – I'm sure a lot of people did love him dearly, but they were also terrified of him.'[12]

The ballet staff that remained – Somes, Larsen, Gregory, Edwards, Shaw – represented stability and, on a day-to-day level, most dancers took the changes in their stride. 'When you are a young dancer,' Mason confessed,

---

11 Interview with author
12 Interview with author

'you see it in terms of what it means to you and you need to be selfish and grab what you can from whoever is there and the moment they're not there, you think "Now who's going to help me." Always me. Me, me, me ...'[13] Lesley Collier didn't sense much change: '... privately, I guess ... it was the end of something rather glorious for him ... and I don't think he liked it too much. But it didn't affect how he worked with us – there was no way he was going to drop any standards at all – which was marvellous. I think he suffered quite a lot inside. He was irritated by people who didn't know as much as he knew,'[14] and as time went on, people knew less and less. As Coleman remarked, 'he maintained his position and he was always respected ... He could say what he liked but the buck stopped somewhere else.'[15]He must have felt very isolated without Ashton or Hart, and Dowell had the uneasy feeling that he was trying to get closer to the dancers. Fortunately, former Company Manager, Michael Wood, was now Director of the School, which was in the same building as the Barons Court studios, and Somes could always wander down the corridor and find a sympathetic ear.

The pressing problem was to maintain standards at Covent Garden while merging the companies and provide a changing roster of dancers for the new touring group without damaging Somes' hard-instilled standards, as one performance on tour could mean three days away from London. Somes' view was that touring benefited more experienced dancers, as young dancers did not get the proper discipline on the road, resulting in 'big heads and slack standards and it was only under the rigorous supervision which was available in London that dancers improved'.[16] Fortunately, several principals were eager to get back on the road where they could perform every night and not wait in the queue for an occasional performance at the Opera House.

The new touring policy got off to a rocky start. Even selecting possible dancers was not straightforward: Jerome Robbins was mounting *Dances at a Gathering* and wanted access to the whole company all the time (famously, he never announced his final casting until the very last moment) and a sizeable contingent were involved in filming Ashton's *Tales of Beatrice Potter.* Regional audiences complained that there were no classics and the repertory was unfamiliar[17] and the dancers, including Park, Sibley and Dowell, were hardly known outside London. Even the first tour of the whole company, taking large-scale ballets to the few cities with suitable theatres, was not a

13 Interview with author

14 Interview with author

15 Interview with author

16 James Kennedy (Monahan), *Somes' Hindsight, Arts Guardian*, 1 February 1974

17 Although it had been argued that the classics could not be adequately shown on smaller stages, the touring repertory now included *Symphonic Variations*, which needed as large a stage as any of the classics.

success. Gradually, the situation became untenable and the companies split. Under Peter Wright, the touring section grew, becoming first the Sadler's Wells Royal Ballet and then, in 1990, Birmingham Royal Ballet, with Wright applying all those hard-learned lessons from Somes on programming and planning.

Major changes in Somes' professional life coincided with equally major changes in his private life. In 1971 Ethel died and he continued to look after his father until his death a year later. Much as he mourned them and though his brother remained a problem, for the first time in his life, he was free. He found stability in his developing relationship with Wendy Ellis, one of the former Touring Company dancers, who came to his notice during the 1971 regional tour when he kept bumping into her sightseeing in the various cities and art galleries. She was eminently sensible, practical, an expert gardener and a good cook, although Somes would take over for his specialities – curry or stuffed pheasant.

The cottage became a much needed retreat from London pressures and here he began to relax. He blended into country life, happy to get involved with the local church and community; he joined the local farmers' shoots, which ended in convivial gatherings, drinking the local version of shandy – a lethal cocktail of rhubarb wine topped up with whisky. The wine was supplied by their next-door neighbours, three brother farm labourers who taught Wendy everything about growing vegetables; they had never travelled further than the local town, until Somes took them to Covent Garden to see *La Fille mal gardée*. 'Whoever he was with, he was on their level,' declared neighbour Darren McLagan. 'Fred (the eldest brother) was a real country bumpkin, he'd never left Lindsell, didn't go to Dunmow (about five miles away), he and Michael were best mates, you'd turn up, (and) they'd be in some ditch together looking at this or whatever, not a care in the world and yet he'd probably be meeting the Queen later.' Few knew anything about his London life until he took them to performances and they saw how their unassuming friend was revered within The Royal Ballet.

He was always interested in what people did and how. McLagan, who was a carpenter, recalled Somes watching him work: 'When he was with you, that was the important thing. He was hovering because he was interested and he often wanted to help and said 'I know I'm a nuisance, but I want to learn. He always had good ideas and schemes – he built a (gazebo cum folly) up in the garden and he asked me so many questions, how to cut the wood, who would split it, would it be strong enough? And he was *incredibly* strong.' McLagan recalled him coming along to help remove some wet decking ('and wet wood is pretty heavy'), which Somes flipped over as though it was made of balsa wood.[18]

18 Interview with author

He always looked smart, even when playing the country bumpkin, wandering around in an old jacket tied around the waist with string, though never abandoning his cuff links, of which he had a large collection; Roger Connor recalled helping a neighbour dig out a septic tank: 'I looked down and there was Michael in the bottom of the hole in his wellingtons and a very, very frayed, doggy but very nice and obviously once very expensive, old shirt with his cuff links on. And he was digging all the muck out of the bottom of this pit.'[19]

He was still performing. Although he would only appear as Armand's Father with The Royal Ballet (when Fonteyn danced it abroad, Leslie Edwards mounted it and performed the role), but the continuing popularity of *Romeo and Juliet* meant he was frequently on as Lord Capulet. In New York, he went on at short notice as Nicholas II in *Anastasia*, talked through the performance by Rasputin/Adrian Grater. There was the occasional gala, notably Richard Buckle's *The Greatest Show on Earth* in 1971, organised to raise funds to save Titian's *Diana and Acteon* for the nation. Wearing original Bakst costumes from the 1921 *Sleeping Princess*, Somes and Joy Newton appeared in a Minuet led by Idzikowsky and Ursula Moreton; Dolin and Alexandra Danilova were the King and Queen and Fonteyn and Nureyev danced the pas de deux. In a 1972 charity gala at the Maltings, Snape, he made a riotous debut in the Foxtrot from *Façade* with Edwards, Sheila Humphreys and Deirdre O'Conaire.

In February 1972, Somes and Wright went to Zurich, to see Nureyev's staging of the full-length *Raymonda* and assess its suitability for The Royal Ballet.[20] The company already had Nureyev's superb staging of Act III, and, as that version included the best of the choreography from the other acts, they felt that the three-act version was old fashioned and exactly the type of 19th century ballet against which Fokine had rebelled. Unfortunately, Somes told Nureyev this while they and other guests were having dinner in Zurich's smartest restaurant and 'an unholy row broke out between Rudolf and Michael ... Rudolf started attacking him and saying it's nothing to do with that it's because you hate me – and it was really fisticuffs and the *whole* restaurant was (stunned) – no conversation just this noise going on at our table.'[21] Nureyev insulted Somes and Wright and took the opportunity to drag up all his resentment against The Royal Ballet – that the company

---

19 Interview with author

20 *Raymonda* had long been hovering on the brink of The Royal Ballet repertory. Plans for Sergeyev to mount Act III in late 1939 were, obviously, abandoned and Ashton resisted Karsavina's suggestion of a full length version in the 1950s. In 1964, Nureyev mounted the full ballet for the Touring Company, but it was thought neither strong nor interesting enough for the permanent repertory; his 1966 version of Act III, incorporating the best bits from earlier acts, was, however, dazzling: 'We've got the best of [*Raymonda* and *La Bayadère*] now,' commented de Valois, 'and don't need the full versions.'

21 Peter Wright, interview with author

35 *O.W.*: Somes as Oscar Wilde, Stephen Jefferies as A Young Chap.
Photograph by Anthony Crickmay.

was nothing before he arrived and had done nothing for his career, never created new ballets for him, only used him as a partner for Fonteyn and as an inspiration for the male dancers until they had improved to a point that he could be thrown aside – most of which were demonstrably untrue.

There was one last starring role. Broadway choreographer and director Joe Layton, suggested a follow-up to his crowd-pleasing *The Grand Tour*, choreographed for the touring group.[22] He proposed a ballet on Oscar Wilde, but with one stipulation 'I'll have to have Michael Somes in the leading role, there's no-one else.' Somes' initial reaction was 'I don't want to play that old poof,' but he succumbed. Set to William Walton's Viola Concerto and a suite from *The Quest*, *O.W.* was more production than choreography. Wilde was portrayed as a high camp aesthete and the trial was reduced to a boxing match between Wilde and the Marquess of Queensberry, with Wilde countering his lordship's parries and jabs with the flick of a sunflower. At the end, the broken Wilde, dressed in prison garb, reflected on his life as the voice of John Gielgud read from *De Profundis;* here Somes, with hardly a movement, transformed an unsatisfactory work into a tragedy.

Many of *O.W.'s* young cast had never performed with Somes. Stephen Jefferies, playing a Young Chap, was intrigued by his style: '... it was the old school of dancing and etiquette – he tipped the stage door keeper and little mannerisms like that ... the old technique how he put on his eyeliner, he's got this black stick which he heats up and a make-up tin which he's had for years. And the way he acted was very expansive, very to the gallery ... he had an air I always think of as 'Larry' [Olivier].'[23]

After the premiere on 22 February 1972, Somes cabled the company his thanks: 'Darling children I remembered my counts thanks to all your wonderful messages glorious bullying and dear love stop ever grateful.' He won a gratifying crop of good notices and praise from friends and colleagues, although Michael Wood summed up the general feeling: 'What a truly marvellous performance you gave. It really was exciting and moving. I don't like the ballet one little bit – a thoroughly beastly conception – but it is worth it for what you do.'[24]

His major contribution, however, remained in the studio. Admiration of Ashton never blinded Somes to the merits of others: he was sensitive to a wide range of choreographic styles, equally adept at rehearsing the classics and the finer points of Ashton, MacMillan, Balanchine, Robbins, Massine,

---

22 Layton had been dance director for *The Sound of Music* and the film *Thoroughly Modern Millie*, won Tonys for the choreography of *No Strings* and *George M*, directed Noël Coward's *Sail Away* and won a director's Emmy for Barbra Streisand's television spectacular *My Name is Barbra*.

23 Interview with author

24 Michael Wood to MS 23 February 1972

Nijinska, Nureyev's productions, de Valois, Helpmann ... 'He moved with every stage of the ballet,' stressed de Valois. 'Some of the people who came to visit us did him a lot of good and he was interested, but he took everything for insertion into the company and he threw it out if he didn't approve of it. If any of the modern people really got on the right side of Michael, it would be quite certain they had a genius in them.'[25] A ballet had to be how the choreographer envisaged it, although a Royal Ballet style was always evident: '... choreographers simply fell over themselves to come and work with us', declared Freeman, 'because there were no mannerisms and it was so clear and that did come from Michael's work.'[26] Somes believed that the audience came to see choreography ('or,' qualified Ashley Page, 'what they should be coming to see');[27] he revered choreographers and felt it was an honour to perform in great ballets; the dancer was the choreographer's instrument and stars who changed given steps to make themselves look better were anathema to him.

Company discipline was never more seriously tested than on tour in South America in 1973. In Brasilia, half the audience could not get into the 25,000-seater stadium – partly because of the traffic in duplicate and black-market tickets, partly because tickets had been sold for the whole stadium, including the space needed for the stage: up to 5,000 shut-out ticket holders chanted 'Margot, let us in'. Inside the audience was screaming enthusiastically, drowning out the orchestra for *La Bayadère*, but Sibley and Dowell in the leads, counted for the corps de ballet while carrying on their own performance: their preparation was so secure, that the performance was hardly affected.

By 1974, Somes had become the company's eminence grise, 'a kind of one-man breakwater between management and dancers;' who 'has made what might have been a nebulous task of preserving performance-standards into a fierce, eagle-eyed reality'.[28] For a while, he developed a more eccentric persona. Page remembered him dressed in 'this smart jacket with a mandarin collar and the monocle, silver hair and for a while he did walk very badly with a stick. And the monocle and the stick together was almost a Diaghilev. He made a great show of getting (the monocle) out, putting it in his eye and looking around the room, it was very theatrical ... he did it with great humour ...' He once dyed his greying hair blonde, taking a good deal of chaff until he reverted to distinguished white. He never minded being made fun of and would join in.

---

25 Interview with author
26 Interview with author
27 Interview with author
28 James Kennedy (Monahan), *Somes' Hindsight, Arts Guardian*, 1 February 1974

Somes venerated not only ballet's greats but any dancer from the older generation and former colleagues. Recognising how hard it must be for once-acclaimed stars to feel forgotten, he got the whole company to sign a testimonial to Tchernicheva in admiration and gratitude for her work with them. He organised donations to buy Karsavina a new chair and took Sibley and Ellis to talk to her about roles she had danced. When she had to move into a care home, he helped ensure that her old friend, Dolly Watkin, could visit her on a regular basis.

Although admitting that 'one would like to possess eternal youth and go on being a dancer for ever,' Somes found his new life 'immensely rewarding. I've had the good fortune to work with many of the greatest ballet names in living memory and I enjoy trying to pass on to the younger generation what I learnt.'[29] Dowell paid tribute when accepting the *Dance Magazine* award for 1972: 'He's someone who at one time picked up the very shattered pieces of a dancer at the school dress rehearsal; and from that moment on, he has always believed in me, which has been a primary source of assurance for me and has given me the urge to go on ... he is the most fantastic driving force; not just for me – well, especially to me – but to many dancers in the company.'[30] For his 55th birthday, to aid his 'driving force', the dancers presented him with a full-size stock whip.

Help might be offered obliquely, abruptly – 'You don't know anything about this, I supposed I'd better tell you' – but what he taught was invaluable, as when talking David Walker through *The Sleeping Beauty* or Wright through the intricacies of programme planning. Few knew the extent of his kindness. 'Although he put on this glossy kind of egocentric in the theatre,' declared Ellis, 'He was extremely generous and thought a lot about people in general.'[31] After Mason was off for nine months with a broken foot, it was Somes who came in after class every day to help rebuild her confidence. He worried about corps de ballet dancers who had reached the limits of their talents. When Fonteyn commissioned Alfred Rodrigues' first ballet, he never knew Somes had suggested him, nor did pianist Donald Twiner realise that Somes proposed to the Board that he should try conducting. When Wayne Sleep had the chance of acting Ariel in *The Tempest*, he was told that his return to the company could not be guaranteed, until Somes intervened: 'Michael, who, I thought, did not care for me and who had alternately sat on me and pushed me in rehearsals to the limits of endurance, had stepped in and saved my career with the Royal Ballet. He had my undying gratitude for the ten happy years I had with the company after this.'[32]

---

29 Eric Johns, *A second career for Michael Somes*, The Stage, 16 November 1972
30 Anthony Dowell, interview with author
31 Interview with author
32 Wayne Sleep, *Precious Little Sleep*, Boxtree, London, 1996, p101

He was interested in every member of the company, where they came from, how they got into dancing, where they first learned to dance. He gave away dancers at their marriages, including Vergie Derman, Marguerite Porter to Carl Myers and Rashna Homji to Stephen Jefferies. He provided comfort and support through problems emotional and physical: when Patricia Ruanne was dropped in rehearsal, Somes took charge, commandeered a car and himself held her immobile until they reached the hospital, where he took control, galvanising the staff into action. His help and interest extended to anyone associated with the organisation and to neighbours in Islington and Essex; he might help financially, and often anonymously, or just lend a sympathetic ear to their problems, for he was a good listener. No one, even Ellis, knew how many people he helped or how. 'He was such a gentleman,' declared Collier, 'such a lovely man. He was a big kind of pussy-cat tiger, whose real bark was much louder than his bite. He was so well-meaning. Just at the bottom this madness.'[33]

Although he told interviewers that his walking stick was an intimidating weapon, it was also a necessity as he was in constant pain. In late 1973, he underwent a tibial osteotomy in an attempt to alleviate his arthritic knee: to redistribute the weight of the body, a wedge-shaped portion of bone was cut from the tibia to realign the shin and knee. '... quite a big job,' he wrote to Cyril Beaumont, 'but I am assured I will have more movement and less pain as a result of it'.[34] It brought some relief, but there was no permanent cure.

He contributed to various publications, proudly writing a new foreword to *Theatre Street*, which unfortunately was never published. There were still official functions – a reception at the American Embassy, invitations to Chequers and Royal Academy of Arts Annual Dinners. Only one frequent request elicited immediate refusal: to serve on the jury of international ballet competitions, however prestigious, annotating one invitation: 'Said NO!! Don't agree with competitions!! (Not the Olympic Games!!)' He did, however, serve on several national scholarship panels and gave lecture demonstrations to the ISTD, Cecchetti Congress and BBO (of which he became a Patron), teaching children the 'snake' from *The Rite of Spring*, the 'building' blocks from *Les Noces*, or working with young Royal Ballet dancers in pas de deux master classes, bringing out all the choreography's subtle phrasing and musicality.

Working with outside organisations he was patient and charming, but The Royal Ballet had to be the best and there he gave no quarter. Rehearsing Royal Ballet School performances '... he really did upset youngsters,' recalled Julia Farron. 'He didn't know how to work with students ... He just couldn't

33 Interview with author

34 MS to Cyril W. Beaumont, 9 September 1973, Cyril W Beaumont collection, Theatre and Performance Collections, V&A

36 Demonstration for the Cecchetti Society with Wendy Ellis and Julian Hosking. Photograph by Jack Blake.

understand why they couldn't do it ...'[35] Yet Ashley Page remembered Somes rehearsing Saturday's Child in *Jazz Calendar* 'being very good with us because he would give us a taste of what we were going to get later but tempered with the fact that he was doing it with students'.[36] Asked if he was afraid of Somes, David Ashmole looked incredulous: 'After having Ninette de Valois [at the School] ... She was actually worse ... Ursula Moreton, Barbara Fewster – all from the old school'.[37] For Somes, students were at the end of their apprenticeship and if no one had treated them as professionals before, it was time they understood what to expect in a world that took little account of fragile egos. Some of the students he coached never looked as good again. After seeing the School perform *The Dream* in 1973, Kirstein wrote 'I cannot tell you how moved and impressed I was ... You always shy away from receiving any credit, almost as if it were bad luck to be told people are grateful for your care and attention, but, I ... cannot forbear from saying ... how much I admire your presence and cherish your service.'[38] Kirsten

35 Interview with author
36 Interview with author
37 Interview with author
38 Lincoln Kirstein to MS, July ny

envisioned exchanges between New York City Ballet and The Royal Ballet – '... teachers, students and dancers, – and even jointly produce repertory. Certainly Balanchine also wants this ...'[39] The dream remained a dream.

In 1975, The Royal Ballet's corps de ballet won the *Evening Standard* Dance Award, an acknowledgment of Somes' and Jill Gregory's work in bringing them to what Clement Crisp in the citation called 'a unique and very beautiful ensemble ... a national treasure'.[40] 'The girls of the Royal Ballet's Corps de Ballet are the most wonderful in the world,' Somes told *The Daily Express*.[41] This was what he had wanted since seeing the Rockettes in 1937.

Under pressure to reach wider audiences, the Opera House found The Tent, believing that a less intimidating venue than Covent Garden would win new audiences in London while allowing largel-scale productions to be toured, countering Somes' argument that productions should not be cut down to fit into small regional theatres. Thus in 1975, the Company returned from a successful Far East tour to Battersea Park, where the former circus marquee had been erected. The opening night, in the presence of Princess Margaret, revealed one disadvantage when a torrential storm turned the park into a quagmire and the orchestra was inaudible above the rain on the canvas roof.

Somes still had an input into new works, notably Ashton's *A Month in the Country* in 1976. In search of a score and having rejected Tchaikovsky, Borodin and Scriabin, Ashton consulted Isaiah Berlin, who, to his dismay, suggested the much-used Chopin. Not until Somes found a Claudio Arrau recording combining Chopin's rare Variations on Mozart's 'La ci darem la mano', Fantasy on Polish Airs and Andante Spinata and Grande Polonaise did Ashton see a way into the ballet.

MacMillan mostly rehearsed his own works, but he entrusted several to Somes, especially *The Rite of Spring*, which he never wanted anyone else to work on. When Somes sat in during the creation of *Manon* in 1974, the ballet which revealed a new glamorous allure in Sibley, Mason described him performing the same 'housekeeping' services that he had for Ashton, leaving MacMillan free to concentrate on the choreography: '... in the middle of Act II, the introductions of the various courtesans to the gentlemen ... Kenneth left the room, and Michael said, "Well, I don't know if Kenneth's really set this, so shall we organise this properly on the music?" ... So he made sure the music was broken down – which was exactly what he was used to doing for Fred ... and also made little suggestions about the different gentlemen's reactions to us ...'[42]

39 Lincoln Kirstein to MS, 1 August nd

40 The other nominees were Marcia Haydée, Natalia Makarova, Sibley and Dowell, Nureyev, Twyla Tharp and Dance Theatre of Harlem.

41 *Thirty girls who are leaping way ahead in the beauty stakes, Daily Express*, 21 January 1975

42 Interview with author

In the late 1970s Somes heard Poulenc's *Gloria*. He suggested it to Ashton, who didn't warm to it, then to MacMillan. MacMillan had been reading Vera Brittain's *Testament of Youth* and saw potential in the contrast between the certainty of the score and the horrors of the First World War, in which his father had served. *Gloria*, premiered in 1980, was one of his finest works and one that Somes greatly admired.

By the mid-1970s, however, dancers seemed to be losing what Michael Boulton described as 'a touch of madness'.[43] For a new generation, dance often seemed more job than vocation: 'I could see the girls (mentally) glancing at their wrist watches (waiting) to get away to the nearest disco,' Lady Lunnon reported to Somes after a particularly lethargic *Les Sylphides*. Reviews noted declining technical standards. With few obvious stars emerging from within the company, guests were brought in to boost the box office.

The result was too many dancers in the same roles, leaving little time to work on interpretation. 'It sounds strange,' admitted Somes' protegé Wayne Eagling after his debut as Romeo, 'but I didn't realise until half way through the first performance that there was more to the role than overcoming the technical difficulties. And then I didn't get to dance Romeo again for months.'[44]

Dancers were now less compliant. Eagling was impatient with the 'slow grinding of the System' where the company was almost an extension of the School: 'so we think like kids and are treated like kids. The majority of dancers can't be bothered to fight for change.'[45] He was in the forefront of the increased union activity agitating for parity with the opera company, a campaign which had Somes' sympathy, even if he disapproved the methods.

By 1977 the dual pressures of choreographer and director became unsustainable and MacMillan resigned as Director. In an unexpected move, his successor came from outside the organisation, Norman Morrice, who had choreographed many works for Ballet Rambert and seen its transformation from classical to contemporary company. 'He's too nice,' was de Valois's verdict. 'To be a Director you have to not mind being hated.'[46]

While Morrice appreciated Somes, their personalities were incompatible. Somes was skeptical about the appointment and certainly Morrice lacked experience in running a large company. His brief was to cut back guest artists and bring on the younger dancers, a task which fell to Somes. Unfortunately, the company was not strong in depth at the time and dancers, at all levels, were pushed before they were ready; Anthony Dowson remembered that '...

43 Interview with author
44 Interview with author
45 Jan Murray, *This Ballet Life. So Short, So Selfish*, *Time Out*, 16-22 May 1975, p14
46 Ninette de Valois to Kathrine Sorley Walker

younger people given more opportunity and experimentation with casting meant more rehearsing (and) less people rehearsing the corps de ballet, so the corps de ballet work perhaps was the first thing that suffered because half were rehearsing solo and principal stuff ...(yet) that was also a time when ballets were not being well rehearsed.'[47] The policy led to '... lethargy and lack of interest in all those parts which weren't solos,' remembered Michael Crookes.[48] The group pride in the ensemble, which Somes had done much to create, weakened as emphasis shifted from the company to the individual. For Collier, the erosion of that slow, structured progression of a career from corps de ballet to coryphee to soloist '... made the company very different. It had lost its respect of achievement.'[49]

Maybe to alleviate pressure on Morrice, a condition of his appointment was that he would not create ballets, despite his considerable experience. In the search to find new choreographers inside and outside the company, the native repertory seemed almost wantonly neglected – not just Ashton, de Valois, Cranko and even some of MacMillan's best works, but also the rich historical repertory of Fokine, Massine, Petit, Nijinska, Balanchine, Robbins, that had defined The Royal Ballet, catering for a wide range of talents in programmes that were balanced and varied – choreographically, visually and aurally – stretching dancers and audience alike. As dancers became increasingly obsessed with technique, dance theatre works became undervalued as diluting the 'dance' experience.

Somes had grown up at a time when dance was a serious art for mature audiences and the company was small enough for the dancers to mix with artists and composers like Lambert, Arthur Bliss, Fedorovitch, McKnight Kauffer, Piper and Burra. Sibley felt a change from her own time: '... the lack of Kenneth, Fred, Antony Tudor, Madam, Helpmann – all these *amazing* theatrical geniuses ... *imagine* just sitting having a cup of coffee with Fred on one day, the next day you're talking to Kenneth or the next day Antony Tudor in a corner being weird ... but the one little gem you might get out of him would last a lifetime ... *invention* was around the place ... it was *theatre* ... so when you came to your classical roles you were thinking 'person' not "Is my leg going up at a hundred miles an hour." ... *Imagine* doing *Cinderella* with Bobby and Fred, you *had* to be bloody good just to exist ... It was *fabulous* ... we had so many geniuses around who were all pouring out, fighting off each other. It wasn't all happy atmospheres ... but what it makes is grit for the pearl.'[50]

---

47 Interview with author
48 Interview with author
49 Interview with author
50 Interview with author

The hallmarks of Royal Ballet style – lyricism, accuracy, footwork, épaulement, speed, characterisation, subtlety – came to be undervalued by the dancers, the young generation of critics and the new audience being courted to replace the 'old', who were seen as living on nostalgia and resistant to change. Tradition ceased to be something positive, a resource to be drawn on. Under Merle Park, the School, too, seemed determined to reject the tried and tested, bringing in teachers unschooled in the English style, especially from Soviet Russia. The Royal Ballet had always welcomed guest teachers, but the foundation had been those steeped in company traditions.

With growing globalisation, change was inevitable. With more companies established in the Commonwealth, often by former Royal Ballet dancers, students who had regarded London as their goal, now had the option of working at home, while, after Britain joined the EEC, dancers and students came increasingly from Europe, trained in diverse schools. New dancers, new audiences, new Boards knew little of company traditions and were in no position to take what was of value in the past and marry it to the best of the present. Morale was low. Problems were blamed on lack of money, not lack of ideas. Somes soldiered on, ensuring that every dancer maximised their talent.

In February 1978 MacMillan created *Mayerling*, one of his most powerful ballets, giving Somes his final created role as Emperor Franz Joseph of Austria-Hungary, father of the unstable Crown Prince Rudolf, who dies in a murder-suicide pact with his young mistress, Mary Vetsera. Somes' rigid, unyielding symbol of a dying Empire 'gave those boys doing Rudolf a chance to be febrile and hysterical and frustrated and angry and mad', declared Deborah MacMillan. 'It's terribly important. Kenneth *adored* him as Franz Joseph.'[51] The character was firmly anchored in fine detail – his fury over the practical joke of the exploding cigar or sending a servant to cover the body of the shot beater. As the Emperor walked across the stage hung with family portraits, brooding on the hopelessness of a dynasty without a responsible heir, Somes movingly evoked a dying world. Could he have drawn an analogy with events closer to home? He was also pleased that MacMillan had created a superb role for Ellis as Princess Stephanie, who projected vulnerability and desperation, sensitively expressed through the extremes of the choreography.

And one last role, Catalabutte, in the *The Sleeping Beauty* celebrating de Valois's 80th birthday in July 1978, '… a portrait full of detail, and in its fussy petulant self-importance, exactly right'.[52] The programme credited Michael Soames. De Valois had paid him her own tribute when she dedicated *Step by Step* to him in 1977.

---

51 Interview with author

52 David Dougil, *Sunday Times*, 30 July 1978

37 With Queen Elizabeth the Queen Mother. Photograph by Reg Wilson.

38 In costume as Lord Capulet in *Romeo and Juliet*, giving advice on child rearing to Princess Diana.

At the same time, he was being pursued to do commercials for After Eight Mints, but, despite all entreaties, he felt it would be demeaning, thus turning down a handsome additional income and making him familiar far beyond the ballet world.

Tributes and anniversaries were reminders of time passing. For Fonteyn's 60ᵗʰ birthday on 23 May 1979, Ashton made *Salut d'amour à Margot Fonteyn* – revisiting some of his most beautiful work for her (significantly many roles could be evoked by stance and upper body alone). At the end, led by Somes, the Royal Ballet men each presented her with a single rose, before Edwards brought on a basket making up the 60 and everyone sang Happy Birthday as the flowers rained down and Princess Margaret announced Fonteyn's elevation to Prima Ballerina Assoluta.

Somes' admiration for Sibley never wavered. After they divorced in 1973, she married Panton Corbett and embarked on a career as wife and mother interspersed with triumphant performances. Somes helped with her exercises after the birth of her daughter, Eloise, in 1975, but a problem knee postponed her return. In 1978 she was expecting her second child, and retirement looked inevitable, so she was asked to cut the Taglioni Cake on the last day of the 1978 season.[53] In his tribute, Somes likened her to Taglioni, who had 'had great patience in adversity, & I like to think, also knew how important it is for a dancer to know how to "Live with failure".!!! ... the charm of her dancing was due to the spiritual quality with which she invested all her movements, – her purity of line, and her effortless grace & lightness. – We will always remember these qualities in Antoinette, with which she is blessed in such abundance, & to which can be added so much more, – that wonderful darting speed & brilliance, & the natural musicality & facility of her movement.'[54] Sibley was very moved: 'It was especially good to hear it from you,' she wrote, 'who had always been such a taskmaster ... how grateful I am for all your wonderful help always and your encouragement.'[55]

Several anniversaries fell in 1981. On 6 January, fifty years since the reopening of Sadler's Wells, Somes and Edwards reunited as the Musicians in *The Rake's Progress* orgy scene alongside colleagues from the 1930s and 1940s – Pamela May, Jean Bedells, June Brae, Stella Claire, Jill Gregory, Gwyneth Matthews, Elizabeth Miller, Joy Newton, Alexis Rassine – with only Stephen Jefferies as the Rake representing the current generation. 'I loved the Orgy Scene,' de Valois wrote to Somes, '– everyone looked so

---

53 The Taglioni cake ceremony, instituted by Cyril W. Beaumont, took place between matinée and evening performances on the last Saturday of the season, when a seed cake, supposedly Marie Taglioni's favourite, was cut by a dancer who was leaving the company.

54 MS mss notes

55 Antoinette Sibley to MS, nd (1978)

unbelievably young!'[56] For the souvenir programme, Somes contributed evocative memories about the trials and joys of the 1930s when they all *were* 'so unbelievably young'.

May marked The Royal Ballet's 50th anniversary. With nothing decided, time getting short and Morrice increasingly agitated, Somes offered to put together a retrospective of the two companies, running for three performances over 29 and 30 May. Unlike the Ashton gala, he was on his own. For weeks, days of rehearsal were followed by hours in the Royal Opera House Archives, checking facts, choosing images, writing the script and ensuring that everyone who had contributed to the company was acknowledged.

Some must-haves required a psychological approach. It was unthinkable to omit Sibley and Dowell in *The Dream* pas de deux, but Dowell was injured and Sibley had no desire to return to the stage. Then, after she created Ashton's short, undemanding *Soupirs* pas de deux for a gala in November 1980, 'Somes said "If you can do *that* on pointe, you can do the *Dream* pas de deux." ... I said, I certainly couldn't do it – I could not hop on pointe and I couldn't do a pas de deux of that duration and control. Somes said "So we'll take out a few of the steps that neither of you can do." Fred said "Yes, you can do it even if you are in gumboots."'[57] Somes guided their rehearsals, knowing they would put themselves under pressure to achieve and each day they could do a little bit more. 'Michael played the whole situation wonderfully ... It was an extraordinary trust that could only come with him knowing us so well, and us knowing him so well, that we allowed ourselves even to get into that position. That was the cleverness of Michael.'[58] Thus he ensured another ten years of Sibley's career.

The programme was a remarkable overview of both Royal Ballet companies. As it was Somes' choice, the selection is significant: twelve Ashton excerpts (*Les Rendezvous, Les Patineurs, Nocturne, Cinderella, Daphnis and Chloë, Ondine, The Two Pigeons, La Fille mal gardée, The Dream, Monotones II, Voices of Spring pas de deux* and the Garland Dance from *The Sleeping Beauty*), eight MacMillan (*Danses Concertantes, The Invitation, Song of the Earth, Romeo and Juliet* – not the obvious Balcony pas de deux but the Romeo/ Mercutio/ Benvolio pas de trois – *Manon, Mayerling* – the scene between the Empress and Rudolf – *Gloria* and *Isadora*), three de Valois (*Job, The Rake's Progress, Checkmate*), two Petipa (*La Bayadère* shades, *Paquita*), two Cranko (*Pineapple Poll* and *Prince of the Pagodas*), plus Ivanov (Mirletons from *Casse Noisette*), Fokine (*The Firebird*), Massine (*La Boutique fantasque*), Nijinska (*Les Noces*), Balanchine (*Ballet Imperial*), Tudor (*Shadowplay*), Robbins (*The Concert*),

56 Ninette de Valois to MS, nd (1981)

57 Interview with author

58 Barbara Newman, *Antoinette Sibley*, London, Hutchinson, 1986, p208

Andrée Howard (*La Fête étrange*) and, representing a new generation, David Bintley (*Meadow of Proverbs*), Michael Corder (*Counterpoint*) and Jonathan Burrows (*Song*). Helpmann was missing because, besides being difficult to excerpt, *Hamlet* was revived during the anniversary season, and Somes somehow found time to help in rehearsals. In his script, he tried to mention everyone of note (forgetting only one major name), including a handsome tribute to Nureyev, acknowledging not only his brilliant dancing, but also his part in raising the status of the male dancer in England and contributing to improving standards. He narrated the performances himself. The *coup de théâtre* came in the finale of the third performance when the *Cinderella* Stars took to the stage followed by Fonteyn and Ashton in the pumpkin coach. The audience fell apart.

Somes' script showed his understanding of what went into making a company and its heritage, especially how much was owed to less familiar and non-dancing names – teachers like Plucis, administrators like Michael Wood. 'Like everyone else,' wrote Sir Claus Moser, Chairman of the Royal Opera House Board, 'I was spellbound & and felt terribly proud of the Company.'[59] 'Without you and your determination to succeed' acknowledged Tooley, 'it would never have happened, and we are greatly indebted to you ...'[60] Gratifyingly, everyone said the company looked wonderful and that it was, above all, a company evening.

That autumn, Somes was shocked to learn that Dowell was leaving to join American Ballet Theatre. He alone expressed reservations to Dowell, afraid that this perfect example of Royal Ballet schooling would lose his characteristic style. When Dowell returned in 1986, Somes was displeased to find his protegé had developed ideas of his own and another period of antagonism set in; then Page remembers '... he started to say "Actually Anthony has this way of doing this maybe you should think about it." I think it was just that initial slightly hurt pride that this person who'd learned everything from you, had learned something from someone else.'[61] He always found it difficult to let go.

Professional recognition came in November, when Somes received the Queen Elizabeth II Coronation Award for a lifetime of service to British Ballet. The citation succinctly summed up his achievement: 'Michael Somes has quietly served British Ballet with total dedication and faith from the moment he entered the Sadler's Wells School in 1934 until today ... He is the stern but loving custodian, not only of the Ashton repertory, but also of the Royal Ballet's historical inheritance ... He cares, as few dancers care, about

---

59 Sir Claus Moser to MS, 30 May ny (1981)
60 Sir John Tooley to MS, 1 June 1981
61 Interview with author

inheritance and about ballet's debt to the great artists and great teachers of former years who have made today's achievements possible. He insists that young dancers appreciate the work of the architects of the Royal Ballet.'

As the 1970s became the 1980s, Somes seemed to be mellowing; Fonteyn recalled him as 'unexpectedly warm and lovable',[62] although for Dowell 'I think to those of us who knew him knew that there could be a volcano sleeping but ready to go.'[63] Behind the scenes, however, tensions were building.

In 1980, Ashton created *Rhapsody,* one of his few ballets without Somes' input. The ban on guest artists had relaxed in favour of superstars and *Rhapsody* was created for Mikhail Baryshnikov. Why Ashton did not want Somes around is debatable – maybe he felt insecure in creating for Baryshnikov and didn't want to be exposed to Somes' blunt criticisms in front of a visiting star. In fact, Somes got on well with Baryshnikov, who gave him the very practical gift of an elegant silver-topped cane.

He was not, however, on good terms with Morrice, who did not even have the courtesy to consult Somes on productions he had personally worked on, such as Berthe's mime in *Giselle* which he had learned from Karsavina. Their relationship, however, reached an all-time low when Morrice told him to end his relationship with Ellis. She had for some time sensed charges of favouritism and antagonism towards herself. Somes valued her tenacity, work ethic and reliability and she was a prime example of what his punishing methods could achieve in pushing a dancer beyond their perceived limits.

Company ethos was crumbling as individuals fought for their own territory. There were increasing conflicts with Gregory and Larsen over the execution of movements and Somes was not shy of trespassing on their province if he felt standards were slipping. There may have been resentment that Somes' understanding of a wide range of ballets gave him greater influence. Gregory was an excellent coach for preliminary Ashton rehearsals, but didn't have Somes' intimate knowledge of the details; she rehearsed the girls in the classics with Larsen and the corps de ballet with Rosalind Eyre, but Somes was responsible for the finished product – the last week of studio rehearsals and the transition to stage calls and the dress rehearsal.

There were difficulties with company dancers and guest stars. 'No-one listens to me anymore,' he used to say gloomily. He was not alone. 'I felt very sad,' Pauline Clayden wrote to him after working on the 1981 revival of *Daphnis and Chloë,* '... so little preparation done by 'Chloe', to find out what it was supposed to be, the few things I had said, it appeared, blatantly ignored

---

62 Margot Fonteyn, *Autobiography,* Hamish Hamilton, London, 1989, p145
63 Interview with author

...'[64] Guesting as Princess Aurora, the brilliant, but neurotic, Gelsey Kirkland needed motivation for every flick an eyelash; Somes treated her very gently but, with time running out, had to be firm: 'Darling, let's just get on with it. We're still on the first act.'

There were problems over the increasing use of notators, who could be very dogmatic, even when they had never danced in a ballet themselves. For Somes, dance notation had to be flexible, like musical notation: 'you have got to have the mind that can stretch, without departing from the choreographer's wishes or intentions. Different dancers doing the same roles *should* differ. If they don't then I'm afraid those ballets will die because they would be sent out as carbon copies.'[65]

The Opera House was changing too. He hated audiences dressing casually as friend Patricia Connor remembered: 'I think you're going to a lovely place and all these people are putting on this marvellous time for you, the least you can do is not turn up in jeans and a t-shirt – Michael was *fierce* about that.'[66]

Another knee operation in 1982 left him in agonising pain. Fonteyn, now settled in Panama with her wheelchair-bound husband, wrote of her concern and William Chappell, too, was disturbed: '... sad you have had such a wretched time and it worries me a lot. Do please call me and visit whenever you feel you need to talk. I think it's a good thing now & then to let it all out to someone like me who is outside that enclosed world you are forced to live in.'[67] Yet he remained physically energetic. On the company's first visit to China and Hong Kong in 1983 they sailed to one function on a clipper-style yacht: when the men all climbed up the rigging and out across the spars, Somes doggedly climbed to the top pinnacle.

Tensions increased as Somes saw the foundations being worn away: 'The discipline had been slowly eroded,' recalled Stephen Jefferies. 'Dancers' attitudes had changed so much that they thought they had a lot more freedom – they wouldn't take it. I think towards the end, his frustrations got so great he took on this resigned attitude ... I got a feeling he couldn't care less any more ... after all he was late 60s, though one never thought of him as anything more than this robust, athletic 55 year old.'[68] His friend, Jo Curtis, 'got the impression he got bored with the politics and he just couldn't be bothered with it.'[69] The result was greater irascibility than usual and frustration could turn into aggression, which led some of the Ballet Staff to complain to Sir Claus Moser, who had always been on friendly terms with Somes. Again, it

64 Pauline Clayden to MS, nd (1981)
65 Somes unidentified interview
66 Interview with author
67 William Chappell to MS, 31 December 1983
68 Interview with author
69 Interview with author

was complainants who were heard. As political correctness began to intrude on quality, less forceful people made life easier. Crookes wondered if he knew his days were numbered: 'Certainly he seemed to be reduced in some way – it was like Merlin losing his powers.'[70] Ellis remembers him saying 'What am I doing with my life. Looking back it all seems very meaningless.'[71] Not an unfamiliar feeling as age creeps up, but an unexpected one for Somes.

The denouement came in 1984, 'Kenneth came home looking absolutely stunned,' recalled Deborah MacMillan, 'and said "I've just nearly been punched by Somes."'[72] Somes had run into MacMillan at the Stage Door and started to harangue him about his recent decision to prune some of the older Juliets, including Ellis. He became terribly agitated and MacMillan was 'absolutely terrified ... It was a lot of bluster (and) did get blown up slightly out of proportion. He thought Somes was going to punch him – I know he didn't (though it was) frightening enough.'[73] MacMillan's rehearsals were hastily moved from the Barons Court studios to the Opera House, to keep the antagonists apart.

Rumours spread. On Friday, 18 May 1984, Somes was at the Ballet School rehearsing *The Sleeping Beauty* for the School matinée. At noon he and Gregory took a full company call of *Scènes de ballet* and then, at 1pm he walked into a full call of *The Firebird*. 'He came in and rehearsed us as well as he had always rehearsed us,' remembered Dowson, 'and at the end ... he just stood up and with a tear in his eye said "You know I love this company and I've just been told that I must leave and I wish you all well" and that was that.'[74] Page recalled him talking about what 'he was going to do without being there every day, working with the company his life had been ... and then he couldn't speak any more. He got up and walked out of the door to the canteen, normally he would go the way down to the office, so it was a real exit. It was really weird. There was a silence, probably about twenty seconds; several people burst into tears and we left the studio pretty silently.'[75] Dowson summed it up: 'For a lot of us I think the bottom fell out of our world.'[76]

On his call sheet Somes wrote: 'My *last* Call Sheet after *50* years!!' And by *Firebird* 'Goodbye!!'

The suddenness was shocking. Disgracefully, whatever the reasons, whatever people's private feelings about Somes, there was no official

---

70 Interview with author

71 Interview with author

72 Interview with author

73 Deborah MacMillan interview with author

74 Interview with author

75 Interview with author

76 Interview with author

announcement and no acknowledgment of an extraordinary career of incalculable benefit to The Royal Ballet. Only *The Stage* ran a report, after which *The Times* and *The Mirror* picked up the story: 'A company spokesman would say only that: "After today he is no longer with us."'[77] 'I don't want to talk about it,' Somes commented. 'The company is the most important thing and it must go on to further success. It's very sad, but things do change and one just has to put up with these situations.'[78] The management had not even agreed a position. With breathtaking understatement, Morrice acknowledged that Somes had been an 'invaluable' company member for 'many' years and that 'The way things have worked out is rather unfortunate.' A 'spokesman' for The Royal Ballet refused to discuss reports that '"a violent backstage drama" was the reason, saying ungraciously, "He's left. He was over retirement age, and he went. It was so long ago – about the middle of last month – that I've thrown the note away with the actual date."'[79]

At the annual press conference in June, nothing was said until the *Daily Telegraph* asked if were true that 'there had been a punch-up' between Somes and MacMillan over Ellis dancing Juliet.[80] A clearly unprepared management seemed surprised that the question had been asked. Morris well-meaningly said he was 'sorry that so distinguished career had ended "in the way it did" and that it was unfortunately "part of life in the theatre"' while Tooley commented about 'times when it becomes difficult, or impossible, to collaborate with someone.' Still no one acknowledged Somes' 50-year contribution. Insult was added to injury when Morrice's almost apologetically announced plans to revive *Symphonic Variations* for Ashton's 80th birthday – 'we thought it would be justified to try to bring some of his works back into the repertory,' – when the guardian of those ballets was no longer there.[81]

Somes remained discreet, while hinting in private letters about long-standing disagreements. Even to de Valois he felt it would be 'inappropriate to comment' and instead expressed his 'thanks, admiration and respect for you, without whom there would have been no wonderful years with the Ballet for me, or for so many. I am sad to have had to end my long association on such an unhappy note, but the Company is, of course, the most important thing, its dancers so dear to me. Change must happen, and there is always a time to go.'[82] Thanking John Percival for his *Dance and Dancers* tributes, he added, '... I always tried to teach the value of discipline self imposed & my

---

77 *The Times*, nd, Somes cuttings

78 *The Stage* 24 May 1984

79 Julie Fairhead, *Royal Ballet teacher quits after 'fight'*, *The Standard*, 21 June 1984

80 Nor, until *The Times* asked a direct question, was MacMillan's new commitment to American Ballet Theatre mentioned

81 All quotations in the paragraph from *Curtain Up, Dance and Dancers*, August 1984

82 MS to Ninette de Valois, 30 June 1984

short temper was perhaps the result of frustration over standards and many disagreements with the Staff over the past few years.'[83]

In private letters to Somes, the Covent Garden Board and Governors of the Royal Ballet acknowledged The Royal Ballet's indebtedness and in reply he expressed himself most clearly to their respective Chairmen, Sir Claus Moser and Sir Joseph Lockwood, both of whom he had always admired. To Sir Claus he referred to 'resentment in certain quarters ... but oddly enough, not by the dancers who have always been most exposed to my irascibility and strict discipline ... you can imagine how sad I feel that now they will be deprived of the knowledge & traditions that I was so fortunate to gather & inherit (because of being in the right place at the right time) & which I had hoped to pass on to them as well as I was able ... my loyalty, as always, is to dancers past & present to whom I owe so much & from whom I have received such love & respect right up to the end.'[84]

Replying to Sir Joseph Lockwood, Somes reiterated that his own contribution was a result of 'being a 'sponge' & 'telephone wire' through which to pass the treasury of knowledge I learnt from the "all time greats" of our Art. Added to this I must mention the enormous & boundless privilege granted me in working & learning from Sir Frederick ... (and) partnering our great Margot through her finest years': passing on that knowledge was 'a duty and a privilege.'[85]

He was especially moved by a heartfelt tribute from James Monahan in *Dancing Times*. 'I was even more gratified by your references to my ferocious crustiness yet implying so kindly, & if I may be permitted to say, so rightly, that underneath it I try to be a very loving & loyal person. Yes! I have enjoyed my rows, – they have all been good fun, but I hope, usually to a good purpose, & with no rancour & hard feelings afterwards. I have always felt that all of us dancers, Directors, choreographers & critics were part of a big family, all intent on one obvious purpose & each with his or her own contributions to make ... As with most good families, I have scolded my students, & insulted & yes encouraged believe it or not & drawn tears, but I hope, only to be rewarded by their love & smiles when something for which I have striven with them has paid off. ... I find this talking abt. myself faintly disgusting, so please forgive me if I say very little more except that as you said, it appears no one officially hardly noticed my passing off the scene publicly & I permitted myself a little hurt well hidden I hope that as an old Artist one wonders maybe why? One always tries to make a good exit.'[86]

---

83 MS to John Percival, mss draft letter nd

84 MS to Sir Claus Moser, mss draft letter nd

85 MS to Sir Joseph Lockwood, mss draft letter nd

86 MS to James Monahan, mss draft letter, nd

A distressed Fonteyn wrote to her Sam: '... Leslie (Edwards) said everyone is appalled, and so, you can be sure, am I. Please don't despair ... dearest Michael, you know that the company is not the same as the one we grew up in and had such a wonderful time in ... You have given such a magnificent contribution to ballet and our ballet in particular. You still give wonderful performances. Don't think this is the end. I know there is more for you to do.'[87]

---

87 MF to MS, 24 June 1984

16

Retirement

The company carried on, but ill-feeling about the way Somes' going had been managed simmered below the surface. The dancers were unsettled, not just because Somes had been a constant presence throughout their dancing lives, but he had a way of making everyone feel safe if things weren't going well: 'There was an incredible self-discipline when Somes was there,' recalled Adrian Grater, 'which came to the rescue.'[1] He had been the repository of so much knowledge that no single person could succeed him, and what had been focused in his single artistic intelligence was now diffused and those who took over needed time to grow into their new responsibilities. Ballet Master Christopher Newton picked up some of the pieces and Brian Shaw took on more teaching and coaching. Christopher Carr worked with the corps de ballet while Mason assumed responsibility for much of the MacMillan repertory. MacLeary, who had Somes' intimate knowledge of the major classical roles, became répétiteur to the principal dancers. Nobody, however, had Somes' understanding of the whole, how to develop a dancer's career, or sensitivity to so many choreographic styles. Yet his influence remained: 'In this business people are so much a part of your life and so much a part of how your career has been,' explained Mason, 'that as long as you go on doing it, you hear their voice in your ear all the time,' a tribute echoed by others who passed on what he had taught – Sibley, Collier, Ellis, Page, Jefferies, Dowson and Carr.

Eagling gave his own take on the dismissal in his ballet *Broken Man* for the Choreographic Group: 'because I liked Michael so much ... I ran in and smashed into a brick wall ... based on the fact that I thought Michael had crashed into a brick wall and it was not fair.'[2]

All companies go through fallow periods but some dancers and many who had watched the company over the years felt that Somes' departure coincided with a decline in standards and quality. There was a disastrous revival of *Ballet Imperial* in March 1985, when the company failed to master the Balanchine style, a style which, in 1950, they had performed convincingly after three weeks. Dancers seemed to stagnate; they may have fulfilled their potential, but Somes could push people beyond the obvious. The range of dancers and repertory, which had been one of the joys of The Royal Ballet, seemed diminished. Dancers 'didn't deliver ... a lot of the detail

1 Interview with author
2 Interview with author

evaporated ... everything got evened out', explained Peter Wright. Line became less classically pure, lyrical became angular, jumps and extensions extreme, whatever the dictates of the choreography or music. Steps were well executed, technique developed, but often there was nothing behind the eyes.

The pride in being part of the ensemble evaporated as the aim became only solo roles. With dancers given chances too soon, self-belief could become ego. Young dancers declared themselves bored after only a few performances of a role, or even a new work. Darcey Bussell complained that in *The Sleeping Beauty*, 'It would make the role even more interesting, if Petipa had given Aurora some less obvious steps to dance,'[3] whereas Sibley paid tribute to Somes 'making me hear the music, pull everything out of the choreography that I could, because he knew what you could do with a *Swan Lake*, a *Sleeping Beauty*, *Giselle*.' Jonathan Cope found it hard to express the emotional side 'which is very hard to do with ballet because, um, y'know, it's so silly'.[4] Somes may not always have liked the characters he was asked to portray and recognised how easily ballet could become absurd, but understood that a dancer must believe in them if the audience is to be convinced. Also, as the company became increasingly international, it lost 'a feeling of camaraderie ... it wouldn't be like that if (Somes) was here,' declared Page, 'because he wouldn't put up with it.'

Every day was no longer filled with activity, but Somes kept himself occupied, refusing some invitations on the grounds that he was too busy. In April 1985, he went to report on ballet in Czechoslovakia for the British Council, a rushed tour of schools and performances, interspersed with the inevitable social functions. He was very impressed with the teaching at all levels and greatly enjoyed the performances, which included a balletic *Macbeth*, *Vox clamantis* ('modern work on a leather strapped steep ramp. v. good.'), a circus, the opera *Garrulous Snail*, Ladislav Fialka's Theatre of the Balustrades ('... really marvellous, ... (Fialka's) miming was fantastic') and he was enchanted by a children's ballet about a beetle. He also coached principals of the Czech National Ballet in *The Sleeping Beauty* and *Giselle*. 'These people *really can* dance,' he wrote in his notes, 'We have no-one to touch them – male or female,' adding wistfully, 'They are kind & modest & listen to me & I tell them a few things & they are so attentive & work *so* hard.'[5] Everywhere he saw high standards of costuming, staging and lighting which, for him, Covent Garden had so often failed to achieve.

He also oversaw Ashton ballets as they were increasingly mounted abroad. He had overseen *La Fille mal gardée* for the Hungarian State Ballet in 1971 and

---

3 Darcey Bussell, *Live in Dance*, Centry, London, 1998, p121

4 Jonathan Cope, *The Times Magazine*, London, 8 July 1995 p32

5 MS notes for British Council report

Ballet of the Teatr Wielki in Warsaw in 1977, and *Jazz Calendar* for the Joffrey Ballet the same year. In 1986 he mounted *La Fille mal gardée* in Vienna and 1987 *Cinderella* for Dutch National Ballet, now under the direction of Wayne Eagling, for whom he also mounted *Symphonic Variations* in 1989; the Royal Swedish Ballet acquired *Cinderella* in 1991 and American Ballet Theatre *Symphonic Variations* in 1992. He had a healthy disregard for hierarchy, his first cast for *Cinderella* in Stockholm, included only three principals and two soloists, the remainder he selected from the corps de ballet and the second cast was almost entirely corps de ballet. A notator then set the ballet after which Somes took over rehearsals until the first night.

In September 1986, Dowell became Director of The Royal Ballet, having served as Assistant Director in 1984 and Associate Director to Morrice from 1985. Somes rang him to say 'If you want any help at any time I'm here.' Dowell later wondered if he hoped 'I would use him as an advice figure and everything would go through him ... I thought "I'm Director, now I'm running the show and I've got to do it."'[6] Somes never actively interfered, but he was critical of Dowell's first programmes and later took him to task for engaging Sylvie Guillem as principal guest artist at a time when company morale was low.

Hardly was Dowell installed than Ashton insisted that Somes rehearse the *Sylvia* pas de deux for his 80th birthday gala that October. In December 1987, he was back rehearsing *Cinderella*. His first demand was that Dowell leave his office and watch the full call with him; thus the company witnessed their Director deferring to his former boss, just as Dowell remembered a deferential Somes in the presence of de Valois or Ashton. Most of the dancers were new to him and unused to his methods. They ran the ballet straight through, 'Somes as usual mouthing off throughout,' according to Errol Pickford. 'At the end he went "That was very good. You can all go home."'[7] As there was over an hour of the rehearsal left, the dancers were astounded; they were used to every second being used, whether it was necessary or not. Somes must, however, have been baffled by the mindset of some young dancers, especially one Cinderella, who had been allowed to develop a superstition about dancing a whole ballet through before the performance, and wanted to leave out the solo in the run through.

Rehearsing *Symphonic Variations* in spring 1988, he was again working with Royal Ballet dancers for whom the ballet was unfamiliar. In the cast was American Cynthia Harvey, who had been well primed to expect fire and brimstone. She later declared she had never been so well prepared for any role and, when Ashton popped his head round her dressing-room door on

---

6 Interview with author
7 Interview with author

the first night and waspishly asked 'Nervous?' he was disconcerted when she replied 'Funnily enough, I'm not.' 'Having no prehistory I didn't really have an intimidation factor, so I think that helped.'[8]

Inevitably the passing years were marked by deaths of friends and colleagues: Tchernicheva died in 1976, and the same year he wrote the obituary for company pianist Hilda Gaunt in the RAD Gazette – 'beautifully and perfectly written,' Fonteyn complimented him; he gave the address and read Karsavina's tribute at Idzikowski's memorial service in 1977, Karsavina died in 1978, Phyllis Bedells in 1985. Now came those disconcertingly closer – Helpmann in 1986, his brother Lawrence in 1989. After Helpmann's death Somes acknowledged his greatest gift to the company: '... on the stage & off we owe him hours of laughter' adding wryly 'alas a commodity in short supply these days.'[9] On the upside, in May 1987 he and Ellis quietly married in the country, celebrating with their friends and neighbours.

Dowell scheduled a revival of *Ondine* for May 1988, with himself as Palemon and Maria Almeida as Ondine. Christopher Newton and Douglas Stuart pieced the ballet together from the filmed record made by Edmée Wood, Czinner's in *The Royal Ballet* film being incomplete.[10] After watching a rehearsal with Somes, 'Ashton said "I'm going to leave you in Michael's capable hands ..." and left; Somes turned to the company and said "Right, I know you all think this is probably a load of old-fashioned rubbish and it is. Actually, we shouldn't really be doing it – there are much better things happening now. It's from another era. That's how we have to approach it."'[11] '[H]e was wonderful,' recalled Dowell. 'He enjoyed it and I've got a wonderful letter from him saying well done and the company looked wonderful and he signed it "Good luck from the old timer." So whatever bridges had collapsed it was an amicable time.'[12]

It was, in fact, the end of an era. On 19 August 1988, Ashton died in his sleep. Somes, Grant, his nephew Anthony Russell-Roberts and Tony Dyson arranged the funeral. On 24 August Somes joined Edwards, Grant and Shaw handing out service sheets at Eye church in Suffolk, and they lined up as de Valois arrived and kissed each in sympathy. Somes gave an address: 'I'll *never* forget that.' recalled Sibley. 'He could hardly speak, he was literally choking with grief ... there'd been such a lot that had gone on in all those years – all that loyalty and love and respect for each other.'[13]

---

8 Interview with author

9 MS tribute to Robert Helpmann, *UpROHr*, nd

10 Edmeé Wood filmed many Royal Ballet productions in the 1950s, although union restrictions meant they had to be recorded in practice dress to piano accompaniment.

11 Ashley Page Interview with the author

12 Interview with author

13 Interview with author

Ashton's Memorial Service was held on 29 November at Westminster Abbey, in the presence of Queen Elizabeth the Queen Mother and Princess Margaret. Fonteyn was unable to attend, so Somes read her tribute, which stressed Ashton's understanding of human emotion, the mystery of how he translated motive and character into movement and the paradox at his centre – 'a sophisticated and finely developed taste in all things, yet on the other hand a very simple person at heart ... He was, above all, a very *human* human being, and for that, as much as for his extraordinary talents, he was beloved by all.' Henze conducted Mozart and de Valois gave an extempore tribute. Despite his own grief, Somes was concerned about others and de Valois later thanked him for his help: 'It was – physically – a very painful morning for me. You were very kind & made it so much easier to cope with ...'[14]

He sent Fonteyn a long description of the service. 'Can't you see [Fred] standing behind the curtain after a first night saying to us "But is it a *real* success?"' she wrote back. 'I do so agree with you about preserving Fred's choreography. I happened to see some graduating students – good ones – doing Blue Boy, Pas de Trois and White Pas de Deux from Patineurs at a graduation performance in North Carolina. ... luckily I had three days to work on them first. You cannot imagine what had got lost or distorted horribly – the trouble is no one can just *dance* as we used to do. How often did we think about technique when Fred was choreographing? I never remember it being mentioned, but now they are obsessed by it and can't do a simple relaxed movement to save their lives.'[15]

'I find, like you,' she wrote to Somes later, 'that everything about ballet and ballet dancers these days is so different from our days that I really don't know what is right or wrong ...' She suggested that he use his exceptional musicality to 'concentrate on the problems of getting choreographers and composers together ... What Diaghilev did, by using existing scores very imaginatively ... has also left a legacy of going to existing music instead of finding more composers willing to write ballet scores ... supposing (Arthur Bliss) had written Mayerling ...'[16]

Ashton never planned a Trust to administer his works. '... Michael Somes ... has worked closely with me and he knows my style thoroughly,' he told Hans-Theodor Wohlfahrt. 'I have distributed the rights to many ballets ... – as a distinction for dancers who have something special in a specific part.'[17] He left Somes *Cinderella* and *Symphonic Variations*, Fonteyn *Daphnis and Chloë* and *Ondine*, Grant *La Fille mal gardée* and *Façade*, Shaw *Les Rendezvous* and *Les*

14 NdeV to MS nd

15 MF to MS 19 December 1988

16 MF to MS 4 March ny

17 Hans-Theodor Wohlfahrt, *An Interview with Sir Frederick Ashton*, *Ballett-Journal/Das Tanzarchiv*, 1 December 1988

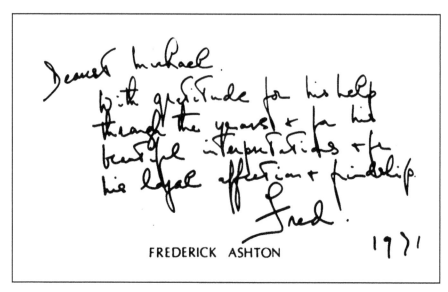

FREDERICK ASHTON

39   Dedication from Ashton in *Frederick Ashton; A choreographer and his ballets* by Zoë Dominic and John Selwyn Gilbert.

Patineurs; the remainder were bequeathed to Russell-Roberts. The will did not address the long-term problems of ownership, copyright and future stagings, and seemed to assume the beneficiaries would live forever.

In Ashton's last years, Somes and Wendy had stayed with him every August. He talked endlessly to her about his ballets, ' ... not just the steps – music, lighting ... the geometrics of how it was placed. I wasn't that interested – though I listened. Especially to do with lighting ... sometimes I wonder if he thought "Well after Michael it will be Wendy" because he used to tell me so many things ...'[18]

In May 1990 Somes made his last stage appearance, performing Lord Capulet alongside Nureyev as Mercutio, to raise money for Fonteyn's medical bills. In October she wrote a last letter from hospital in Houston: 'Dearest 'Sam', I can't really write properly but want to say that I loved your letter. Much love to you and Wendy / Margot'[19] She died in February 1991. Somes hardly figured in her obituaries, but Chappell, understanding what her death meant to him, hastened to write – 'What a glorious *pair* you were!'[20] At the Memorial Service in Westminster Abbey on 2 July, David Wall gave the tribute from her partners.

Ellis often accompanied Somes when he mounted ballets abroad, taking her away from Covent Garden for weeks at a time, until, in 1990, she decided

18 Wendy Ellis Somes in interview with Frank Freeman
19 MF to MS October 1990 ny
20 William Chappell to MS nd

to retire. There followed 'probably the best four years we ever had ... I think he was preparing me ... I learned *so* much in that short time in what to teach, what to look for and it was the most wonderful experience.'[21]

Although Somes' health problems were increasing and he found it hard to be patient, his passion and energy seemed undiminished. Harvey recalled how the 75-year-old, rehearsing *Symphonic Variations* with American Ballet Theatre in 1992, 'would pick me up and partner me ... I couldn't believe it'. He was calm and endlessly patient, 'Mr Charming personified ... he was very gentle, very gentle,' but still demanding on detail, spacing, keeping *something* in the head, stressing performance not steps.[22] He chose twelve dancers and spent a long time mixing them up until he got the two casts he wanted: the first included principal Harvey alongside two girls who were not yet soloists. His first night telegram just said: 'listen to the music'. The dancers were deeply moved when he came back after the performance with tears in his eyes.

His most productive and enjoyable collaborations were now with the 'Touring Trash' which, under Peter Wright's inspired Directorship became the Birmingham Royal Ballet in October 1990. Somes rehearsed *Jazz Calendar* for the inaugural programme. 'I think it amazed him when he came to Birmingham, that there really was a lot of talent there,' recalled Wright, 'and I remember when he watched Balanchine's *Theme and Variations* he was over the moon – "I'm now seeing classical ballet danced as it really should be." He was unhappy, I think, about the way things were going at Covent Garden ... he was very, very supportive of me in Birmingham; he loved coming to performances and his whole attitude changed.'[23]

He hadn't completely mellowed: instead of screaming at the dancers, he now screamed at the staff – 'The trouble is you people don't know how these ballets were meant to be done ... you've never been there – you've never seen the real thing,' but he appreciated how well they were danced, with a style and attention to detail missing at Covent Garden.

He wasn't always happy. In October 1992 he reluctantly agreed to set *Symphonic Variations* on the company, although he felt they hadn't the right dancers. 'He got so bogged down in the accuracy of every arm movement and head movement and unfortunately he got into such a state about it that he wasn't really happy until he'd made everyone in the cast cry,' recalled Wright. 'It was *wonderfully* rehearsed, but ... just before it went on he realised himself that ... it was without soul, without heart, without feeling – all of what Ashton wanted in it. I ... said "You must do something to breathe life into it now – they're all doing it so accurately, they hardly dare move," and

---

21 Wendy Ellis Somes in interview with Frank Freeman
22 Interview with author
23 Interview with author

it was too late and then it became ... superficial because everyone started to smile...'[24]

Job was more successful. De Valois felt it was old-fashioned and only reluctantly agreed to the revival after considerable persuasion from Wright ('Peter' she wrote to Somes 'is my definition of an optimist!'). Unable to oversee rehearsals herself, she was reassured when Somes and Joy Newton became involved. For Newton it was 'an incredible experience ... Your contribution has been invaluable – you brought out something extra from the dancers & made them *live* it! ...'[25] Audiences were enthusiastic, both for the ballet and Michael O'Hare's excellent Satan.

With the company established in Birmingham, the Opera House started to look for Wright's successor. Somes was incensed: for him, age was unimportant when someone still had much to contribute. He dashed off a stiff letter to General Director Jeremy Isaacs, who replied that Wright was past retirement age and they had to look to the future. He showed the letter to Angus Stirling, Chairman of the Royal Opera House, who wrote to Somes 'I remember you extremely well ... so much respect (your) views ...'; when Somes saw Stirling at a performance and thanked him for remembering him and for his reply, Stirling obviously had no idea who he was.

Wright was touched by Somes' support: '(your letter) really makes me feel that all the years of struggle and sheer hard work that my colleagues and I have put into the establishment of BRB (Birmingham Royal Ballet) have been worth it. I shall treasure your letter for always ... even if it doesn't change people's minds it really has done me a power of good ...' His PS 'I have raised *hell* at the ROH about the way you were treated on the 'phone – I am shocked,' speaks volumes about the changing Opera House.[26]

William Chappell died on 1 January 1994: Somes read Byron's 'So we'll go no more a-roving' at the Memorial Service. His vitality and enthusiasm seemed undiminished. Maybe it was just increasing age that led him to make a nostalgic trip to Gregynog Hall, visit old friends and re-read all his accumulated papers and letters and wonder what should happen to them. He started destroying them, but Wendy intervened, though not before Ashton's letters had been consigned to the flames.

In autumn 1994 Somes was busier than ever, mounting *Enigma Variations* for Birmingham with help from Sibley, Dowell and Bergsma, rehearsing *Symphonic Variations* at Covent Garden and working with Pauline Clayden on reviving the Air pas de deux from *Homage to the Queen. Enigma Variations* was an extraordinary event. 'He was *wonderful*,' recalled Wright. '... his

---

24 Interview with author
25 Joy Newton to MS 14 June 1993
26 Sir Peter Wright to MS 18 March 1994

whole attitude to the work and his approach to the dancers was absolutely magnificent: wonderful feeling at all the rehearsals and none of the screaming and bullying, and he got (from) all the characters wonderful, wonderful performances. He was very proud of it. He was very good at pointing out what was wrong (and) that's what was so marvellous in Birmingham – he suddenly started pointing out what was right and became very positive about everything and was so encouraging.'[27] Desmond Kelly, cast as Elgar, recalled the experience as exciting and incredible, though admitting 'he could be a bugger'. On one moving, magical day, Somes, Edwards and Wendy visited the cottage at Broadheath where Elgar was born, with its stunning view of the Malvern Hills which had inspired so much of his music.

No one who had seen the original cast thought it could ever be equalled, but the first performance on 11 October was astonishing. Kelly was superb as Elgar, with Sherilyn Kennedy a gracious 'Lady'; Alain Dubreuil was Jaeger, and Leslie Edwards in his original role of Basil Nevinson linked past and present. At the curtain call, Somes touched each member of the cast in thanks and brought Edwards forward in acknowledgement of their long friendship. The press was universally excellent.

Symphonic Variations at Covent Garden was a different story; neither he nor the ballet was given due respect: '... everybody was in everybody else's ballet as well' remembered Collier, 'and here was this wonderful masterpiece and he didn't have a cast. Rehearsals were put down and so and so was somewhere else and I remember him being quite frustrated ...'[28] A new generation was amazed, not only by how demanding the ballet was, but also by the rigour of his rehearsals: many coaches slow down with age, but '(for) a man of his age to push you so hard for stamina was surprising,' recalled Pickford, one of the side boys: 'You didn't see a lesser Somes, he was older and maybe a tiny bit more mellow, he didn't reach for the chairs, they were getting a bit heavy for him. But you saw that he was the same person.'[29]

So the end was entirely unexpected. On 22 October he felt unwell, but refused to see a doctor, saying he would be better after a night's sleep. The next day he didn't know Wendy and was rushed to hospital. Nine days later he was diagnosed with a brain tumor but refused to have an operation. He returned home and died as midnight struck on Saturday 19 November. After the matinée of *Enigma Variations* that day in Bristol, Kelly announced his death to an audience in the city where he had performed in all those eisteddfods decades before; the same night a visibly moved Dowell made the announcement after *The Sleeping Beauty* at the Royal Opera House.

---

27 Interview with author
28 Interview with author
29 Interview with author

All the major British newspapers carried obituaries, many clichéd and dismissive, reiterating that his dance career had been erased by Nureyev, but few acknowledged how much Fonteyn owed to his partnering and how much The Royal Ballet owed to him as dancer and teacher. Only Barbara Newman in *Country Life* acknowledged his role in Sibley's career and the Sibley-Dowell partnership. Sibley was distressed: 'I thought "People are now trying to whitewash this out of the way." ... It was one of the things he *really* was about ... I was, and I think Anthony was too, really shocked. He was more loyal to that company than anybody other than de Valois – more because he was in there for everybody all the time.'[30]

Throughout his life, Somes had attended church regularly, and always marked the major festivals at Easter and Christmas. For the last year, he had attended Sunday Choral Matins at the Queen's Chapel at the Savoy, one of London's last strongholds of traditional Anglicanism, using the Book of Common Prayer, although the primary attraction was probably the high musical standards under William Cole, a musician he knew and admired. Wendy approached the Chapel's Chaplin, John Robson, to take Somes' funeral, a very intimate affair at Golders Green with only her, Sibley, Edwards and a few very close friends.

The Royal Ballet's autumn schedule included Ashton ballets that had seen Somes' finest performances, *Symphonic Variations, Daphnis and Chloë*, and pas de deux from *Birthday Offering* and *Sylvia*; three performances at the end of November were dedicated to his memory.

There was a last altercation between those at the Opera House who thought the Memorial Service should be at St Paul's, Covent Garden, a church Somes disliked, and Wendy, who wanted the Savoy Chapel, which only seated 150. On 9 February 1995 the Chapel was packed: at the core of the congregation were his contemporaries – de Valois, now wheelchair bound, Alicia Markova, Joy Newton, Beryl Grey, Julia Farron, Alfred Rodrigues, Moira Shearer – alongside a huge contingent from The Royal Ballet and Birmingham Royal Ballet and his Essex friends. Ellis's reading was followed by tributes from Wright, Page and Eagling; Dowell read the lesson. It was a real celebration.

Wendy gave John Robson Somes' favourite cream and pink striped tie and a very grand portrait photograph. Some years later, Robson told Carlos Acosta of his connection with Somes and when Acosta said 'I just wish I'd met people like that,' Robson gave him the photograph. Somes would have been pleased. Not quite forgotten then.

---

30 Interview with author

17

The Method [1]

No artist is pleased. There is no satisfaction whatsoever at any time. There is only a queer divine dissatisfaction, a blessed unrest that keeps us marching and makes us more alive than the others.

Martha Graham to Agnes de Mille

The concept of discipline & vocation ... so deeply underlined and taught to us in the past, were the guidelines of my ... stewardship. I know, that only by this can you expect the dedication and respect required by so exacting a profession ...

Michael Somes to Sir Joseph Lockwood, mss draft letter undated (1984)

To survive a heritage needs more than solid foundations; it has to be maintained and cherished. Here Somes was supreme. Great dancers are rare, but rarer still are those who so magnificently hand on the torch. Somes' influence spanned what many saw as The Royal Ballet's greatest years and, although all the ballet staff must be acknowledged, it was his ethic that prevailed. As Brian Pollitt, one-time press officer for the touring group, observed, 'If Fonteyn was the heart of The Royal Ballet, Somes was its soul and moral centre.' [2]

A ballet company is full of rivalries, disappointments, unfulfilled ambitions stoked in a hothouse atmosphere where individual egos fight for attention. Like all performers, the first thing a dancer has to develop is a thick skin in a world of disappointments, unfulfillment, roles lost, roles learned but never performed, a world where small slights can be magnified, never free from anxiety and stress, which can either have a negative effect or, as Judi Dench remarked, be the 'petrol' that ignites the performance. Luckily, Somes never had to deal with social media which, while revealing injustices and malpractice, can also magnify the insignificant and be stoked by input from those ignorant of the context in which events occur.

Somes' description of himself as a dynamo applied to his rehearsal methods

---

1   Unless otherwise stated, quotations are from interviews with author
2   Brian Pollitt, 'Absolutely the first dancer ...' *Llandudno Advertiser* 1 March 1991

as much as his partnering, transforming the mechanical power of technique into the energy of performance. Often dressed formally in a suit (removing the jacket for action), he commanded immediate respect from the moment he entered the studio, autocratic, charismatic and in complete control, 'so much *there*' as Ashley Page put it.

Marking was not permitted. He demanded total concentration (fortunately, he never had to contend with the smartphone). Learning by watching was as important as dancing and meant that everyone knew exactly what everyone else was doing. 'There was only one way,' declared Dowell. '... to do it full out to give it full value and believe in it.' 'Convey, portray,' he urged, 'You've got a quarter of a mile to go up to the gallery at the top of Covent Garden.' The dancers had a responsibility beyond themselves – to their colleagues on stage and the audience: '... his commitment to what went on behind those lights for the audience was what it should all be about,' declared Deborah MacMillan, 'and sometimes that thinking's missing now.'

For Somes, a choreographer was a major or a minor god, and the integrity of each individual creator had to be maintained, but, within that, a unique Royal Ballet style had to be preserved. While he used 'the Russians' as a generalised perfection to spur on the dancers, he never wanted The Royal Ballet to be a copy, believing audiences went to see different companies because they *were* different. 'There was a style and a clarity and that Englishness that was slightly reticent and *that* I think Michael was largely responsible for,' declared Frank Freeman. His maxim was 'keep it clean, keep it simple, finish it': precision, accuracy, attention to detail, speed, no fudging, no blurring of the edges, no cheating. '... how you'd do that simply, do this more extravagantly, and his *timing*, everything was impeccable,' explained Sibley. 'The way you presented yourself, the way you start a variation, the way you finish a variation.'

In Ashton's ballets, he was manic about dancers preserving the musicality, subtle details, épaulement and, especially, the bending, all so necessary to achieve the 'briskness, swiftness, nonchalance and sophistication' of the Ashton style.[3] For Christine Aitken, 'Michael was to me and a lot of people the lynchpin between Fred and the ballets.' His passion for the choreography, for the company, for dance itself communicated itself to the dancers and helped create the high energy levels needed for Ashton's deceptively lyrical ballets like *La Valse* or the peasant dances in *La Fille mal gardée* and rehearsals ended with him as soaked in sweat as the dancers.

Errol Pickford's breathless memories of Somes rehearsing the Blue Bird and Prince Florimund for the 1984 School matinee of *The Sleeping Beauty* Act III encapsulated the experiences of many. 'He did the whole thing as one – style,

---

3 *Ivan Lika, Ballet Director Bavarian State Ballet Dancing Times, ?June/July 2012*

musicality, stamina, the physical ability ... (Other) teachers would just come in and go "This is the music, and you do this to that count, and you go dir-dir-dir and finish." I'll never forget the first day with him, coming out covered in bruises, literally ... I didn't mind at all, it was comical at first ... everything you did was wrong, every step you made ... he would talk about the way you were carrying yourself, portraying yourself in front of an audience ... what's going through your head ... no one (in my experience) had ever approached a role in such a way ... No one had ever made me stand and just listen ... and go through in my mind what I'm doing with the music ... The rehearsals were agony, your concentration was endless ... he didn't stop talking the whole time ... the physical punishment was absolutely endless, he would just drive you into the ground ... (but) worth it. He kept everything very masculine ... I enjoyed what he was making me do because I saw the improvement. Every minute was a challenge ... Things got thrown, chairs came across the room ... He really would push it to the limit, and sometimes you thought he'd go over that – and you did wonder how far he could actually go – but he always had a way of bringing it around, so you didn't get too upset. ... Yes, he'd make girls cry ... he would then back down a bit, and try and build (them) up. It was a shame, I joined the Company and Somes had gone. The only way I can really think of him is great. I think he's irreplaceable.'

The clichéd brutal, driven ballet master has some basis in reality: Taglioni's father drove her to exhaustion every day, even denying her a drink when working; in Russia, Christian Johannsen's motto was 'Work not only till the sweat comes, but till the blood comes through the pores of the skin – only then you'll be a dancer'; Preobrajenska's pupils trembled with fright before she came into the studio; Marie Rambert's advice to Alan Carter on handling dancers was 'You must insult them'; Fokine and John Cranko, like Somes, sometimes hurled chairs across the room: Dowell recalled being taught by Claude Newman 'physical abuse, mental abuse, harassment – whatever, you name it, but we accepted it'. As Broadway star Chita Rivera observed, 'As a dancer if we didn't have that teacher – that one teacher to really scare the heck out of us where would we be? We wouldn't have tried it. It made you who you are.'

Somes came from a robust generation which was merciless in the drive for perfection, not just in the ballet world – there were famously intimidating theatre directors like John Dexter, film directors like John Huston and William Wyler. '... this steaming machine ... he screamed for 14 hours' could be Somes, but it's *Sun* editor Kelvin MacKenzie, when 'the paper had this pulsating energy and danger ...'[4] In his own terms, Somes would have agreed with the great newspaper editor Arthur Christiansen: 'Show me a contented editor

---

4 Emma Brockes, *Piers Morgan's Life Stories: Radio Times*, 16-22 April 2011, p18.

[ballet master] and I'll show you a bad newspaper [performance].'

Working in the theatre demands a thick skin, but dancers who went direct from school into a company and spent their whole careers there often didn't develop the resilience of show dancers, always open to public rejection in auditions or a production failing. While Royal Ballet dancers obviously had a stake and interest in a new work and did everything possible for its success, a failure didn't mean unemployment the next week. To counteract the complacency that can come from security, Somes made them fight, if only him. If it took brutal methods to get a reaction, if only anger, to push a performance beyond good technique, so be it. His fury was 'born of frustration, not malice,' insisted Stephen Jefferies. 'But look at the results. Dancing is hard work and his message was "Nothing is easy."' Deborah MacMillan saw the positive side: 'his expectation of talented people was the highest and he was absolutely disappointed if they didn't give it ... it does actually gee people up, because you believe in his belief.'

Somes was professional and unsentimental. 'You crawled out of that studio on all fours absolutely exhausted, mentally and physically by this man physically beating you at times,' recalled Jefferies. 'Somes would walk out, go to the canteen – charming.' Whatever happened in the studio stayed there. 'It all came from wanting the best for The Royal Ballet,' explained Dowell. 'It wasn't about individuals – it was the ballet, the art form.' He was a great leveller, applying the same strictures to everybody, even Fonteyn if he felt she was not giving her all.

'You can't teach anybody unless you care about them,' declared leading voice coach Patsy Rodenberg. 'That doesn't mean you're strokey, strokey – no teacher should want to be liked. ... You are going to be disliked if you ask somebody to go further.' A few always felt hard done by: 'He was less generous with some,' admitted Page. 'He could be a bully, as could Fred. There could have been an element that liked to reduce people to tears to know that he'd got them – he wanted to level you,' something he would have observed in Ashton. He reserved his special wrath for talented but lazy dancers, who were going to throw it all away, and those he called 'sliders', who only worked when they thought they would be noticed.

'People would say, "How could you stand there and take it?"' recalled Jefferies, 'There were times when you said "I'm walking out and not coming back," he could really, really get to you, but one always took it. I always felt he was doing it for *me*, he was trying to make *me* dance better. He did it to needle you, but actually it produced a better performance ... He hated lethargy and he would *whip* you into shape ... get the fire in the belly again.' As Collier admitted, 'It was always worse watching him with another person than experiencing it yourself. I used to be absolutely flabbergasted the way he treated some people. Absolutely shocked. But it was no different to the way he behaved with me and I loved it. If you were just an onlooker it was appalling and yet I got so much joy from it.' If asked, Somes would modify the screaming – for a while. Eagling never remembered him 'really shouting. He could be loud, but I don't remember him being out of control, ever.' If Freeman's experience was of him as 'a tyrant', Kathryn Wade 'never had anything but kindness from him – good and generous. He cared so passionately for the dancers and the ballets.' 'We understood how he worked and how he thought and, even in his bad moments, there was no animosity at all; we just loved Michael,' declared Aitken, though admitting there were times they hated him too.

Whatever the dancers suffered paled beside his fury if all his careful preparation was marred in performance by sloppy conducting, a lethargic orchestra or careless technical departments. As one stage-manager admitted after a very public rebuke, 'Oh that's just Michael. But he was right.' No one let his dancers or the audience down.

He had to work out how to approach each dancer and how far they were willing to go: while he drove Sibley, she never recalled him shouting at Dowell. Michael Crookes' experience was that '(Somes) understood my shyness immediately and looked after me.' Page saw him rehearsing *Cinderella* with Tetsuya Kumakawa '... doing not quite the right steps ... throwing in a few flash things. Normally that would have sent Michael spare, but he knew when someone was that talented, how to meet them half way. He had a charm and he knew how to use it and he could always use it at the right time.' As he told Barbara Newman, 'You must approach every single person differently, some need to be jolted and pushed, others encouraged and drawn. You must change your approach for everyone, and even change how you approach any one depending on the situation. You must be very patient ...'[5]

He loved finding a dancer's potential and testing their limits, which is why, even after years and years of rehearsing the same roles, he was never bored: 'It's a question of trying to amass the largest combinations of Can Do's. It's fascinating to try and find these combinations and master them.'[6] Coaching David Ashmole '... he would maybe raise his voice at one time or be nice another time. He tried a variety of things ... to get ... something that I don't think I ever did give him ... a part of my soul, myself. (When) I went on the road and ... matured ... then I realised what he was trying to get out of me.' Somes knew it was there from the start. Listening to him give corrections to others was always enlightening: '... even if it was all the things he had said to you,' declared Page, 'you'd see it as applied to a different personality, a different talent and that was endlessly fascinating ... watching him working

5   Kay Lundeen, *Royal Ballet Inspires Dedication, Eugene Register-Guard*, 30 June 1963
6   Barbara Newman, *Antoinette Sibley*, Hutchinson, London, 1986 p109

with Anthony (Dowell) you could see how different he was with more mature people – who'd heard it all before from him and he would speak much more quietly and just suggest things.'

'He gave such an *enormous* amount to young dancers,' declared Peter Wright. 'He was terribly good at making dancers, (they often) 'begged to have rehearsals from him, because they *knew* that he would get them through it.' Lynn Seymour disliked Somes' rigid approach, yet, when MacMillan wanted her to do *Swan Lake* after a gap of several years, she only agreed if Somes rehearsed her: 'He'll kill me and it'll be tears and everything but that's the only way I'll get through it,' she told Wright.[7]

'He could be quite frightening,' admitted Wayne Sleep, 'And perversely, we rather revered him – particularly when we realised (as we grew with the company) that he only leaned heavily on those dancers he respected and whom he thought had talent.'[8] Sibley understood: '... he drove and he drove because he could see farther. He could see you can go that far, you can go that much further ... Some people said it was cruel and didn't like it. It was very, very depressing and debilitating: how did you pull yourself up even to try to get on and do it, but in the end and after *years* of working with him you knew that ... the only reason he was pushing you was he knew you *could* do it.'

Yet 'so calming' was Anthony Dowson's experience of rehearsing ensembles, like Ashton's pas de douze in *Swan Lake*: 'Michael was so masterly at almost coaxing you into it ... Each phrase of music was taken apart and rehearsed so that after about 45 minutes you'd only be half way. You would not actually get to do the whole dance until the third or fourth rehearsal.' He had an 'exceptional way of counting even a 3/4 to make you on the music. I was used to counting 1,2,3, but he would count in a 12 or in a 6, so that every piece of your body knew what it was doing on each ½ note, each ¼ note even ...' Everyone had to be in exactly the same shape, every head, every focus, épaulement, every arm, every hand, every finger, the amount of 'bend'. 'Every eyelash had to be right,' sighed Freeman. 'You couldn't get away with anything.'

He was expert in rehearsing the corps de ballet: '(Others) didn't have this 100% awareness of where we all needed to be and also technically how to put us there,' explained Crookes. 'He made us feel good about working as a team, that it was good to move as one, (that) the corps de ballet was the most important part ... without making you feel you were wasting your time because you were stuck directly behind someone.' That did not mean an ensemble of clones: Somes 'had a grasp of what almost each corps de ballet girl should do to bring out the best they could', recalled Aitken, which is

7 Peter Wright, interview with author
8   Wayne Sleep, *Precious Little Sleep*, Macmillan, London, 1996, pp49-50

why the company was so strong in depth, with every dancer feeling valued and giving to the best of their ability. 'He made what you did be important,' stressed Cynthia Harvey. 'He made you know it was important.' He gave dancers at every level a respect for their work, showing great concern for the long-serving solo and corps de ballet dancers. He knew how much a company relies on 'backbone dancers ... on the stage every night and delivering', declared Christopher Carr. 'You were aware he liked you because you were reliable ...' Hard work within the group did not go unnoticed: in his first year in the company, Page danced in the Waltz of the Flowers in Nureyev's *The Nutcracker*: '... (Michael) said "I was watching you last night and I think you did that very nicely and I hope you always work like that." Just to *know* that you'd been noticed in a corps de ballet role, you knew it was worth ... being one of (a group) and doing it to the best of your ability.' He encouraged young dancers to learn roles far ahead of their current abilities which gave them an aim and strengthened their general work.

His approach to rehearsing the big productions was the same as the ensembles, breaking down each element and then gradually building up to performance level, melding everything into a seamless whole – 'make it seamless' was a favourite saying. 'We've never had anyone since who really got to the root of the way ballets were rehearsed,' declared Wright. 'The way they were put together, the way dancers were prepared for roles ... he was second to none, not just coaching dancers but also rehearsing ballets like *Rite of Spring*: Kenneth didn't want anyone else to touch it.' The ballet was centred accurately in the studio, so that it transferred smoothly to the stage, leaving time for placing, ensuring that every dancer could be seen from anywhere in the theatre: 'Everyone has paid for their seat' he would say, 'and has a right to see.'

He spent a lot of time on the tricky sequences which could so easily go wrong, like the Princesses throwing the golden apples in *The Firebird* or Kolya playing with his ball in *Month in the Country*. A performance was never just waiting around for the solos; a dancer had to know exactly what they were doing all the way through – every mime gesture, walking about, or standing on the sidelines. Dancers liked working with him, declared de Valois, because 'he was the one person who would bother to give them the details of everything'.

Somes knew how to work with the music: rehearsing Page as Beliaev in *Month in the Country*, he showed how to '(squeeze) every drop out of that Chopin music, how you could loop the phrasing across several passages of music and think of that as one package ... like the solo's actually making this shape ...' Harvey never forgot him singing *Symphonic Variations*, to give not 'what you hear in the piano directly ... more the *essence* of what Sir Fred wanted ... the nuance ... I've had fantastic ballet mistresses and ballet masters ... but *none* ... so distinctive with the musicality that he was.'

Eagling particularly appreciated what he learned about partnering: 'awareness of where a ballerina's weight is; he made me aware that you had to know what she was doing not what you were doing ... how to really take care of a ballerina.' Somes took pride in knowing that the success of a pas de deux rested with the man and he understood that the more the audience concentrated on the ballerina the more successful the partner.

Collier described two rehearsal methods which she and others went on to use: 'he had this wonderful technique of working backwards, so that you practised the end more than the beginning – it's very easy to keep going back to the beginning and then you're exhausted by the end ... It is the finish people remember ...'; the dancer could also experience what it was like to approach the end fresh and thus know how much to keep in reserve. He also liked to take dancers outside their comfort zone by repeating a piece in different tempi, a useful preparation for performance when tempo could easily differ from rehearsal.

Everyone dreaded hearing 'Do it again. Again. No not good enough, why don't you listen?' The male Blue Bird solo was hard enough to do once, difficult twice, torture three; Somes even made selected dancers do it five times. 'We were all pretty tough,' admitted Collier, 'and if you could take it the performance was a joy. You knew you only had to do it once,' and the dancers radiated confidence of having so much in reserve.

Facility must never become complacency. Somes told Mason to always do double or triple pirouettes, even if they didn't always come off. He hated everything evened out: 'In the Black Swan solo he absolutely loathed it if the pas de bourrée was the same speed as the renversé and the same speed as the glissade,' recalled Mason. 'He would stand up and bang the chair and say "Oh you're so *boring* it's driving me mad."' He also knew all the tricks, as Dowson discovered: 'What you forget is that I had a big jump when I was a very young man and I learned all the tricks in the book about how to make myself look as though I was jumping higher than everybody else, so, Dowson, I can stop you from doing that now. You take off on the same beat as everybody else.'

Blank faces he abhorred. He encouraged dancers to have something in their heads. Page recalled him saying 'I don't care what it is, it can be anything, it could be what you had for supper last night, perhaps something about trying to get the musicality or the timing right – say something that goes with the music.' His suggestions were apt, understandable and memorable: correcting a transition step in *Symphonic Variations* with American Ballet Theatre he explained 'I don't want to see old Cadillacs working, I want to see Rolls-Royce gear changes,'[9] and on the same ballet with The Royal Ballet,

---

9 Anon, *Dance, The New Yorker*, 20 April 1992

Harvey remembered him 'pushing down Ravenna (Tucker) and saying "You're smelling the flowers."'

Somes wanted dancers who took responsibility for their work and came to rehearsal prepared. Before notation and video, dancers learned the roles from watching in rehearsal and performance or from other dancers, as he himself had passed on his roles to others before he became a teacher; Philip Chatfield remembered learning *Symphonic Variations* in the 1940s: 'I can honestly say that I could never have coped with it without Michael's guidance ... In later years he was exactly the same caring person ...' That generosity in passing on knowledge and roles ran through the company and experienced dancers had the confidence to help the less experienced without feeling threatened. Deborah MacMillan recalled Julie Lincoln mounting *The Rite of Spring* on English National Ballet and bringing in other Royal Ballet dancers, many of whom had been senior to her but deferred to her current status: 'The most fantastic example of collaborative work I've seen. I think that way of working has come directly from their association with Somes, if you are going to tie it to any one person. The respect for the work and the respect for the performance of the work and the commitment to the performance, and energy levels.'

Another asset Somes had 'in great depth, he had that in spades' declared John Lanchbery, 'the *motivation* of the ballet, the motivation of the choreography ... It wasn't just the steps (but) through the steps.' He didn't work on individual interpretation but on getting the maximum from the choreography. After 'getting you to a (point) where you could go on and do it four times,' recalled Dowson, 'he'd say "Of course, I've only given you the bare bones it's for you to do with it now what you will and make it your own."' 'I had to find my own way' declared Sibley, 'and you could only do that in a performance ... He told me what didn't work, which is fine.' Collier used him as a sounding board: 'Juliet – I remember telling him I knew how I felt, but I didn't know if it was coming over and I wanted him to tell me.' If he felt something wasn't working he would make suggestions: in Act II of *Swan Lake* he told Mason 'You need to find a way for that (moment) to feel a little more vulnerable, a little softer, a little more lyrical.'

While striving for perfection, Somes knew that it was elusive. He wanted a sign over the entrance to the School: 'All Ye That Enter Here, Be Prepared for Ninety-Nine-Per-Cent Failure Every Day.'[10] He accepted that people had limits, but refused to accept anything below that limit, making them 'aware of their special abilities and make them learn to think for themselves rather than relying on all the things fed to them.'[11] At the same time, he subscribed

10 John Gruen, *The Private World of Ballet*, Penguin Books, London, 1976, p166
11 Barbara Newman, *Antoinette Sibley*, Hutchinson, London, 1986, p108

to Karsavina's dictum that 'it is the sign of a true artist, always to want something higher that is out of reach, always to think to himself that he could do better.'[12] He believed that 'The better, the greater dancer you're eventually going to be, the greater sense of failure you're going to suffer, because the knowledge of what you might accomplish makes the failing all the sharper ...' so dancers had to learn to overcome 'what seems like failure at any given time.'[13]

'Failure' could include things going wrong in performance – dancing, technical or accidental. Somes alone taught that 'the moment it's happened, it's history, you are involved with the moment and you think ahead but never look back,' recalled Mason. 'He did that in rehearsals all the time. "Today we're going through from A to Z. We're not going to stop no matter what goes wrong, you deal with it and get on with it." That was an amazing lesson – the firmness of mind and the ability get through a show when things are going wrong.'

There was a destructive downside. 'He could give a dancer great confidence and take it right away in one single rehearsal ... just when he'd got them to their peak, suddenly he'd find little faults,' declared Wright. He had a habit of watching from the downstage wing (watching a performance out front was painful for him and for anyone sitting near him, as he squirmed and suffered at what he saw as a lack of perfection): John Gruen described him standing there 'admonishing ballerinas as they leap offstage, curtly telling them they were "miserable", danced "dreadfully",'[14] or even commenting during their performance. 'It shouldn't distract you,' he told Mason, 'If you said "It does" "Well, don't let it."' The dancers simply got used to it. 'I wouldn't say it was destructive,' Collier admitted, 'but it was sometimes a bit painful. I think if you allowed it to destroy you, you wouldn't go on the stage. I always rose to it as a challenge.' Some dancers simply told him to go away.

Rehearsals were not all fraught intensity. He could have everyone crying with laughter. If necessary, he would play the clown and never minded looking ridiculous so long as he made his point. 'He had no sense of pomposity, no sense of importance,' insisted Emanuel Young and he liked the dancers who laughed with him. There was a feeling of normality in the studio. 'There wasn't room for anyone to be precious especially his ballerinas,' declared Pickford. 'Precious it can get and he wouldn't have that.' Cleverly, he left the men with the impression that he gave the girls the worst time, and vice versa. If the girls had the advantage of what Mason called 'the twinkle factor' (Crookes recalled 'that smile that used to come over him,' rehearsing

12 Zoe Dominic & John Gilbert *Frederick Ashton*, George G. Harrap & Co Ltd., London, 1971, p232

13 Barbara Newman, *Antoinette Sibley*, Hutchinson, London, 1986, p109

14 John Gruen, *The Private World of Ballet*, Penguin Books, London, 1976, p162

the Princesses in *The Firebird* ...), he was equally a master of dealing with the male ego.

Somes was always interested in the person behind the dancer. He loved connections: he sought out Clover Roope, daughter of Rita Watts, Kathleen Blotts' partner of his dance school in Weston- super- Mare, when she joined the Sadler's Wells School and company pianist Philip Gammon recalled his interest when he found that Gammon was also from the West Country and had studied at the Royal Academy of Music with Harold Craxton, father of *Daphnis and Chloë*'s designer John Craxton.

'He was a little, shall I say, bigoted over the people he liked,' admitted de Valois, 'but then who isn't if they're very good ... if he believed in anyone he was marvellous. He'd push them all he could and help them all he could.' He adored Sibley and Collier and Ellis because they 'always gave 100% ... devoted to the company, devoted to the ballets, just 100% for the Royal Ballet,' declared Mason. 'That's what he was and that's what he expected.'

'It was the ones who were... becoming shall I say positive artists in their own right,' noted de Valois, '(who) didn't get on with him very well because he so wanted to keep them down there ... It was a natural problem for the up and coming company, who had quite a lot to say and he very rightly saw at once that they weren't ready to say it and wouldn't listen.' 'You didn't have the freedom to grow,' admitted Collier. 'Later when I realised there was a further out – I began to really love dancing more.' For some, that dogmatism and desire to keep control made him the worst kind of teacher.

In fact, he liked to be challenged and always enjoyed a good row; what he could not bear was not being listened to: after three steps of a *Swan Lake* Pas de quatre rehearsal, he shouted 'Dreadful', threw his chair across the studio and walked out. When he came back he said: 'You haven't done a thing I asked you do to in the last rehearsal.' Page recalled him saying 'time and again "I don't mind if you're not a virtuoso as long as it's clear that you've applied what we talked about and I haven't wasted my time."'

Sometimes he really hit a nerve. After a girl in *Serenade* persistently made a mistake, that movement became 'the girls' folly'. He would run the whole Pas de quatre in *Swan Lake* and deliberately not watch: 'you wouldn't dare not do it full out because he might glance up,' bemoaned Collier. 'You *knew* you were going to have to do it again. It was really mean.' One long-remembered and often recalled grudge (always prefaced by 'I'll tell you an awful story about Somes') was when he said 'again' once too often and one dancer walked out; Somes called a full rehearsal on a Saturday, then, once everyone was in the studio, said 'You know who's to blame for you being here. You can go now.' He was reasserting his authority.

'You weren't working with a dancer,' observed pianist Donald Twiner. 'You were talking to a complete artist in every aspect of the theatre.' De

Valois described him as 'head of the academic side of a company. He had incredible knowledge, more knowledge than any of them ... the ballets as well as the school. ... it was born in him. We always said if we didn't know go and check it with Michael. He was like an encyclopaedia.'

Having worked with so many ballet greats, Somes keenly felt his responsibility to pass on what he had learned. 'Traditions must not die' ... was Mike's outlook,' declared Young. 'He was not against innovations, but the old, great traditions should be preserved ...' He brought Tchernicheva to work on *Firebird* revivals, May on *Symphonic Variations*, Seymour to coach *The Two Pigeons*. 'You must pay attention to what has been done in the past,' he declared, 'and to the original dancer and what her qualities were, and embody as much as you can, but you've still got to add something yourself.'[15] The company absorbed style and a code of behaviour by watching the dancers of the earlier generations: 'All of those dancers had style,' declared Eagling, 'and even in the studio you could pick (it) up from just the way somebody stands – they were stylish people. It was something that was innate in their personalities.'

Pickford enjoyed the richness of working with him: 'His passion was always trying to ... make people understand the sense of history, where things came from and more than just you're up here dancing. He'd say "Have you seen the great – this person or that person? ... Well, you should have. What are you doing this for? You want to build roads?"' Tradition for Somes didn't just mean the past greats; he saw everyone as contributors to a living tradition, consulting corps de ballet dancers as well as principals when he wasn't sure of a movement or a sequence.

Somes gave his time, his knowledge, passion, standards, loyalty, tradition, the hot line into the past, the insight into the choreography, especially Ashton's. For those who rose to the challenge, rehearsals with Somes were exciting, inspiring, invigorating, stimulating, immensely satisfying, *never* boring.

That does not mean that the legendary rages were not real. 'He had such mood swings' Barbara Fewster remembered. 'I used to look at the eyes and keep away on certain days.' It was all extremes, all technicolour. He was unpredictable. While he could ruin an expensive photocall at Covent Garden by taking up the time for yet more corrections, on tour he would happily participate in publicity stunts, like cutting the 50th anniversary cake in Leeds with Albrecht's sword. There were stories of irrational behaviour, pouring water over Alexander Grant, tearing Jane Edgeworth's dress, pushing Gerd Larsen, breaking Ashton's finger (he applied too much force when trying to remove a ring). At full moon everyone trod warily; there is no consensus

15 Clarson Reach, Robert, *Ballet, Life as it really is in a dance company*, Artmusicque Publishing Co, London, 1986, p27

among psychiatrists about a link between the full moon and mental states, but Somes believed there was.

'Life was very different then,' mused Mason, '(now) Union rules would drive him insane, he thought you either want to work or you don't. I think he was used to a very black and white world and he couldn't have stood any of those shades of grey, which we have now. He would have been hauled up before the Unions, there would have been all sorts of sexual discrimination and physical batterings.' A more judgmental century now condemns such an approach; certainly he could go too far and while some dancers could not cope, others blossomed. Page, who became Director of Scottish Ballet, admitted that 'It's very difficult sometimes to get the work done and still adhere to a lot of these rules and dancers don't always respect that; sometimes they like to be pushed a bit and sometimes they don't even realise they need it; the truth hurts and you have to be told – it's a very public job.'

Harvey sympathised with his approach. 'I think it was necessary and a lot of what I think is wrong now is everybody trying to be so nice and careful ... he just spoke his mind.' Peter Wright agreed, with reservations: '... In a way I agree with some of his philosophy – it's a waste of time telling dancers they're wonderful all the time, you've got to tell them about their faults – make sure they put their faults right then the rest will come, which is true, but you do need a bit of psychology sometimes.' Most appreciated his directness. 'You knew where you stood and you knew it was for one common cause, there was no other motive,' declared Jefferies.

How much was it an act? 'I think he was a very shy person,' Carr surmised, 'and a lot of the big voice and the big manner ... actually you need; there needs to be a focus at the front of the room or else nothing is going to happen ... I now know, having gone into a studio to face eighty or a hundred people, what courage it does take ... you can act that you are angry, or you're not angry ... you have to play a role.'

Inevitably stories of temper, violence, bullying, intimidation and 'destroyed' dancers were relishingly received by the ballet gossips, who grudgingly admitted the high standards but qualified praise with 'But I couldn't stand his methods'. There was no fun in gossiping about his positive qualities – indeed, few outside the company knew about his endless patience. No one was afraid to approach him with a problem and even after an exhausting rehearsal, he never said 'Come back later,' but always 'Let's find a corner and sort this out.' Sibley paid tribute to his generosity with his time, 'with his effort his spirit, with the degree he goes into things. He would rehearse you on a Sunday if you wanted, he would come in at 6:00 in the morning, he would do anything to make the end result right, for you, for the ballet, for everyone concerned.'[16] 'There was nothing you couldn't ask him, and you never doubted that he didn't know the answer ...' recalled Crooks, '... when Somes went so did a lot of technique.' He was a kind, sympathetic listener, not just to the dancers' problems but anyone associated with the company.

'I think there was a sort of purity in Michael,' declared David Walker, who worked with Somes on mounting *Cinderella* in Stockholm and Amsterdam. 'He was not a corrupt person at all. ... I found (him) very good company. And he was a gossip, like some men are. He liked to gossip and to analyse things (though) not a word of scandal was breathed about Margot. He would tell you about a figure from the past like Mathilde Kschessinska and hit them off exactly. His observations about people were perceptive and shrewd. He was very naughty. He could tease the living daylights out of you – and at the same time he had another side ... there was a sort of funny conventional gentleman about him.'[17]

Somes commanded respect for the reasons expressed by Robert Irving when he left the company – that he had stood for the highest integrity and sincerity as well as the highest artistic standards. 'Always a great dansur (sic) noble on the stage and such a rare being in life,' was Anton Dolin's tribute.[18] As his beloved Karsavina wrote about Diaghilev '... his harsher traits ... were but the faults of his virtues. His devotion to his art was his virtue, one of absolute integrity, a sacerdotal flame.'[19]

Successive Chairmen of the Royal Opera House Board, Lord Drogheda and Sir Claus Moser, who worked at the highest echelons of media and Government, saw Somes more objectively than those working in the hothouse atmosphere of the studio and they recognised the company's debt. 'To Michael Somes more than to anyone else is due the credit for the maintenance of standards of performance,' declared Drogheda in his memoirs, '... everyone in Britain should realise our indebtedness to him for the enormous care and attention which he brought to his work, his refusal to be satisfied with the second best, and his unswerving loyalty to the Royal Ballet ... regardless of the vicissitudes through which it might be passing.'[20] Sir Claus was equally forthright: '... a *terrific* lot of the standards of the Royal Ballet during those years were due to him. It's all very well having Margot and Rudi out front, but it's what happening in the background. He has been undervalued ... it's easy to say Kenneth MacMillan, Fred – but there's that solid steel in the middle, that core in every sense, and that was Michael

---

16 Barbara Newman, *Antoinette Sibley*, Hutchinson, London, 1986, p168.

17 Interview with author

18 Anton Dolin to MS 25 April 1966

19 Tamara Karsavina, *Theatre Street*, Readers Union, 1950, p285-6

20 Drogheda, Charles Garrett Ponsonby Moore, *Double Harness*, London, Weidenfeld & Nicholson, 1978, p296

Somes, it really was. No compromises, no short cuts. To find the highest standards and bloody well get there and if it means that you are very tough on the young kids, OK.'

Tough he was on student Erroll Pickford, who, while admitting the rough treatment, mused 'Why do I miss him, why do I miss all of that? Isn't it an easier life now? But at the end of the day, you're not better in yourself and you're going out on the stage ...'

Working with Frederick Ashton

By Michael Somes. Published *Ballet Annual* 1961

To start working with Frederick Ashton on a new ballet is like setting out on some exciting voyage of discovery. Sometimes there will be promises of luscious lands to conquer when Nature's rich inventions come pouring out in profusion, or sometimes the musical charts will warn us of rocks ahead. Often the navigation of the rocks proves to be the most rewarding, but always we know that the genius of our captain will unearth hidden treasures of movement, and teach us how to exploit and use them to the utmost advantage.

I said 'to work with' Frederick Ashton, and *with* is the operative word. Although his are the ideas, the basic overall plan and unerring taste, one always has the knowledge that whatever artistic talent one possesses will be sought out, what is bad rejected, or at worst transformed and miraculously turned to good account. Whatever seed of talent there is will be magnified, embellished and polished to an extent of refinement of which one would never have imagined oneself capable. For me, this extreme understanding of his artists, together with his ability and humility to realise that the newest member of the *corps de ballet* has a 'dancing soul' to be won and coaxed to a perfection beyond its possessor's dream, is Ashton's great teaching contribution to British ballet.

Added to this, is his wide knowledge of all forms of our art; his sensitive memory of everything he has seen in the theatre or has experienced in his own personal everyday life; all find expression in his wide range and versatility. Ashton is a fine exponent of the value of mastering one's art by long apprenticeship in the basic classical ballet, which he understands and loves so well. As an example, his study of the use and importance of *port de bras* has resulted in that fluency of line, exemplified in all the roles created by him for Margot Fonteyn. Ashton also possesses an extremely sensitive ear, and a brand of 'movement musicality' that continually delights the eye.

Many times, as a dancer, I have been fortunate enough to be present at the very first meetings with his collaborator, the composer of the music. If it is to be specially commissioned or arranged from some existing score, a rough indication of the requirements of the action is outlined by Ashton. Firstly, he has a very sure sense of the time needed for the creation of atmosphere and the requirements of dramatic action. Secondly, he has a shrewd awareness of the visual limitations of the audience, of how much they can absorb and for how long without tedium. Repose is as important to him as an exciting climax yet, on the other hand, he will know exactly when to repeat a formula of action if the occasion demands. He will deliberately slow down a movement, if it is essential that it should be followed by a display of speed, in order to heighten the contrast; similarly, he will build up the entrance of a soloist by increasing or diminishing, the action of the *corps de ballet*, as in the ballroom scene in *Apparitions*. He will also indicate the smallness of a movement when wishing to emphasise a larger movement later.

Although modest by nature, Ashton has the necessary confidence of the creative mind. That is, he will not desperately discard a poor choreographic idea, but will pass on and return later to replace or perfect it. I have known him arrive at rehearsal apparently without a thought in his head, and the first few minutes will be spent in some good-humoured badinage about his failure to learn to drive a car, or some fascinating anecdote or reminiscence of Pavlova, whom he adored. Then we get down to the rehearsal; his explanation of the next movement to be choreographed will begin with 'I dreamt last night', followed by a description of some human waterfall or massive pyramid effect. When it is pointed out –not always politely – that this cannot possibly be achieved without the aid or wires, and at least six pairs of hands and feet, he is not in the least deterred, and accepts the challenge. Then comes the long process of mechanics, trial and error, addition and subtraction, and invariably at the end of the rehearsal what was meant to be a pyramid has turned into a waterfall; and some beautiful effect, at first thought impossible, has been produced. But not always. A whole morning of rehearsal may reveal little, but Ashton is content that even if there is nothing positive to show, the research done will finally produce the answer – and very often the answer is so simple that one wonders why nobody had ever thought of it before.

Ashton is a master of the *pas de deux*, and in it he finds a perfect medium for his imagination. A high proportion of his extensive list of ballets remains in the repertoire, but it is sad to know that many of his loveliest *duo* creations have been lost to us because the remainder of the ballet has not endured. In his group movements and patterns he has a strong eye for symmetry and it is this which makes such ballets as *Symphonic Variations* and *Scènes de Ballet* so difficult to perform. How often he entreats us to watch our 'spacing' above all else! For once creation is over, Ashton demands perfection in the performance of his ballets. He is not so happy when confronted with group character dances – 'another peasant dance' often brings forth a sigh. The variety of his creations for the ballerina is shown by his many beautiful soli for Margot Fonteyn, for Nadia Nerina in *La Fille mal gardée* and for the ballerinas in

Birthday Offering. Again he will find the particular *métier* of the individual, be it long line, *adagio* work, quicksilver *allegro*, *pointe* work, *pirouettes* or jumps, and will graft his own invention on to the personality of the performer. He has shown by his fine choreography for the male dancer in *La Fille mal gardée* (superbly executed by David Blair), that he by no means regards the *danseur* merely as a 'prop' and supporter, but he needs an excellent dancer to measure up to his demands.

Ashton's speed of creation is remarkable as its variety, and he counts his progress in pages of music covered even if not completely filled in. Of course the presentation of a ballet does not end at the choreography of steps to selected music. The mounting of the ballet in the theatre, the special lighting, the addition of the orchestra, not only require the full range of the theatrical artist but also that of the diplomat. While attentive to the demands of his dancers, Ashton possesses the faculty to blend and integrate all these elements of a production into a complete whole.

Not many people who have watched and loved his work over many years realise that he has a 'signature step' inspired by the *Gavotte Pavlova*, which I think I can say has become traditional in every new ballet he has composed. Even when a new work is complete, room must somewhere he found for it in one form or another. I will leave it to my readers to discover it for themselves, but that 'signature step' has become dear to all of us who have had the privilege of working with Frederick Ashton. For us, it is a symbol of the reverence and the high esteem that we have for him.

Music for Dancing – the Part it Plays
With special reference to 'Daphnis and Chloe'

A lecture delivered by Michael Somes at the Royal Academy of Dancing (sic)
London Music Course in 1961

There are four types of dancers:

(1) Dancers who derive inspiration from the sounds and rhythm often with disregard to the visual aspect of what they are doing.

(2) Dancers who are so concerned with the visual aspect that they ignore the music and rhythm.

(3) Dancers who have long since learnt the music by ear and tend to listen to their own music in their heads.

(4) Those who can balance all three – in other words, who know the music by ear, and can anticipate its sound and rhythm, yet still actually listen, at the same time leaving enough of their mind to think about the visual correctness and precision of their movement and line.

Therefore, as always, we come down to early training and the necessity to recognise, as teachers, these various types and trends in students, and to train them accordingly. I am a great opponent of the teacher who takes her class by beating a stick on the floor to beat out the rhythm – very often out of the correct time and rhythm herself. This is usually the teacher who encourages the student to work too visually. In the end, and that would seem the object, all the student hears is the stick; then why have a pianist? As for any subtlety or nuance of phrasing, that becomes completely swamped, and so the student is never trained to dance *to* the music.

This is most important when later on the student has to distinguish cross-rhythms or tunes which they may be using alone, in opposition to the rest of the dancers in the ballet – all using, perhaps, a more predominant one. Also to listen for a particular instrument, not only for this more practical purpose aforementioned, but also so as to invest the movement with the character of the instrument, be it loud and strident, or soft and melting; to know how to use pauses and breaths in music, and later be able to phrase a movement through music, or against the predominant rhythm. A simple illustration of this is simply being able to walk or run to the character of the music without actually being in strict tempo. A great danger to the student who listens to the music in his own head – the one who has learnt it by ear – can be the undoubted attribute, which, of course, we never discourage – that of practising *without* music. They start taking liberties according to their needs, out of all relation to what they will hear if they are listening when they come to the performance; stretching out Adagio phrases or hurrying them to relieve aching legs on held developpés, slowing quick batterie steps and indulging in overlong balances – all of which can produce a dangerous contented feeling of achievement, rudely shattered by the orchestral rehearsal and resulting in pleas for 'slower' or 'faster', until the music bears no resemblance to the composer's intentions or even those of the choreographer. Again, I am all against those last-minute compromises with the conductor. Ideally, he should be present at the first rehearsals of a new work, and have the authority to lay down what *is* and *is not* possible – firstly to the choreographer and, secondly, to the performer. Apart from his obvious knowledge of the composer's intention, as marked in the score, as in the case of classical ballets, the tempos for traditional choreography, he knows how fast the flute can fly those runs – as in the last act of *Swan Lake* – or how much wind the brass have left for those final chords of the Rose Adagio. This is the time for discussion and compromise, and dancers should know what they are in for *before* the orchestral rehearsal, when they have to cope with the sound from many instruments and not just *one* piano. Nowadays tapes, or even gramophone records, are used by choreographers and in the case of very complex scores, this is an undoubted advantage in being able to learn the orchestration and hear what predominates or otherwise, not only in actual volume, but in the colour of the sound. But I am inclined to think that in all but perhaps the *most* difficult of scores, and those practically unplayable on a single piano, the old method is best (shades of the Musicians Union!) and tapes and records should only be used as a reference. Again, it teaches us to listen and imagine what this or that particular theme *will* sound like on the oboe, or how much of our mind must be diverted to keep attention to that insistent rhythm on the kettle-drum!

The spirit of the music and all that it gives you is most important. As you see, everything again depends on early training and no pianist should watch the dancers and give them leeway, such as that extended chord to allow for those two extra fluke pirouettes in class which will probably never happen on the stage. If a conductor is present, he conducts the pianist – if not, the tempo is set by the teacher or *répétiteur* taking the rehearsal, and no 'messing about'! Pauses tend to become longer and longer and sustained passages hurried through. All that should be necessary is to indicate the tempo, either vertically or musically, by what we irreverently call a 'Till ready'. Tchaikovsky employed this method in almost all his solos and adagios. Very often, alas, they are used as a mere introduction without any relation to the tempo or rhythm of the dance which follows. I am against all use of the teachers' '*and*', which can be stretched or contracted according to whether, on the one hand, the pianist has found his place in the music and the dancers are ready balanced on the right foot – or, on the other hand, merely if time is short. I think it is essential to use different and varied music for classes *not* always a march for Grand Battement – why not mazurka or tango? Also, use pauses in the movement of a set enchaînement – the pause to be set, to take a simple example, first on (1) – (2-3-4), then 1 (2) 3-4, 1 2 (3) 4 and 1 2 3 (4), in sequences. Very few dancers can do this the first time, and it is an excellent exercise in rhythm and listening. Make the students sometimes set their own adagio or allegro and explain its relation to the music. Enchaînement and exercises in 5/4 or 7/4 tempo should also *not* be neglected – it is surprising how perplexed even professional dancers can be when confronted by not having that '6' or '8' (123456) or (12345678). All this, and many more complicated rhythms are to be found in the modern repertoire of ballet, and the student must be trained and equipped to cope with them. Although I think it is essential that the student should be taught to count, and *made* to count, in the first stages of learning a ballet, this system should be discarded as soon as the work has been learnt by ear, otherwise the dancers will listen to his or her counts and *not* to the music, and often they will bear very little relationship, even in tempo. Naturally, technical musical knowledge can be a great advantage to the student, although sometimes *this* does not necessarily produced the best 'ears'. A keen musical ear and overall interest in music, composer's styles and their intentions, can be more valuable, to my mind. I have known, to their everlasting shame, those training to be professional dancers who do not know who wrote the music for *The Sleeping Beauty*. This is, of course, an extreme and absurd case, but there are many who could not tell you of works for the ballet by Constant Lambert (*Tiresias, Horoscope, Rio Grande, Pomona, Romeo and Juliet*) or the names of three ballets by Sir Arthur Bliss (*Checkmate, Adam Zero* and *Miracle in the Gorbals*). In these days of libraries and recorded Ballet music there is no excuse for this ignorance.

In regard to what music to use for choreography, I say, be simple in your choice. This does not necessarily mean it is any easier – very often the reverse. To watch a good Strauss waltz with movement that is in the spirit of the music, but not banal like many apparently simple things, can be the most difficult yet the most effective. On the other hand, someone will take the latest piece of 'musique concrete' and quite honestly, utterly defeated by the composer's intentions (if any), produces some parallel in dance completely obscure, tedious and with no attraction for the eye. Avoid too much paralleling of the music; this can also become a bore visually. Remember, a phrase can be usually acceptable when repeated four times, but not necessarily *visually*. The eye seems to tire quicker than the ear. Nevertheless never be afraid to let the music become visual itself. Sometimes it so transcends all improvement, and being impossible to match, complete immobility is the only answer. Avoid the association of certain steps with certain rhythms, and certain instruments of the orchestra for the male and female dancer. The ballerina, tripping prettily to the melody on the flute, need not necessarily be followed by a spate of entrechats and double tours from the gentleman, accompanied by the tuba and trombones and loud crashes on the timpani and cymbals – although in this crude situation it would probably seem most odd the other way round. I think you will find that the most successful choreographers steep themselves in the music they have chosen and then 'forget it' and do not try to parallel every note with a movement. Remember the value of repose; sometimes stillness can be the most eloquent movement in a ballet.

This leads me to the ballet about which I have been asked to talk to you – *Daphnis and Chloe*.

We have heard Dr. Cole brilliantly examine the score for us and explain the composer's intentions, and I feel I can only give you an impression of how Mr. Frederick Ashton set about composing the choreography and the atmosphere within that framework which we dancers tried to convey. Of course, I did not see the original Fokine version and I cannot say in any detail how much it differed from Mr. Ashton's, but I can imagine the difference must have been considerable. Mr. Ashton freely adapted the libretto to his own conceptions – the most striking of which was the more modern costumes, particularly for the men, and the break from Grecian tunics. He also dispensed with the dance actually in honour of the God Pan, which became just a joyful finale of celebration. I think he saw his Chloe full of sweet innocence and charm, and yet with a slight sense of naughtiness, plenty of spirit when captured by the pirates. Dorkon was the blundering, resentful, rather oafish character; yet even he is allowed a few bars in the final celebration to remind us of his vanity in both senses of the word – his vain bid for Chloe's hand earlier in the ballet. Lykanion was just sheer sex appeal; the virility of the Pirate's chief with his agitated movements and sadistic pleasure as he taunts Chloe. Which leaves me with Daphnis, with whom I have lived personally since the ballet's presentation, who I must admit, on most occasions, I felt early lost the dance competition anyway, and throughout seemed to me to be a bit of a 'drip'!

The ballet opens with the entry of pairs of dancers walking quite relaxed and, if I may use the term, 'flat-footed' through the quiet spring music (as I have said earlier, one of the most difficult things to do gracefully and with natural rhythm), until they join in lines of girls and boys, standing shoulder to shoulder. Then follows a slow moving country dance, almost reminiscent of a Kola; smooth and unruffled, yet keeping the underlying rhythm going all the time. Here Ashton employed a particularly striking example of his use of the head – so simple yet so beautiful – the boys and girls alternately laying them on each other's shoulders in unison. Next we have (I think it is actually Daphnis's theme) as the two lovers enter one after another at the back of the stage, tenderly seeking each other. Yet Ashton subtly conveyed the feeling that although in love all was not quite well yet, and there were trials ahead for both of them. They walk up an avenue of dancers to Pan's Grotto, where they pay respectful homage and Daphnis offers Chloe an apple which she accepts but declines to pay the price of a kiss – just for an old apple – Daphnis will have to exert himself a great deal more than *that*! Then follows the dance in 7/4 time – oh *how* we always longed at first to count **8** and not **7**, but devising steps for that rhythm becomes a strange fascination, which made the music for the little Swans' dance of *Lac des Cygnes* – itself a masterpiece – seem, after such long acquaintance, strangely banal. This dance brings Daphnis literally face to face with Lykanion who, in spite of Daphnis's love for Chloe, at least seems to bear a second look – or should I say a 'wolf-whistle'! This was brought about by the formation of arches by the dancers, in and out of which Daphnis, Chloe and Lykanion play a sort of hide and seek, and Chloe turns up just in time to see Daphnis give Lykanion a very full gaze! By now Dorkon has also entered the scene and here follows a very clever pas de quatre – still the 7/4 time, in which the four characters get thoroughly mixed up (sometimes quite unintentionally)! I must say, if I ever heard an **8** in my ear, I was lost for good! The quarrelling reaches a climax and jealousy rears its ugly head, and the competition by dance is to decide who shall win Chloe's kiss. Dorkon's dance – so extremely difficult to give the impression of clumsiness and yet do it *gracefully*, was full of sudden stops, in which he seems to be looking at Chloe to see if she is admiring him. But, of course, *she* is rooting for Daphnis! After Dorkon's clumsy end – a most difficult grand pirouette – he is ignominiously hauled away by the crowd, as if they had had more than enough. Daphnis shows *his* exploits, with what I remember being told by Mr. Beaumont was once a wand and is now a crook – he is a goatherd – across his shoulders. Most awkward, I can assure you – full of pirouettes and double turns en l'air to the chords of a harp. Of course, he ends *his* dance with a triumphant flourish on to the floor. Throughout this dance Ashton used many frieze positions in profile, with everything turned in (a godsend to some dancers I won't name!). Chloe implants her kiss on his lips as a prize and Daphnis is left alone on the stage – except for Lykanion lurking in the background. She moves towards him in a tentatively yet purposeful way – she is on pointe – and begins her short dance of seduction. Daphnis is ashamed and, finally, after having gone a *little* (or should I say, a *great deal* too far?) repulses her. In this dance Ashton invested many what might be called suggestive movements, yet never crude or vulgar – one particularly affecting, when Daphnis turns Lykanionn around on pointe in a back-bend, whilst she does a ronde-de-jambe developpé movement en dedans with her raised leg. Soon after we have the first rumbling thunder-like music, rising in crescendo for the pirate invasion, and the abduction of Chloe by the Chief, while Dorkon just looks on his seeming revengeful way – that if he cannot get Chloe, certainly Daphnis will not either. He restrains Daphnis from rescuing Chloe and, after a very brief encounter, is thrown to the ground by Dorkon and falls in a faint in the corner! Now comes one of the most lovely moments in the wonderful score – the three Nymphs, who enter singly. I always lie there listening and hoping the horns will reach those, to me, seemingly *impossible* high notes. Ashton always used his most musical dancers for this – because *here*, ear was of prime importance – in fact I am sure they needed at least *three* each! But the whole impression is one of a lovely cool breeze, quality of space, and of an ethereal air. The employment of a wind machine helps to create this. Daphnis is brought to the Grotto by the Nymphs and Pan arises and sends him off to find and rescue Chloe. That is the end of Scene 1.

Scene 2 – the Pirates' encampment – opens with the wives and girl-friends awaiting the return of the plundering boys. Their chief trophy, being Chloe, is carried high around the stage. In this most exuberant dance Ashton invented many fine steps and formations – what we call a 'character dance'. Often he pauses the main body of dancers to allow the pirates' chief some dazzling leaps and spins, thereby emphasising both that and the mass movements that follow. Inevitably Chloe is forced to dance with her wrists still tied. A beautiful number this, terrified and pleading, and yet with that touch of defiance I have already mentioned, but with plenty of terror too. Ashton used many beautiful arabesques which 'fell' off the pointe in this dance. In what seems the nick of time, Pan comes up through the trap door and terrifies and disperses the bandits, rescues Chloe, and movingly places a wreath on her head, and her on his shoulders; we hear the beginning of 'day break'. A drop curtain falls and here the music, so descriptive and utterly lovely, is allowed our whole attention to sing for itself. About half-way through the drop curtain rises disclosing Daphnis again having a good rest! He is awakened by his friends, to find Chloe restored to him. They do at first a gentle pas-de-deux of apparent relief and love at their reunion. She tucks her head into his shoulder and he swings her in ever-faster circles and slow, slight lifts just off the floor, in which Ashton obviously beat the Russians to it by giving Chloe a sense of 'weightlessness'. She merely moves her legs but does not jump, all the weight being carried from start to finish of the lift by her partner. Next we have her dance to Daphnis's flute. This was almost oriental in character and one almost expects her to wear those baggy trousers and little cymbals between her fingers. Finally, Daphnis and Chloe are lifted into the air and brought together and a fountain effect is produced as he lifts her up and down to the undulating music which almost immediately precedes the finale.

Now we have to count **5** instead of **6** (and for a very long time)! Streams of dancers enter in a kind of step-hopping rhythm which continues almost throughout, joined by handkerchiefs. Formation succeeds formation, avenues and groups are made, Daphnis and Chloe enter, flitting in and out, Dorkon gets his deserved shove and finally, to the sound of the kettle-drum beating 10, all form up for the very last dance. We listen carefully for that 10, otherwise we never catch up for the rest of the ballet! Ashton increases and increases the momentum by cleverly adding just an extra twist here and there to step up the pace until the whole stage is going at it hammer and tongs. This, I think I can honestly say, I have found one of the most exciting passages to dance in the whole of our repertoire. And one just *cannot* help being carried along with the gloriously exciting music and draining the last drop of energy for the last final twirl as the curtain descends.

How was it choreographed? I wish I knew the answer! Fred himself could not tell us, I know. All I can say is that he has a tremendously perceptive ear and capability of seeing the broad line of the music and its infinite shades of colour, and these are indispensable to its choreographic creation.

Many of the steps for the company he worked out with just a few of us, and experimented with different accents of the rhythm until he found the one the most satisfyingly balanced – aurally and visually. Many were the arguments – no two people hear the same things it seems – but we admitted he was invariably right. .

I can now only recommend you to see the ballet!

INDEX OF PERSONS AND PRODUCTIONS

Italics indicate an illustration: n reference in footnote
Dates in ( ) refer to Sadler's Wells/Royal Ballet productions
ch: choreography
* indicates ballets in which Somes appeared/rehearsed

Achcar, Dalal   224
Acosta, Carlos   306
Adam Zero   96, 327
Addison, Errol   4, 186
Agon   206, 212
Aïda   24, 27n41
Aitken, Christine   308, 311, 312
Albery, Donald   72
Alexandre le Grand   42
Almeida, Maria   300
Amis, Kingsley   197
Anastasia   272, 276
Andersen, Hans   51
André, Grand Duke   41
Ansermet, Ernst   182
Anthony, Gordon   36, 254
* *Antigone*   161, 174, 221-2, 235,
   242
Antoinette, Princess of Monaco   191
Appleyard, Beatrice (Mrs Mithat
   Fenman)   205
* *Apparitions*   31-32, 36, 41, 51, 70,
   119, 122, 127, 159, 160, 229,
   269, 323
Après-midi d'un faune, L'   57
Argyle, Pearl   26, 51,
Argyll, Jill   14, 15
Arias, Roberto   178, 187, 188, 189,
   203, 214, 217
Armstrong-Jones, Antony (Lord
   Snowdon)   226
Arnold, Malcolm   23, 187
Arova, Sonia   239
Arrau, Claudio   283
Ashbridge, Bryan   150, 186, 193,
   201, 202, 219
Ashcroft, Peggy   223n119
Ashmole, David   238, 258, 282, 311
Ashton, Frederick   1, 3n3, 17,
   20-24,26, 28-32, 35-42, 44-47,

49-52, 53-59, 61-69, 71-74, 75,
76, 77, 78-82, 85-89, 91, 95, 96-
98, 100-102, 107, 108, 111, 112,
116, 118-120, 123, 125, 127,
131, 134, 135, 136, 138,142,
143, 145, 146, 150, 152, 154-55,
156-61, 168, 170, 174, 175, 177-
79, 187-91, 193-94,196, 200,
201, 203, 204, 207-8, 212, 222,
225, 226, 228, 229, 231-33, 235,
236, 240-43, 245-48, 251, 253,
256, 258, 259, 260-63, 264-65,
266, 267-70, 272-274, 276n20,
278, 283-85, 288-91, 294, 295,
214, 298-302, 304, 306, 308,
310, 312, 313, 318, 320, 322-24,
328-31
Asquith, Anthony   39
Astafieva, Seraphina   4
Astaire, Fred   84, 142
As You Like It (film)   32
As You Like It   140n28
Ataturk, Keman   205
Atkins, Ian   194
Atlee, Clement   96
Auld, John   273
Auriol, President   157
Aurora pas de deux see Sleeping Beauty,
   The
* *Aurora's Wedding*   135
Ayrton, Michael   22, 102

Babilée, Jean   100
Bach, Johann Sebastian   66
Baddeley, Hermione   190
Bailey, James   103, 140n28, 200
* *Baiser de la fée, Le* *
− (Ashton) 29, 120, 269
− (MacMillan) 174, 223
Baker, Josephine   42

Bakst, Leon 56, 127, 276

Balanchine, George 124, 125, 127, 128, 131, 134, 135, 165, 226, 254, 255, 278, 283, 285, 289, 297, 303

Bal des voleurs 245

* *Ballet Imperial* 131, 134-35, 160, 196, 218-9, 289, 297

Banting, John 35,

* *Barabau* 28

Barnes, Clive 149, 158, 162-63, 164, 155, 172, 188, 191, 194, 201, 206, 207, 209, 218, 219, 229, 235

Baronova, Irina 11, 34, 56

Bartered Bride, The 24, 92

Bartòk, Béla 196

Baryshnikov, Mikhail 291

* *Bayadère, La, Kingdom of the Shades* 237, 246-47, 268, 279, 289

Baylis, Lilian 11, 15, 16, 17-8, 19n7, 27, 35, 53, 138

Beaton, Cecil 31, 101

Beaumont, Cyril W. 109, 113, 114, 115, 118, 135, 152n9, 155, 159, 163, 184, 281, 288n53, 329

Bedells, Phyllis 5, 81, 300

Bedells, Jean 288

Beecham, Thomas 39

Beethoven, Ludwig van 35

Benois, Alexandre 56

Benois, Nadine 56

Bérard, Christian 97, 115

Bergner, Elisabeth 32

Bergsma, Deanne 199n51, 246, 264, 267, 304

Beriosova, Svetlana 159, 182, 187, 188, 192, 193, 209, 215, 218, 221, 239, 240, 241, 259, 264

Berkley, Busby 244

Berlin, Irving 257

Berlin, Isaiah 283

Berlioz, Hector 22, 31, 127, 226

Berners, Lord 39, 57, 101

Bevin, Ernest 78

* *Biches, Les* 251-52, 253, 254

Bintley, David 290

Birds, The 80

* *Birthday Offering* 193-4, 200, 269, 324

– *Pas de deux* 199, 223, 235, 306

Blair, David 132, *133*, 150, 163, 190, 192, 193, 217, 221, 225, 230, 232, 234-35, 238, 239, 240, 243, 254n74, 255, 324

Blake, William 85

Bland, Alexander 154, 221

Bliss, Arthur 285, 301, 327

Bloom, Sheila 250

Blott, Katharine 13, 15, 16, 25, 317

* *Blue Bird pas de deux* 20, *43*, 44, 45, 57, 198

Bohen, Max von 35

Bolero (Ravel) 76

Bolm, Adolph 4, 141

Boosey and Hawkes 86-7

Boris Godunov 24, 28

Borodin, Alexander 283

Borovansky, Edouard 203

Botticelli, Sandro 66, 85

Boulez, Pierre 223

Boult, Adrian 223, 265

Boult, Lady 265

Boulton, Catherine 175

Boulton, Michael 116, 118, 170, 179, 284

Bournonville, August 200, 238, 241

* *Boutique fantasque, La* 20, 104, 108, 109, 289

Bradley, Lionel 44, 45, 51-52, 53, 57, 66, 90, 102, 113, 131, 132, 161

Brae, June 22, 55, 56, 58, 63, *64*, 73, 288

Brahms, Caryl 102, 109, 204, 271

Brazil, Angela 272

Britten, Benjamin 79

Brittain, Vera 284

Britton, Donald 240, *262*

Broken Man 297

Brook, Peter 120

Browne, Louise 192

Browning Version, The   120
Brownlee, Peter   273
Bruhn, Erik   239
Brunvoll, Jonas   192
Buckle, Richard   26-27, 102, 122, 124, 131, 132, 135, 153, 155, 163, 182, 221-22, 241, 242, 253, 276
Bulganin, Nicolai   193
Bumbry, Grace   257
Burne, Gary   221
Burra, Edward   23, 83, 85, 116, 285
Burrows, Jonathan   290
Bussell, Darcey   298
Butler, R. A.   65
Byron, Lord George Gordon   304
Byron, John   26

Caine, Michael   257
Callas, Maria   218
Carnival of the Animals, The   79
Capriol Suite   269
Carmen (opera)   25
Carmen (film) 120
* *Carnaval*   20, 28, 38, 86, 89, 120
Caron, Leslie   223n119
Carr, Christopher   297, 313, 318, 319
Carter, Alan   20, 21, 22, 29, 33, 35, 39, 40, 41, 42, 45, 49, 50, 51, 55, 56-57, 58, 66, 74, 75, 76, 89, 208, 238, 309
* *Casse-noisette*   19, 24, 26, 28, 34, 52, 55, 76, 289
– *Pas de deux*   200, 201, 205, 225
   Milan   200
   see also The Nutcracker
Cecchetti, Enrico   4, 20, 118, 241
Chabukiani, Vakhtang   35, 96, 199, 232
Chaplin, Charlie   140, 141, 142
Chappell, William   23, 24n30, 31n54, 37, 39, 74, 155, 269, 270, 292, 302, 304
Charisse, Cyd   141n30
Charrat, Janine   157
Chase, Lucia   128

Chatfield, Philip   150, 159, 167, 192, 193, 244, 315
Chatting, Harry   29
Chauviré, Yvette   193, 239
* *Checkmate*   40, 41, 44, 52, 59, 60, 62, 67, 109, 122, 136, 157, 289, 327
Checkpoint   272
Chekhov, Michael   72
Chevalier, Maurice   42
Chopin, Frédéric   283, 313
Choreartium   25
Christiansen, Arthur   309-10
Churchill, Winston   6, 191
* *Cinderella* Ashton: *117*-119, 120, 122, 127, 131, 160, 188, 191, 200, 201, 209, 226, 229, 241, 259, 263, 269, 285, 289, 290, 299, 301, 311, 320
– Act II   215
– Act II *pas de deux*   179, 226
– pantomime: 24
– school show: 9
City Lights   140
Claire, Stella   288
Clark, Kenneth   61-62n6, 78,
Clarke, Arthur C.   12
Clarke, Mary   52, 56, 69, 73, 90, 94, 98, 103, 104, 105, 109, 113, 154, 155, 167, 201, 204-5, 226, 245
Clayden, Pauline   143, 146, 160, 179, 291, 304
Clegg, Peter   148, 256
* *Clock Symphony*   115-16
Cochran, Charles Blake   29, 37, 39
Colbert, Claudette   141
Cole, William   306, 328
Coleman, Michael   246, 260, 267, 274
Collier, Lesley   260, 267, 274, 281, 285, 297, 305, 310-11, 314, 315, 316, 317
Colman, Ronald   141
Colyer-Fergusson family   7n2
Concert, The   289
Connolly, Billy   202n61
Connor, Patricia   292

Connor, Roger   276
Conquest, Mrs   2
Conti, Italia   3
Cooper, Gary   36
Cope, Jonathan   298
* *Coppélia* (1933)   24, 28, 34, 55, 60
– (1940)   66, 70, 80, 84
– (1954)   219, 266
Corbett, Eloise   288
Corbett, Panton   288
Corder, Michael   290
Cormani, Lucia   5
Coton, A. V.   50, 119, 122, 203-4
Cotten, Joseph   141
Counterpoint   290
Couperin, François   55
Coward, Noël   278n22
Cranko, John   95, 154, 174, 218,
   221, 222, 260, 266, 285, 289,
   309
Craske, Margaret   4, 45, 127
Craxton, Harold   317
Craxton, John   152, 153, 317
Crazy Gang, The   223n119
Creaking Princess, The   190
Cripps, Stafford   81, 129n36
Crisp, Clement   283
Crookes, Michael   285, 293, 311,
   312, 316, 320
Cunard, Lady Emerald   80
* *Cupid and Psyche*   51, 57-8, 269
Curtis, Jo   292
Czinner, Paul   32, 169, 225, 300

Dale, Margaret   223
Dame aux camélias, La   242
Dammer, Karl   92
Dance Dream, The   3
Dances at a Gathering   274
Danilova, Alexandra   34, 124, 125,
   276
Danses Concertantes   289
* *Dante Sonata*   63-4, 67, 74, 80, 90,
   106, 111, 136, 138, 269
Danton, Henry   97, 99
* *Daphnis and Chloë*   83, 150-52,
   160, 172, 184, 188, 223, 235,
   241, 268, 269, 289, 291, 301,
   306, 317, 325, 328-331
   Scene 3 268
Dark of the Moon   120
Davies, Dudley   198
Davies, Gwendoline   85, 88
Davies, Margaret   85, 88
da Vinci, Leonardo   85
Day, Doris   142
de Basil, Colonel W   56
de Falla, Manuel   179
de Gaulle, General   193
Delibes, Léo   158
Delius, Frederick   36
Demery, Felix   11, 12
de Mille, Agnes   307
Demoiselles de la nuit, Les   115
Denby, Edwin   118
Dench, Judi   307
de Nobili, Lila   207, 247, 266
Derain, André   55, 108,
Derman, Vergie   251, 281
de Valois, Ninette   1, 5, 11-16, 18-
   22, 24-27, 31-36, 38-41, 44, 51,
   55, 56, 60, 61-62, 65, 67-74, 76-
   80, 82, 84-88, 90, 94-96, 103-6,
   108, 109, 113, 115, 117, 119,
   120-27, 130, 131, 134-36, 141-
   43, 146, 154-56, 157, 159, 166,
   167, 171, 174, 177, 185, 187,
   188, 194, 197, 200, 203-6, 209,
   218, 219, 221, 229, 230-38, 242,
   245-48, 252, 260, 261, 263, 271,
   272, 276n20, 279, 282, 284-86,
   288, 289, 294, 299-301, 304,
   306, 313, 317, 318
Devil's Holiday   58, 61n4
de Walden, Lord Howard   71
Dexter, John   309
de Zoete, Beryl   111, 132
Diaghilev, Serge   3, 4, 11, 12, 20,
   23, 39, 55, 56, 104, 124, 126,
   127, 141, 150, 165, 173, 180,
   182, 193, 224, 251, 254, 265,
   279, 301, 320
Diana, Princess of Wales   *287*
Dido and Aeneas   134

Dietrich, Marlene   34, 190
Dixon, Deirdre   159, 190, 194, 196,
    206, 212, 214, 215-7, 218, 221,
    224, 226, 250, 251
Doboujinski, Mstislav   34
Dolin, Anton   4, 22, 26, 115, 119,
    135, 138, 161, 165-66, 187, 194,
    276, 320
Don Giovanni   25
Don Juan   83, 116, 118, 269
Don Quixote   136, 138
Doré, Gustav   63
Douanes   28, 34
Doubrovska, Felia   127
Dowell, Anthony   152, 169, 228,
    238, 242, 246, 249, 250, 253,
    254, 255, 258, 264, 266, 267,
    268, 274, 279, 280, 283n40,
    289, 290, 291, 299, 300, 304,
    305, 306, 308, 309, 310, 3311,
    312
Dowson, Anthony   284-85, 293,
    297, 312, 314, 315
Doyle, Desmond   150, 193, 239,
    264m 267, 272, 273
Drake, Alfred   127
Dream, The   248-50, 256, 268,
    269, 282, 289
Drogheda, Lord   246, 260, 26, 320
Dryden, John   102
du Boulay, Christine   143, 175
Dubreuil, Alain   305
Dukas, Paul   191
Dumas, Alexandre   242
Duncan, Isadora   63, 150
Dyson, Tony   300

Eagling, Wayne   169, 284, 297,
    299, 306, 311, 314
Eckman, Sam   80
Edgeworth, Jane   318
Edward VII, King   194
Edwards, Leslie   21, 24, 25, 27n41,
    32, 35, 40, 41, 42, 58, 59, 62, 68,
    70, 74, 76, 84, 105, 142, 146,
    148, 167, 188, 236, 250, 261,
    264, 269, 273, 276, 288, 296,
    305, 306
Edwards, Winifred   97, 109, 113,
    114, 115, 251
Eglevsky, André   39, 100, 121
Egorova, Lubov   11
Elgar, Edward   85, 264, 265, 305
El Greco   85
Elizabeth, Queen, the Queen Mother
    96, 208, 275, *287*, 301
Elizabeth II, Queen   161, 214-5, 275
– as Elizabeth, Princess   96, 149
Ellis, Richard   24, 25, 34, 35, 38,
    49, 57, 66, 70, 74, 76, 85, 175
Ellis, Wendy   104, 188, 263, 275,
    280, 281, *282*, 286, 291, 293,
    294, 297, 300, 302-3, 304, 305,
    306, 317
Elmhirst, Dorothy   72
Elmhirst, Leonard   72
Elvin, Violetta (Prokhorova)   96,
    113n50, 134, 150, 159, 160,
    161, 184, 192, 193, 203, 238
Emperor's New Clothes, The   51
Enigma Variations   264-65, 266,
    269, 304-5
Entrée de Madame Butterfly   192
Espinosa, Edouard   5, 10, 12,
Euclid   111
Eyre, Rosalind   291

Façade   38, 62, 67, 70, 72-73, 127,
    136, 138, 172, 193, 268, 269,
    301
– *Foxtrot*   276
– *Popular Song*   84, *262*
Fadeyechev, Nicolai   198
Faery Queen, The   79
Fairy Queen, The   102, 120, 161
Fancy Free   100
Farren, Brigadier   76
Farrington, J. R.   193
Farron, Julia   21, 25, 27, 34, 50,
    51, 57, 60, 91, 103, 116, 206,
    207, 254, 281-82, 306
Faust   25
Fedorovitch, Sophie   23, 37, 47, 63,
    71, 81, 82, 97, 131, 133-34, 155,

159-60, 285
Feinstein, Martin   124
Fenman, Mithat   205
Fenman, Mrs Mithat   *see* Appleyard, Beatrice
Ferguson, Howard   132
Fête étrange, La   219, 243, 290
* *Fête Polonaise*   24, 73
Fewster, Barbara   164, 166, 282, 318
Fialka, Ladislaw   298
Fidelio   92
Field, John   96, 149, *151*, 153, 155, 157, 159, 161, 171, 187, 204, 205, 236, 246, 260-61, 262, 263, 271
Field, Lila   3
Fifield, Elaine   95, 131-32, *133*, 160, 192, 193, *195*, 196, 203, 218
* *Fille mal gardée, La*   37, 173, 225, 232, 236, 241, 269, 275, 289, 298, 299, 301, 308, 323, 324
Fillery, Phil   76
* *Firebird, The*   160, 165, 173, 174, 180-84, 188, 189, 200, 209, 223, 224, 225, 230, 232, 235, 236, 241, 242, 259, 289, 293, 313, 317, 318
Fisehri, Oska   35
Fisher, Hugh *see* Swinson, Cyril
Flaxman, John   63
Fledermaus, Die   24
Flindt, Fleming   193
* *Flower Festival at Genzano pas de deux*   241
Flynn, Errol   189, 214
Fokine, Michel   38, 90, 150, 152, 158, 165, 180, 198, 232, 254, 276, 285, 289, 309, 328
Follow the Sun   29
Fonda, Henry   127
Fonteyn, Felix   217, 224
Fonteyn, Phoebe   217, 224
Fonteyn, Margot   1, 20-24, 26, 27, 29, 31n55, 32, 33, 36, 37, 40, 41, 44-47, 49-52, 56, 58, 59, 63-4,

66- 67, 69, 73, 77-83, 85, 86, 90, 95, 97-104, 107, 108, 111-15, 117-26, 129, 130, 131, 134-136, 138-50, 152, 156-64,166-69, 170, 172-75, 178, 179-82, 184-94, 197-215, 217-19, 222, 223-28, 230-33, 234-40, 242-45, 247, 250, 254, 255, 258-60, 266- 69, 276, 278-80, 288, 290-92, 295, 296, 300, 301-2, 306, 307, 310, 320, 322, 323
Fountain of Bakhchisarai, The   198
Franck, César   82, 96
Frank, Elizabeth   192
Franklin, Frederic   124
Freeman, Frank   258, 266, 269, 279, 308, 311, 312
Fricassée   193n36 *see Birthday Offering*
Friedman, Murray N   128
Fry, C. B.   187
Furse, Roger   70

Gable, Christopher   240, 246, 254
Gable, Clark   141
Gabovich, Mikhail   231, 232
Gainsborough, Thomas   85
Gammon, Philip   317
Garbo, Greta   127
Gardner, Ava   141, 175
Garrulous Snail   298
Garson, Greer   141
Gaunt, Hilda   32, 62, 226, 300
Gavotte Pavlova   324
Gavrilov, Alexander   4
Gavrilov, George   4
Geltzer, Ekaterina   3
Geneé, Adeline   3, 5, 42, 81, 241
George V, King   31
George VI, King   96
George M.   278n22
Georgiadis, Nicholas   209
Gielgud, John   278
Giesking, Walter   83 n32
Gilbert, Jean   100, 120, 126, 146, 148, 175, 188, 190, 229
Gilpin, John   193, 218, 239, 241

Giselle 39, 197, 298
- (1934) 19, 24, 26, 38, 55
- (1946) 95, 99-100, 103, 108,
  136, 138, 146, 159, 160, 161,
  162, 213, 226
- (1960) 228-29, 235, 236, 237,
  239, 240, 241, 247, 291
- *Peasant pas de deux* 249n56, 269
- Argentina 190, 227
- Brazil 190, 217, 227
- Chile 190, 227
- Czech National Ballet 298
- Finnish National Ballet Helsinki
  190, 226
- Japan 190
- Montevideo 227
- Munich 208
- Uruguay 190, 227
Glazunov, Alexander 193
Gloria 284, 289
Glyn, Leo 15, 16, 24, 37-38, 40,
Gods go a'Begging, The 28, 38, 44,
  62
Goodliffe, Arnold 12
Goodman, Arnold 263n112
Goodwin, Noël 197
Gordon, John 33
Gordon, Kathleen 13
Gore, Walter 85
Goudin, Alexandre 4
Grace, Princess of Monaco 6, 193,
  224
Graham, Martha 222, 307
Grand Tour, The 278
Grant, Alexander 27, 89-90,
  95, 109, 115, 118, 120, 122,
  124, 146, 150, 153, 154, 179,
  186, 187, 193, 196, 207, 225,
  240n26, 264, 267, 300, 301, 318
Grant, Cary 141n30
Granville-Barker, Harley 18
Grater, Adrian 276, 297
Greatest Show on Earth, The (gala)
  276
Green, Sarah *see* Somes, Sarah
Gregory, Jill 206, 241, 273, 283,
  288, 291, 293

Grenfell, Joyce 223n119
Grey, Beryl 84, 90, *101*, 102, 103,
  107, 109, 159, 161, 187, 192,
  193, 203, 306
Grigoriev, Serge 180, 182, 201
Gruen, John 316
Guillem, Sylvie 299
Gustav, King of Sweden 107
Guthrie, Tyrone 27, 60, 62, 65, 72

Haakon, King of Norway 107
Hailey, Arthur 257
Haines, Alfred 23
Hall, John 51
Hall, Stanley 74
Hamby, Greta 142
Hamilton, Gordon 77
Hamlet (ch: Helpmann) 76, 105,
  106, 107, 122, 127, 290
Hamlet 77, 83
Harlequin in the Street 51, 53-55,
  62
Hart, Ann 271
Hart, John 73, 96, 103, 107, 150,
  157, 161, 171, 204, 236, 246,
  248, 255, 256, 259, 260, 261,
  262-63, 266, 268, 271-72, 273,
  274
Harvey, Cynthia 98, 299-300, 303,
  313-14, 315, 318
Haskell, Arnold 4, 5, 13, 14, 26,
  102, 161, 166, 188, 194, 197,
  222
Haunted Ballroom, The 26, 90
Hawkins, Margot 10
Haydée, Marcia 283n40
Haydn, Josef 115
Hayward, Betty 9
Hayward, Kathleen 8, 10
Hayworth, Rita 84
Healey-Kay, Patrick *see* Dolin, Anton
Heaton, Anne 120, 159
Henie, Sonja 141
Helpmann, Robert (Bobby) 22, 23,
  26-7, 31, 33, 37, 40, 41, 45, 51,
  52, 53, 56, 63, *64*, 66, 68, 70, 71,
  72, 73, 74, 76, 77, 78, 79, 80-1,

82, 83, 86, 90, 91, 92, 96, 99,
100, 102, 103, 106, 108, 112,
115, 118-19, 125, 127, 131, 136,
138, 141, 142, 143, 149, 164,
193, 194, 234, 247, 269, 270,
279, 285, 290, 300
Henry V (film)   77
Henze, Hans Werner   116, 207,
248, 301
Hepburn, Katharine   140n28
Herf, Estelle   217
Heston, Charlton   223n119
Hitchins, Ivon   191
Hitler, Adlof   92
Hoffmannsthal, Alice von   37, 42,
61n6, 82,
Hoffmannsthal, Raimund von   37
Holden, Stanley   225
Hollingsworth, John   146
Holmes, Lieutenant Robert   75, 76
Holst, Gustav   85
* *Homage to the Queen*   102, 161,
173, 184, 269
– *Air pas de deux*   191, 304
Homji, Rashna   281
Honer, Mary   26, 38, 44, 67,
Hookham, Mrs Hilda   44-45, 77, 81,
115, 205, 217, 224
Hooper, Gerald   12
Hope-Wallace, Philip   97, 111, 155
* *Horoscope*   36, 45-50, 51, 53, 62,
66, 69, 84, 86, 90, 98, 109, 119,
120, 152, 153, 154, 190, 193,
269, 327
Hosking, Julian   *282*
Howard, Andrée   290
Howe, George RSM   98
Hudson, Rock   36, 221
Hughes, Herbert   142
Humphreys, Sheila   276
Hunt, Martita   127
Hurok, Sol   86, 121, 122, 124, 129,
136, 140n28, 141-42, 145, 146,
147, 148, 171, 172, 175, 176,
177, 200, 254, 255, 256
Hurry, Leslie   83, 222
Hussey, Dyneley   50, 55, 73

Huston, John   309
Hutton, Betty   141n30
Hynd, Ronald   206, 239, 264

Icare   42
Idzikowski, Stanislas   4, 20-21, 186,
276, 300
Ile des sirèns   134
Inglesby, Mona   79f
Invitation, The   222, 243, 289
Ironside, Christopher   158
Ironside, Robin   158
Irving, Henry   3
Irving, Robert   *123*, 140n28, 146,
148, 175, 204, 206-7, 320
Isaacs, Jeremy   304
Isadora   289
Isherwood, Christopher   257
Ivanov, Lev   200, 289

Jackson, Rowena   95, 160, 191,
193, 201
Jar, The   24, 28
* *Jazz Calendar*   259, 269, 282, 299,
303
Jeanmaire, Zizi   223n119
Jefferies, Stephen   *277, 278*, 281,
288, 292, 297, 310, 319
Jenner, Ann   260, 267
* *Job*   24, 26, 28, 37, 119, 122, 127,
265, 289, 304
Johannsen, Christian   309
John of the Cross, Saint   97
Johns, Eric   115
Johns, Glynis   11
Johnson, President   257
Johnson, Richard   155
Johnson, Van   141
Jones, Inigo   2
Jonson, Ben   2
Judd, Sally   218
* *Judgement of Paris, The*   51, 52, 269

Kalioujny, Alexander   157
Karinska, Barbara   31
Karsavina, Tamara   4, 5, 11-12,
33, 38, 83, 150, 153, 165-66,

180-182, 200, 222, 228-29, 231,
   276n20, 280, 291, 300, 316, 320
Kauffer, E McKnight   285
Kavanagh, Julie   61n6
Kaye, Danny   141, 175, 190
Kaye, Nora   124
Kelly, Desmond   305
Kelly, Gene   142
Kelly, Grace *see* Grace, Princess of
   Monaco
Kennedy, Jacqueline   245
Kennedy, President   245
Kennedy, Sherilyn   305
Kerner, Leighton   255
Kerr, Deborah   25n33
Kersley, Leo   21, 50, 89, 91, 100,
   116, 153
Keynes, Maynard   65
Khruschev, Nikitina   193, 231
Kidd, Michael   100
Kingdom of the Shades, The see
   Bayadère, La
King John   112
Kirkland, Gelsey   292
Kirstein, Lincoln   124, 126, 128,
   134, 135, 174, 212, 267, 282-83
Kiss Me Kate   127
Knight, Dennis   242
Komaki, Masahide   210-212
Kriza, John   100, 124, 127
Kschessinska, Mathilde   11, 32-33,
   41, 42, 320
Kumakawa, Tetsuya   311
Kyasht, Lydia   158

Lac des cygnes, Le see Swan Lake
La Meri   24
Lambert, Constant   1, 22, 23, 31,
   34, 35, 36, 37, 45, 46, 47, 61n6,
   62, 63, 65, 66, 69, 72, 74, 77, 78,
   82, 96, 102, 108, 113, 122, 124,
   125, 126, 135, 154, 155, 156,
   159, 188, 285, 327
Lament of the Waves   269
Lanchbery, John   23, 69, 132-3,
   229, 233, 246, 248, 261, 265,
   267-68, 315

Lander, Toni   193
Lane, Maryon   240
Lang, Harold   127
Laing, Hugh   100
Langley, A. G.   84
Larsen, Gerd   95, 144, 241, 273,
   291, 318
Laura Theresa, Sister   138
Lavrovsky, Leonid   226, 228
Layton, Joe   278
Lazovsky, Leonide   127
Lebrun, President   57
LeClerq, Tanaquil   124, 226
Legat, Nicholas   4, 13, 35, 39
Legerton, Henry   58n146, 273
Leigh, Vivien   141, 202, 223n119
Lejeune, Caroline   225
Leslie, Doris Niles   254
Levasseur, André   191-92, 194, 209
Lifar, Serge   4, 21, 35, 42, 100, 135,
   155, 193, *224*
Lincoln, Julie   315
Linden, Anya   160, 179, 184, 223,
   239
Liszt, Franz   31
Little Ballerina, The   103
Lloyd, J. L.   14, 15, 16, 37-38
Lockwood, Joseph   295, 307
Longus   150
Lopokova, Lydia   81
* *Lord of Burleigh, The*   52, 120, 269
Loring, Eugene   142
Lorrayne, Vyvyan   246, 264, 267
Louis II, Prince of Monaco   105
Loves of Mars and Venus   2
Lunnon, Lady   284
Lupino, Ida   141
Lynne, Gillian   146

Macbeth (opera)   226
Macbeth (ballet)   298
MacKenzie, Kelvin   309
MacLeary, Donald   221, 236, 239,
   241, 254, 267, 297
MacMillan, Deborah   254, 272, 273,
   286, 293, 308, 310, 315
MacMillan, Kenneth   142, 143, 146,

150, 174, 200, 201, 206, 209, 218, 222, 223, 241, 254, 260-61, 262, 267, 271, 272, 273, 278, 283, 284, 285, 286, 289, 293, 294, 297, 312, 313, 320
Macrae, Frances   257
Macready, William Charles   2
McLagan, Darren   275
Madame Chrysanthème   187
Madwoman of Chaillot, The   127
Magic Flute, The   194
Mahler, Alma   223
Mahler, Anna   223
Mahler, Gustav   222-23
Makarova, Natalia   246, 283n40
Malenkov, Georgy   193
* *Mam'zelle Angot*   108-9, 111, 120, 184
Manchester, P. W.   27, 40, 55, 58, 64, 74, 77, 95, 104, 109, 114, 132, 133, 150, 174
* *Manon*   272, 283, 289
Mansfield, Jayne   223n119
Margaret, Princess   96, 119-20, 208, 226, 269, 283, 288, 301
* *Marguerite and Armand*   169, 242-43, 269
Markova, Alicia   4, 19, 20, 22, 26, 115, 138, 160, 161, *162*, 187, 306
Marks, Alicia *see* Markova, Alicia
Marriage of Figaro, The   25
Martin, John   114, 121, 124, 126, 174, 184
Martin, Mary   127
Martin, Tony   141n30
Mary, Queen   96
Marx, Groucho   257
Mason, Monica   206, 231, 238, 246, 251-53, 267, 273-74, 280, 283, 297, 314, 315, 316, 317, 319
Massine, Leonide   4, 11, 20, 25, 35, 104, 105, 108-9, 115-16, 165, 167, 198, 226, 245, 278, 285, 289
Matchaloff   28

Matthews, Gwyneth   288
Matthews, Jessie   24
May, Pamela   20, 22, 26, 36, 39, 45, 49, 50, 51-2, 56, 58, 59, 63, *64*, 70, 72, 73, 81, 90, 97, *99*, 107, 137, 142, 144, 288, 318
Mayer, Daniel   19, 61
* *Mayerling*   286, 289, 301
Mead, Robert   264
Meadow of Proverbs   290
Meistersinger, Die   24,
Mendel, Lady   41
Mendelssohn, Felix   248
Merman, Ethel   127
Merrie, Eileen   76
Messel, Oliver   95, 96, 124, 266
Messerer, Asaf   232
Midsummer Night's Dream, A   102, 248
Milborne, Kathleen   8
Milhaud, Darius   209
Miller, Elizabeth   22, 26, 38, 44, 50, 288
Miller, Patricia   95, 132, *133*, 198
Milligan, Leslie   211, 212
Mills, John   190
Millet, Jean-François   85
* *Miracle in the Gorbals*   91, 92, 99, 100, 106, 107, 122, 127, 327
* *Miraculous Mandarin, The*   161, *195*, 196-7
Miss Hook of Holland   68
Mister Roberts   127
Mistinguett   41
Modigliani, Amedeo   85
Monahan, James   295
Monnet, Jean   257
Monotones   269, 289
* *Month in the Country, A*   283, 313
Moore, Doris Langley   79
Moore, Lilian   201
Montresor, Beni   247
Mordkin, Mikhail   3
Moreton, Ursula   13, 21, 34, 55, 62, 276, 282
Morosoff, Serge   4
Morrice, Norman   284, 285, 291,

294, 299
Morris, Marcus   187
Morrison, Angus   62
Moser, Claus   261, 290, 292, 295,
   320-21
Mossetti, Carlotta   158
Mossford, Lorna   241
Mozart, Wolfgang Amadeus   301
Munnings, Hilda *see* Sokolova, Lydia
Mutiny on the Bounty   24
Myers, Carl   281

Napoli pas de six   241
Nash, Walter   213
Negus, Ann   146
Nemchinova, Vera   124, 125, 126-
   27, 174-75, 244
Nerina, Nadia   95, 143, 159, 160,
   161, 175, *183*, 184, 192, 193,
   200, 219, 225, 232, 239, 240,
   323
Newman, Barbara   221, 306, 311
Newman, Claude   26, 33, 37, 186,
   309
Newman, Paul   36, 221
Newton, Christopher   297, 300
Newton, Joy   45, 56, 62, 66, 95,
   108, 120, 142, 187, 188, 276,
   288, 304, 306
Nicholson, John   85
Nijinska, Bronislava   251-54, 279,
   285, 289
Nijinsky, Vaslav   4, 21, 38, 45, 57,
   90, 100, 135, 150, 152, 165, 174,
   182, 253
Noces, Les   251, 252-53, 281, 289
Nocturne   36-37, 51, 86, 90, 99,
   269, 289
Nolan, Sydney   247
No Strings   278n22
Novikoff, Laurent   4
Nureyev, Rudolf   46, 167, 229, 232,
   235-36, 237-39, 242-43, 244,
   245, 246-47, 254, 255, 256, 258,
   259, 260, 263, 266, 268, 276,
   278, 279, 283n40, 290, 302,
   306, 313, 320

Nursery Suite   38
Nutcracker, The   244
− excerpts 162
− BBCtv   209
− (1968)   237, 264, 313
   see also Casse-noisette
Nye, Palma   66, 70, 103, 116
Nyholm, L   189

Oboukhov, Anatole   124, 125, 127
O'Conaire, Deirdre   276
O'Dwyer, William, Mayor of New York
   125
Ogawa, Ayako   211
O'Hare, Michael   304
Oistrakh, David   257
Oklahoma!   127
Olivier, Laurence   32, 77, 120, 141,
   190, 202, 223n119, 278
Olrich, April 179
Onassis, Aristotle   191, 209
Ondine   169, 173, 207-8, 225,
   226, 230, 232, 235, 236, 241,
   242, 248, 269, 289, 300, 301
− *Pas de deux*   208, 209
Orfeo   119
Orledge, Ann   169
Ormondy, Eugene   129
Orpheus and Eurydice   73-4
Osborne, John   197
O.W.   277, 278

Page, Annette   239, 240, 254
Page, Ashley   237, 279, 282, 290,
   293, 297, 298, 306, 308, 310,
   311-12, 313, 314, 317, 319
Pakhomov, Vassily   233
Paltenghi, David   77, 91, 96
Paquita   289
Park, Merle   246, 254, 267, 274,
   286
Parkinson, Georgina   232, 246,
   264, 267
Parsons, Alice *see* Somes, Alice
Partriège, Elizabeth   51, 55
Passport to Pimlico   120
Patineurs, Les   24, 38, 39, 40, 51,

58, 62, 67, 72, 74, 120, 136, 138, 150, 269, 289, 301, 302
Pavlova, Anna   3, 4, 11, 20, 38, 42, 158, 191, 323
Penney, Jennifer   260, 267
Percival, John   51, 64, 98, 119, 294
* *Péri, La*   173, 191-92, 226, 227, 230, 232
* *Persephone*   241, 269
Petipa, Marius   28, 55, 119, 156-57, 222, 231, 244, 246, 268, 289, 298
Petit, Roland   100, 115, 223n119, 285
Petrouchka   155, 201
Pfister, Prosso   90, 241
Phillips, Ailne   19
Piano Concerto No 2   135n17
Pickford, Errol   299, 305, 308-9, 316, 318, 321
Pickford, Mary   128
Pilgrim, Miss   35
Pineapple Poll   289
Pinza, Ezio   141
Piper, John   79, 81, 82, 285
Pius XII, Pope   185
Plisetskaya, Maya   226, 264
Plucis, Harjis   112, 113n50, 148, *166*, 185, 290
Poème tragique   235
Pollitt, Brian   307
* *Pomona*   38, 40, 42, 44-45, 327
Poole, David   95,
Porter, Andrew   235
Porter, Marguerite   281
Portman, Eric   120
Poulenc, Francis   284
Powell, Ray   138, 144, 146, 148, 196
Preobrajenska, Olga   11, 210, 309
Presages, Les   25
Pridham, Ethel, *see* Somes, Ethel
Pridham, Mrs   14
Prince of the Pagodas, The   289
Prokhorova, Violetta *see* Elvin, Violetta
Prokofiev, Serge   117, 118

* *Promenade*   90
* *Prometheus*   35, 36
Prospect Before Us, The   70, 74, 90, 143
Pruzina, Anna   4, 20
Purcell, Henry   102, 134

* *Quest, The*   80-82, 91, 269, 278

* *Rake's Progress, The*   25, 26, 28, 34, 62, 80, 84, 106, 120, 127, 136, 140, 146, 193, 232, 288, 289
Rambert, Marie   5, 11, 13, 24, 81, 155, 194, 309
Rainier III, Prince of Monaco   193, 224
Rassine, Alexis   77, 83, 96, 100, 161, 190, 192, 288
Rathbone, Basil   128
Rattigan, Terence   120
Ravel, Maurice   76, 83, 150
Raymonda 276n20
Raymonda (Nureyev after Petipa) 276
* *Raymonda scène d'amour*   222, 225, 226, 227, 258
* *Raymonda pas de deux*   241
* *Raymonda Act III*   237, 276
Red Shoes, The   105, 108, 118, 124, 125
* *Rendezvous, Les*   20, 24, 26, 44, 66, 70, 269, 289, 301
Respighi, Ottorino   131
Rêve de Léonore, Le   120
Reymond, Paul   40, 42, 74
Rhapsody   291
Riabouchinska, Tatiana   11, 56
Richard III   120
Richardson, Philip J. S.   4
Richardson, Ralph   223n119
Rigoletto   24
* *Rinaldo and Armida*   23, 161, 173, 174, 187-88, 209, 230, 232, 242
* *Rio Grande*   22, 24, 120, 269, 327
* *Rite of Spring, The* (MacMillan) 241, 243, 281, 283, 313, 315
Rivera, Chita   309

Robbins, Jerome   100, 124, 274, 278, 285, 289
Robbins, Lord   262
Robeson, Paul   223n119
Robson, John   30
Rockettes   42, 127, 283
Rodenberg, Patsy   310
Rodeo   100
Rodrigues, Alfred   134, 146, 185, 196, 200, 222, 280, 306
Rogers, Ginger   257
Roi nu, Le   51
* *Romeo and Juliet*
– ch: Lavrovsky   198, 200
– ch: MacMillan   254, 255, 276, 289
Romeo and Juliet (Lambert)   327
Rona, Viktor   236
Roope, Clover   13, 112, 317
Rosai, George   4
Rose, Francis   57
Roslavleva, Natalie   231
Rossini, Giacomo   119
Round, Roy   232
Rowlandson, Thomas   70
Royal Ballet, The (film)   225, 300
Ruanne, Patriaia   281
Ruskin, John   2
Russell-Roberts, Anthony   84, 270, 300, 302
Russell-Roberts, Edith   80, 81, 84, 234, 235, 270
Rutland, Harold   62

Sachs, Leslie   76
Sail Away   278n22
* *Salut d'amour à Margot Fonteyn*   288
Sanguine Fan, The   265
Santlow, Hester   2
Sassoon, Victor   257
* *Scènes de ballet*   111, 116, 136, 161, 185, 207, 241, 265n116, 269, 293, 323
Schubert, Franz   72
Scofield, Paul   223n119
Scriabin, Alexander   235, 283
Seasons, The (Glazunov)   193

Senior, Evan   155
* *Serenade*   317
Sergeyev, Nicholas   28, 55-56, 62, 73, 114, 244, 276n20
Seven Brides for Seven Brothers   193n36
Seventh Symphony   20
Seymour, Lynn   240, 246, 254, 267, 312, 318
Shabelevsky, Yurek   227
Shadowplay   289
Shaffer, Peter   257
Shahanshah of Iran   193, 215
Shakespeare, William   17, 24, 33, 53, 85, 102, 248
Shankar, Uday   72
Sharp, Cecil   9-10
Shaw, Brian   97, 150, 174, 179, 193, 223, 232, 264, 267, 273, 297, 300, 301
Shaw, George Bernard   18, 24, 65
Shearer, Moira   84, 90, 95, 97, 99, 105, 109, 118, 120, 122, *123*, 124, 125, 127, 131, 134, 160, 306
Sholto-Douglas, Air Chief Marshal   92
Siam, ex King of   71
Siam, Prince of   71
Sibley, Antoinette   112, 166, 167-69, 190n28, 206, 216, 218-221, 223, 228, 229, 231, 236, 237, 239, 240, 243, 246, 247, 248-51, 254-58, 259, 263, 264, 266, 267, 268, 274, 279, 280, 283, 285, 288, 289, 297, 300, 304, 306, 311, 312, 317, 319-20
Sickert, Walter   85
Singaevsky, Nicholas   251
* *Sirènes, Les*   101-2
Sitwell, Osbert   155
Skeaping, Mary   189
Skibine, George   161
Sleep, Wayne   259, 264, 280, 312
* *Sleeping Beauty, The*   55, 298, 327
– (1946) 95, 96, 104, 109, *110*, 115, 121, 122, 126, 127, 136,

138, 139, 141, 147, 149, 150,
156, 157, 160, 162, 175, 176,
179, 184, 185, 192, 219, 230,
231, 232, 235, 239, 241, 243
- (1968) 248, 259, 266,
- (1977) 280, 286, 293, 298, 305
- Act III 194, 308
- *Aurora pas de deux* 72, 142, 145,
  193
- *Awakening pas de deux* 269
- *Garland Dance* 289
- *Rose Adagio* 201
- BBCtv (1959) 223
- Czech National Ballet 298
- Finnish National Ballet Helsinki
  189, 193
- Maryinsky 28
- Masahide Komaki Company 210,
  211
- Royal Danish Ballet Copenhagen
  190
- Swedish National Ballet Stockholm
  189
  see also *Aurora's Wedding*
  Blue Bird pas de deux
* *Sleeping Princess, The*
- (1921) 124, 165, 276
- (1939) 55- 57, 58, 63, 76, 190
Slingsbury, Simon 2
Smith, Mr 84
Snowdon, Lord *see* Armstrong-
  Jones, Antony
Snow Maiden, The 24
Soames, Christopher 6
Sokolova, Lydia 4, 13, 14, 253
Solti, Georg 260
Somes, Alice (grandmother née
  Parsons) 7, 14, 16, 24,
Somes, Edwin (father) 7, 8, 10, 30,
  82, 100, 105, 137, 138, 140, 160,
  174, 190, 250, 267, 275
Somes, Ethel (mother née Pridham)
  7-8, 10, 12, 13, 14, 24, 25, 29,
  30, 31, 33, 38, 40, 45, 47, 49, 60,
  61, 75, 82, 86, 91, 100, 105, 111,
  116, 126, 137, 138, 140, 148,
  156, 160, 174, 176, 179, 190,

196, 204, 228, 250, 255, 257,
  260, 266, 267, 275
Somes, Joseph (ancestor) 6, 7n2,
  213
Somes, Joseph (grandfather) 7
Somes, Lawrence (brother) 7, 14,
  82, 84, 86, 275, 300
Somes, Maria, 6
Somes, Samuel 6, 36*f*, 213
Somes, Sarah (née Green) 6, 213
Song 290
Song of the Earth 222-23, 265, 289
Sorley Walker, Kathrine 116
Sound of Music, The 178n22
Soupirs 289
South Pacific 127
* *Spectre de la rose, Le* 20, 83, 90,
  135
Spenser, Edmund 79
Spessiva, Olga 26, 175, 244
Staff, Frank 25, 57, 58
Stanford, Charles Villiers 24
Stanislavsky, Konstantin 238
Strauss, Johann II 45
Strauss, Richard 83, 226
* *Strauss-Tanze* 45
Stravinsky, Igor 29, 111
Steele, General GOC 101
Steele, Tommy 257
Stein, Gertrude 39, 57
Stirling, Angus 304
Streisand, Barbra 278n22
Stuart, Douglas 300
Stuart, Mark 226, *227*
Stubbs, Philip 1-2
Sullivan, Ed 148
Sullivan, Frank 256
* *Summer Interlude* 131-34, 198,
  204
Sutherland, Graham 73
* *Swan Lake* 180, 58n146, 298,
  326, 329
- (1934) 19, 24, 26, 28, 33, 37, 52,
  55, 56, 66, 72
- (1943) 83, 90, 103, 105, 106,
  112-15, 116, 120, 122, 126, 129,
  136, 138, 143, 145, 147, 150,

157
– (1952) 160, *173*, 174, 175, 178,
    179, 184, 185, 190, 213, 219,
    221, 223, 228, 238, 239, 241
– (1963) 247, 255, 256, 266, 269,
    312, 315, 317
– *Act III* 26, 129
– *Act II pas de deux* 145, 178, 190
– *Neapolitan Dance* 269
– Borovansky Ballet 201
– Festival Ballet 191
– Finnish National Ballet 189, 190,
    193
– Masahide Komaki Company 210
– Norwegian Ballet 190, 192
– South Africa 198, 199
– Swedish National Ballet 190
– Turkish State Ballet 205
– Warsaw 190, 215
– Yugoslav National Ballet 179, 190
Swan Lake Act II 66, 73, 131, 160,
    169, 193, 209, 225, 230, 236,
    259
Swinson, Cyril 188
* *Sylphides, Les* 38, 39, 51-52, 62,
    72, 74, 90, 102, 103, 120, 162,
    165, 173, 190, 239, 284
* *Sylvia* 158-59, 173, 176, 190,
    200, 208, 223, 269
– Act III pas de deux 178, 179,
    191, 192, 226, 227, 299, 306
* *Symphonic Variations* 82, 96-98,
    99, 100, 102, 104, 111, 119, 122,
    126, 127, 129, 136, 157, 178,
    179, 192, 223, 235, 268, 269,
    274n17, 294, 299, 301, 303-4,
    305, 306, 313, 314-15, 318, 323
Symphonie fantastique 25, 31
Symphony 243

Taglioni, Filippo 309
Taglioni, Marie 2, 288, 309
Tales of Beatrix Potter (film) 274
Tales of Hoffman (film) 136
Tallchief, Maria 124
Tamayo, Rufino 221
Tannhauser 25

Tchaikovsky, Pyotr Ilyich 28, 55,
    124, 135, 231, 244, 283, 326
Tchernicheva, Lubov 180, 182,
    201, 280, 300, 318
Tempest, The 280
Tenterden, Lady 34
Teresa of Avila, Saint 97
Terry, Walter 255
Tharp, Twyla 283n40
That Forsyte Woman 129
Theme and Variations 303
Theodorakis, Mikis 221
Thoroughly Modern Millie 278n22
Thorpe, Edward 260
* *Three-Cornered Hat, The* 20, 25, 104,
    106, 116, 167, 198
    Miller's Dance 192
Three Juvenile Delinquents 190
Tierney, Gene 141
Tikhomiroff, Vasili 3
Tiller, John   3
* *Tiresias* 154-55, 161, 173, 174,
    178, 184, 185, 188, 327
Titian 276
Tito, Marshal 160
Todd, Arthur 138, 172, 229
Toms, Carl 247
Tooley, John 261, 262, 263, 272,
    290, 294
Toscannini, Arturo 127
Toumanova, Tamara 11, 56
Travelling Companion, The 24
Trecu, Pirmin 132, *133*, 196, 218
Trevett, Reginald 12
* *Triad* 273
*Tricorne, Le   see Three-Cornered Hat,
    The*
Trimmer, Deborah *see* Kerr, Deborah
* *Tritsch-Tratsch* 120
Truman, President 129
Tucker, Ravenna 315
Tudor, Antony 210, 285, 289
Turner, Harold 21, 23-24, 26, 29,
    38, 51, 53, 66, 106, 107, 120,
    131, 136, 186, 194
Turner, Joseph Mallord William 85
Twiner, Donald 23, 253, 258, 280,

317

Two Pigeons, The   240, 243, 269, 289, 318

Tyson, Dorothy   *186*

Ulanova, Galina   198

Usher, Graham   206, 231

Valse, La   212, 308

Variations on a Theme of Purcell   187

Vaughan-Jones, Sergeant G   76

Vaughan Williams, Ralph   85

Velmar, André   127

Verdi, Giuseppe   119, 226

Vestris, August   2

Vestris, Gaetan   2

Villella, Edward   165

Visconti, Luchino   198

Vladimirov, Pierre   124, 125, 165

Voices of Spring   289

Volinine, Alexander   3, 40, 42, 157-58, 159

Volkova, Vera   89, 112

Vox clamantis   298

Vyroubova, Nina   193

Wade, Kathryn   311

Wadsworth, Pauline   142

Wakehevitch, Georges   247

Walker, David   21, 29, 36, 247-48, 280, 320

Wall, David   264, 267, 302

Walter, Bruno   223

Walton, William   61-2n6, 66, 79, 82, 207, 278

*Wanderer, The   72, 73, 80, 90, 269

Waters, General   34

Watkin, Dolly   280

Watts, Rita   13, 317

Waugh, Evelyn   242

Wayne, John   175, 214

Weaver, John   2

Webster, David   91, 97, 141, 145, 147, 176, 177, 204, 254, 256, 260, 261, 263, 267-68, 269, 272

*Wedding Bouquet, A   39-40, 72, 122, 127, 135, 136, 138, 172,

270

Weiller, Louis   185

Wellington, Duke of   6

Wells, Doreen   264

Wells, H. G.   252

Whistler, Rex   66, 67, 85

White, Franklin   148

Wigman, Mary   159

Wilde, Oscar   278

Williams, Esther   141

Williams, Peter   149, 154, 161, 163

Williamson, Audrey   116

Wilson, Edmund   94

Wilzak, Anatole   165, 174

Winston, Harry   130

Winter, Marian   106

* *Wise Virgins, The*   66-67, 120

Wohlfahrt, Hans-Theodor   301

Woizikowski, Leon   4, 23, 35, 47, 106

Wood, Edmée   300

Wood, Michael   192, 217, 218, 245, 255, 270, 274, 278, 290,

Wright, Peter   134, 166, 209, 223-24, 225, 266, 271, 273, 275, 276, 280, 298, 303, 304-5, 306, 312, 313, 316, 319

Wyler, William   309

Yank in Rome, A   120

Young, Emanuel   23, 230, 257, 316, 318

Young, Leo   74

Young, Loretta   141

Youskevitch, Igor   161

You Were Never Lovelier   84

Yudkin, Louis   147

Yugoslav folk dance   179

Zakharoff   231

Zanfretta. Francesca   21

Zefferelli, Franco   198

Zeller, Robert   142, 146

Zorina, Vera   124, 125

Milton Keynes UK
Ingram Content Group UK Ltd.
UKHW022312131123
432489UK00005B/205/J

9 781852 731878